W9-ADF-654

Down-East Spirituals And Others

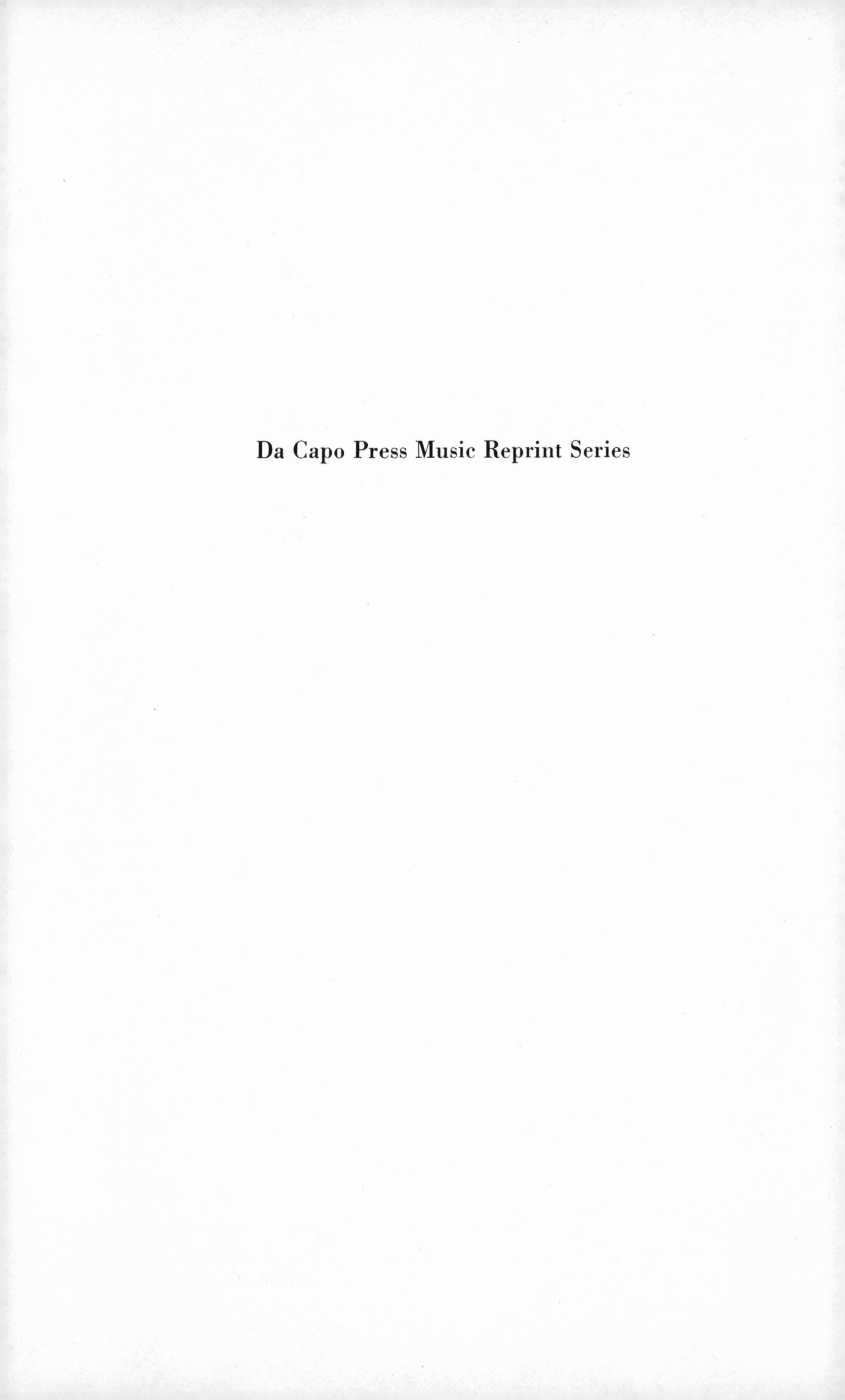

Da Capo Press Music Reprint Series

Down-East Spirituals And Others

Three Hundred Songs
Supplementary to
The Author's

SPIRITUAL FOLK-SONGS
OF EARLY AMERICA

Collected and Edited
by
GEORGE PULLEN JACKSON

DA CAPO PRESS • NEW YORK • 1975

Library of Congress Cataloging in Publication Data

Jackson, George Pullen, 1874-1953, ed.
Down-east spirituals, and others.

(Da Capo Press music reprint series)
Reprint of the 1st ed., 1943, published by J. J. Augustin, New York.
Includes indexes.
1. Folk-songs, American. 2. Ballads, American. 3. Hymns, English. 4. Hymns, English–History and criticism. I. Title.
M1629.J147D6 1975 784.4'973 74-34317
ISBN 0-306-70666-0

This Da Capo Press edition of *Down-East Spirituals And Others* is an unabridged republication of the first edition published in New York in 1943. It is reprinted from an original in the collections of the Memorial Library, University of Wisconsin.

Published by Da Capo Press, Inc.
A Subsidiary of Plenum Publishing Corporation
227 West 17th Street, New York, N.Y. 10011

Manufactured in the United States of America

DOWN-EAST SPIRITUALS
AND OTHERS

62 SATAN'S KINGDOM IS TUMBLING DOWN.*
This hymn and the original melody, which have been so useful in revival seasons for more than half a century, and which, it is believed, have never before been published together, were lately procured after considerable search, from the diary of an aged servant of Christ, bearing the date of 1810.
Shout, shout, we are gaining ground, Halle, halle - lu - jah!
End.
Satan's kingdom is tum - bling down, Glo-ry; Hal-le - lu jah!
* In view of the prejudices and feelings of christians in relation to the alteration of old hymns, the hymn has been published in full like the original, except a very few words. It will perhaps be found sufficiently long if the verses inclosed in brackets are omitted.
REVIVAL HYMNS
REVIVAL TUNES
MILLENNIAL HARP
WESLEYAN HARP
REVIVALIST
CHRISTIAN LYRE
RELIGIOUS SONGS
DIVINE HYMNS
SPIRITUAL SONGS

A TYPICAL DOWN-EAST SPIRITUAL (center) dated 1810. From *Revival Hymns*, Boston, 1842. See song No. 240 in this volume.

TITLE PAGES of some of the many pocket-sized booklets of spiritual folk-songs. All were published and sung down east.

Down-East Spirituals And Others

Three Hundred Songs
Supplementary to
The Author's

SPIRITUAL FOLK-SONGS
OF EARLY AMERICA

Collected and Edited
by
GEORGE PULLEN JACKSON

1632

J. J. AUGUSTIN PUBLISHER
NEW YORK

PRINTED IN U. S. A.

TO MY DEAR FRIENDS

JOHN AND LOUISE POWELL

INSPIRED AND TIRELESS WORKERS ON
THE EDIFICE OF AMERICAN CULTURE

Table of Contents

Illustrations

Introduction

> Die Kunst ist lange bildend, ehe sie schön ist, und doch so wahre, große Kunst, ja oft wahrer und größer als die schöne selbst.
> Goethe

What Songs Are These?

In my recently published collection, *Spiritual Folk-Songs of Early America*,[1] only about one half the song material then known was used. The present volume presents the other half augmented by scores of songs found during the past two years largely in the tradition of the Northeast.

The down-east spirituals make up a little more than one third of the present collection. Their number would have been far greater but for the purely accidental fact that many of them had been found first in the Southeast and published in *Spiritual Folk-Songs* at a time when the existence of the northeastern tradition was a mere hypothesis. The one-time richness of the singing custom in the eastern New York and New England region is now sure. I make this assertion after a careful search of a number of representative source collections identified with that section and the finding of no less than 272 examples of spiritual folk-song.[2]

Despite all these discoveries, or perhaps by reason of them, the search for this type of song is becoming less fruitful. Old books appear from time to time to be sure; and good variants of known songs are not rare among their pages; but the scarcity, among the new-found booklets, of songs thus far completely unknown leads me to believe that the 550 songs in the foregoing and present volumes represent the great bulk of the extant religious folk-songs of this land.

I do not mean that there is nothing left for other collectors to do. That would be presumptuous and untrue. There are three different environments where this type of song has been and still may be sought: in the *old song books*, in rural *group singings*, and in the homes of *individual singers*. My work and the two compilations resulting from it have touched only the first two of these environments. I have gleaned from hoary books of song and have been a studious observer at many of the "big singings" of the southern *Sacred Harp* and *Southern Harmony* folk, the chief bearers today of the ancient tradition in its group-singing aspects.[3]

My part in the tilling of the third angle of the religious folk-song field — that of the individually sung song — has been almost negligible; and others have done but little. Those few who had collected songs from the individual singer

[1] New York, J. J. Augustin, 1937. The book is called here *Spiritual Folk-Songs.*

[2] The books yielding these songs were *The Christian Harmony* (Vermont, 1805), *The Christian Lyre* (New York, 1832), *The Wesleyan Harp* (Boston, 1834), *Revival Hymns* (Boston, 1842), *Revival Melodies* (Boston, 1842), *The Millennial Harp* (Boston, 1843), and *The Revivalist* (Troy, New York, 1868).

[3] See *White Spirituals in the Southern Uplands,* Chapters vi, ix, and x.

up to the time of publication of *Spiritual Folk-Songs* were spoken of in the Introduction of that book.[1] Those who have carried on the work since then are Annabel Morris Buchanan, L. L. McDowell, and Winston Wilkinson. Mrs. Buchanan's contribution consists chiefly in her recording of 20 songs accurately remembered from the singing of her parents and grandparents in northern Alabama.[2] Mr. McDowell has contributed a booklet compiled from the oral tradition as he found it in a small area in the Tennessee foothills of the Cumberland Mountains.[3] Mr. Wilkinson's part was the excellent recording of 14 songs in the Virginia uplands during the years 1935 and 1936. They form small parts of his own private collection and of the large unpublished *University of Virginia Collection of Folk-Music* made by him. Mr. Wilkinson and Dr. John Lloyd Newcomb, president of the University of Virginia, have kindly consented to my publishing this valuable cluster of songs in the present volume.[4] — Thus it will be seen that the field of the individually sung religious folk-songs is broad and apparently rich, and that its surface has hardly been scratched.

Arrangement of the Songs

The songs are presented here, as in *Spiritual Folk-Songs*, in three large groups; Religious Ballads, Folk-Hymns, and Revival Spiritual Songs, and in this order. The Ballads group includes bible-story songs (carols) and songs of religious experience exhortation and farewell, all of which are intended chiefly for, and are thus suited to, singing by individuals, not groups. The Folk-Hymns are largely songs of praise suited to group singing. The Revival Spirituals might be called sung-to-pieces hymns; the "pieces" then being patched together with the help of repetitions, refrains and choruses. Although the classifying of some songs has not been easy, these three general divisions of the material have seemed worth holding to.

Within each of the three general divisions, too, I have followed the same plan of song sequence as in the preceding volume; that is, the songs are all considered

[1] P. 2ff.

[2] Published under the title *Folk Hymns of America*, New York, J. Fischer and Brother, 1938. It consists of 50 songs beautifully harmonized, about two thirds of which were drawn from the same song books which had served me in *Spiritual Folk-Songs* and are still serving me in the present book.

[3] His collection, is entitled *Songs of the Old Camp Ground*, Ann Arbor, Michigan, Edwards Brothers, 1937. It contains 36 songs which are variants of those in my two volumes, and 9 which have not been previously recorded. He gives texts and tunes and valuable data as to the habitat of songs and singers.

[4] The titles of the songs are 'Dying Californian', 'Salvation', 'Fairfield (B)', 'Zion's Light', 'Messiah (B)', 'Sweet Prospect (B)', 'Poor Pilgrim', 'O Hallelujah', 'Judgment Day (B)', 'I Went Down to the Valley', 'Joys of Mary', 'Sunny Bank', 'Cherry Tree Carol', and 'Windham'.

as being transposed into a key with two flats as its signature. Those tunes beginning on *b*-flat are placed first; those beginning on *c*, *d*, etc., follow. Among the many tunes beginning on the same note, the pitch of the next following notes, from lowest to highest, in diatonic sequence, determines the order of the song. It will be noted however that I have violated this order in a few instances where the grouping of *related* tunes has seemed more important.

Treatment of the Songs

With few exceptions the tunes and texts are reproduced here exactly as found in the sources. In some instances however and after some hesitation, I have made alterations in some of the old tune notations. I have, for example, corrected the mistake, made commonly a hundred years ago by compilers in rural parts, of barring a three-two-time tune in even time. Indeed, it has been in the matter of barring that most of my alterations have been made. Some will call this indefensible meddling. Others will feel that while it is meddling, it is justified. I did none of this in the tunes of *Spiritual Folk-Songs* and was severely censured by some of my best critics for "reverence for old mistakes." I now see that the critics were right.

I have paid a little closer attention to the texts here than in the former volume, by reproducing them more fully and giving more data as to their sources.[1] No changes in the original texts have been made except occasionally in orthography and punctuation.

Sources in the "Deep North" and England

In *Spiritual Folk-Songs* I stated that these songs were from the British Isles and came to us in the eighteenth century with the Methodists.[2] The finding of much new source evidence and a reinterpretation of old evidence which has somehow been neglected or misinterpreted makes it now certain that this statement must be revised.

That the parent song movement began in the British Isles is still easily demonstrable, as is also their eighteenth century advent in America. The revision of ideas formerly held touches only the decision as to which of the many dissenting religious groups in Albion was chiefly responsible for the importation. With the determination to answer this question I have examined more closely the part taken by other denominations, more particularly the Baptists, and compared

[1] Fairly reliable data has been found as to the authorship of about one third of the song texts in this volume.

[2] See the Introduction to that volume, p. 6.

it with that of the assumed chief participants, the Methodists. It may be well to summarize here the pertinent items of evidence.

(1) The Baptists of England were from their beginnings a *folk-sect*, one in which a folky singing practice would most naturally take root; whereas the Methodists, springing from the womb of the dignified Established Church did not provide that sort of song soil.

(2) The English Baptists grew to numerical power practically without any central authority, a condition which would tend to foster a *freedom of development* for any singing tradition which might once have sprung up; whereas the Methodists were thoroughly organized from the start, and the denominational authority extended specifically to the songs they sang, channeling them in the unfolky style set chiefly by the prolific hymnwriting Wesleys, John and Charles, and keeping this singing practice in the channel.

(3) The hymn books made by and for English Baptists contain scores of folky texts (no tunes at all, unfortunately) which reappear in subsequent American Baptist books of the eighteenth century; whereas the English Wesleyan hymn books, as far as I have examined them, seem to be practically devoid of such texts, and their few *tune* books show only one or two melodies which fall into the folk category.

(4) The Baptists have always been ahead of the Methodists in point of time. In Britain they had become numerically strong long before the first little group was gathered in Oxford by John Wesley.

(5) The Baptists maintained their time lead also in America. They multiplied in the Northeast in almost the earliest Colonial times; and around the beginning of the eighteenth century their numbers were augmented by the influxes of "free-singing" Welsh and English of the same sect into New Jersey and Pennsylvania; all of this long before the "prescribed-singing" Wesleyans even appeared on the northeastern scene.

(6) The Baptists still held their headstart over the Methodists when their northern itinerant preachers invaded the Southeast after the Revolutionary War. They followed Baptist Daniel Boone into the Kentucky-Tennessee region where they, not the Methodists, were the leading sect at the turn of the century, — that is, at the time and the place of the outbreak of the Great Southern and Western Revival.

Baptists as Folk-Hymn Singers

The above pieces of pertinent evidence, a few out of many, point to the conclusions, first, that it was primarily among the Baptists that the folk-hymn-singing tradition came to western shores over 200 years ago; second, that the Baptists spread the tradition first in the Northeast — New England, New York, New Jersey, and parts of Pennsylvania; and third, that they later brought the songs into the Southeast and what was then called the "Western Territory" where they became the song-tinder for the Great Revival of 1800, a movement which was to become sc important in the subsequent development of the same tradition.

The probability is that this song-tinder consisted of the old hymns, sung to the folk-tunes with which we find them associated later. But the *folk-tunes* part of this assumption is still technically unproved; for I have as yet been unable to find any appreciable number of folk-tunes in English or American religious song books before 1805.

Folk-Hymns Manhandled in Camp Meetings

Thusfar I have tried to make clear the revision of my previously held ideas as to the source and early development of religious folk-songs. It will be noted however that all observations have been confined to one variety,[1] the folk-hymn, and to the period ending with 1800. But what happened then? What influences were then brought to bear on the folk-hymn tradition in the environment of the wilderness camp meetings which were born at that time near the Kentucky-Tennessee state line?

Much happened. The conditions during this revival were unique. Overwrought men and women had been subject to religious "exercises" before. There had been cases of weeping, shouting, and falling unconscious among Baptists, Presbyterians, Evangelicals, and Methodists; even in supposedly unemotional New England; even in stolid England. But these untrammeled backwoods throngs went the limit, danced, jerked, barked, fell to the earth, and rolled. And they did all this not singly but by scores and hundreds on a single occasion.

This radical loosening of crowd-behavior patterns stood in causal relationship to the practices of the "wild" preachers. And since the preachers were also usually the song leaders and often song makers, the spread of the disintegrating influences also to the songs they sang would seem quite natural. We have ample evidence, indeed, that this was precisely what took place, — that many old folk-hymns were sung-to-pieces and that great numbers of new songs (new texts wedded to old tunes) came to life in the new revival patterns, songs which have been called collectively the Revival Spiritual Songs.[2] The dating of the beginning of this development at around 1800 is justified not alone by the circumstantial evidence just mentioned, but also by the fact that not a single revival spiritual song has yet been found in any printed record *before* that date, and by the fact that songs of this sort begin to appear promptly in the camp-meeting "songsters" *after* that date.

[1] The much smaller variety, the religious ballads, being for individual rather than group singing, are harder to coordinate with definite religious movements and denominational trends. There is some internal evidence of source in some of the ballads; but I shall be content to call attention to this merely in my notes on the individual ballads.

[2] The Revival Spiritual Songs are described in some detail in the Introduction to *Spiritual Folk-Songs*, p. 7ff.

Revival Spirituals Take to Road

The better understanding of the eighteenth century period in the development of the songs under discussion sheds new light also on their subsequent trend. Knowing their northeastern Baptist past we understand better why they appear in the earliest nineteenth century compilations of that region. It was merely their old "unwritten" music now come out into the open and recorded, tunes and all. This explains, I think, the otherwise mysterious *Christian Harmony* of the Vermonter, Jeremiah Ingalls, in 1805. And when we see revival spiritual songs in the New England books of somewhat later date, we seem justified in looking on them as echoes from the camp meetings, — the Yankees' old melodic friends come home again, with a southern or western air about them.

Knowing of the Baptist folk-hymn invasion of the Southeast in George Washington's time, we recognize why the camp-meeting offspring of these songs were welcomed with open arms in the Carolinas and Georgia. And we see why it was two musical Baptists, William Walker and Benjamin Franklin White, who compiled somewhat later practically the whole body of their beloved traditional song including many camp-meeting spirituals in their *Southern Harmony*, *Southern and Western Pocket Harmonist*, *and Sacred Harp* and laid it in harmonized form before the Fasola Folk (largely Baptists) of that region. We see better why L. L. McDowell was able quite recently to tap such a rich vein of oral song of this type among the Baptists of the Cumberland Highlands; and why Primitive Baptists still hold fast to their 200-years-old songs. When we reflect that the eighteenth-century Baptists chose their hymn texts largely from the works of Isaac Watts, John Cennick, and four Baptist writers, John Leland, Robert Robinson, Edmund Jones, and Samuel Stennett, we understand better why it happens that the eight most widely sung texts of the early nineteenth-century folk-singers were written by precisely these men.[1]

Knowing that the Methodists found out in 1800 how successfully the devil could be fought with Baptist song-fire, it is easier to see why the songs then went along with the Wesleyan revivalists everywhere until they even became known as "Methodist music". This understanding clears up the case of the Methodist *Revivalist* of Troy, N. Y., 1868. We now know that its 185 revival

[1] The first lines of these texts are:

Jesus, my all, to heaven is gone (Cennick)
O when shall I see Jesus (Leland)
Alas, and did my Savior bleed (Watts)
Come, thou fount of every blessing (Robinson)
Come, humble sinner in whose breast (Jones)
On Jordan's stormy banks I stand (Stennett)
Children of the heavenly King (Cennick)
When I can read my title clear (Watts)

They appear in 18 folk-hymns and 39 revival spirituals.

spirituals songs and folk-hymns reflect a rich strong Yankee Methodist singing tradition of long standing, one which was essentially the same then as that of the northeastern Baptists, but of later adoption by the Methodists. We also understand better why the negroes, south and north (Methodists or Baptists, by and large, since their Christianizing) have made this folk-song tradition their own for a century now.

Knowing finally of the electric nature of this song current, we understand why its sparks leaped the Atlantic with the camp meetings in the very first years of the last century and gave new song-life to the "Ranters", as the English Primitive Methodists were called.

> The Lord a glorious work begun,
> And thro' America it run,
> Across the sea it flies;
> This work is now to us come near,
> And many are converted here,
> We see it with our eyes.
>
> The little cloud increases still
> That first arose upon Mow Hill,
> It spreads along the plain.
> Tho' men attempt to stop its course,
> It flies in spite of all their force,
> And proves their efforts vain.[1]

Modal Nature of Tunes

The modal aspects of the tunes are about the same as those of the melodies in *Spiritual Folk-Songs* as Hilton Rufty found them.[2] This will be seen by comparing the Table of Modal Incidence on page 8 of this Introduction with the data on page 16f of the preceding volume. A few comments on the Table may be in place here.

It will be noted that mode 1, in full and gapped forms, occurs in only 6% of the tunes; mode 2, 31%; mode 3, 46%; mode 4, 10%; and mode 5, only 1%.[3] Mr. Rufty's Classification Chart of Tunes, inserted at the end of *Spiritual Folk-*

[1] From *Hymns and Spiritual Songs for the use of Primitive Methodists Generally Called Ranters*, hymn No. 41. It is attributed (Benson, p. 276) to Hugh Bourne who, under the influence of the American evangelist Lorenzo Dow, started camp meetings in England. Most of the hymns (no tunes are given) in this book are duplicates or variants of those found in American "songsters" of the early nineteenth century period.

[2] Mr. Rufty determined the modal nature also of some two thirds of the tunes in the present collection.

[3] About 6% of the tunes fail, for one reason or another, to fit into the Rufty classification scheme.

TABLE OF MODAL INCIDENCE

		Tones Represented							Number of Songs	
MODE 1	Pentatonic...........	I	II	—	IV	V	VI	—	6	
	Hexatonic A	I	II	III	IV	V	VI	—	3	
	Hexatonic b	I	II	—	IV	V	VI	7	3	
	Heptatonic ionian	I	II	III	IV	V	VI	VII	1	
	Heptatonic mixolydian	I	II	III	IV	V	VI	7	5	18
MODE 2[1]	Pentatonic...........	I	—	3	IV	V	—	7	13	
	Hexatonic A	I	II	3	IV	V	—	7	36	
	Hexatonic b	I	—	3	IV	V	6	7	5	
	Heptatonic dorian	I	II	3	IV	V	VI	7	7	
	Heptatonic aeolian....	I	II	3	IV	V	6	7	33	94
MODE 3	Pentatonic...........	I	II	III	—	V	VI	—	43	
	Hexatonic A.........	I	II	III	—	V	VI	VII	28	
	Hexatonic b	I	II	III	IV	V	VI	—	33	
	Heptatonic ionian	I	II	III	IV	V	VI	VII	32	
	Heptatonic mixolydian	I	II	III	IV	V	VI	7	1	137
MODE 4	Pentatonic...........	I	II	—	IV	V	—	7	2	
	Hexatonic A.........	I	II	—	IV	V	VI	7	5	
	Hexatonic a	I	II	—	IV	V	6	7	2	
	Hexatonic b	I	II	3	IV	V	—	7	6	
	Heptatonic dorian	I	II	3	IV	V	VI	7	5	
	Heptatonic aeolian....	I	II	3	IV	V	6	7	10	30
MODE 5	Pentatonic...........	I	—	3	IV	—	6	7	2	
	Heptatonic phrygian ..	I	2	3	IV	V	6	7	1	3
	Songs which do not fit the classification scheme									18
	Total									300

Songs, shows 40 possibile varieties of modal-melodic structure. Only 23 of these varieties are found in the present collection; and if we counted out those represented by only one or two songs each, the varieties would be reduced to 18.[2] Just which varieties fail to appear may be ascertained by comparing the Table with the Rufty Chart.

The incidence of gapped and full tunes is also about the same here as in the previous collection. The five-tone (two-gapped) tunes are 25% of the 283 class-

[1] Among the 94 songs cast in the second mode, 13 were minorized, presumably by their editors.

[2] These empty spaces — failures of actual tunes to fill out the ample Rufty framework — will counteract the surprise registered by Miss Anne G. Gilchrist (in her incisive review of *Spiritual Folk-Songs*, JFDS, iii, 214) at the expansion in America of the modal scheme which she drafted for Gaelic tunes back in 1910. See JFSS, v, 150ff.

ifiable ones; the six-tone (one-gapped) melodies, 40%; and the full seven-tone, 35%.

The often observed tendency of folk-singers to flatten the seventh of the scale[1] is shown here clearly by the presence of 154 songs with that feature as opposed to 61 with the raised seventh or leading tone.[2] Eighty-five tunes have no seventh at all.

I shall leave the analysis of the finer points of modality to those more competent in the field. I refer, for example, to such matters as determining which songs, among those classified as ionian, are really major; and which of those classed as mixolydian are perhaps merely ionian (major) ending on the fifth, and so on.

One more note on modality. There seems to have been a distinctly stronger trend in the South than in the North in olden times toward the reinstatement, or the preservation, of the modes. A clear indication of this is the fact that most of the mixolydian and dorian tunes in this volume are from the southern region. Another is that most of the minorized tunes — originally probably aeolian and dorian — have been found in northern books. This is not due, I think, to a regional difference in folk-singing manner, but merely to a difference in the amount of editorial "correcting" of tunes which the editors recorded from actual singing, — the southern editors doing less of it.

Acknowledgements

I wish to acknowledge the valuable help of Miss Mary O. Eddy, Mr. John Lair, Mrs. Annabel Morris Buchanan, and Mr. Edward Deming Andrews for laying rare song books in my hands and allowing me to draw from them. I have been greatly aided by the generous cooperation of Dr. Harold Spivacke, Chief of the Music Division, Library of Congress; Dr. Carleton Sprague Smith, Chief of the Music Division, New York Public Library; Mr. Clarence S. Brigham, Director, The American Antiquarian Society, Worcester, Massachusetts; and Dr. Kenneth S. Gapp, Librarian of the Theological Seminary, Princeton, New Jersey.

For allowing me to use certain songs which appear also in their published collections I am endebted to Miss Maud Karpeles and the Oxford University Press, and Professor Arthur Kyle Davis and the Harvard University Press. For permitting me to record and/or publish rare songs of theirs I am in debt to Professor A. M. Harris, Miss Helen Hartness Flanders, Professor Josiah H. Combs, Mr. Keith Mixson, and Dr. Sam L. Clark. For permission to use songs from the Denson Revision of the *Original Sacred Harp* I wish to thank especially Mr. Paine Denson and Mr. Howard Denson. My greatest debt of gratitude for song

[1] In actual folk singing the seventh is often neutral. The old recorder-compilers, however, made no note of this fine distinction; and I have taken their recordings without question.

[2] This number would be larger if we included tunes which were obviously minorized by their compilers.

acquisitions is due Mr. Winston Wilkinson and Dr. John Lloyd Newcomb, president of the University of Virginia, for permission to publish here the cluster of songs recorded by Mr. Wilkinson and listed on page 2 above.

Mr. John Powell, Miss Anne G. Gilchrist, Mr. Winston Wilkinson, and Mr. Hilton Rufty have been my most highly valued critics and helpers in the preparation of this book. Whatever may be its value, a good share of it is due to their musicianship, knowledge of folklore, and friendly generosity.

Equally generous co-workers have been my sister, Mrs. Genevieve Jackson Beckwith; my daughter-in-law, Mrs. Jane Neil Jackson; and my daughter, Mrs. Frances Jackson Parker. For their critical reading and correction of manuscript and proofs I wish to record my affectionate gratitude.

George Pullen Jackson
Vanderbilt University

Nashville, Tennessee, April 1, 1939

Sixty Religious Ballads

Including Carols and Songs of Farewell, Religious Experience and Exhortation,
Intended Chiefly for Individual Singing

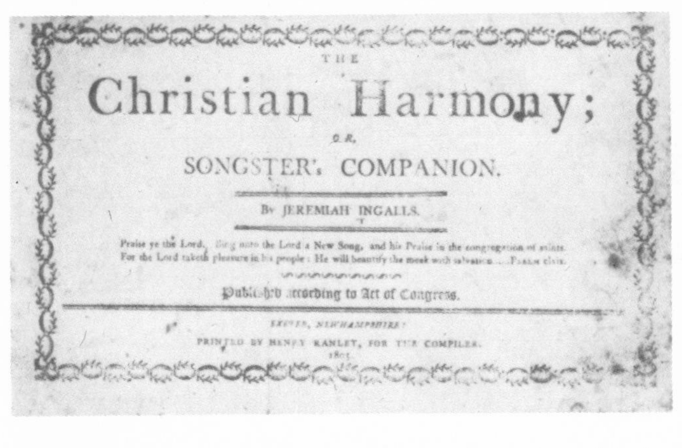

THE

Christian Harmony;

OR,

SONGSTER's COMPANION.

By JEREMIAH INGALLS.

Praise ye the Lord. Sing unto the Lord a New Song, and his Praise in the congregation of saints. For the Lord taketh pleasure in his people: He will beautify the meek with salvation.....Psalm cxlix.

Published according to Act of Congress.

EXETER, NEWHAMPSHIRE:

PRINTED BY HENRY RANLET, FOR THE COMPILER.

1805.

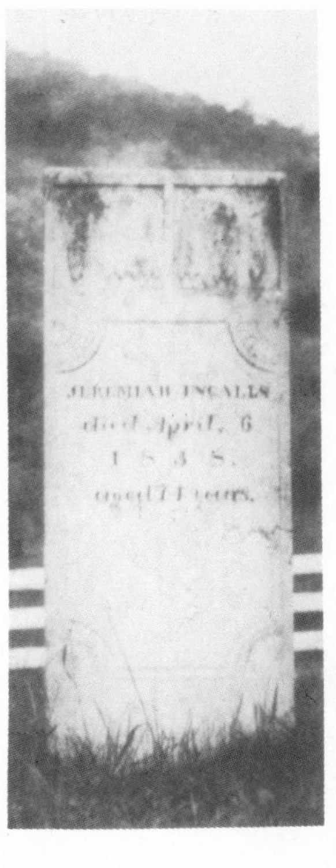
JEREMIAH INGALLS
died April, 6

TITLE PAGE OF THE OLDEST KNOWN BOOK of American spiritual folk-tunes. It appeared in New Hampshire in 1805.

JEREMIAH INGALLS, author of *The Christian Harmony*, rests since 1838 in the Old Cemetery in the cross-roads neighborhood called Hancock in a mountain valley of Vermont.

'INNOCENT SOUNDS' was the song which rationalized the turning of "drunken or lewd or light" lays to spiritual ends. It is on page 71 of *The Christian Harmony*. See song No. 156 in this volume.

Innocent Sounds. 71

Enlisted in the cause of sin, Why should a good be evil, Music, alas! too long has been Press'd to obey the devil.

Drunken or lew'd or light they lay, Flows to their soul's undoing, Widen and strew'd with flow'rs the way, Down to eternal ruin.

[illegible] on the part of God, will rise,
[illegible] recover;
[illegible] the prey, and seize the prize,
[illegible] the carnal lover;
[illegible] every moving strain,
[illegible] melting measure;
[illegible]
[illegible]

3 Come let us try if Jesus' love
Will not as well inspire us;
This is the theme of those above,
This upon earth should fire us:
Try if your hearts are tun'd to sing?
Is there a subject greater?
Harmony all its strains may we bring,
Jesus' name is sweeter.

4 Jesus the soul of music is,
His is the noblest passion;
Jesus' name is life and peace,
Happiness and salvation;
Jesus' name the dead can raise,
Show us our sins forgiven,
Fill us with all the life of his grace,
Carry us up to heaven.

5 Then let us in his praises join, Triumph in his salvation, Heaven already is begun, Open'd to each believer,
Glory ascribe to love divine, Worship and adoration. Only believe, and still sing on, Heaven is ours for ever.

No. 1

METHODIST AND FORMALIST, HH 454

Hexatonic, mode 3A (I II III — V VI VII)

Methodist

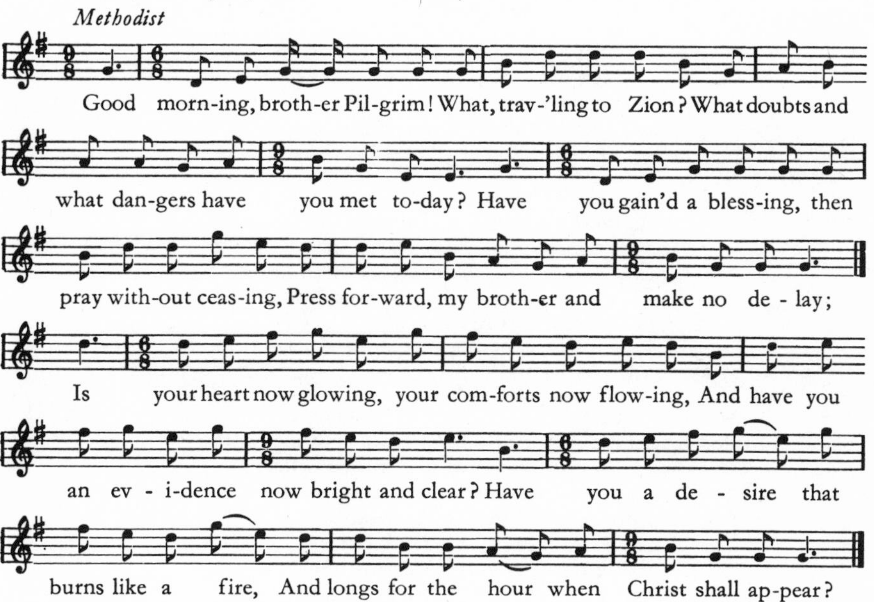
Good morn-ing, broth-er Pil-grim! What, trav-'ling to Zion? What doubts and
what dan-gers have you met to-day? Have you gain'd a bless-ing, then
pray with-out ceas-ing, Press for-ward, my broth-er and make no de - lay;
Is your heart now glowing, your com-forts now flow-ing, And have you
an ev - i-dence now bright and clear? Have you a de - sire that
burns like a fire, And longs for the hour when Christ shall ap-pear?

Formalist

I came out this morning, and now I'm returning,
Perhaps little better than when I first came,
Such groaning and shouting, it sets me to doubting,
I fear such religion is only a dream.
The preachers were stamping, the people were jumping,
And screaming so loud that I nothing could hear,
Either praying or preaching — such horrible shrieking!
I was truly offended at all that was there.

Methodist

Perhaps, my dear brother, while they prayed together
You sat and considered, but prayed not at all:
Would you find a blessing, then pray without ceasing,
Obey the advice that was given by Paul.
For if you should reason at any such season,
No wonder if Satan should tell in your ear,
That preachers and people are only a rabble,
And this is no place for reflection and prayer.

Formalist

No place for reflection — I'm filled with distraction,
I wonder that people could bear for to stay,
The men they were bawling, the women were squalling,
I know not for my part how any could pray.
Such horrid confusion — if this be religion
I'm sure that it's something that never was seen,
For the sacred pages that speak of all ages,
Do nowhere declare that such ever has been.

Methodist

Don't be so soon shaken — if I'm not mistaken
Such things were perform'd by believers of old;
When the ark was coming, King David came running,
And dancing before it, in Scripture we're told.
When the Jewish nation had laid the foundation,
To rebuild the temple at Ezra's command,
Some wept and some praiséd, such noise there was raiséd,
'Twas heard afar off and perhaps through the land.

And as for the preacher, Ezekiel the teacher,
God taught him to stamp and to smite with the hand,
To show the transgressions of that wicked nation
To bid them repent and obey the command.
For Scripture collation in this dispensation,
The blesséd Redeemer has handed it out —
"If these cease from praising," we hear him there saying,
"The stones to reprove them would quickly cry out."

Formalist

Then Scripture's contrasted, for Paul has protested
That order should reign in the house of the Lord —
Amid such a clatter who knows what's the matter?
Or who can attend unto what is declared?
To see them behaving like drunkards, all raving,
And lying and rolling prostrate on the ground,
I really felt awful, and sometimes felt fearful
That I'd be the next that would come tumbling down.

Methodist

You say you felt awful — you ought to be careful
Lest you grieve the Spirit, and so he depart,
By your own confession you've felt some impression,
The sweet melting showers have soften'd your heart.
You fear persecution, and that's a delusion
Brought in by the devil to stop up your way.
Be careful, my brother, for blest are no other
Than persons that "are not offended in Me."

As Peter was preaching, and bold in his teaching,
The plan of salvation in Jesus'es name,
The Spirit descended and some were offended,
And said of these men, "They're filled with new wine."
I never yet doubted that some of them shouted,
While others lay prostrate, by power struck down;
Some weeping, some praising, while others were saying:
"They're drunkards or fools, or in falsehood abound."

As time is now flying and moments are dying,
We're call'd to improve them, and quickly prepare
For that awful hour when Jesus, in power
And glory is coming — 'tis now drawing near.
Methinks there'll be shouting, and I'm not a-doubting,
But crying and screaming for mercy in vain;
Therefore, my dear brother, let us pray together,
That your precious soul may be fill'd with the flame.

Formalist

I own prayer's now needful, I really feel awful
That I've grieved the Spirit in time that is past;
But I'll look to my Savior, and hope to find favor,
The storms of temptation will not always last.
I'll strive for the blessing, and pray without ceasing,
His mercy is sure unto all that believe. —
My heart is now glowing! I feel his love flowing!
Peace, pardon, and comfort I now do receive!

This falls into the category of "dialog" songs which are discussed briefly in this volume under 'Calvary or Gethsemane'. It is unique in the clear way in which it presents both sides of the argument which developed in the Methodist Church and in other dissenting sects during their formative periods in America, the argument between the intransigents and the progressives. Differences of opinion like this often grew and in time became the causes of denominational divisions, the conservatives becoming known eventually as the Old or Primitive branches with a stronger hold in the country parts, and the progressives — the Formalists above — developing gradually into the various Protestant denominations as we see them today in towns and cities.

The tune is of that Celtic-dance sort which is spoken of under 'South Union' in this volume.

No. 2

CHRISTIAN WARFARE, GOS 603

Hexatonic, mode 1 b (I II — IV V VI 7)

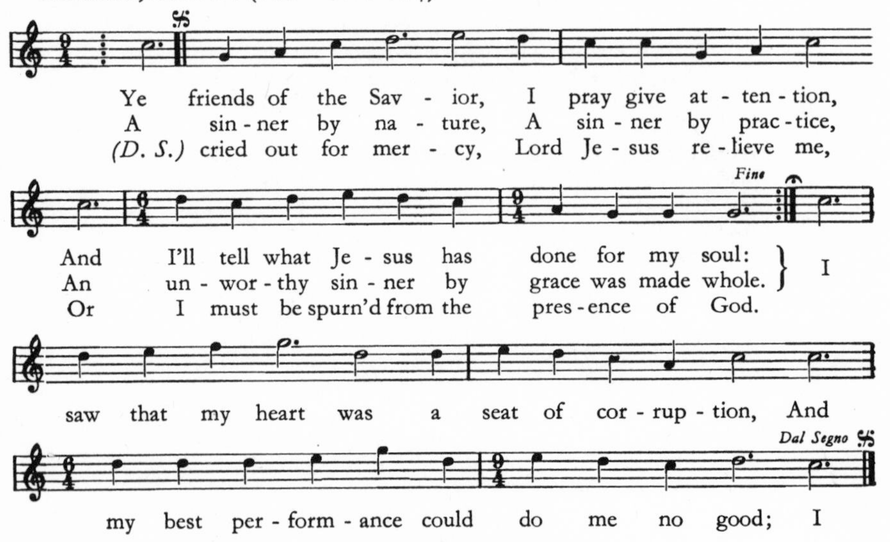
Ye friends of the Sav - ior, I pray give at - ten - tion,
A sin - ner by na - ture, A sin - ner by prac - tice,
(D. S.) cried out for mer - cy, Lord Je - sus re - lieve me,
Fine
And I'll tell what Je - sus has done for my soul:
An un - wor - thy sin - ner by grace was made whole.
I
Or I must be spurn'd from the pres - ence of God.
saw that my heart was a seat of cor - rup - tion, And
Dal Segno
my best per - form - ance could do me no good; I

But mercy, free mercy, that still interposes,
And pleads for the vilest of sinners like me;
God's goodness appear'd in the suff'rings of Jesus,
And open'd the way for to set my soul free.
God's justice requiréd a sinless obedience,
And I was asham'd and I fell to the ground;
Then Jesus appearéd and quickly relieved me,
And that very moment the pardon I found.

I soon did discover my guilt was removéd,
And I was deliver'd from under the law;
For Christ's pure obedience, when strictly examined
By justice, it would not admit of one flaw.
On this I depend for my justification,
When I must appear in the judgment to come,
And for my adoption and sanctification
And true perseverance, until I get home.

Now, if I have told you a Christian experience,
In token of fellowship give me your hand;
We'll join in sweet union, in Christian devotion,
And glorify Jesus as well as we can.

And if you'll agree to my short experience,
And join in a compact to serve my dear Lord,
My soul will rejoice and I'll call you my kindred,
And patiently wait for my glorious reward.

And when we've accomplish'd our days as a hireling,
We then shall lay down these vile bodies of clay;
We'll join with those spirits who've enter'd before us,
To sing of redemption through Jesus'es blood;
We'll cease to complain of temptation and sorrow,
We'll enter the city and there we'll get home;
All glory, all glory, all glory to Jesus,
The saint is at rest and set down on his throne.

The text presents a remarkably complete and typical example of conversion according to the Arminian method. *Good Old Songs* credits it to William Walker; but in Walker's *Southern Harmony* (1835) he lays no claim to it.

The strong assertive tune is one which has been found in variant forms in the British Isles associated with secular ballad texts. References to these are given in *Spiritual Folk-Songs*.[1] 'Louisiana' and 'Zion's Walls' in this volume are melodically related. The time designation in *Good Old Songs* is straight six-four. The above alterations in that metrical pattern are mine.

No. 3

BOWER OF PRAYER, HH 327

Pentatonic, mode 3 (I II III — V VI —)

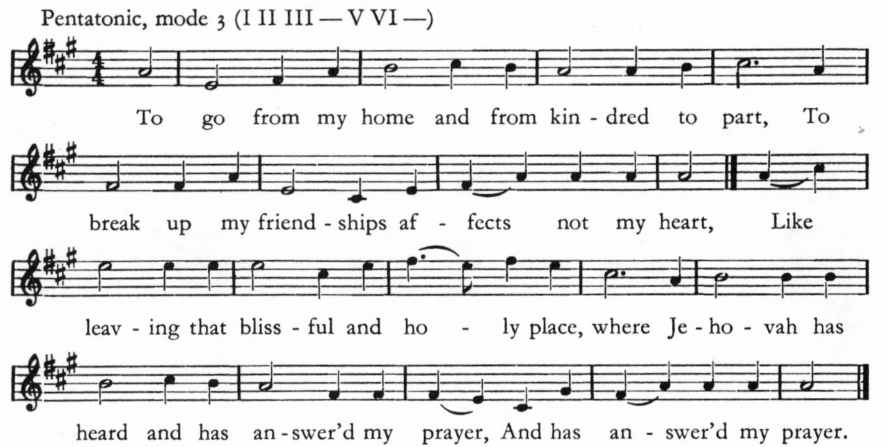
To go from my home and from kin - dred to part, To
break up my friend - ships af - fects not my heart, Like
leav - ing that bliss - ful and ho - ly place, where Je - ho - vah has
heard and has an - swer'd my prayer, And has an - swer'd my prayer.

[1] No. 28. Add to those references 'Lord Ullin's Daughter', *Our Familiar Songs*, p. 331.

Sweet bower! where the vine and the poplar o'erspread,
Have woven their branches a roof for my head.
How oft have I knelt by the evergreen there,
And poured out my soul to the Savior in prayer.

The early sweet notes of the lov'd nightingale,
My hours of devotion would faithfully tell —
Would call me to duty, while birds in the air
Sang anthems of praises as I went to prayer.

How sweet were the zephyrs perfum'd by the pine,
The ivy, the balsam, the wild eglantine!
But sweeter, O sweeter, the pleasure which there
I often have tasted while offering my prayer.

But soon I must bid my lov'd bower adieu.
And leave for a region that's distant and new.
Yet, O blessèd thought! I've a friend everywhere,
Who will, in all places, give ear to my prayer.

His love and his pow'r he will daily impart,
To strengthen my mind and to gladden my heart;
And when on my death-bed, he'll be with me there,
And take me to heaven in answer to prayer.

And high in the mansions of glory and joy,
My soul shall be blest with delightful employ —
Be freed from all sorrow, and anguish and care,
And bask in his smile who has answered my prayer.

There is no clue to the source of this song excepting that the words nightingale, balsam, and wild eglantine point to the British Isles. The song is found in many southern rural song books.

No. 4

DYING PENITENT, VH 50

Hexatonic, mode 3A (I II III — V VI VII)

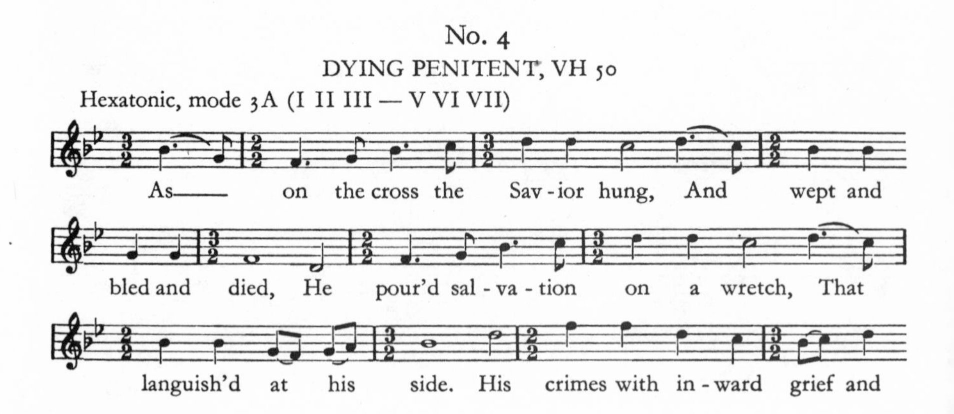
As— on the cross the Sav-ior hung, And wept and
bled and died, He pour'd sal-va-tion on a wretch, That
languish'd at his side. His crimes with in-ward grief and

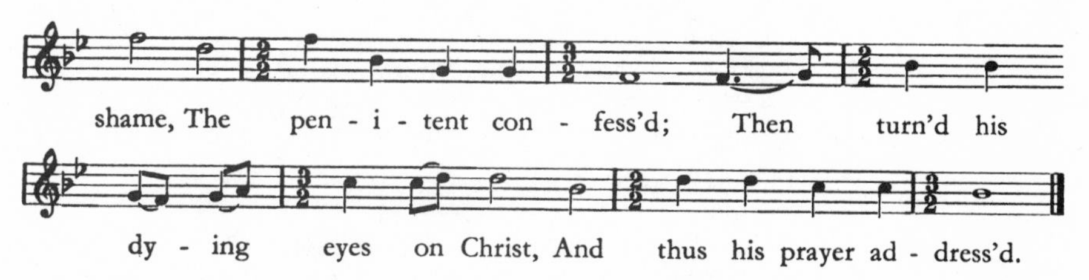
shame, The pen - i - tent con - fess'd; Then turn'd his
dy - ing eyes on Christ, And thus his prayer ad - dress'd.

The complete text, which is anonymous, is given with 'Deep Spring' in *Spiritual Folk-Songs*. The *Virginia Harmony* gives the source of the tune as "Carrell", meaning James P. Carrell, compiler of that song book. I have found it and its many variants to be an eighteenth century secular folk-tune from the British Isles. References to these are given in *Spiritual Folk-Songs* under 'Separation'. A related tune in this volume is 'Foster'.

No. 5

SOUTH UNION, OL 201

Pentatonic, mode 3 (I II III — V VI —)

Ho - san - na to Je - sus! I'm fill'd with his praises; Come, O my dear
brethren, and help me to sing! No theme is so charming, no love is so
warming; It gives joy and glad - ness and com - fort with - in. Ho-
san - na is ring-ing, I'm hap - py while sing - ing, There's nothing so
sweet as the sound of his name; The an - gels in glo - ry repeat the glad sto - ry Of Je - sus - 'es love which is made known to men.

Hosanna to Jesus! He suffered to save us;
We'll love him and serve him wherever we go;
Ascended to heaven, the spirit he's given
To quicken and comfort his children below.

Hosanna forever! His grace, like a river,
Is rising and spreading all over the land.
His love is unbounded; to all it's extended;
And sinners are joining the heavenly band.

Hosanna to Jesus! the soul how it pleases
To see sinners falling and crying to God!
Believing in Jesus their agony ceases;
Their souls are all cleans'd in Emmanuel's blood.

Hosanna is ringing! O how they are singing
The praises of Jesus and tasting his love!
The sound goes to heaven; the spirit is given,
And rolls through the soul from the mansions above.

The musical time designation accompanying texts in this dactylic meter is usually six-eight. The above two-part time is thus abnormal.[1] The Gaelic flavor in tune and words is unmistakable. Miss Anne G. Gilchrist was the first to call attention to the Gaelic assonances and rhymes of the sorts which appear in most of the above lines and to point to their probable source. Such songs, she states, "imitate with more or less success in an alien tongue the assonantal Gaelic rhymes with which their makers, whether hedge-schoolmasters or peasants, were doubtless familiar."[2] Examples of such features in the above song are

Hosanna to *Jesus* [pron. *Jases*], the s*o*ul how it *pleases* [*plaises*].
The *praises* of *Jases* and *tast*ing his love.
And *rolls* through the *soul* from the mansions above.
Be*lav*ing in *Jases* their agony *sayses.*

The editor of the *Olive Leaf* stated that he got the song from "Maj. Wm. Denny, of Guilford County, N. C. He learned this tune [song] at South Union, a Shaker village in Kentucky." This seems to indicate that it is a real Shaker song. South Union is in that section of Kentucky where the Scotch-Irish Revival (as the Great Southern and Western Revival was often called) was kindled and where camp meetings were born. This settlement not only dates from the time of that movement (about 1805) but also was founded by those who were active in the revival itself.

[1] Compare in this regard 'Hosanna is Ringing', 'Transport', 'Come Christians', and 'Royal Band' in this volume.

[2] See JFSS, v, 46. I made the regrettable error, when quoting Miss Gilchrist's statement on page 70 of my *Spiritual Folk-Songs*, of attributing it to Cecil Sharp.

No. 6

REDEEMING GRACE, UHH 65

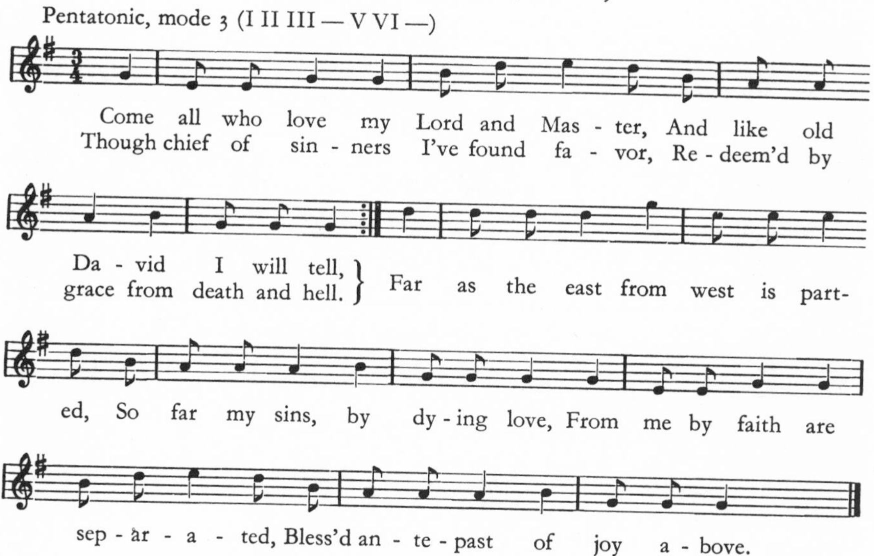
Pentatonic, mode 3 (I II III — V VI —)
Come all who love my Lord and Mas - ter, And like old
Though chief of sin - ners I've found fa - vor, Re - deem'd by
Da - vid I will tell,
grace from death and hell.
Far as the east from west is part-
ed, So far my sins, by dy - ing love, From me by faith are
sep - ar - a - ted, Bless'd an - te - past of joy a - bove.

I late estranged from Jesus wander'd,
And thought each dangerous poison good,
But he in mercy has pursued me,
With cries of his redeeming blood.
Though like Bartimeus I was blinded,
In nature's darkest night conceal'd,
But Jesus' love removed my blindness,
And he his pardoning grace reveal'd.

Now I will praise him, if he spares me,
And with his people sing aloud,
Although opposed, and sinners mock me,
In rapturous songs I'll praise my God.
By faith I view the heavenly concert,
They sing high strains of Jesus' love;
O! with desire my soul is longing,
And fain would be with Christ above.

No. 7

WAY TO CANAAN, SWP 18

Hexatonic, mode 2A (I II 3 IV V — 7)

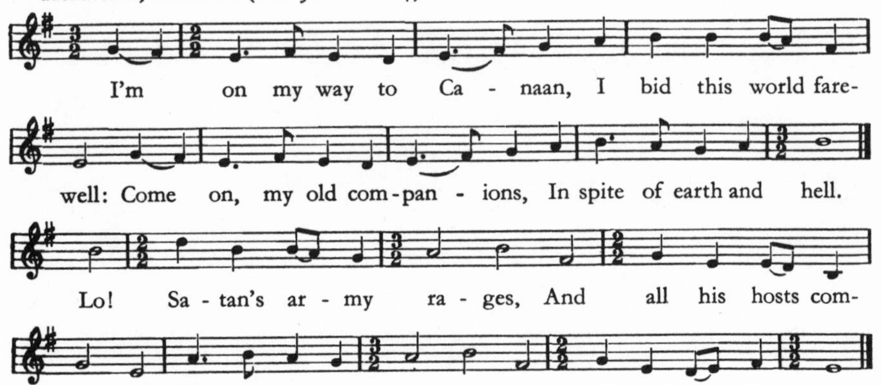
I'm on my way to Ca - naan, I bid this world fare-
well: Come on, my old com-pan - ions, In spite of earth and hell.
Lo! Sa - tan's ar - my ra - ges, And all his hosts com-
bine! Yet Scrip-ture doth en - gage us, The strength of grace di - vine.

I'll blow the silver trumpet, and on the nations call,
For Christ hath me commissioned to say he died for all.
Come try his grace and prove him, you shall the gift obtain;
He will not send you empty, nor let you come in vain.

And if you want a witness, here are some just at hand,
Have lately felt the sweetness now flowing from that land.
It comes in copious showers our bodies can't contain;
It fills our ransomed powers — and now we drink again.

The glories of that kingdom my soul cannot describe;
I feel it is within me, I feel the blood supplied.
O come unto the Savior's arms, and you shall feel his love.
'Tis sweeter than all other charms, it comes from heaven above.

The glories of that heavenly place I've ofttimes felt before,
But what I've felt is but a taste, which makes me look for more.
Had I the pinions of the dove, I'd fly and be at rest;
Then would I soar to worlds above, and be forever blest.

There are three more stanzas of this text in the *Southern and Western Pocket Harmonist.* Of a close variant of the above melody, Frank Kidson stated, "This air is one of the finest as well as one of the most commonly known in British folk-music. It appears to have been sung for narrative ballads for a great length of time."[1] As witness he pointed to 'Gilderoy', a florid tune in D'Urfey,[2] and to

[1] JWF, i, 142. [2] *Pills to Purge Melancholy*, Vol. v.

'Ah! Chloris' in the Johnson collection.[1] A branch of this tune family, usually found in six-eight time, is called the 'Lazarus' group in the British Isles[2] and is represented in America by 'Lazarus and Dives'[3] which is reproduced in this volume by permission. Other related tunes found in the British Isles, and in connection with which still further references are given, are 'Irish Air',[4] 'Our General Bold Captain',[5] and 'Murder of Maria Martin'.[6]

No. 8

WHEN I AM GONE, PB 256

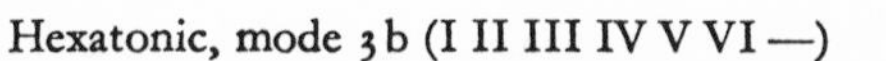

Hexatonic, mode 3b (I II III IV V VI —)

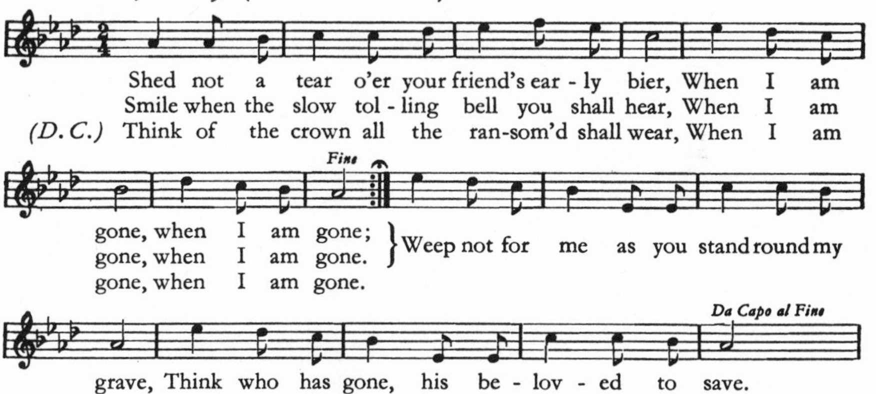
Shed not a tear o'er your friend's ear - ly bier, When I am
Smile when the slow tol - ling bell you shall hear, When I am
(D. C.) Think of the crown all the ran-som'd shall wear, When I am
Fine
gone, when I am gone;
gone, when I am gone.
gone, when I am gone.
Weep not for me as you stand round my
Da Capo al Fine
grave, Think who has gone, his be - lov - ed to save.

Plant you a rose that shall bloom o'er my grave,
When I am gone, when I am gone;
Sing a sweet song such as angels may have,
When I am gone, when I am gone.
Praise ye the Lord that I'm freed from all care,
Pray ye the Lord that my joy you may share;
Look up to heaven and believe that I'm there,
When I am gone, when I am gone.

This is an adaptation of 'Long, Long Ago', a secular song which has enjoyed enduring popularity and has been flattered by much parodying. The adapter in this case was Mary Stanley Bunce Dana Shindler. The song appeared first on page 76 of her *Southern Harp*, a collection of songs utilizing her own poetic works and published by Parker and Ditson, Boston, 1841. She gives T. H. Bayly as the composer of the music. Thomas Haynes Bayly (1797–1839) was an English composer of popular songs.

[1] *Scots Musical Museum*, p. 5.
[2] See JWF, i, 139ff.
[3] Davis, p. 566.
[4] JFSS, i, 238.
[5] *Ibid.*, i, 136.
[6] *Ibid.*, ii, 118.

No. 9

COME SAINTS AND SINNERS, SWP 69

Hexatonic, mode 3A (I II III — V VI VII)

Come, saints and sin - ners, hear me tell The won-ders of Im-
man - u - el Who snatch'd me from a burn - ing hell, And brought my
soul with him to dwell, To dwell, in sweet - est un - ion.

When Jesus from his throne on high
Beheld my soul in ruin lie,
He looked on me with pitying eye,
And said to me as he pass'd by,
"With God you have no union."

This information made me cry,
I strove salvation hard to buy,
And with my tears to satisfy;
I looked this way and that to fly,
For still I lacked this union.

But when depress'd and lost in sin,
My dear Redeemer took me in,
And with his blood he wash'd me clean,
And O what seasons I have seen!
Since first I felt this union.

I prais'd the Lord both night and day,
And went from house to house to pray,
And if I met one in the way,
Something I always found to say
About this heavenly union.

O come, ye lukewarm, come away,
And learn to do as well as say,
And bear your cross from day to day,
And mind to walk the narrow way,
And then you'll feel this union.

I wonder that the saints don't sing,
And make the hills and valleys ring
With loud hosannas to their King,
Who sav'd their souls from hell and sin,
And brought about this union.

We soon shall leave these climes below
And every scene of pain and woe,
We all shall then to glory go,
And there we'll see and hear and know
And join in perfect union.

Come heaven and earth unite your lays,
And give Jehovah-Jesus praise,
And thou, my soul, look up and gaze,
He bleeds, he dies, thy debt he pays
To give thee heavenly union.

O were I like an angel found,
Salvation through the earth I'd sound,
The devil's kingdom to confound,
I'd triumph on Immanuel's ground,
And spread this glorious union.

This song, with its insistent text burden of union of man with God, seems peculiarly Baptistic and Methodistic. It appeared in the very earliest American recordings of spiritual folk-songs, that is, in Ingalls' *Christian Harmony* of 1805.[1] With its usual ten stanzas as above (though we find in different places as many as 24 entirely different stanzas all built on the same unique plan and ending in "union") the song romped through the more than six decades following the time of the Ingalls book and up to its appearance in the *Revivalist* of post-Civil War times.[2] Its appearance also in the English Ranters' (Primitive Methodists') *Hymns and Spiritual Songs* of around 1820[3] and in *Richard Weaver's* (English) *Tune Book* of 1861[4] shows that its popularity was not confined to America.

No. 10

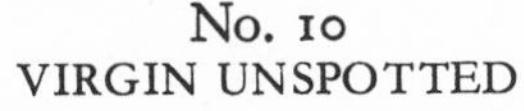

VIRGIN UNSPOTTED

Hexatonic, mode 1A (I II III IV V VI —)

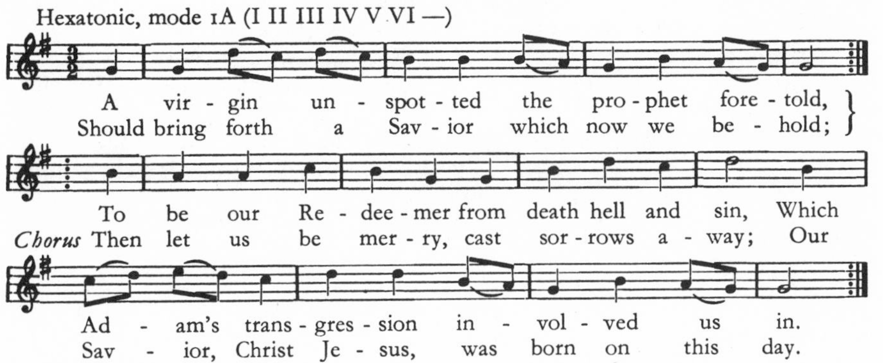
A vir - gin un - spot - ted the pro - phet fore - told,
Should bring forth a Sav - ior which now we be - hold;
To be our Re - dee - mer from death hell and sin, Which
Chorus Then let us be mer - ry, cast sor - rows a - way; Our
Ad - am's trans - gres - sion in - vol - ved us in.
Sav - ior, Christ Je - sus, was born on this day.

[1] Page 30. See also CL, i, 74.

[2] Reproduced in *Spiritual Folk-Songs*, No. 37, with a variant tune.

[3] Hymn No. 8. [4] Reproduced by Miss Gilchrist, JFSS, viii, 80. It has a variant tune.

Through Bethlehem city in Jewry it was,
That Joseph and Mary together did pass;
And for to be taxéd when thither they came,
Since Caesar Augustus commanded the same.
(Chorus) Then let us be merry *etc.*

But Mary's full time being come, as we find,
She brought forth her first born to serve all mankind.
The inn being full for this heavenly guest,
No place there was found for to lay him to rest.

But Mary, blest Mary, so meek and so mild,
Soon wrappéd in swadlings this heavenly child.
Contented she laid him where oxen [did] feed,
The great God of nature approv'd of the deed.

Then presently after, the shepherds did spy
Vast numbers of angels to stand in the sky;
So merrily talking, so sweet they did sing:
All glory and praise to our heavenly King.

The song was found in Catherine Alderice's manuscript four-shape-note song book, made at or near Emmittsburg, Maryland, between 1800 and 1830, p. 198. The only other American recording of this undoubtedly Old World carol is the slightly variant tune found by Annabel Morris Buchanan in Wyeth's *Repository of Sacred Music* of 1813 and reproduced — along with the text which I lent her from the above song — in harmonized form in her *Folk Hymns of America.*[1] Of the four English versions of the tune which were given by Cecil Sharp,[2] the fourth is most like the above. A version which is musically and textually the same as the Alderice song was found in J. Arnold's *Compleat Psalmodist* of 1750.[3] I have found a close variant of the tune associated with an Annunciation text in a recent collection of folk-songs from the Bavarian Highlands entitled 'Der englische Gruß'.[4]

Dr. Ralph Vaughan-Williams told me, on seeing the Alderice song, that he looked on the tune as one which had wandered freely in Europe for a long time. My Bavarian find tends to support his opinion.

[1] No. 40.
[2] JFSS, v, 24f.
[3] *Ibid.*, v, 325.
[4] Kurt Huber und Kiem-Pauli. *Altbayerisches Liederbuch.* Mainz, Edition Schott, 1937, p. 37.

No. 11

LAZARUS AND DIVES, Davis, p. 566.

Pentatonic, mode 3 (I II III — V VI —)

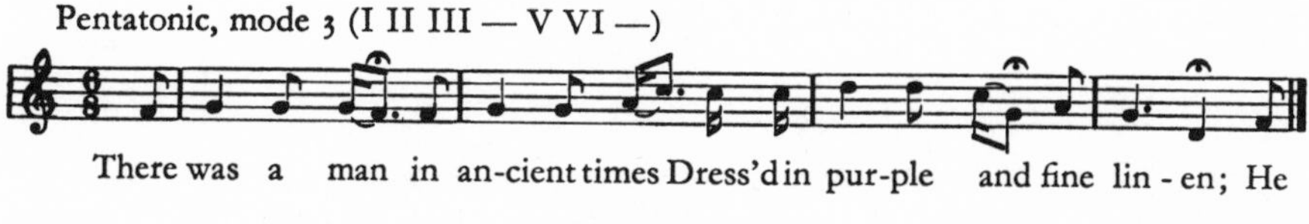
There was a man in an-cient times Dress'd in pur-ple and fine lin - en; He

ate, he drank, but scorn'd to pray, Spent all of his days in sin - ning.

This song is reproduced with kind permission from Arthur Kyle Davis' *Traditional Ballads of Virginia*. The text, as Davis points out, has nothing but the biblical-story background in common with that of the Child ballad with the same title, No. 56. The outstanding characteristic of this text, the prevalence of feminine rhymes — *linen, sinning; condition, damnation* — and of other similar line endings not rhyming, a characteristic not at home in English verse, has led me to suspect that the text came into the English language environment from some Celtic version. This suspicion was strengthened when I noted a close relationship of the above tune to an 'Irish Air' in the *English Folk-Song Journal*[1] and to the Welsh 'The Beauties of Conway',[2] both of which have the same rhythm and type of endings. It was further strengthened when I noted that the Virginia tune was recorded in a part of the state, Alleghany County, where Scotch-Irish influence was marked,[3] and that a recent recording of a close variant of the tune was made by Edwin Capers Kirkland and Mary Neal Kirkland in eastern Tennessee.[4] It seems hardly to be doubted therefore that the song came to the Appalachian Mountains region with the Celtic settlers.[5]

This type of tune is called in England the 'Lazarus' type. I have considered an American branch, or side line — most of the examples of which are found in six-eight time — as the 'Babe of Bethlehem' tune family.[6]

[1] JFSS, i, 238.

[2] JWF, i, 141.

[3] Note the names of some of the settlements in that county: Griffith, Flynn, Glen Wilton, Callaghan, McDowell, Gala, and Lemon.

[4] SFQ, ii, 67.

[5] A further American variant of the tune is Sharp-Karpeles, ii, 29.

[6] For references to the wider 'Babe of Bethlehem' tune connection see 'Old Israelites' in this volume.

No. 12

CHRIST IN THE GARDEN (A), RHD 48

Hexatonic, mode 3A (I II III IV V VI —)

Fine
When na - ture was sink - ing in still - ness to rest,
The last beams of day - light shone dim in the west,
(D.C.) The moon cast her pale - ness in lone sol - i - tude.
Da Capo al Fine
In deep med - i - ta - tion I wan - der'd a - broad,

While passing a garden I lingered to hear,
A voice, faint and plaintive, from one kneeling there;
The voice of the suppliant affected my heart,
While pleading in anguish, the poor sinner's part.

In offering to heaven his pitying prayer,
He spake of the torments the sinner must bear;
His life as a ransom he offered to give,
That sinners redeemèd in glory might live.

I listened a moment, then turned me to see
What man of compassion this stranger could be;
When lo! I discover'd, knelt on the cold ground,
The lovliest being I ever had found.

His mantle was wet with the dews of the night —
His locks by pale moonlight were gliss'ning and bright;
His eyes, mildly beaming, to heaven were rais'd,
While round him in grandeur stood angels, amaz'd.

So deep was his sorrow, so fervent his prayers,
That down o'er his bosom roll'd blood, sweat, and tears!
I wept to behold him, and asked him his name —
He answered, "'Tis JESUS! From heaven I came.

"I am thy REDEEMER — for thee I must die;
The cup is most bitter, but cannot pass by;
Thy sins, which are many, are laid upon me,
And all this sore anguish I suffer for thee!"

I heard with deep sorrow, the tale of his wo,
While tears of repentance mine eyes did o'erflow;
The cause of his sorrows to hear him repeat,
Pierc'd deeply my bosom — I fell at his feet.

In humble contrition I poured out my cry,
"Lord, save a poor sinner! O save, or I die!"
He smiled, when he saw me, and said to me, "Live!
Thy sins which were many, I freely forgive!"

How sweet was that sentence! — it made me rejoice!
His smiles, how consoling! How *charming* his voice!
I ran from the garden to spread it abroad,
And shouted — "*Salvation! O glory to God!*"

I'm now on my journey to mansions above —
My soul's full of glory, of light, peace, and love;
I think of the garden, the prayers and the tears
Of my blessèd Jesus, who banish'd my fears.

The day of bright glory is rolling around,
When Gabriel, descending, the trumpet will sound.
My soul to the Savior, in raptures shall rise,
And see him forever, with unclouded eyes.

This song appeared, in forms which varied tonally and textually only a little, in a number of the early hymn collections of the Northeast; but I have not met with it in any of the southern fasola books. The tunes all seem folky.[1] My guess is however that the text had an individual maker and did not enjoy much revision by singers.

No. 13
CHRIST IN THE GARDEN (B)

Heptatonic ionian, mode 3 (I II III IV V VI VII)

Fine
As I pas - sed the gar - den I sor - row'd to hear
A voice of con - tri - tion from one kneel - ing there.
(D. C.) That down on his fore-head roll'd the sweat, blood and tear.
Da Capo
So deep was his sor - row And so fer - vent his prayer,

[1] See RHK 24 and 'Christ in the Garden (B)' in this volume.

Miss Helen Hartness Flanders kindly permits me to use the above song as transcribed from a dictaphone record made from the singing of Mrs. Nellie Richardson, Springfield, Vermont. A fuller text will be found under 'Christ in the Garden (A)' in this volume. The latter has a variant tune.

No. 14
HOSANNA IS RINGING, SOC 227

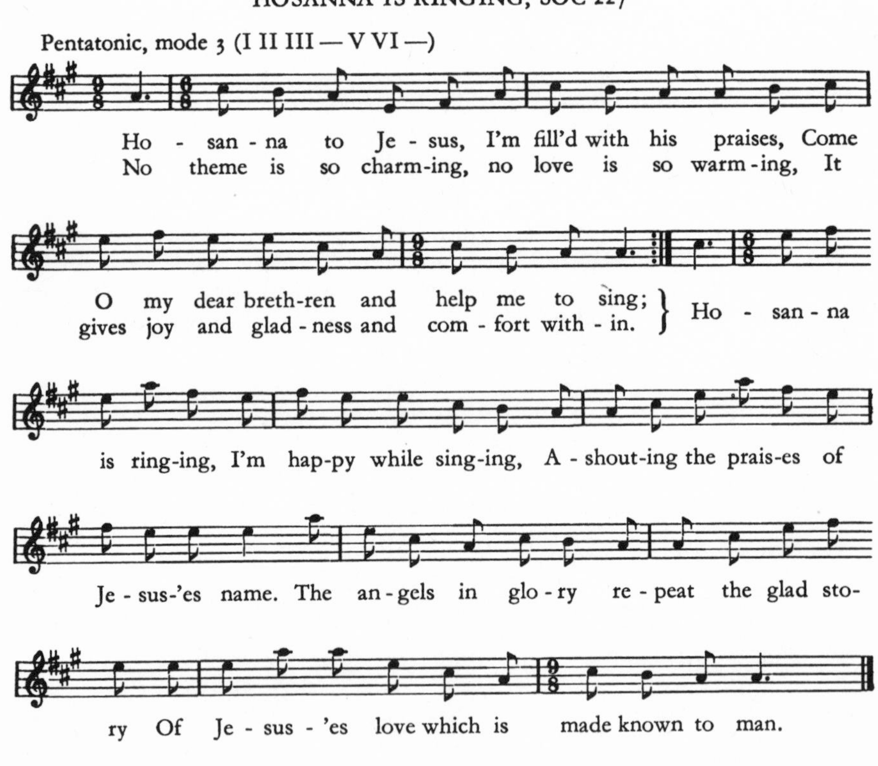
Pentatonic, mode 3 (I II III — V VI —)
Ho - san - na to Je - sus, I'm fill'd with his praises, Come
No theme is so charm-ing, no love is so warm-ing, It
O my dear breth-ren and help me to sing;
gives joy and glad - ness and com - fort with - in.
Ho - san - na
is ring-ing, I'm hap-py while sing-ing, A - shout-ing the prais-es of
Je - sus-'es name. The an - gels in glo - ry re - peat the glad sto-
ry Of Je - sus - 'es love which is made known to man.

The compiler of the *Social Harp*, John G. McCurry, claims the song and dates it December 1, 1853. The full text is given with 'South Union', in this volume, where I discuss this peculiar type of movement and rhyme. 'Royal Band' in this volume has a variant text and similar melodic-rhythmic character.

No. 15
YOUNG PEOPLE ALL, CHH 201

Pentatonic, mode 3 (I II III — V VI —)

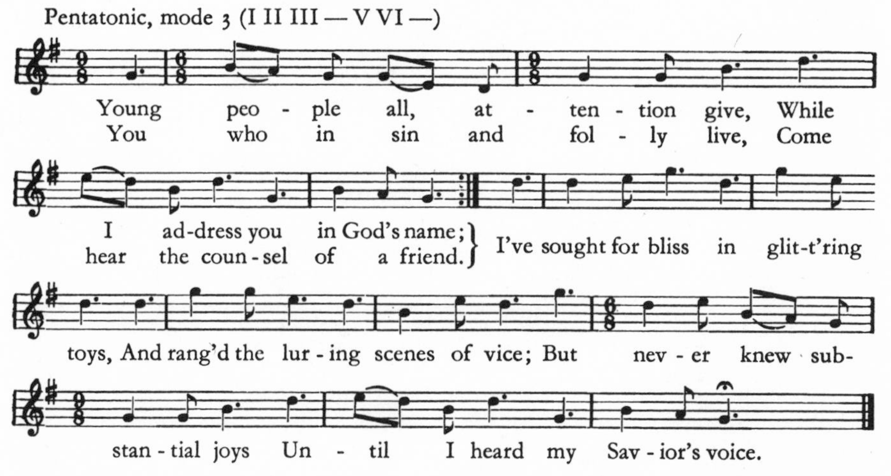
Young peo - ple all, at - ten - tion give, While
You who in sin and fol - ly live, Come
I ad-dress you in God's name;
hear the coun - sel of a friend.
I've sought for bliss in glit-t'ring
toys, And rang'd the lur - ing scenes of vice; But nev - er knew sub-
stan - tial joys Un - til I heard my Sav - ior's voice.

The song is attributed to "Rev. A. Grambling, of Spartanburg, S. C." The same text and a variant of the tune are 'Patton' in *Spiritual Folk-Songs*.

No. 16
PARTING HAND, OSH 62

Pentatonic, mode 3 (I II III — V VI —)

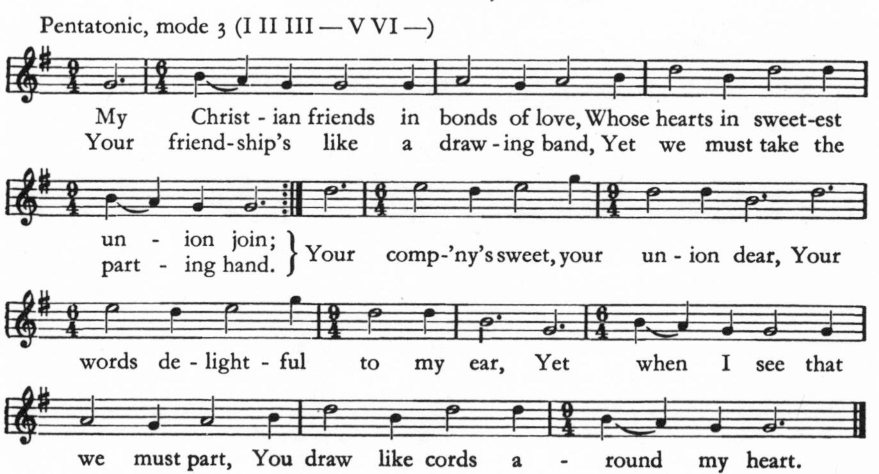
My Christ - ian friends in bonds of love, Whose hearts in sweet-est
Your friend-ship's like a draw - ing band, Yet we must take the
un - ion join;
part - ing hand.
Your comp-'ny's sweet, your un - ion dear, Your
words de - light - ful to my ear, Yet when I see that
we must part, You draw like cords a - round my heart.

How sweet the hours have passed away
Since we have met to sing and pray;
How loath we are to leave the place
Where Jesus shows his smiling face.
O could I stay with friends so kind,
How would it cheer my drooping mind!
But duty makes me understand
That we must take the parting hand.

And since it is God's holy will,
We must be parted for a while,
In sweet submission, all as one,
We'll say, our Father's will be done.
My youthful friends, in Christian ties,
Who seek for mansions in the skies,
Fight on, we'll gain that happy shore,
Where parting will be known no more.

The editor of the *Original Sacred Harp* and other song book compilers ascribe this song to Jeremiah Ingalls, 1764–1838, a singing school master who lived in Massachusetts and Vermont. It is significant, however, that this song does not appear in Ingalls' only song compilation, the *Christian Harmony* of 1805.[1] 'Parting Hand' is sung regularly by Primitive Baptist gatherings and *Sacred Harp* singing conventions at the close of their meetings while everyone moves around informally and engages in a general hand-shaking.

No. 17
STRANGER, SWP 20

Hexatonic, mode 3 A (I II III — V VI VII)

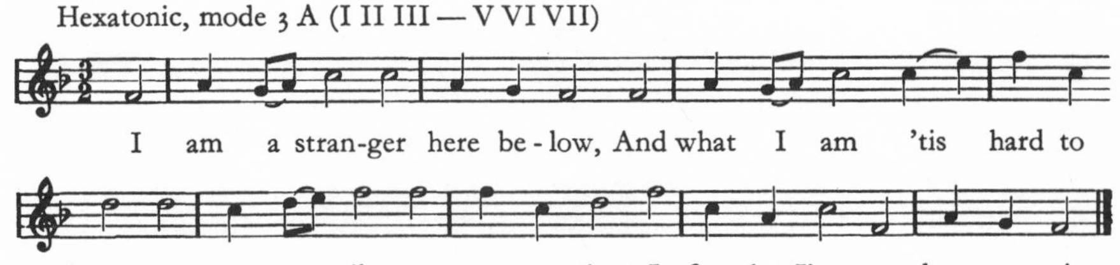
I am a stran-ger here be-low, And what I am 'tis hard to
know; I am so vile, so prone to sin, I fear that I'm not born a-gain.

When I experience call to mind,
My understanding is so blind —
All feeling sense seems to be gone,
Which makes me think that I am wrong.

[1] More about this notable man is given under 'Redeeming Love' in this volume. Burrage finds the first appearance of 'Parting Hand' to have been in the *Baptist Harmony* of 1834. He ascribes the text to John Blain (1795–1879) and states that it was written in 1818.

I find myself out of the way,
My thoughts are often gone astray;
Like one alone I seem to be —
O is there anyone like me!

'Tis seldom I can ever see
Myself as I would wish to be;
What I desire, I can't attain,
And what I hate, I can't refrain.

So far from God I seem to lie,
Which makes me often weep and cry;
I fear at last that I shall fall,
For, if a saint, the least of all.

I seldom find a heart to pray,
So many things step in my way;
Thus filled with doubts, I ask to know,
Come tell me, is it thus with you?

So by experience I do know,
There's nothing good that I can do;
I cannot satisfy the law,
Nor hope, nor comfort from it draw.

My nature is so prone to sin,
Which makes my duty so unclean,
That when I count up all the cost,
If not free grace, then I am lost.

The tune is a member of the 'Lord Lovel' family. References are given under 'Eden' in this volume.

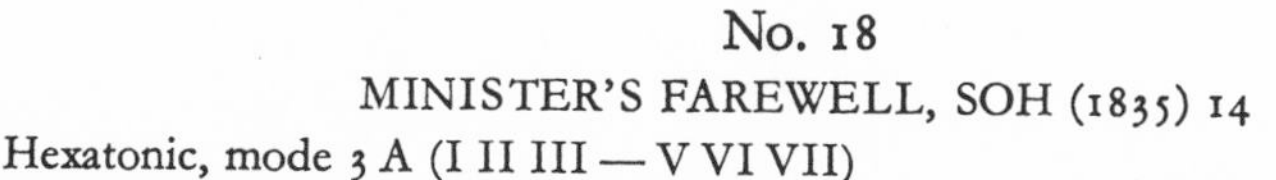

No. 18

MINISTER'S FAREWELL, SOH (1835) 14

Hexatonic, mode 3 A (I II III — V VI VII)

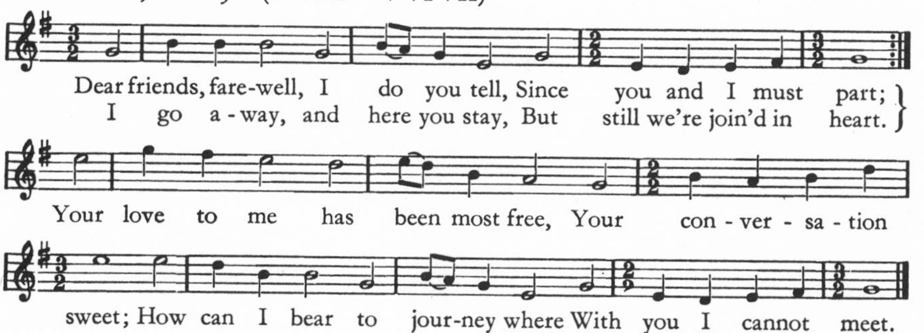
Dear friends, fare-well, I do you tell, Since you and I must part;
I go a-way, and here you stay, But still we're join'd in heart.
Your love to me has been most free, Your con-ver-sa-tion
sweet; How can I bear to jour-ney where With you I cannot meet.

Yet I do find my heart inclin'd
To do my work below;
When Christ doth call I trust I shall
Be ready then to go.
I leave you all, both great and small,
In Christ's encircling arms,
Who can you save from the cold grave,
And shield you from all harm.

I trust you'll pray, both night and day,
And keep your garments white,
For you and me, that we may be
The children of the light.
If you die first, anon you must,
The will of God be done,
I hope the Lord will you reward,
With an immortal crown.

If I'm call'd home whilst I am gone,
Indulge no tears for me;
I hope to sing and praise my King
To all eternity.
Millions of years over the spheres
Shall pass in sweet repose,
While beauty bright unto my sight
Thy sacred sweets disclose.

I long to go, then farewell wo,
My soul will be at rest;
No more shall I complain or sigh,
But taste the heavenly feast.
O may we meet, and be complete,
And long together dwell,
And serve the Lord with one accord;
And so, dear friends, farewell.

The song is found in many of the southern fasola song books.[1] The type of stanza, with medial rhyme in an unusually short line, is found also in 'Address for All' in *Spiritual Folk-Songs.*

[1] Among them, KNH 75, OSH 69, SOC 124, HH 106.

No. 19
VERNON, OSH 55

Hexatonic, mode 2 A (I II 3 IV V — 7)

Come, O thou Trav - el - er un-known, Whom still I hold but can - not see;
My com-pan - y be - fore is gone, And I am left a - lone with thee.

With thee all night I mean to stay, And wres-tle till the break of day.

I need not tell thee who I am,
My misery and sin declare;
Thyself hast call'd me by my name,
Look on thy hands and read it there.
But who, I ask thee, who art thou?
Tell me thy name, and tell it now.

In vain thou struggl'st to get free,
I never will unloose my hold;
Art thou the Man that diedst for me?
The secret of thy love unfold.
Wrestling, I will not let thee go,
Till I thy name, thy nature know.

This is all that appears in the *Sacred Harp* of the eleven-stanza poem by Charles Wesley. James, the 1911 editor of that book, states that the tune is by F. F. Chopin. Evidently he involved the Polish composer's name through some slip in a handwritten name that was intended to be "Chapin"; and "Chapin" is the Man of Mystery in southern song. We find his name as composer affixed to many songs in many books, and the tunes he "composed" are mostly folk-melodies of hoary age; but nothing definite has been found out about the man. Frank J. Metcalf hazards the guess that he is Amzi Chapin, a New Englander who ranged through Virginia and Kentucky and into Ohio where, in Northfield, he died. Here is a biographical chore for some Ohioan.

No. 20
SISTER'S FAREWELL, UHP 152

Pentatonic, mode 3 (I II III — V VI —)

Fare-well, dear broth-ers, fare you well, Pray do not weep for
me, I'm go-ing home with Christ to dwell Through-out e-ter-ni-
ty. When I get home to that bright world, And meet my Sav-ior
there, And all the lov'd ones gone be-fore, I'll no more shed a tear.

Dear sister, thou art left alone,
But thou art kind and true,
And when God calls you to come home,
I hope to meet you too;
Thus we'll surround the great white throne,
And dwell forever there,
And sing God's praise through endless days,
From sorrow, pain and care.

Dear father, you've been kind to me
When I was young and wild,
But now, dear father, do not weep,
Forgive your loving child.
O may we all together meet,
And shout and praise and sing
Hallelujah then to our God,
Our Savior and our King.

My loving mother, fare you well,
But do not fear alarm;
The Savior dear is ever near
To shield you from all harm.
Yet may we meet and be complete
With all the blood-wash'd throng,
And cast our crowns at Jesus' feet
And sing redemption's song.

The tune and its words are accredited to A. J. McLendon, of Georgia, and the song is dated 1905. McLendon evidently recorded here the orally preserved tune which was used in the two revival spiritual songs, 'Resurrected' in *Spiritual Folk-Songs* and 'Away Over Jordan' in this volume. All three songs show the same textual theme, that of the loved one gone or going to heaven; but the two revival spiritual songs handle their texts in the repetitive manner. All three, moreover, are members of the 'Roll Jordan' tune family, to which references are given under 'Glorious Day' in this volume.

No. 21

IMANDRA NEW, OSH 54

Hexatonic, mode 3 b (I II III IV V VI —)

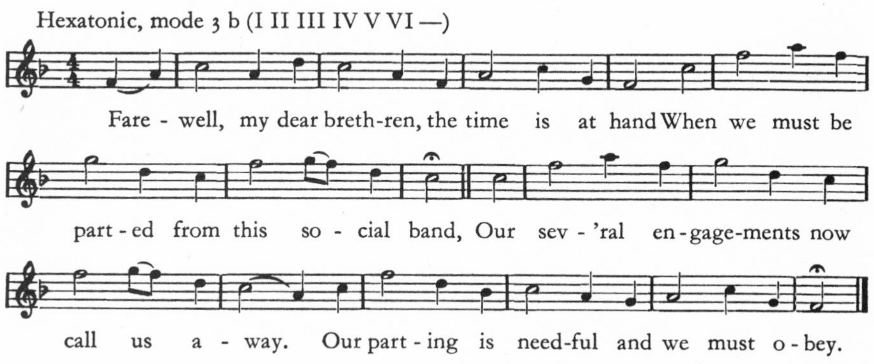
Fare - well, my dear breth-ren, the time is at hand When we must be
part - ed from this so - cial band, Our sev - 'ral en - gage-ments now
call us a - way. Our part - ing is need-ful and we must o - bey.

Farewell, my dear brethren, farewell for a while,
We'll soon meet again if kind Providence smile;
But while we are parted and scatter'd abroad
We'll pray for each other and trust in the Lord.

Farewell, faithful soldiers, you'll soon be discharged,
The war will be ended, the bounty enlarged.
With shouting and singing, though Jordan may roar,
You'll enter fair Canaan and rest on the shore.

The first appearance of this song in the fasola books was in the *Southern Harmony*.[1] The tune is clearly derived from that of 'Braes o' Balquhidder' as are also 'Sinner's Invitation', 'Florence', 'Orphan Girl', and 'Lone Pilgrim'.[2] See 'Sinner's Invitation' for further song-relationship references.

[1] Edition of 1835, p. 34.
[2] *Spiritual Folk-Songs*, Nos. 80, 82, 19, and 18, respectively.

3*

No. 22

HOPE HULL, HH 363

Pentatonic, mode 3 (I II III — V VI —)

Fine

Ye souls who are now bound for heav-en, Pray join and as - sist me to sing
An an-them of praise un - to Je - sus, My Pro-phet, my Priest and my King;
(D.C.) When Je - sus him-self is the lead-er, Who draws you with cords of his love.

Da Capo

These notes are so soft and mel - o-dious, They'll help you most sweet-ly to move,

When Jesus beheld me in nature,
Pursuing the road unto pain,
He brought me my sins to discover,
Then cleansèd my soul from the stain:
How sweet were the accents of pardon!
How quickly my guilt did remove,
When I could behold with sweet wonder,
That God such a sinner could love!

And now I am pressing for Canaan,
Though Jordan is rolling before;
It causes me almost to tremble,
To hear how its billows do roar;
But Jesus can calm the dread ocean,
And cause its loud ragings to cease;
If Faith, Hope, and Love are in motion,
I'll walk through the valley in peace.

His rod and his staff shall console me.
His Shepherd-like voice I shall hear,
Why then should its raging affright me,
Since Jesus will be with me there?
On seraphic wings I'll be soaring,
To join the bright spirits above;
There ever to praise and adore him,
Who brought me to feast on his love.

O Christians, I feel myself happy
In anticipating this joy!
We shortly on love shall be feasting,
Which never, no never, can cloy.

O sinners, it grieves me to leave you,
Once more I entreat you to go;
O hasten and fly unto Jesus,
The Gospel's inviting you now.

In the tune we see the rhythmic and tone-trend formula which, in its major phase, is so well exemplified by the widely sung and often adapted 'Old Rosin the Bow'[1] and, in its minor phase, by 'Help Me to Sing' in this volume. See the last-named song for a variant text and further tune references. The New England preacher, Hope Hull, was instrumental in the conversion of the noted evangelist, Lorenzo Dow, in the latter part of the eighteenth century. This may account for the above title.

No. 23

WEARY SOULS, OSH 72

Pentatonic, mode 3 (I II III — V VI —)

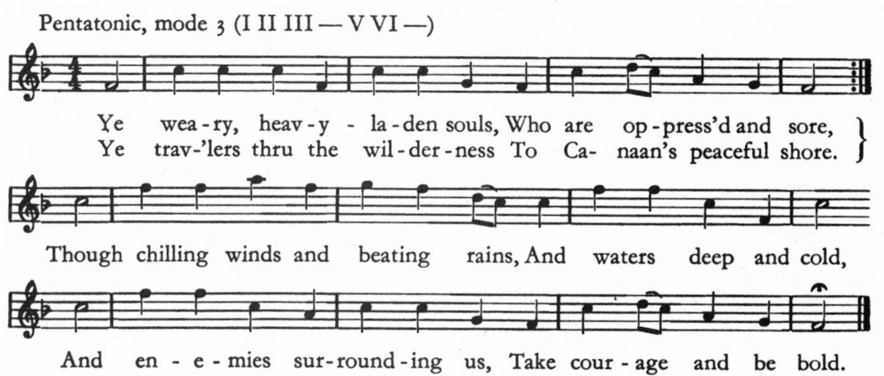
Ye wea-ry, heav-y - la-den souls, Who are op-press'd and sore,
Ye trav-'lers thru the wil-der-ness To Ca- naan's peaceful shore.
Though chilling winds and beating rains, And waters deep and cold,
And en - e - mies sur-round-ing us, Take cour - age and be bold.

Farewell, my brethren in the Lord,
Who are for Canaan bound,
And should we never meet again
Till Gabriel's trump shall sound,
I hope that I shall meet you there
On that delightful shore,
In mansions of eternal bliss,
Where parting is no more.

A variant of this tune is 'Florence', *Spiritual Folk-Songs*, No. 82. See 'Foster' in this volume for more about the above text.

[1] *Spiritual Folk-Songs*, No. 129.

No. 24
SEPARATION NEW, SOC 23

Pentatonic, mode 3 (I II III — V VI —)

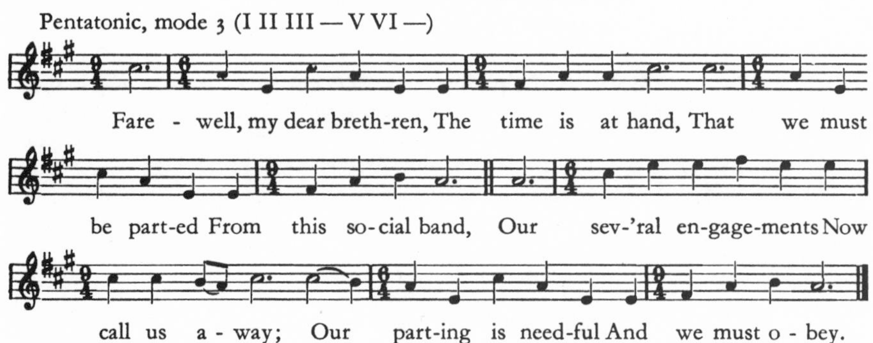
Fare - well, my dear breth-ren, The time is at hand, That we must
be part-ed From this so-cial band, Our sev-'ral en-gage-ments Now
call us a - way; Our part-ing is need-ful And we must o - bey.

A fuller text is given under 'Imandra New' in this volume. In the *Social Harp* the tune is attributed to B. G. Stalnacker and is dated 1854. Variants of the tune are 'St. Denio', a Welsh hymn melody in the *Christian Science Hymnal*,[1] and 'John Adkins' Farewell' in *Spiritual Folk-Songs*.[2]

No. 25
OLD CHURCHYARD (A), PB 262

Heptatonic aeolian, mode 2 (I II 3 IV V 6 7)

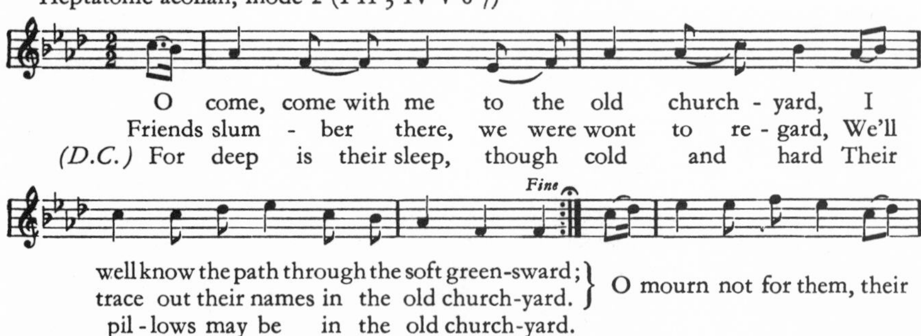
O come, come with me to the old church - yard, I
Friends slum - ber there, we were wont to re - gard, We'll
(D.C.) For deep is their sleep, though cold and hard Their
Fine
well know the path through the soft green-sward;
trace out their names in the old church-yard.
pil - lows may be in the old church-yard.
O mourn not for them, their

Da Capo
grief is o'er, Weep not for them, they weep no more;

[1] No. 150.
[2] No. 11.

I know it seems vain, when friends depart,
To breathe kind words to the broken heart;
I know that the joys of life seem marr'd,
When we follow our friends to the old churchyard.
But were I at rest beneath yon tree,
Why should you weep, dear friends, for me?
I'm wayworn and sad, O why then retard
The rest that I seek in the old churchyard?

Our friends linger there in sweetest repose,
Released from the world's sad bereavements and woes;
And who would not rest with the friends they regard
In quietude sweet, in the old churchyard?
We'll rest in the hope of that bright day,
When beauty shall spring from the prison of clay,
When Gabriel's voice and the trump of the Lord,
Shall waken the dead in the old churchyard.

O weep not for me, I am anxious to go
To that haven of rest where tears never flow;
I fear not to enter that dark lonely ward;
For soon I shall rise from the old churchyard.
Yes, soon shall I join that heavenly band
Of glorified souls at my Savior's right hand;
Forever to dwell in bright mansions prepared
For saints, who shall rise from the old churchyard.

I find the tune with a song entitled 'Burns' Farewell' and designated as "the original air" on page 103 of *The Masonic Harp;* its first line reading,

Adieu, a heart-warm fond adieu!

Miss Gilchrist tells me that its full title is 'The Farewell to the Brethren of St. James' Lodge, Tarbolton', a village near Ayr. She adds, "It is highly probable that Burns did write it to the tune of the 'Freemason's March' [above] with which he would be familiar (an early name for this tune was 'The Peacock') — though in both my editions of Burns its tune is given as 'Guid Night and Joy be wi' you a''. This 'Farewell' (Burns wrote many of them) seems to have been written when Burns was short of money and contemplating emigrating to Jamaica (which however he never did, so the farewell was rather premature!)." Influence from this tune is apparent in 'Good Old Way (B)' in *Spiritual Folk-Songs.*

No. 26

JOSEPH AND HIS BRETHREN, USH 107

Heptatonic aeolian, mode 2 (I II 3 IV V 6 7 [VII])

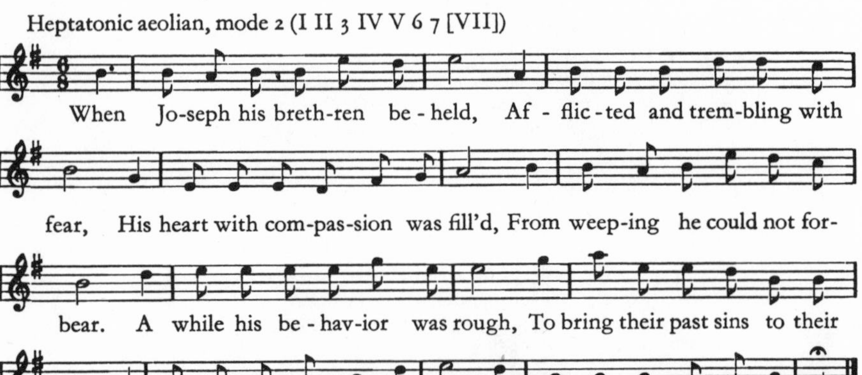
When Jo-seph his breth-ren be-held, Af-flic-ted and trem-bling with
fear, His heart with com-pas-sion was fill'd, From weep-ing he could not for-
bear. A while his be-hav-ior was rough, To bring their past sins to their
mind: But when they were hum-bled e-nough, He hast-en'd to show him-self kind.

How little they thought it was he,
Whom they had ill treated and sold!
How great their confusion must be,
As soon as his name he had told!
"I am Joseph, your brother," he said,
"And still to my heart you are dear:
You sold me and thought I was dead,
But God, for your sakes, sent me here."

Though greatly distresséd before,
When charged with purloining the cup.
They now were confounded much more
Not one of them durst to look up.
"Can Joseph, whom we would have slain,
Forgive us the evil we did?
And will he our households maintain?
O, this is a brother indeed!"

After these three ballad stanzas the maker of the text — John Newton, 1725–1807 — goes on to tell, in four more stanzas, of his own religious experience, one suggested by the biblical story. I have found the text in a number of American collections dating from 1784 onward.[1]

[1] Winchester, *Choice Collection* etc., 1784; Dupuy, *Hymns and Spiritual Song*, 1812; Scott, *Hymns and Spiritual Songs*, 1812; Himes, *A Selection of Hymns* etc., 1818; *The Dover Selection*, 1828; Carden, *The United States Harmony*, Nashville, 1829 (the song used here); and Taylor, *Revival Hymns and Plantation Melodies*, 1883. The tune has been found with different text in the *Christian Lyre*, 1830, ii, 156.

No. 27

CHRIST WAS BORN IN BETHLEHEM, *Sacred Harp*, Ed. 1859

Hexatonic, mode 1 A (I II III IV V VI —)

Christ was born in Beth - le - hem, Christ was born in Beth - le - hem,
Christ was born in Beth - le - hem, And in the man - ger lay.
And in the man - ger lay, And in the man - ger lay;
Christ was born in Beth - le - hem, And in the man - ger lay.

This ballad appeared with one stanza of text in the early editions of the *Sacred Harp* but was removed from the edition of 1869 and subsequent ones. The fuller text appears as follows in *The Christian Songster*.

Christ was born in Bethlehem, *(three times)*
And in the manger laid;
But he rose, he rose, yes, he rose,
And went to heaven in a cloud.

His life was our example,
His death our only hope; For he rose, *etc.*

Peter he denied him,
And sadly he did weep; Till he rose, *etc.*

Judas he betrayed him,
With a deceitful kiss; But he rose, *etc.*

The Jews they crucified him,
And nailed him to the cross; But he rose, *etc.*

Joseph begg'd his body,
And laid it in the tomb; But he rose, *etc.*

Mary came a-weeping,
To see her loving Lord; For he rose, *etc.*

Down came a shining angel,
And roll'd away the stone; Then he rose, *etc.*

Christ came forth triumphant,
And conquered death and hell; For he rose, *etc.*

Go tell John and Peter,
I'm risen from the dead. Jesus rose, *etc.*

Shout, shout the victory,
We're on our journey home; For he rose, *etc.*

The folk-singers could and did add details to the story, as the following stanzas from the *Revivalist* version (No. 482) indicate.

'Tis the very same Jesus, *(three times)*
The Jews crucified; But he rose, *etc.*

The grave it could not hold him,
For he was the Son of God.

The earth began to tremble,
The Roman soldiers fell.

Poor Mary came weeping,
And looking for her Lord.

Two men in shining raiment,
They sat within the tomb.

O where have you laid him?
He's not within the tomb.

Go preach to every nation.
And tell to dying men. That he rose, *etc.*

But oh! he said he'd come again,
And take his people home; For he rose, *etc.*

Other less complete texts are in Sharp-Karpeles (vol. ii, 293) and *Folk Hymns of America* (No. 21).

No. 28

END OF THE WORLD, WHM 210

Heptatonic aeolian, mode 2 (I II 3 IV V 6 7 [VII])

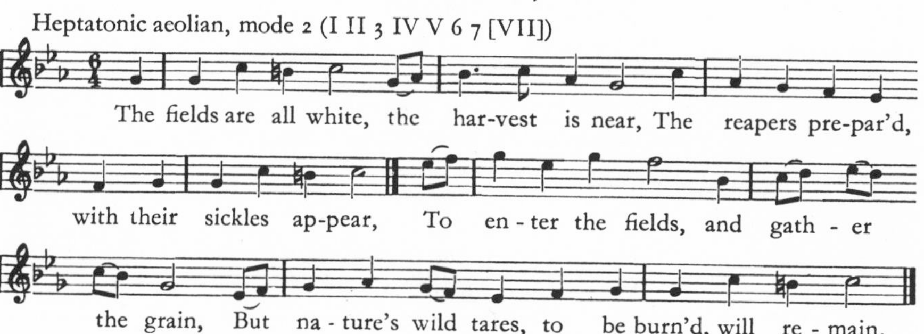
The fields are all white, the har-vest is near, The reapers pre-par'd,
with their sickles ap-pear, To en - ter the fields, and gath - er
the grain, But na - ture's wild tares, to be burn'd, will re - main.

Come then, dying sinner, O think on that day,
When all things in nature shall haste to decay;
When the trumpet shall sound, and the angels appear,
To reap down the earth, both the wheat and the tare.

In four more stanzas the maker of the text goes on to tell the biblical story of Judgment Day. The tune has a trend which I have not seen elsewhere.

No. 29

EXPERIENCE, CHI 89

Heptatonic phrygian, mode 5 (I 2 [II] 3 [III] IV V 6 7)

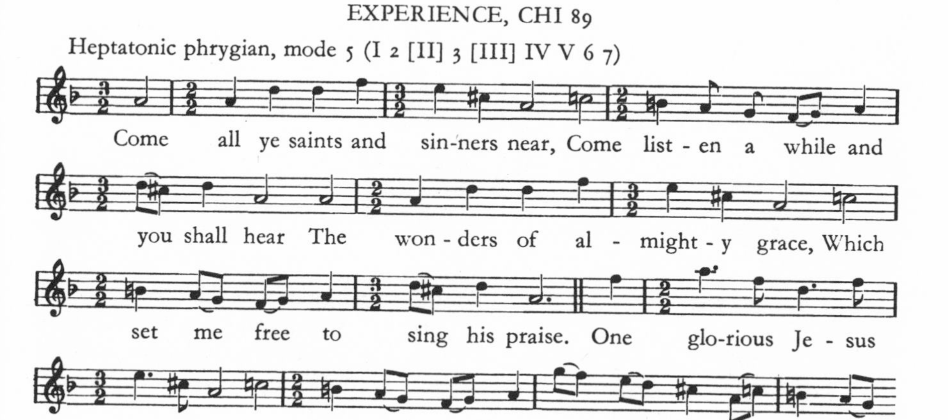
Come all ye saints and sin-ners near, Come list - en a while and
you shall hear The won - ders of al - might - y grace, Which
set me free to sing his praise. One glo-rious Je - sus
from the sky, He said to me as he pass'd by, A - wake, a -
rise, de - part and fly, Go hence, or you will sure - ly die.

Mine eyes he open'd to behold
The wonders I have never told;
Heaven and hell I thought I saw,
And my poor soul in ruin lay.
I heard of Jesus who, they say,
Could wash a sinner's sins away.
How to find him I did not know,
Nor how to meet with him below.

My flesh did war against my soul,
Temptation did me much control;
The weeping saints I could not slight,
Who sought their Jesus day and night.
The scandal of his cross I see,
That scandal it would fall on me.
But still I thought I did behold,
I wanted Jesus more than gold.

I laid me down to take my rest
Bemoaning of my dreadful case.
I thought I would for mercy wait,
But then I fear'd I'd come too late.
I little thought he'd been so nigh,
His speaking made me smile and cry.
He said: I'm come to you, my love,
I have a place for you above.

This glorious news I did believe,
My sins and sorrows did me leave;
My soul enraptur'd in his love,
In hopes to go with him above.
There for to sit and sing and tell
The wonders of Immanuel.
While we shall join in songs divine,
To praise him all his saints combine.

The text was cobbled by one who had far more religious zeal than poetic ability, or even "book larnin'". The tune's the thing. It is strangely agile and independent. I find not the slightest relationship of its trend to that of any other folk-tune. In interpreting it as a phrygian tune I have assumed that the *b*-flats and *c*-naturals are organic and that the *b*-naturals and *c*-sharps are not.

No. 30

SWEET MESSENGER, SWP 21

Heptatonic aeolian, mode 2 (I II 3 IV V 6 7)

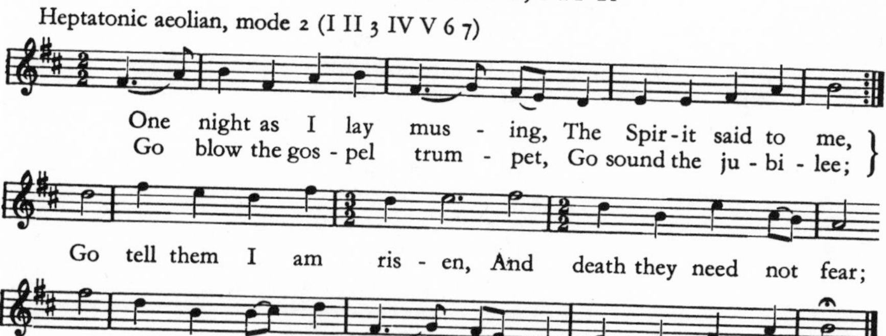
One night as I lay mus - ing, The Spir-it said to me,
Go blow the gos - pel trum - pet, Go sound the ju - bi - lee;
Go tell them I am ris - en, And death they need not fear;
I've turn'd the aw - ful sum - mons To a sweet mes - sen - ger.

The harvest fields are ripening,
The laborers are few;
When Zion she doth languish,
O watchman, where are you?
Their blood will cry against you,
If idle you should be;
You see the sword is coming,
Then sound the jubilee.

Come, O my Father's children,
Redeem'd for liberty;
Why stand you here so idle,
And wasting all the day?
Remember some are teaching,
While others preach the word;
Go labor in the vinyard,
I'll give a sure reward.

Come, brethren all and sisters,
Though but a little band,
The victory I'll ensure you;
Stand fast with sword in hand.
Then wield the sword with pleasure,
The battle goes aright;
Thus Israel gained the victory
Against the Amalekite.

Come, all ye sons of vanity,
Who are exposed to death,
Who've listed under Pharaoh,
Th' Egyptian king beneath.

Although you serve with rigor,
He will not set you free,
Then harken to the gospel,
The sound of jubilee.

Come, ye who're bound for Canaan,
And give me your right hand;
Who've turn'd your backs on Egypt,
And join'd our little band.
I pray you hold out faithful,
Your crown it will be sure;
You'll reign with Christ your Savior,
In bliss for evermore.

How beauteous are the garments,
The bride of Christ doth wear!
He adorns her with his presence,
And clothes her with his care.
He decks her with rich jewels,
And crowns her with his love;
And by his mighty power,
He'll bear her safe above.

No. 31

OLD ISRAELITES, GH 105

Hexatonic, mode 4 b (I II 3 IV V — 7 [VII])

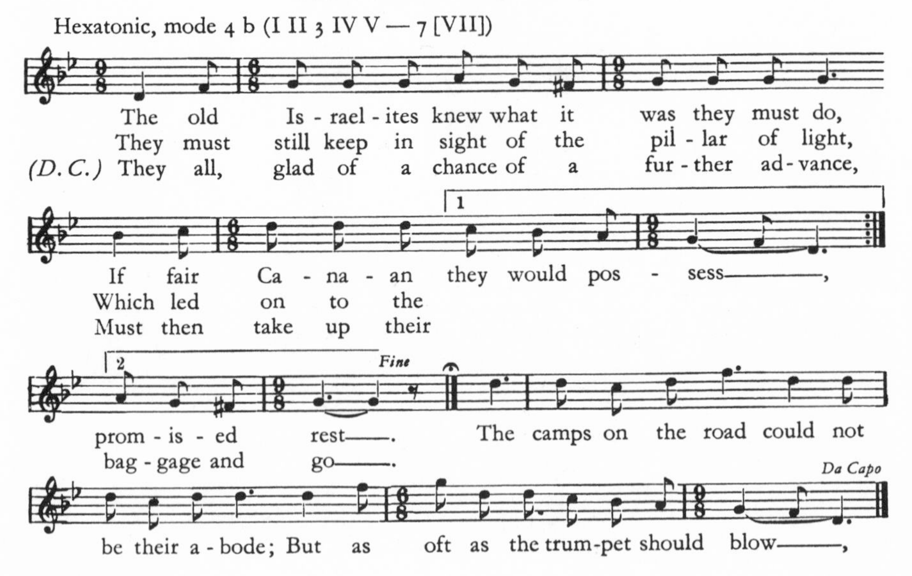
The old Is - rael - ites knew what it was they must do,
They must still keep in sight of the pil - lar of light,
(D. C.) They all, glad of a chance of a fur - ther ad - vance,
1
If fair Ca - na - an they would pos - sess,
Which led on to the
Must then take up their
2
Fine
prom - is - ed rest.
bag - gage and go.
The camps on the road could not
Da Capo
be their a - bode; But as oft as the trum-pet should blow,

I am thankful indeed for the Heavenly Head,
Which before me has hitherto gone;
For that Pillar of Love which doth onward still move,
And doth gather our souls into one.
Now the cross-bearing throng are advancing along,
And a closer communion doth flow;
Now all who would stand on the promiséd land,
Let them take up the cross and go.

The way is all new as it opens to view,
And behind is a foaming Red Sea;
So none now need speak of the onions and leeks,
Or talk about garlics to me.
On Jordan's near side I can never abide,
For no place here of refuge I see,
Till I come to the spot, and inherit the lot
Which the Lord God will give unto me.

What though some in the rear preach up terror and fear,
And complain of the trials they meet?
Though the giants before with great fury do roar,
I'm resolved I will never retreat.
We are little, 'tis true, and our numbers are few,
And the sons of old Anak are tall;
But while I see a track I will never go back,
But go on at the risk of my all.

Now the bright morning dawns for the camp to move on,
And the priests with their trumpets do blow.
As the priests give the sound and the trumpets resound,
All my soul is exulting to go.
If I'm faithful and true and my journey pursue
Till I stand on the heavenly shore,
I shall joyfully see what a blessing to me
Was the mortifying cross which I bore.

All my honors and wealth, all my pleasures and health,
I am willing should now be at stake;
If my Christ I obtain, I shall think it great gain,
For the sacrifice which I shall make.
When I all have forsook, like a bubble 'twill look,
From the midst of a glorified throng,
Where all losses are gain, where each sorrow and pain
Are exchang'd for the conqueror's song.

This is apparently the only occurrence of the above ballad text in American songlore. It is of course, far from a consistent ballad. Its maker relapsed, after a stanza, into the first person of religious experience and the implied second person of exhortation, using the bible story simply as a figurative back-ground.

It is interesting to note that this typical ballad tune — current presumably in the Northeast where the *Golden Harp* appeared — was associated also, in only slightly varying form, with the 'Babe of Bethlehem',[1] which was recorded twenty years earlier (1835) in the far Southeast. Another New York appearance of the tune was in the *Revivalist* (1868)[2] where it was associated rather inappropriately with a hymn text. Other variant member-tunes of the 'Babe of Bethlehem' family in this collection are 'Help me to Sing', 'Staunton', 'Repose', and 'Brownson'.

No. 32

NATIVITY, SAM 226

Pentatonic, mode 1 (I II — IV V VI —)

You na - tions all, on you I call, Come hear this dec - lar- a - tion;
And don't re - fuse the glo - rious news Of Je - sus and sal- va - tion.
To roy - al Jews came first the news Of
Christ the great Mes - si - ah, As was— fore - told by
pro - phets old—, I - sai - ah, Jer - e - mi - ah.

The rest of the text is identical with that given in *Spiritual Folk-Songs* under 'Babe of Bethlehem'. The tune is of the 'Lazarus' family which is explained in this volume under 'Lazarus and Dives'. It is quite a coincidence that this 'Babe' text and 'Lazarus' tune have mated; this in view of the fact that, although the two melodic types have been found *somewhat* similar, their texts have otherwise never been found deserting their own tune-group and going over to the other.

[1] See *Spiritual Folk-Songs*, No. 51.

[2] No. 7, entitled 'Howland'.

No. 33

SONS OF WAR, SWP 152

Heptatonic aeolian, mode 2 (I II 3 IV V 6 7)

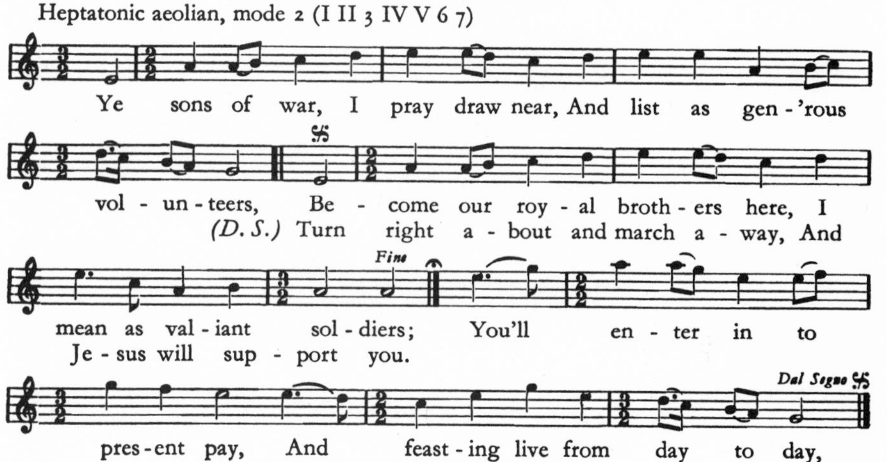
Ye sons of war, I pray draw near, And list as gen-'rous
vol-un-teers, Be-come our roy-al broth-ers here, I
(D. S.) Turn right a-bout and march a-way, And
Fine
mean as val-iant sol-diers; You'll en-ter in to
Je-sus will sup-port you.
Dal Segno
pres-ent pay, And feast-ing live from day to day,

Ye careless sons of Adam's race,
Who long have trod in folly's ways,
O turn about to Zion's face,
And meet Apollyon's forces.
Gird on your sword and glittering shield,
And with your helmet take the field,
And fight your way and never yield,
And Jesus will support you.

The bounty you shall have in hand,
If you will list in Jesus' band,
Your Captain in the front will stand,
And beat your foes before you.
Come throw your rebel weapons down,
And seek for honors and renown,
And you shall wear a starry crown,
For Jesus will support you.

You long have been the slaves of sin,
With dire corruption deep within;
The Christian warfare now begin,
And face Apollyon's forces.
The breastplate take of righteousness,
Your feet be shod with gospel peace,
Be daily at the throne of grace,
And Jesus will support you.

Desert the cause of heaven's foe,
Before you plunge in endless woe;
Now courage take, to Jesus go,
And he will now receive you.
From sin and Satan you'll get free,
And happy seasons you shall see,
And gain the Christian's liberty,
For Jesus will support you.

No more in Satan's ranks appear,
But to our banner pray draw near,
We'll win the day, you need not fear,
Though earth and hell oppose us.
Our Captain he is always brave.
And able still his men to save,
He conquered death, hell and the grave,
And he will still support you.

Let not sinners you affright,
Although they rage and vent their spite,
Wear but the Christian's armor bright,
And none can stand before you.
Although your parents should oppose,
Your dearest friends become your foes,
Yet sweetly with the gospel close,
And Jesus will support you.

And when the war is at an end,
Our Captain still will be our Friend,
We'll wing our way and up ascend
To reign with him in glory.
Then shall our tears be wiped away,
Our night be turned to endless day,
And on our golden harps we'll play
The joyful song of heaven.

William Walker's name affixed to the song indicates that he recorded it from unwritten sources. The text looks like a parody of some secular song intended to encourage army enlistment. The prevalence of tied eighth-notes points to a source tune of instrumental nature.

No. 34

RICH MAN, CHI 113

Heptatonic aeolian, mode 2 (I II 3 IV V 6 7 [VII])

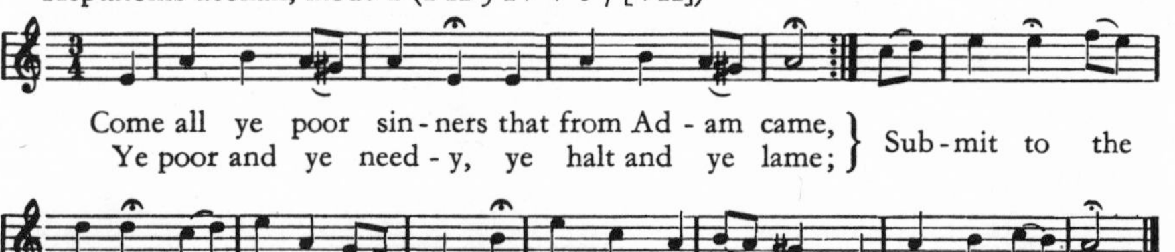
Come all ye poor sin-ners that from Ad-am came,
Ye poor and ye need-y, ye halt and ye lame;
Sub-mit to the
gos-pel up-on its own terms, Or you'll burn for-ev-er like poor mor-tal worms.

We read of a beggar, a rich man likewise,
The beggar he dy'd and attain'd to a prize;
The rich man he dy'd and to his surprize,
In hell he awakéd, and lift up his eyes.

See'ng Abram a far off, in mansions above,
And Laz'rus in his bosom in raptures of love,
He cries, Father Abram, send to my relief,
For I am tormented with pains and in grief.

He said, Son, remember when you liv'd so bold,
Dress'd in your fine linen, and boasted of gold;
The beggar lay at your door, wounded and poor,
The dogs had compassion and lickéd his sore.

Besides, there's a gulph *(sic)* fix'd between us, you see,
That those who would, cannot pass from thence to me;
Therefore you must lie and lament your sad state,
For now you are sending your cries up too late.

He cries, Father Abram, I pray you provide,
Send one from the dead, I've five brothers beside;
In hearing from me, and believing my state,
Perhaps they will repent, before it's too late.

They have a rich gospel that spreads far and wide,
They've Moses, the prophets, and 'postles beside;
And if they don't adhear *(sic)* unto them, and repent,
They will not believe, tho' one from the dead went.

Now therefore, dear sinners, take warning by this,
Since death will soon fix your unchangeable state;
Prepare to meet Jesus and give him your love,
So when he appears, he'll receive you above.

I have given the text exactly as it appears in the rural Vermont *Christian Harmony* of 1805. Jeremiah Ingalls, the recorder of the song, noted the first half of the melody in two-four time. Neither text nor tune has any relationship to 'Dives and Lazarus' in this volume except that they both draw on the same biblical story.

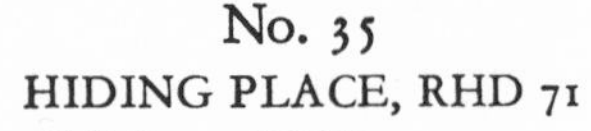

No. 35

HIDING PLACE, RHD 71

Hexatonic, mode 2 A (I II 3 IV V — 7 [VII])

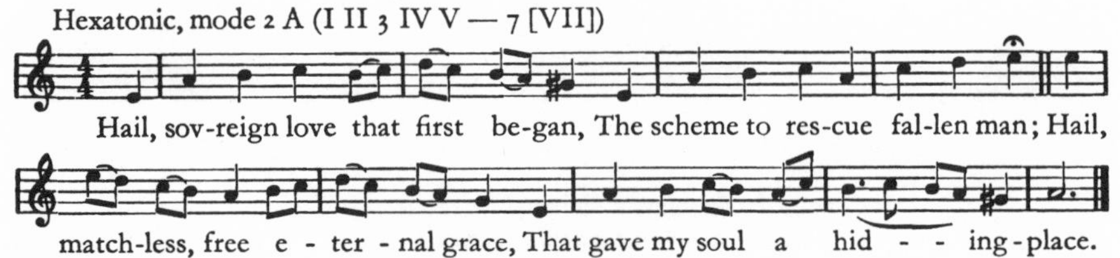
Hail, sov-reign love that first be-gan, The scheme to res-cue fal-len man; Hail,
match-less, free e - ter - nal grace, That gave my soul a hid - - ing-place.

Against the God that built the sky,
I fought with hands uplifted high;
Despis'd the mansions of his grace,
Too proud to seek a hiding-place.

Enwrapt in dark Egyptian night,
And fond of darkness more than light;
Madly I ran the sinful race,
Secure without a hiding-place.

But lo! the eternal council ran;
Almighty love, arrest the man;
I felt the arrows of distress,
And found I had no hiding-place.

Vindictive justice stood in view,
To Sinai's fiery mount I flew,
But justice cried, with frowning face,
This mountain is no hiding-place.

But lo! a heavenly voice I heard,
And mercy's angel soon appeared;
Who led me on a pleasant pace,
To Jesus Christ, my hiding-place.

The tune is related to 'Consolation (A)' in this volume and to 'Bourbon' in *Spiritual Folk-Songs*.[1] Among its secular relatives are 'The Bailiff's Daughter of Islington',[2] 'Heart's Ease',[3] and 'Gernutus the Jew of Venice'.[4]

[1] No. 109. See also *Folk Hymns of America*, p. xiv, Notes on No. 3.

[2] JFSS, i, 125.

[3] Gibbon, p. 46f.

[4] The tune, discovered by Dr. Rimbault, to the Percy's *Reliques* ballad which is related, in turn, to the Shakespeare *Merchant of Venice* story. See Elson, *Shakespeare in Music*, p. 225.

No. 36

DYING CALIFORNIAN, UVW 159

Heptatonic dorian, mode 2 (?) (I II 3 IV V VI 7)

a
Lay up near - er, broth-er, near - er, For my limbs are grow-ing cold,

b
And thy pres-ence it seem - eth near - er When thine arms a - round me

fold. I am dy - ing, broth-er, dy-ing, Soon you'll miss me in your berth,

c
For my form will soon be ly - ing Be-neath the o-cean's brin-ey deep.

a
b
c

The song was recorded by Winston Wilkinson in Harriston, Virginia, October 9, 1935, from the singing of Nathaniel Melhorn Morris. It is No. 159 of the *University of Virginia* (manuscript) *Collection of Folk-Music* and is used here by kind permission.

The rest of the text is much the same as that of the song with the same title in *Spiritual Folk-Songs*.[1] A comparison will show however that the two melodies are independent. Mr. Wilkinson has no less than four variants of the above song, tune and words, in his private collection, all recorded in Virginia.

[1] That the 'Dying Californian' story is based on fact is evident. It first appeared as a poetic contribution to *The New England Diadem*, December 21, 1854, headlined *Touching and Beautiful Lines* and prefaced by: "The New England Diadem gives its readers the following beautiful stanzas, which were suggested by hearing read an extract of a letter from Capt. Chase, giving an account of the sickness and death of his brother-in-law, Mr. Brown Owen, who died on his passage to California. We have seldom met anything so painfully interesting in every line, and it will be read with 'teary eyes' by many who have lost brothers, fathers, husbands, or sons, upon their way to, or after having reached, the land of Gold and of Graves."

The folk singers have done away with the hiatus "thy arms", made the artificial "'neath" into "beneath", and have changed the last word in the above stanza from the "surf" of the original.

No. 37

DYING MINISTER, OSH 124

Hexatonic, mode 3 A (I II III — V VI VII)

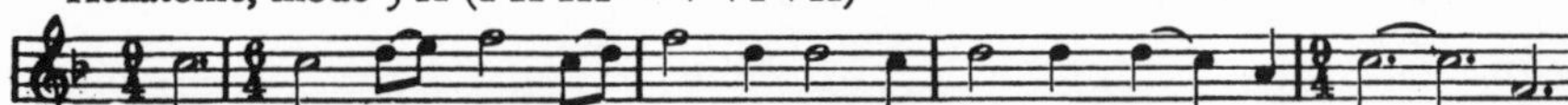

The time is swift - ly roll-ing on, When I must faint and die; My

bod - y to the dust re-turn, And there for - got - ten lie.

The rest of the text is given under 'Farewell'.[1] The tune has some relationship to that of 'I'll Never Turn Back (A)'.[2]

No. 38

ON THE WAY TO CANAAN, REV 137

Pentatonic, mode 2 (I — 3 IV V — 7)

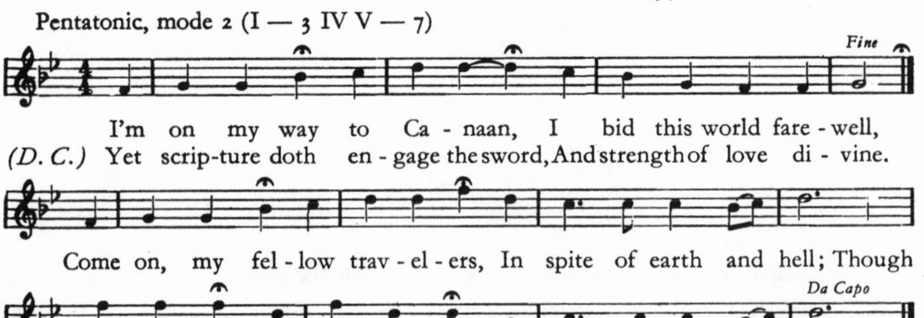
Fine
Da Capo

I'm on my way to Ca - naan, I bid this world fare - well,
(D. C.) Yet scrip-ture doth en - gage the sword, And strength of love di - vine.

Come on, my fel - low trav - el - ers, In spite of earth and hell; Though

Sa - tan's ar - my ra - ges hard, And all his hosts com-bine.

I'll blow the gospel trumpet loud,
And on the nations call,
For Christ hath me commissionéd
To say he died for all.
Come try his grace, come prove him now,
You shall the gift obtain,
He will not send you empty away,
Nor let you come in vain.

And if you want more witnesses,
We have some just at hand,
Who lately have experienced
The glory of that land.

[1] *Spiritual Folk-Songs*, No. 25. [2] *Ibid.*, No. 217.

It comes in copious showers down —
Our souls can scarce contain;
It fills our ransomed powers now,
And yet we drink again.

Says Faith, look yonder, see the crown
Laid up in heaven above!
Says Hope, it shortly shall be mine,
I'll wear it soon, says Love.
Desire says, this is my home,
Then to my place I'll fly,
I cannot bear a longer stay,
My rest I fain would see.

But stop, says Patience, wait a while,
The crown's for those who fight,
The prize for those who run the race
By faith and not by sight.
Then Faith doth take a pleasing view.,
Hope waits, Love sits and sings,
Desire flutters to be gone,
But Patience clips her wings.

The tune is related to 'Poor Sinner Come to Jesus' in this volume and to 'Good Physician' in *Spiritual Folk-Songs*.[1]

No. 39

HOLY CITY, OL 366

Pentatonic, mode 3 (I II III — V VI —)

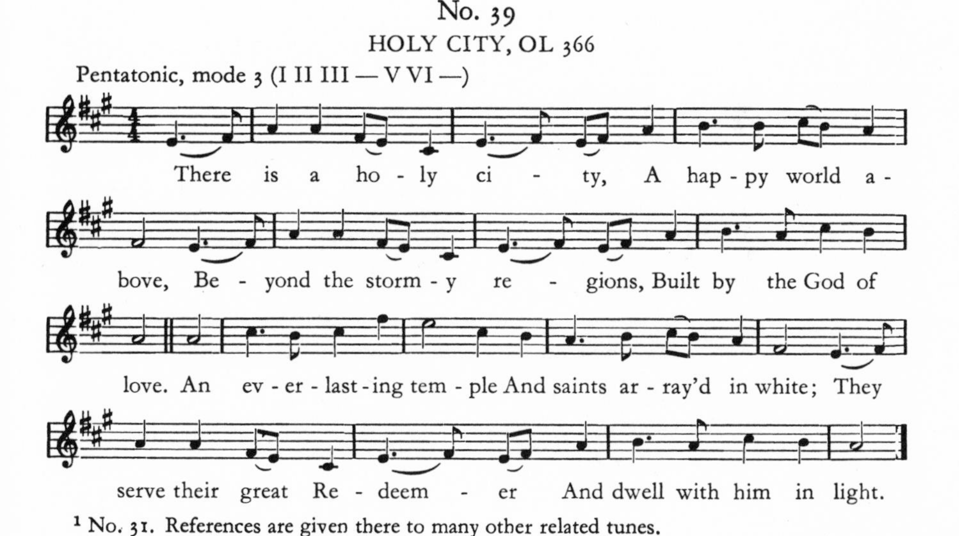
There is a ho - ly ci - ty, A hap - py world a -
bove, Be - yond the storm - y re - gions, Built by the God of
love. An ev - er - last - ing tem - ple And saints ar - ray'd in white; They
serve their great Re - deem - er And dwell with him in light.

[1] No. 31. References are given there to many other related tunes.

This is no world of trouble, the God of peace is there;
He wipes away their sorrows, he banishes their care.
Their joys are still increasing, their songs are ever new;
They praise th'eternal Father, the Son and Spirit too.

The meanest child of glory outshines the radiant sun;
But who can speak the splendor of that eternal throne,
Where Jesus sits exalted in godlike majesty?
The elders fall before him, the angels bend the knee.

Is this the man of sorrows who stood at Pilate's bar,
Condemn'd by haughty Herod and by his men of war?
He seems a mighty conqueror who spoil'd the pow'rs below,
And ransom'd many captives from everlasting wo.

The hosts of saints around him proclaim his work of grace;
The patriarchs and prophets and all the godly race.
They speak of fiery trials and tortures on their way;
They came from tribulation to everlasting day.

Now, with a holy transport they tell their sufferings o'er,
Their tears and their temptations, and all the pains they bore.
They turn and bow to Jesus who gain'd their liberty:
"Amid our fiercest dangers our lives were hid in thee."

Long time was I invited to gain that heavenly rest;
Grace made no hard condition, 'twas only to be bless'd.
But earth's bewitching pleasures inclined me long to stay;
I sought her dreams and shadows and joys that pass away.

But now it is my purpose the better way to find,
To serve my great Creator and leave my sins behind.
In guilt's seducing mazes I will no longer roam;
I'll give my soul to Jesus who brings the ransom'd home.

And what shall be my journey, how long I'll stay below,
Or what shall be my trials, is not for me to know.
In every day of trouble I'll raise my thoughts on high;
I'll think of the bright temple and crowns above the sky.

William Hauser compiler of the *Olive Leaf* attributed the tune to "Rev. Stephen Bovelle, perhaps." It is related to 'Romish Lady', *Spiritual Folk-Songs*, No. 1.

No. 40

MARTIAL TRUMPET, OL 252

Pentatonic, mode 3 (I II III — V VI —)

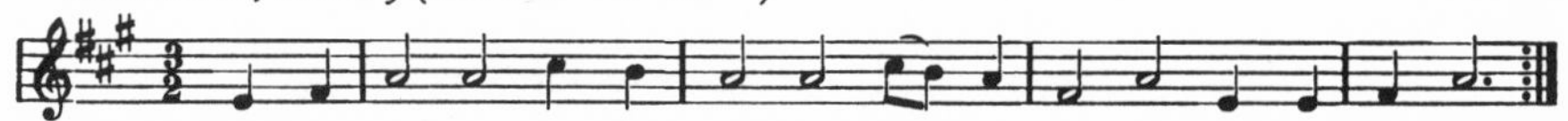

Breth-ren, don't you hear the sound? The mar-tial trum-pet now is blow-ing;
Men in or - der list - ing round, And sol-diers to the stand-ard flow-ing.

Boun-ty's of-fer'd, joy and peace, To ev-ery sol - dier this is given. When from

toils and war they cease, A man - sion bright pre-par'd in hea-ven.

Those who long in sin have lain,
And felt the hand of dire oppression,
Are releas'd from Satan's chain,
And then endow'd with long possession:
Lo, the sick, the blind, the lame!
The maladies of all are healéd:
Outlaw'd rebels, too, may claim
And find a pardon freely sealéd.

Vict'ry is not to the strong,
The burden's on our Captain's shoulder;
None so agéd, or so young,
But may enlist and be a soldier:
Those who cannot fight or fly,
Beneath his banner find protection:
None who on his arm rely,
Shall be reduced to base subjection.

Do not fear, the cause is good;
Come, who will to the crown aspire?
In this cause the martyrs stood,
And shouted victory in the fire.
In this cause let's follow on,
And soon we'll tell the pleasing story,
How by faith we gain'd the crown,
And fought our way to life and glory.

Lo! the battle is begun;
Behold the armies now in motion!
Some, by faith behold the crown,
And almost grasp their future portion.
Hark! the vict'ry's sounding loud!
Emmanuel's chariot wheels are rumbling!
Mourners weeping through the crowd,
And Satan's kingdom down is tumbling.

No. 41

CHERRY TREE CAROL

Heptatonic mixolydian, mode 1 (I II III IV V VI 7)

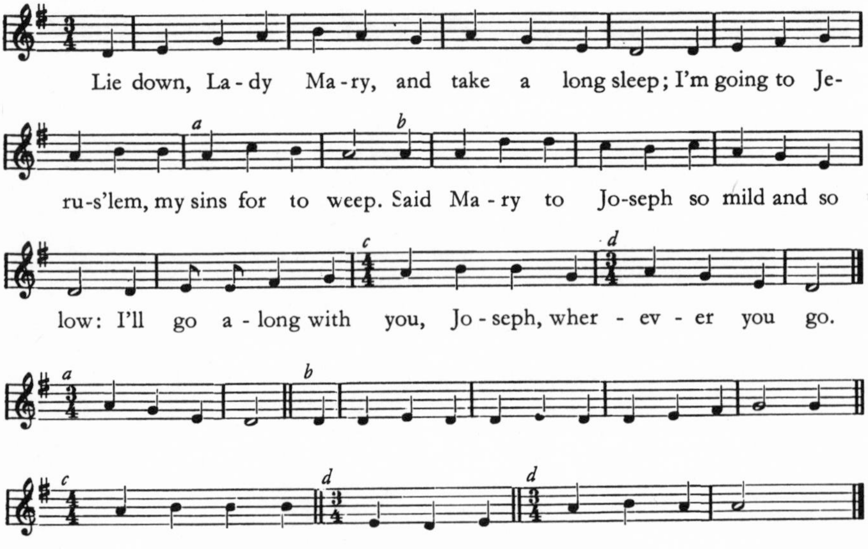

Lie down, La - dy Ma - ry, and take a long sleep; I'm going to Je-

ru-s'lem, my sins for to weep. Said Ma - ry to Jo-seph so mild and so

low: I'll go a - long with you, Jo - seph, wher - ev - er you go.

As Mary and Joseph were walking the green,
Said Mary to Joseph so mild and serene:
Joseph, pull me a cherry, I'm surely with child.
— — — — — — — — — — — — — — — —

Said Joseph to Mary so stubborn and unkind:
Let the father of your baby pull cherries for you.
— — — — — — — — — — — — — — — —
— — — — — — — — — — — — — — — —

Well bespoke our blessèd Savior in his mother's womb:
Cherries, bow down, till my mother gather of you.
The highest of the branches bowed down to the ground;
Mary gathered cherries till her apron overflowed.

Winston Wilkinson recorded this old and beautiful carol in Lynchburg, Virginia, May 15, 1933, from the singing of Miss Agnes O'Halloran. It is No. 200 in Book vii of Mr. Wilkinson's personal collection of folk-songs and is used here with his kind permission. I reproduce also some of the recorder's many song-comparative references in footnote.[1] A glance at these references makes clear that the 'Cherry Tree Carol' has been equally widely sung in the British Isles and America.

No. 42

REDEMPTION, HH 295

Hexatonic, mode 3 b (I II III IV V VI —)

Come friends and re - la-tions, Let's join hearts and hand, The

voice of the tur - tle Is heard in our land. Come let's join to - geth - er And

fol - low the sound And march to the place Where re - demp-tion is found.

The full text is given with 'Redemption (B)'.[2] A related tune is 'Redemption (C)'.[3]

[1] See Sharp-Karpeles, i, 90ff., six variants; JAFL, xlv, 13; xxix, 293 and 417; JFSS, iii, 260; v, 11 and 321-323; viii, 111 and 229; Greig-Keith, No. 23, etc. etc.
[2] *Spiritual Folk-Songs*, No. 46.
[3] *Ibid.*, No. 12.

No. 43

JOYS OF MARY, UVW 184 A

Heptatonic ionian, mode 1 (I II III IV V VI VII)

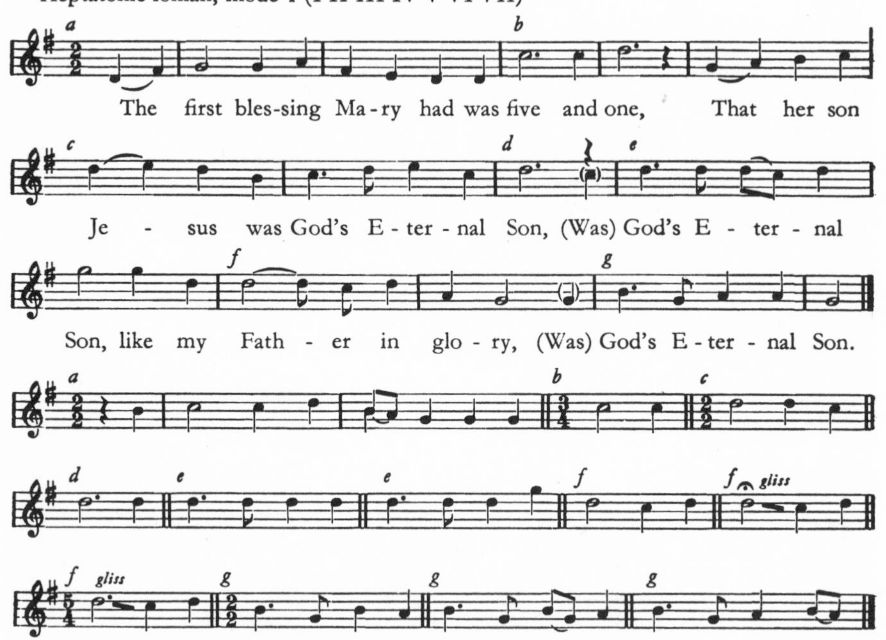
a
b
The first bles-sing Ma-ry had was five and one, That her son
c
d
e
Je - sus was God's E-ter-nal Son, (Was) God's E - ter - nal
f
g
Son, like my Fath - er in glo - ry, (Was) God's E-ter - nal Son.
a
b
c
d
e
e
f
f gliss
f gliss
g
g
g

The second blessing Mary had was five and two,
That her Son Jesus could read the Bible through,
Could read the Bible through, like my Father in glory,
Could read the Bible through.

The third blessing Mary had was five and three,
That her Son Jesus could make the blind to see, *etc.*

The fourth was five and four,
make the rich man poor, *etc.*

The fifth was five and five,
make the dead man rise, *etc.*

The sixth was five and six,
relieve the sick, *etc.*

The seventh was five and seven,
That her Son Jesus carried the key of heaven, *etc.*

The eight	was five and eight, went through the pearly gate, *etc.*
The ninth	was five and nine, could turn the water to wine, *etc.*
The tenth	was five and ten, bring the world to an end, *etc.*
The eleventh	was five and eleven, turn the world to heaven, *etc.*

The twelfth blessing Mary had was five and twelve,
That her Son Jesus could turn the sick to well,
Could turn the sick to well, like my Father in glory,
Could turn the sick to well.

This carol was recorded in Evington, Virginia, October 19, 1935, by Winston Wilkinson, as sung by Mrs. Kit Williamson. It is No. 184A in the *University of Virginia* (manuscript) *Collection of Folk-Music* and is used here by kind permission. It is one of the oldest English carols; the versions covering the period from the fifteenth century to the present, and found in the British Isles and in America. Richard Chase has a version from Kentucky with a somewhat better text.[1] See the *Oxford Book of Carols* for comprehensive references.[2]

No. 44

SUNNY BANK UVW, No. 183

Hexatonic, mode 3 A (I II III — V VI VII)

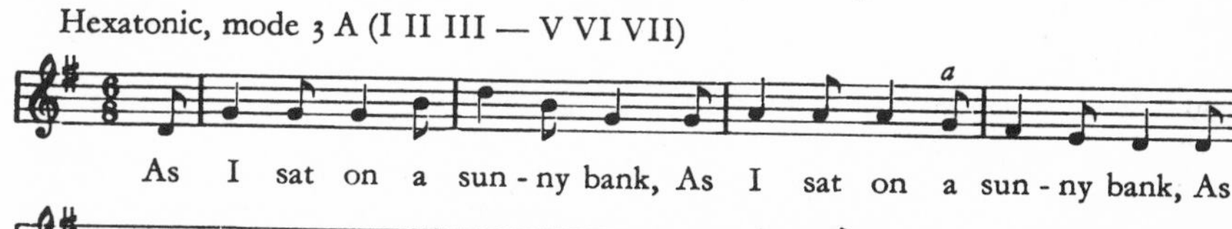
a
As I sat on a sun - ny bank, As I sat on a sun - ny bank, As

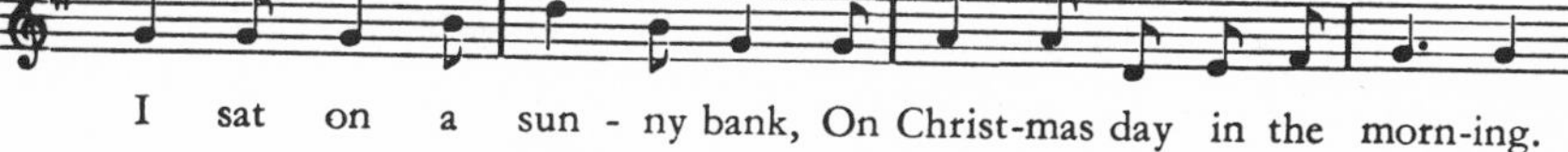
I sat on a sun - ny bank, On Christ-mas day in the morn-ing.

a

I saw three ships come sailing, *thrice*
On Christmas day in the morning.

And who do you think was in those three ships, *thrice*
But Joseph and his fair lady?

[1] *Old Songs and Singing Games*, p. 29. [2] P. 152.

Then he did whistle and she did sing, *thrice*
On Christmas day in the morning.

And all the bells on earth did ring, *thrice*
On *etc.*

For the joy of the new-born King, *thrice*
On *etc.*

This carol was recorded February 17, 1936, in Charlottesville, Virginia, by Winston Wilkinson from the singing of Arthur Morris.[1] The oldest version of 'Sunny Bank' dates from 1666. This Virginia variant is practically identical with those found during recent years in various parts of the British Isles.[2] The tune is a variant of 'Lancaster' in this volume, where further song-comparative references are given.

No. 45

COMPLAINER, SOH (1835) 18

Hexatonic, mode 3 A (I II III — V VI VII)

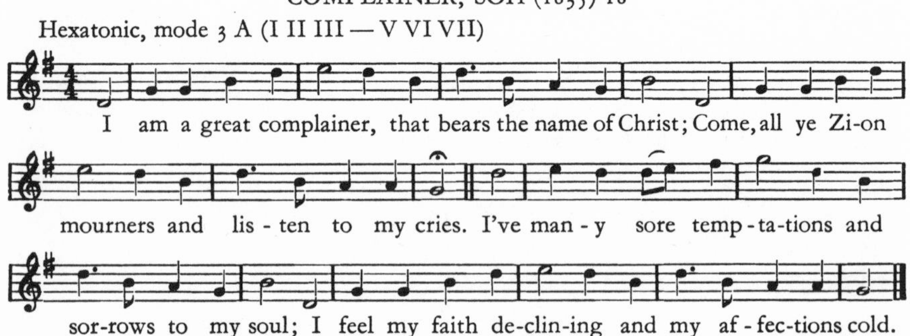
I am a great complainer, that bears the name of Christ; Come, all ye Zi-on
mourners and lis - ten to my cries. I've man - y sore temp - ta-tions and
sor-rows to my soul; I feel my faith de-clin-ing and my af - fec-tions cold.

O Lord of life and glory, my sins to me reveal,
And by thy love and power, my sin-sick soul be heal'd.
I thought my warfare over, no trouble I should see,
But now I'm like the lonely dove that mourns on the wavering tree.

I wish it was with me now as it was in the days of old,
When the glorious light of Jesus was flowing in my soul.
But now I am distresséd and no relief can find,
With a hard deceitful heart, and a wretched wandering mind.

It is great pride and passion beset me on my way,
So I am fill'd with folly and so neglect to pray.
While others run rejoicing and seem to lose no time;
I am so weak, I stumble , and so I'm left behind.

[1] It is No. 183 in the *University of Virginia* (manuscript) *Collection of Folk-Music*, and is used here by kind permission.

[2] See *Oxford Book of Carols*, Nos. 3 and 18.

I read that peace and happiness meet Christians in their way,
That bear their cross with meekness and don't neglect to pray.
But I, a thousand objects me beset in my way,
So I am filled with folly, and so neglect to pray.

This song of the dejected back-slider is claimed by William Walker. Its tune is found with various texts in most of the southern fasola song books.[1] Related tunes are 'Horn Fair'[2] and a "Welsh Hymn Melody" in the *Methodist Hymnal* of 1935.[3]

No. 46

AS ON THE CROSS, RHD 30

Hexatonic, mode 3 b (I II III IV V VI —)

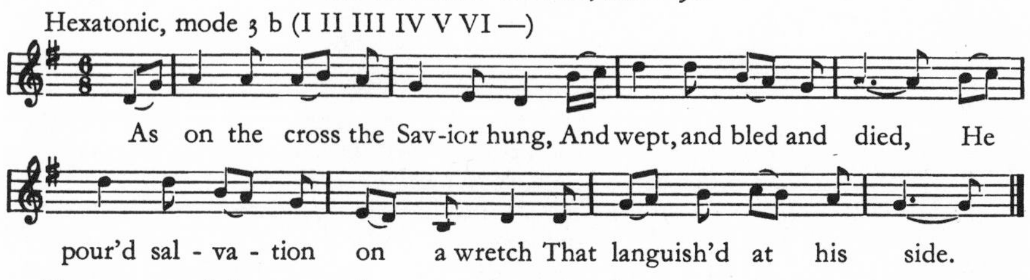
As on the cross the Sav-ior hung, And wept, and bled and died, He
pour'd sal - va - tion on a wretch That languish'd at his side.

Six stanzas of the text and a somewhat related tune are 'Converted Thief (B)', *Spiritual Folk-Songs*, No. 35.

No. 47

AS SHEPHERDS IN JEWRY, CHI 56

Heptatonic ionian, mode 3 (I II III IV V VI VII)

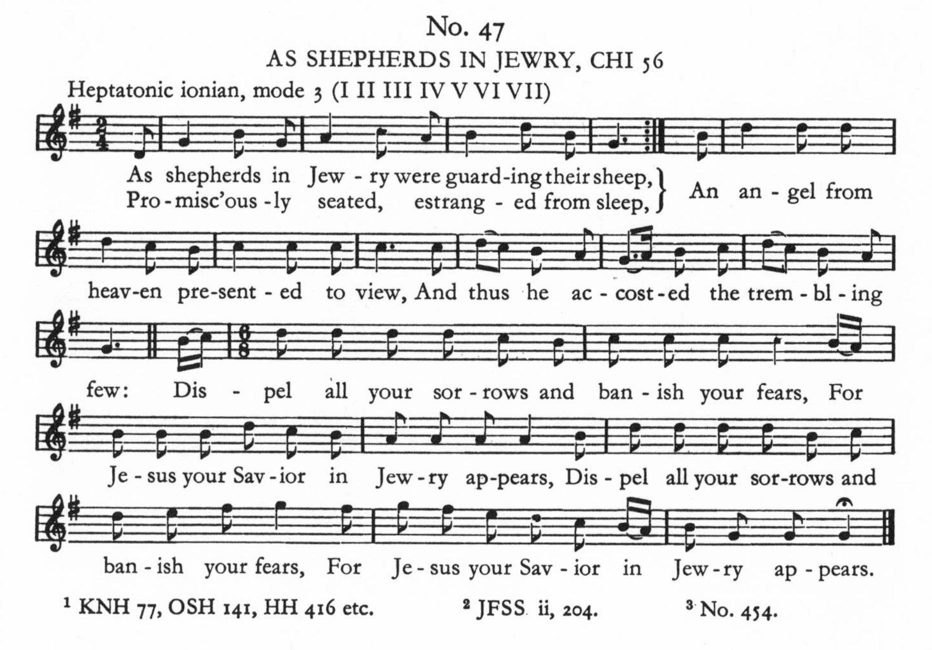
As shepherds in Jew - ry were guard-ing their sheep,
Pro - misc'ous - ly seated, estrang - ed from sleep,
An an - gel from
heav-en pre-sent - ed to view, And thus he ac - cost - ed the trem - bl - ing
few: Dis - pel all your sor - rows and ban - ish your fears, For
Je - sus your Sav - ior in Jew - ry ap-pears, Dis - pel all your sor-rows and
ban - ish your fears, For Je - sus your Sav - ior in Jew - ry ap - pears.

[1] KNH 77, OSH 141, HH 416 etc. [2] JFSS ii, 204. [3] No. 454.

Though Adam the first in rebellion was found,
Forbidden to tarry in hallowéd ground;
Yet Adam the second appears to retrieve
The loss you sustain'd by the devil and Eve.
Then shepherds be tranquil, this instant arise,
Go visit your Savior and see where he lies.

A token I leave you whereby you may find
This heavenly stranger, this friend to mankind:
A manger his cradle, a stall his abode,
The oxen are near him and blow on your God.
Then shepherds be humble, be meek and be low,
For Jesus your Savior's abundantly so.

This wonderful story scarce reachéd the ear,
When thousands of angels in glory appear,
They join in the concert, and this was the theme:
All glory to God, and good will towards men.
Then shepherds go join your glad voice to the choir,
And catch a few sparks of celestial fire.

Hosanna! the angels in ecstacy cry,
Hosanna! the wandering shepherds reply;
Salvation, redemption are center'd in one,
All glory to God for the birth of his Son.
Then shepherds adore, we commend you to God,
Go visit the Son in his humble abode.

To Bethlehem city the shepherds repair'd,
For full confirmation of what they had heard;
They enter'd the stable, with aspect so mild,
And there they beheld the Mother and Child.
Then make proclamation, divulge it abroad,
That both Jews and Gentiles may hear of the Lord.

This is the sole recording apparently of this simple and beautiful version of the nativity story and of the tune as well. Its language, its tune and its rhythm all point to its being traditional.

No. 48

TRANSPORT, UHH 82

Pentatonic, mode 3 (I II III — V VI —)

Ye child-ren of Je-sus who're bound for the king-dom, At-tune all your
Sweet an-thems of prais-es to my lov-ing Je - sus, For he is my

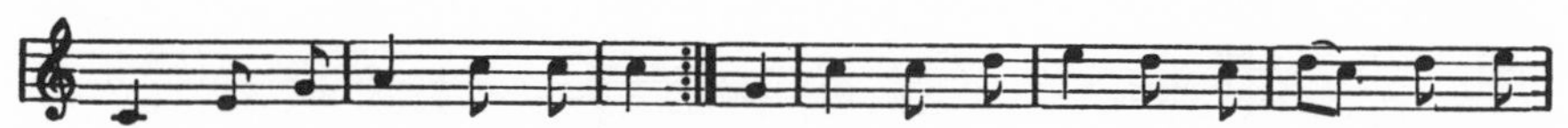

voic - es and help me to sing,
pro-phet, my priest and my king. } When Je - sus first found me, a - stray I was

go-ing, His love did sur-round me and sav'd me from ru - in, He kind-ly em-

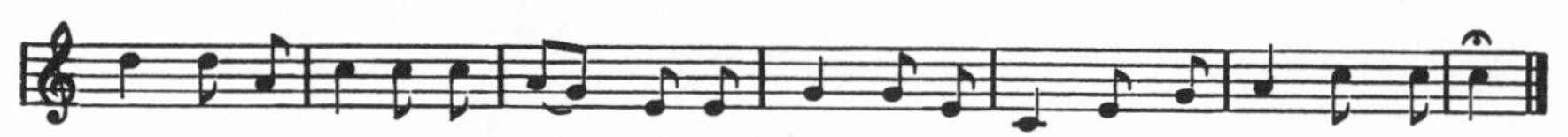

brac'd me and freely he bless'd me, And taught me a-loud his sweet prais-es to sing.

Why should you go mourning from such a physician,
Who's able and willing your sickness to cure;
Come to him believing, though bad your condition,
His Father has promis'd your case to ensure.
My soul he hath healéd, my heart he rejoices,
He brought me to Zion to hear the glad voices,
I'll serve him and praise him and always adore him,
Till we meet in heaven where parting's no more.

The song is ascribed to White and Davisson. We do not know White. Davisson is the compiler of the *Kentucky Harmony* and its *Supplement*.[1] In the text we see another example of the Gaelic assonance and rhyme which is described briefly under 'South Union' in this volume.

In Hendrickson's *Union Harmony* the tenor voice (the melody) is the only moving part, the other two parts, the treble and the bass, droning on the note *c* (an octave apart) from beginning to end. I am at a loss to account for this. Was Davisson trying to reproduce, with voices, a bagpipe effect? Was the tune originally for that instrument?

[1] The above song is in the *Supplement*, p. 76. It is also on page 152 of the *Southern Harmony* of 1835.

No. 49
BLESSED BIBLE, OSH 347

Hexatonic, mode 4 a (I II — IV V 6 7)

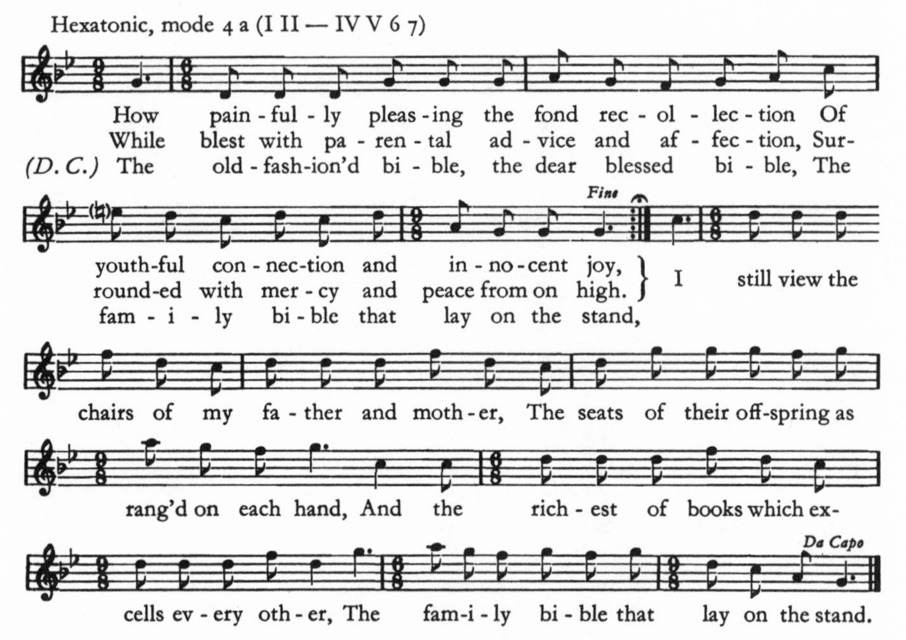
How pain - ful - ly pleas - ing the fond rec - ol - lec - tion Of
While blest with pa - ren - tal ad - vice and af - fec - tion, Sur-
(D. C.) The old - fash-ion'd bi - ble, the dear blessed bi - ble, The
Fine
youth-ful con - nec-tion and in - no - cent joy,
round-ed with mer - cy and peace from on high.
fam - i - ly bi - ble that lay on the stand,
I still view the
chairs of my fa - ther and moth - er, The seats of their off-spring as
rang'd on each hand, And the rich - est of books which ex-
Da Capo
cells ev - ery oth - er, The fam-i - ly bi - ble that lay on the stand.

Though age and misfortune press hard on my feelings,
I'll fly to the bible and trust in the Lord;
Though darkness should cover his merciful dealings,
My soul is still cheer'd by his heavenly word.
And now from things worldly my soul is removing,
I soon shall shout glory with heaven's bright band,
And in raptures be forever adoring
The family bible that lay on the stand.
The old-fashion'd *etc.*

My parents, though dear, are safe landed in glory,
Escaped to the mansions of heavenly rest,
Where seraphs and angels repeat the glad story
Of Jesus'es mercy to sinners confess'd.
They range the bless'd fields on the banks of the river,
Surveying the breadth of Immanuel's land;
And they love him and praise him forever and ever.
The family bible that lay on the stand.
The old-fashion'd *etc.*

The bible, that volume of God's inspiration,
At morning and evening could yield us delight;
The prayers of our father, a sweet invocation,
For mercy by day and for safety by night;
O hymns of thanksgiving with harmonious sweetness,
As warm'd by the hearts of the family band,
Hath rais'd us from earth to that rapturous dwelling
Describ'd in the bible that lay on the stand.

The maker of this text parodied the rhythmic form and textual trend of 'The Old Oaken Bucket'.[1] There are two other songs in the *Sacred Harp* which differ from the above simply in the tunes which are used; they are 'Family Bible' and 'Old-Fashioned Bible'. I have pieced out the above text with stanzas from these other songs. The tune was probably originally dorian, the sixth having been lowered here by an editor who felt he had to make a natural minor (aeolian) tune out if it.

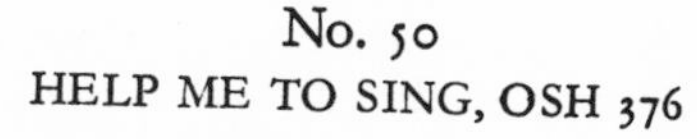

No. 50

HELP ME TO SING, OSH 376

Pentatonic, mode 2 (I—3 IV V — 7)

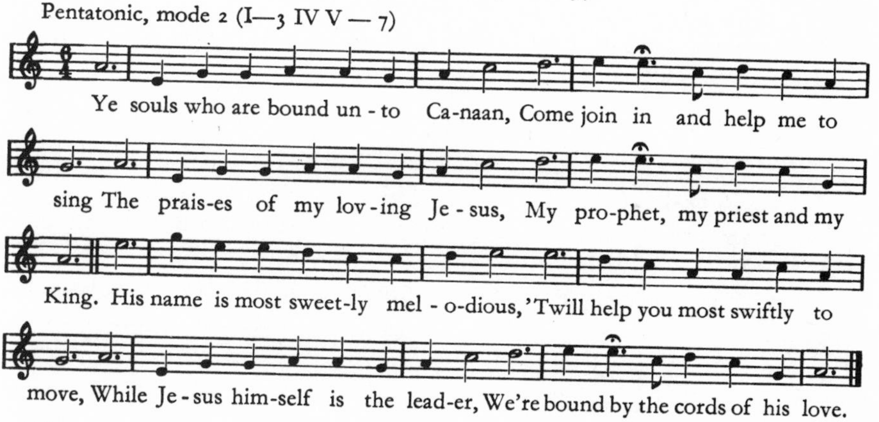
Ye souls who are bound un - to Ca-naan, Come join in and help me to
sing The prais-es of my lov-ing Je - sus, My pro-phet, my priest and my
King. His name is most sweet-ly mel - o-dious, 'Twill help you most swiftly to
move, While Je - sus him-self is the lead-er, We're bound by the cords of his love.

We are fortunate in finding numerous close and distant relatives of this text and tune. We must first interpret B. F. White's claim to it in the *Sacred Harp*[2] as pertaining merely to his harmonic arrangement of what he must have considered an "unwritten" song.[3] The text seems to be of American origin. The tune stems

[1] The song, long popular, whose text was written by Samuel Woodworth and whose tune is supposedly based on an old Scottish air.

[2] Page 376.

[3] An earlier recording of the same traditional song was made, as it happens, by "Monday" and it appeared in *The Supplement to the Kentucky Harmony*, p. 135.

from the British Isles. In England its close relatives appear under such titles as 'Sally Gray'[1] and 'Ratcliffe Highway';[2] in Scotland as the old tune 'The Mucking o' Geordie's Byre' which Robert Burns used for his 'Tam Glen'.[3]

Its somewhat less close melodic kindred are in England 'The Banks of the Lea',[4] in Wales 'Llanarmon', a hymn version,[5] 'The Green Pool',[6] and 'The Pretty Girl Milking her Cow'.[7] In Ireland they are 'The Rose of the Vale',[8] 'The Lass With the Bonny Brown Hair',[9] and 'The Pretty Girl that Milks the Cows' which was found in the Bunting Collection of 1796.[10]

Some members of this tune family, appearing in four-four time, tend to merge with the 'Gilderoy' melodies which reach back at least to 1719.[11] Those with texts in iambic meter sometimes touch the 'Babe of Bethlehem' tune family, as does 'Enquirer';[12] and *major*-keyed versions of this predominantly aeolian and dorian formula approach the popular 'Old Rosin the Bow' group of tunes.[13] So the tune above may be said to swim in the middle of our broad stream of national melody.

The *fermate* in the above tune do not appear in the *Sacred Harp*. They are introduced by me to show a feature of the actual singing tradition of this melody as I heard it in the convention of the United Sacred Harp Singing Association in Atlanta, September 10, 1938.

The following song in this collection, 'Poor Pilgrim', is still another variant of 'Help Me to Sing'.

No. 51

POOR PILGRIM, UVW No. 174

Pentatonic, mode 2 (I — 3 IV V — 7)

I am a poor pilgrim of sor - row, Toss'd out in this wide world to roam. I've

heard of a ci - ty call'd heav - en, I'm striv - ing to make it my home.

[1] From the North of England, JFSS, iii, 41.
[2] From Norfolk, JFSS, ii, 172.
[3] *Ibid.*, iii, 42.
[4] From Norfolk, *ibid.*, iv, 91; from Essex, *ibid.*, ii, 150; from Wiltshire, *ibid.*, ii, 210.
[5] *Ibid.*, iv, 91.
[6] JWF, i, 55.
[7] *Ibid.*, i, 56.
[8] From County Waterford, JIFS, xii, 19.
[9] *Ibid.*, volume and page not available.
[10] *Ibid.*, xxv, 26.
[11] See *Spiritual Folk-Songs*, No. 54.
[12] *Ibid.*, No. 87. See also 'Old Israelites' in this volume for further references to 'Babe of Bethlehem' tunes here.
[13] *Ibid.*, No. 129.

Sometimes I feel weak and weary,
Sometimes I know not where to roam,
But Jesus, my blesséd Redeemer,
Says: Pilgrim, I'll take you home.

My sisters nor brothers won't own me,
I'm out in this wide world alone.
I have no hopes of tomorrow,
I'm striving to reach a fair home.

Hark, hark at the message I hear,
One trouble is over my brain.
The old ship draws nearer and nearer,
Says: Pilgrim, I'll take you in.

My mother has reached the fair glory,
My father still walks in his sin.
But Jesus, my blesséd Redeemer,
Says: Pilgrim, I'll take you in.

This song was recorded by Winston Wilkinson, October 31, 1935, in Grottoes, Virginia, as sung by R. H. Mace.[1] As to its relationships, it seems to lie on middle ground between 'Banks of the Lea', of which it is tonally a variant and textually a parody, and a negro song from Virginia by the same title, 'Poor Pilgrim', found in Dett's collection. The 'Banks of the Lea' begins:

When first in this country a stranger,
Curiosity caused me to roam;
Over Europe I resolved to be a ranger,
When I left Philadelphia my home.[2]

The negro song runs:

I am a poor wayfaring stranger,
I sometimes know not where to roam;
I heard of a city call'd heaven,
I'm striving to make it my home.

Sometimes I'm both tosséd and driven,
(Next three lines are same as in first stanza)

My friends and relations forsake me,
And troubles roll round me so high;
I thought of the kind voice of Jesus,
Saying "Poor pilgrim, I'm always nigh."[3]

[1] It is No. 174 in the *University of Virginia* (manuscript) *Collection of Folk-Music* and is used here by kind permission.

[2] JFSS, ii, 120. Frank Kidson recognized "Philadelphia" as made over from "dear Ireland".

[3] See *Religious Folk-Songs of the Negro*, p. 169.

The three songs, Wilkinson's, Dett's, and 'Banks of the Lea' are close kin. Their relationship to 'Help me to Sing', the preceding song in this volume, lies chiefly in the melody, the text of the latter following merely the general theme of weary wayfaring which is common, in some form, to all the texts in this song group, especially to those cited as secular variants of 'Help Me to Sing'.

No. 52

SARDINIA, SOH (1835) 126

Heptatonic aeolian, mode 2 (I II 3 IV V 6 7)

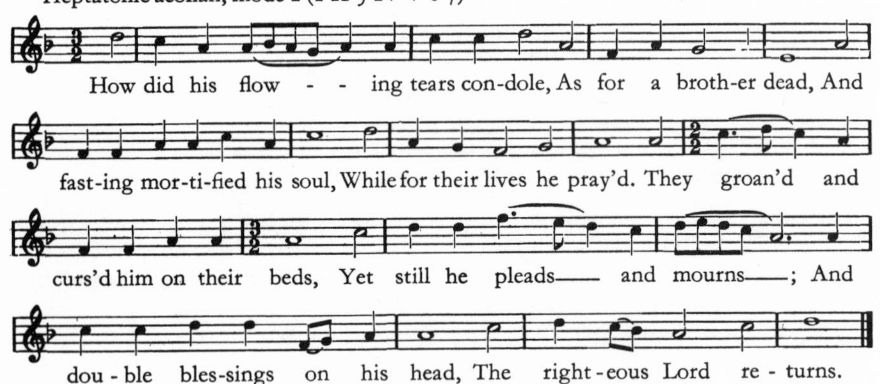
How did his flow - - ing tears con-dole, As for a broth-er dead, And
fast-ing mor-ti-fied his soul, While for their lives he pray'd. They groan'd and
curs'd him on their beds, Yet still he pleads—— and mourns——; And
dou - ble bles-sings on his head, The right - eous Lord re - turns.

The biblical story connection of the above text fragment will become evident with the two following stanzas which are taken from the *Hesperian Harp*. They are the first and third stanzas of the poem while the above is the second.

Behold the love, the generous love
That holy David shows!
Behold his kind compassion move
For his afflicted foes!
When they are sick his soul complains,
And seems to feel the smart;
The spirit of the gospel reigns
And melts his pious heart.

O glorious type of heavenly grace!
Thus Christ, the Lord, appears;
While sinners curse, the Savior prays,
And pities them with tears.
He, the true David, Israel's king,
Bless'd and belov'd of God,
To save us rebels, dead in sin,
Paid his own dearest blood.

The *Hesperian Harp* editor gave the name "Castle", top right. The 1911 *Original Sacred Harp* editor calls "G. Castil" the author of the tune and states that the text was found in *Mercer's Cluster.*

No. 53

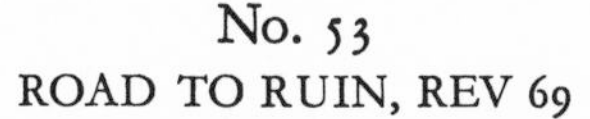

ROAD TO RUIN, REV 69

Pentatonic, mode 5 minorized (I — 3 [III] IV — 6 7 [VII])

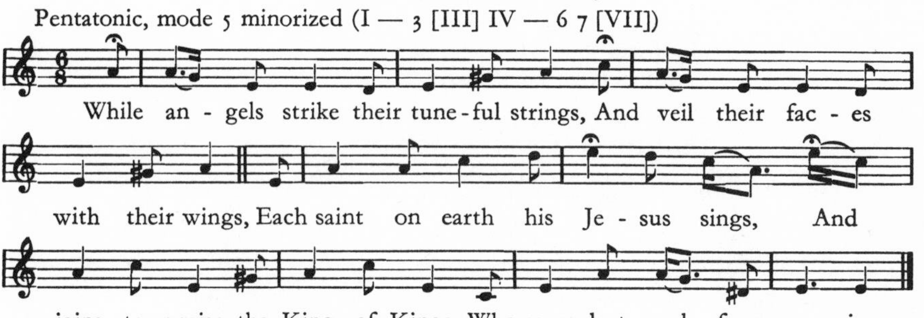
While an - gels strike their tune - ful strings, And veil their fac - es
with their wings, Each saint on earth his Je - sus sings, And
joins to praise the King of Kings, Who saves lost souls from ru - in.

But sinners, fond of earthly toys,
Mock and deride, when saints rejoice;
They shut their ears at Jesus' voice,
And make the world and sin their choice,
And force their way to ruin.

The preachers warn them night and day;
For them the Christian weeps and prays;
But sinners laugh and turn away,
And join the wicked, vain, and gay,
Who throng the road to ruin.

Ofttimes in visions of the night,
God doth their guilty souls affright;
They tremble at the awful sight,
But still again with morning light
Pursue the road to ruin.

Sometimes by preaching, sinners see
They're doom'd to hell and misery;
To turn to God they then agree,
But oh! their wicked company
Allures them on to ruin.

Ofttimes when nothing else will do,
Affliction will their danger show,
And bring the haughty sinners low;
Then they'll repent, and pray, and vow,
But turn again to ruin.

When every way is tried in vain,
No more the spirit strives with man,
But full of guilt and fear and pain,
Death strikes the blow, the sinner's slain,
And sinks to endless ruin.

Oh sinners, turn! ye long have stood
Opposed to truth and all that's good;
You may be saved through Jesus' blood,
Lay down your arms, submit to God,
And thus be saved from ruin.

Turn, sinners, neighbors, friend or foe,
The terrors of the Lord we know;
Oh tell us, friends, what will you do?
We cannot bear to let you go
To everlasting ruin,

The stanzaic pattern, four rhyming lines followed by one which ends regularly in the word "ruin", is the same as that found in 'Come Saints and Sinners' in this volume where the recurrent word is "union".

This tune and 'Night Thought', a variant, and 'Experience' are the only ones in the entire collection cast in the fifth mode and having phrygian implications. 'Ho Every One That Thirsts' is also a variant, but it is in a different mode.

No. 54

GLORY IN MY SOUL, REV 351

Heptatonic aeolian, dorian influence, mode 4 (I II 3 IV V 6 [VI] 7)

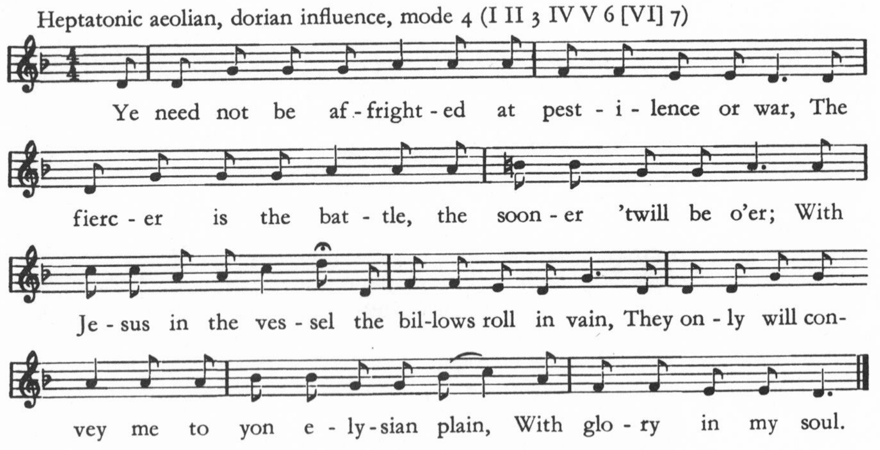
Ye need not be af-fright-ed at pest-i-lence or war, The
fierc-er is the bat-tle, the soon-er 'twill be o'er; With
Je-sus in the ves-sel the bil-lows roll in vain, They on-ly will convey me to yon e-ly-sian plain, With glo-ry in my soul.

Though sinners do despise us and laugh at what we say,
We find a little number walk with us in the way;

Come on, come on, my brethren, they laughed at Jesus too,
The kingdom is before us and heaven heaves in view;
And glory's in our souls.

I feel that Jesus loves me, but why I do not know,
To him I'm so unfaithful in what I have to do;
I grieve to see my failings, but he does all forgive,
Which makes me love him more, and by faith in him I live;
With glory in my soul.

We soon shall reach fair Canaan, and on that peaceful shore,
Beyond the reach of Satan, we'll sing our suff'rings o'er;
We'll walk the golden pavements and blood-washed garments wear,
And to increase our pleasures our Jesus will be there,
And glory in our souls.

My song I must conclude, though it is against my will,
I long to have the power to sing what I do feel;
I long to see the day when immortal I shall be,
And sing and praise my Jesus to all eternity,
With glory in my soul.

A note in the *Revivalist* states that the song was recorded "as sung by the Auburn Praying Band." The *b*-natural (raised sixth) in the fourth measure indicates dorian influence. The tune is quite like 'God Bless You Merry Gentlemen', Sharp, *English Folk-Carols*, No. 6, and 'New Year's Carol', No. 20.

No. 55

ROYAL BAND, OSH 360

Pentatonic, mode 4 (I II — IV V — 7)

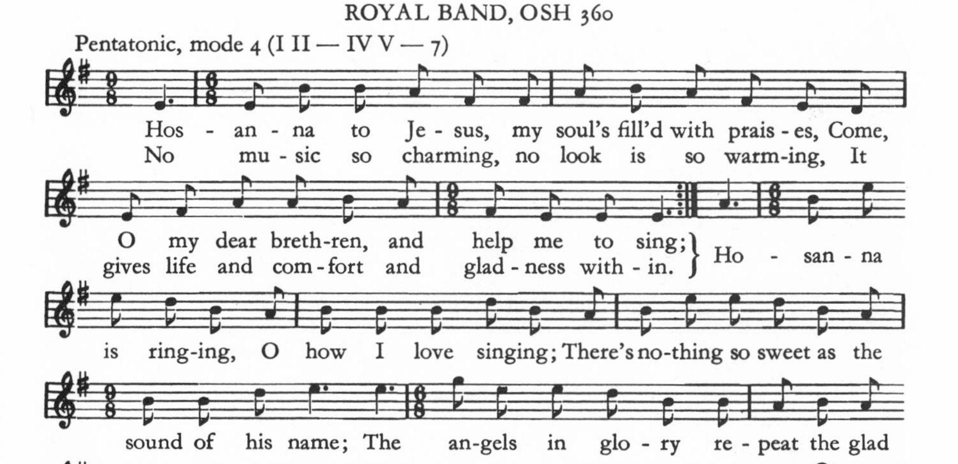
Hos - an - na to Je - sus, my soul's fill'd with prais - es, Come,
No mu - sic so charming, no look is so warm-ing, It
O my dear breth-ren, and help me to sing;
gives life and com - fort and glad - ness with - in.
Ho - san - na
is ring-ing, O how I love singing; There's no-thing so sweet as the
sound of his name; The an-gels in glo - ry re - peat the glad
sto - ry Of love which in Je - sus is made known to man.

Hosanna to Jesus, my soul, how it pleases,
To see sinners falling and crying to God;
Then shouting and praising, they cry, "'Tis amazing,
We've found peace and pardon in Jesus'es blood."
Hosanna is ringing, hark, how they are singing,
"All glory to Jesus, we've tasted his love."
The kingdom of heaven to mortals is given,
And rolls through my soul from the mansions above.

See 'South Union' in this volume for remarks on this type of Gaelic movement and rhyme.

No. 56

WEDLOCK, *Sharp-Karpeles*, ii, 272

Pentatonic, mode 4 (I II — IV V — 7)

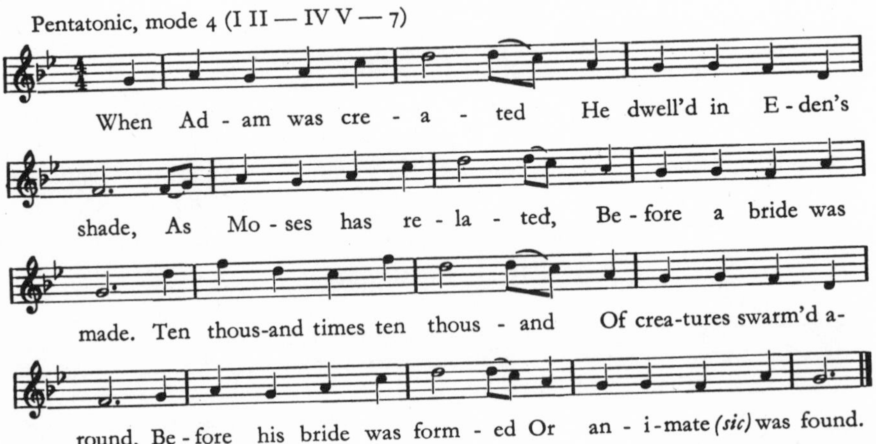
When Ad - am was cre - a - ted He dwell'd in E - den's
shade, As Mo - ses has re - la - ted, Be - fore a bride was
made. Ten thous-and times ten thous - and Of crea-tures swarm'd a-
round, Be - fore his bride was form - ed Or an - i-mate (sic) was found.

In the lore of Abraham Lincoln a tale was told, and has persisted, that he was the author of this song; that he wrote it for the occasion of the marriage of his sister Sarah to Aaron Grigsby in 1826. Vannest, one of his more recent biographers, denies the Lincoln genesis of the song. This on the basis of his finding traces of its English provenience in a southern Indiana tradition whence, as he suggests, it probably came to Lincoln.[1]

Vannest is correct in denying the Lincoln authorship and in pointing to England for its source. I find a version of it from the north of England in Baring-Gould,[2] where there are references to other English texts dating as early as 1740. Miss Anne G. Gilchrist, in a letter to me, adds: "Your hymn [referring to the variants

[1] *Lincoln the Hoosier*, pp. 226–228.
[2] *Songs of the West*, No. 100.

under the same title, 'Wedlock', in *Spiritual Folk-Songs*, Nos. 13 and 43] is a re-cast in a different metre of an old English song on this theme, beginning

> Both sexes give ear to my fancy[1]

but more often

> When Adam was first created
> And lord of the universe crowned.

This is in Dixon's *Songs of the Peasantry of England* and was long a favourite in the northern counties. F. Kidson has a copy with tune in *Traditional Tunes.* But the conceit of Eve being taken out of Adam's side instead of his head or his feet, and for the reasons given — that she was neither 'to triumph or rule over man', but 'taken out of his side, his equal and partner to be' goes back to the 'Parson's Tale' in Chaucer's *Canterbury Pilgrims!*"

The conceit mentioned by Miss Gilchrist is contained in the following couplets which, for the convenience of the reader, I reproduce here from *Spiritual Folk-Songs*, No. 43.

> This woman was not taken from Adam's head, we know;
> And she must not rule o'er him, 'tis evidently so.
>
> This woman she was taken from near to Adam's heart,
> By which we are directed that they should never part.
>
> This woman she was taken from under Adam's arm,
> And she must be protected from injury and harm.
>
> This woman was not taken from Adam's feet, we see;
> And she must not be abuséd, the meaning seems to be.
>
> The husband is commanded to love his loving bride,
> And live as does a Christian, and for his house provide.

The striking analogy in the 'Parson's Tale', written nearly 500 years before the time when the above couplets were recorded in Georgia, will appear from the following quotation. "For he [God] ne made hir nat of the heved of Adam, for she sholde nat clayme [too] greet lordshipe. / For ther-as the womman has the maistrie, she maketh to much desray; ther neden none ensamples of this. The experience of day by day oughte suffyse. / Also certes, god ne made nat womman of the foot of Adam, for she ne sholde nat been holden to [too] lowe; for she can nat paciently suffre: but god made womman of the rib of Adam, for womman sholde be felawe [fellow] un-to man. / Man sholde bere him to his wyf in feith, in trouthe, and in love, as seith seint Paul."

[1] For its tune see *Spiritual Folk-Songs*, No. 60.

But not even Chaucer was the author of the head-rib-foot observation and interpretation. Sister Mariella, in looking for Chaucer's sources, has come upon parallels in a Latin sermon of the twelfth century, in another of the thirteenth century, and in an English sermon of the fifteenth century. These, grouped with the fourteenth-century Chaucerian use of it, determine her statement that "it was a commonplace in mediaeval religious literature."[1] She cites my *White Spirituals* version of 'Wedlock' and assumes, correctly, I believe, that this rationalisation of the marital state, as male man would have it, lived on in song — we would say in *folk*-song — to present times.

The Sharp-Karpeles tune above, found in North Carolina in 1918, and the variant which I found in the Georgia *Sacred Harp* of 1844 have a close relative in the Irish capstan chanty 'The Banks of Newfoundland'.[2]

No. 57

COME CHRISTIANS, SOH (1835) 81

Heptatonic aeolian, mode 2 (I II 3 IV V 6 7)

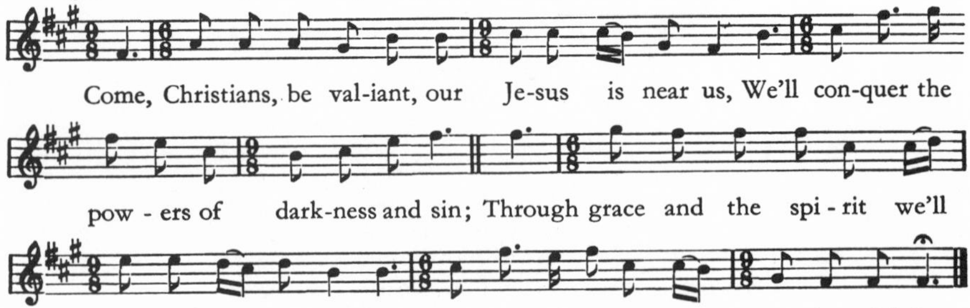
Come, Christians, be val-iant, our Je-sus is near us, We'll con-quer the
pow - ers of dark-ness and sin; Through grace and the spi - rit we'll
glo - ry in - her - it, And peace, like a riv-er, give com-fort with-in.

We've trials and cares and hardships and losses,
But heaven will pay us for all that we bear;
We'll soon end in pleasure and glory forever,
And bright crowns of glory forever we'll wear.

Young converts , be humble, the prospect is blooming,
The wings of kind angels around you are spread;
While some are oppressèd with sin and are mourning,
The spirit of joy upon you is shed.

Live near to your Captain and always obey him,
This world, flesh, and Satan must all be denied;
Both care with diligence and prayer without ceasing,
Will safe land young converts to riches on high.

[1] *Modern Language Notes*, liii, 251ff.
[2] JFSS, v. 300.

O mourners, God bless you, don't faint in the spirit,
Believe, and the Spirit our pardon he'll give;
He's now interceding and pleading his merit,
Give up, and your souls he will quickly receive.

If truly a mourner, he's promised you comfort,
His good promises stand in his sacred word;
O harken and hear them, all glory, all glory,
The mourners are fill'd with the presence of God.

O sinners, my bowels do move with desire;
Why stand you gazing on the works of the Lord?
O fly from the flames of devouring fire,
And wash your pollution in Jesus'es blood.

Brethren, in sweet gales we are all breezing,
My soul feels the mighty, the heavenly flame;
I'm now on my journey, my faith is increasing,
All glory and praises to God and the Lamb.

No. 58

DYING FRIEND, SHD 399

Hexatonic, mode 2 b (I — 3 IV V 6 7)

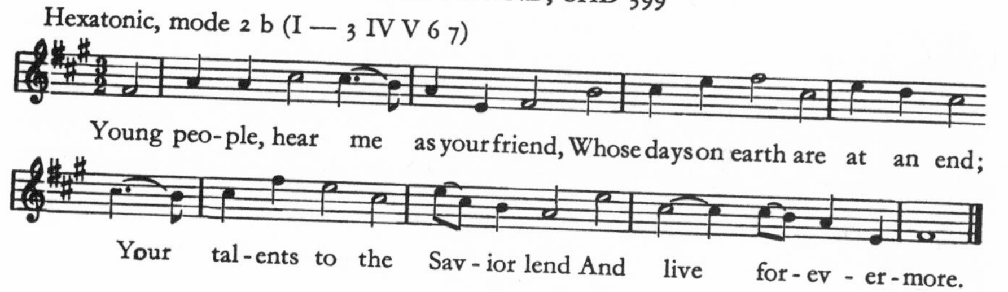
Young peo-ple, hear me as your friend, Whose days on earth are at an end;
Your tal-ents to the Sav-ior lend And live for-ev-er-more.

His word will guide you here below,
Great love and mercy he will show;
And then with Jesus you may go
And live forevermore.

With you no longer I may dwell,
But his great love for you I tell;
I'm ready now to bid farewell
And live forevermore.

The song is by Lee Wells who is at present a young and zealous *Sacred Harp* singer and leader. It was composed in 1935 and introduced into the *Sacred Harp, Denson Revision*, of 1936. When one compares the tune with those of 'The Wife of Usher's Well',[1] one is reassured that the feeling for racial melody is not yet dead among the rural musical folk of the South. 'Horton', another recently composed tune in the present volume and a variant of the one above, is a melody to which the same observation applies. The 'Dying Friend' tune belongs to the 'Kedron' family.[2]

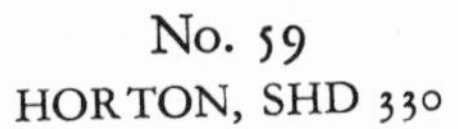

No. 59
HORTON, SHD 330

Hexatonic, mode 2 A (I II 3 IV V — 7)

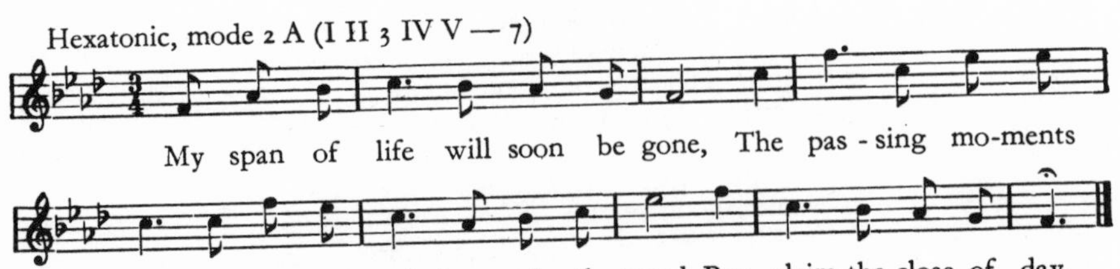
My span of life will soon be gone, The pas - sing mo-ments
say; As length'ning shad-ows o'er the mead Pro - claim the close of day.

My Christian friends to whom I speak,
I have a crown in view;
My sinner friends, now will you seek,
How stands the case with you?

The love of Christ constraineth me,
Sin's evil ways to shun,
And in the paths of righteousness,
My race with patience run.

The cross of Christ inspires my heart
To sing redeeming grace;
Awake my soul and bear a part
In my Redeemer's praise.

How long, dear Savior, oh how long
Shall this bright hour delay?
Fly swift around, ye wheels of time,
And bring the promised day.

When we've been there ten thousand years,
Bright shining as the sun,
We've no less days to sing God's praise
Than when we first begun.

[1] See Sharp-Karpeles, i, 150ff.
[2] See 'Distress' in this volume and No. 57 in *Spiritual Folk-Songs*.

The song was composed for the 1936 *Denson Revision* of the *Original Sacred Harp* by Paine Denson, one of the editors of that edition, an attorney in Birmingham, Alabama, and son of the notable fasola musician, the late T. J. (Uncle Tom) Denson. He drew the stanzas of the text from various other fasola songs. Compare the tune with 'Detroit' and 'Kedron' in *Spiritual Folk-Songs*,[1] 'Fellowship',[2] various tunes given with 'The Wife of Usher's Well'[3], 'Wagoner's Lad',[4] 'The Royal Charter',[5] 'The Royal Oak',[6] 'Come Father Build Me'[7] and, in this volume, 'Dying Friend' and 'Distress'. It would seem undeniable that Mr. Denson, in composing this tune, was treading the well-beaten path of his racial melodic past.

No. 60

CALVARY or GETHSEMANE, REV 23

Hexatonic, mode 2 b minorized (I — 3 IV [IV♯] V 6 7 [VII])

Come, prec-ious soul, and let us take A walk be-com-ing you and me, And

whither, my friend, shall we our foot-steps bend, To Cal-v'ry or to Geth-sem-a-ne?

O Calvary is a mountain high;
'Tis much too hard a task for me,
And I had rather stay
In the broad and pleasant way
Than to walk in the garden of Gethsemane.

O! it would not appear such a mountain high;
Nor yet so hard a task for thee,
If thou didst love the man
Who first laid the plan
Of climbing the mountain of Calvary.

I had rather abide in the pleasant plain,
My gay companions there to see,
And to tarry a while
In the joys of the world,
Than to climb up the mountain of Calvary.

[1] Nos. 147 and 57 respectively.
[2] *Sacred Harp* (Denson), p. 330.
[3] Sharp-Karpeles, i, 150ff.
[4] *Ibid.*, ii, 125.
[5] JFSS, vii, 6.
[6] *Ibid.*, v, 167.
[7] *Ibid.*, viii, 212.

Thy gay companions ere long will be gone,
Poor blinded souls, could they but see!
And if ever thou wouldst stand
On Canaan's happy land,
Thou must first climb the mountain Calvary.

There is no pleasure that I can behold,
'Tis a sad and dreary path to me,
And I have heard them say,
There are lions in the way,
And they lurk in the mountain Calvary.

True, it is a straight and narrow road,
And lions lurk there for their prey,
But thou shalt have a guard,
Yea, the angels of God,
Shall conduct thee up to Calvary.

I had rather have peace and live at my ease,
Than to be afflicted thus by thee,
When blooming youth is gone,
And old age comes on,
I will then go with thee to Calvary.

There is no time so good as youth,
To travel this mountain, you must see,
For when old age comes on,
With a great load of sin,
How then canst thou climb up Calvary?

O conscience, thou art ever making a noise,
I cannot enjoy any peace for thee,
There is time enough yet,
And the journey's not so great,
I can soon climb the mountain Calvary.

Oh hark! I hear a doleful sound,
And thou shouldst greatly alarméd be,
A blooming youth is gone,
And is sleeping in the tomb,
Who refuséd to climb up Calvary.

Alas! I know not what to do,
For thou hast greatly alarméd me,
In sin I have gone on,
Till I fear I am undone,
Lord help me to climb up Calvary.

Tarry not in all the plain,
Lest it prove a dangerous snare to thee,
But look up to the man
Who was bruiséd for thy sin,
And he'll help thee to climb up Calvary.

The song-debate between Soul and Conscience furnishes a good example of the type called the "dialog" song. Such songs were favorites during the eighteenth century and were sung, in Baptist and Methodist gatherings, by two sections of the congregation, each singing alternate verses. The practice of seating the women on one side of the meeting house and the men on the other, seems to have been the incentive to the development of this dramatic type. The first record we have of this sort of hymn is in *Sacred Hymns .... Generally Composed in Dialogues*, compiled by John Cennick, the Baptist, Bristol, 1743. And it is supposed that Cennick was also the actual author of the dramatic hymns there.[1] The seating practice and the dialog songs came to America and persisted, even in the camp-meeting environment.[2] Other dialog songs in this volume are 'Methodist and Formalist' and 'Mariner's Hymn'.[3]

The *Revivalist* editor printed the song "as sung by Rev. G. C. Wells", or from oral tradition, as we should say. It is a question, however, whether the accidentals shown in the tune were actually sung by the Reverend Wells or were "arranged" into the essentially modal tune. The suspicion of tampering rests more heavily on the *Revivalist* editor since Winston Wilkinson discovered the secular analog to this tune in 'A Song of the Sea' which is cast in the pure dorian mode.[4]

[1] See Benson, *The English Hymn*, p. 317, and Lightwood, *Hymn-Tunes and Their Story*, p. 144.
[2] See Bennett, *Memorials of Methodism in Virginia*, pp. 392 and 437.
[3] Songs of this type elsewhere are 'Brother and His Soul', SWP 148; 'Female Pilgrim', SWP 149; 'Watchman', HH 188; 'Zion's Pilgrim', REV 409; 'The Better Land', REV 423; and 'Shout for Joy', REV 288.
[4] See Chapple, *Heart Songs*, p. 67.

One Hundred and Fifty-Two Folk-Hymns

Songs of Praise for Assemblages

SACRED HARP singers take time out for the traditional dinner-on-the-grounds, Liberty Church, Helicon, Winston County, Alabama.

"Women on that side, men on this, please!"

NINETEEN MEMBERS OF THE MUSICALLY NOTED DENSON CLAN and a few friends at the July 4th, 1938, *Sacred Harp* Singing at Liberty Church. Densons have sung, taught, and composed *Sacred Harp* music for four known generations. The Liberty Church singings have gone on without interruption for 58 years. See *White Spirituals in the Southern Uplands*, pp. 107—109.

No. 61

FLORILLA, SOH (1835) 47

Pentatonic, mode 3 (I II III — V VI —)

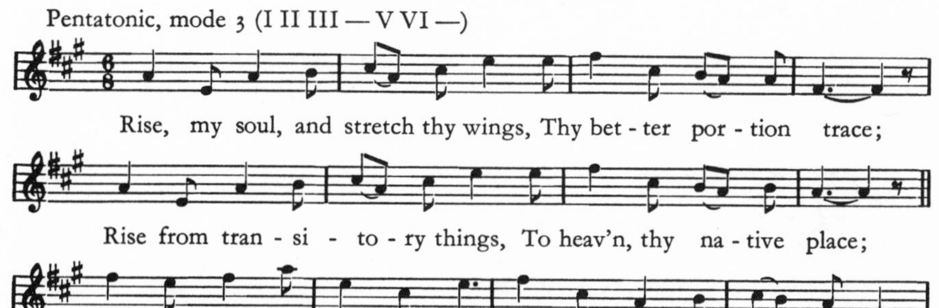
Rise, my soul, and stretch thy wings, Thy bet - ter por - tion trace;
Rise from tran - si - to - ry things, To heav'n, thy na - tive place;

Sun and moon and stars de - cay, Time shall soon this earth re-move;

Rise, my soul, and haste a - way To seats pre - pared a - bove.

The words, by Robert Seagrave, 1693–1756(?), and the tune were widely sung in early country music circles;[1] but no secular use of the melody has been found.

No. 62

AWFUL DAY, OL 121

Hexatonic, mode 2 A (I II 3 IV V — 7 [VII])

That aw - ful day will sur - ly come, Th'ap-point - ed hour makes
Chorus And pass the sol - emn test———, And pass the sol - lemn

Da Capo for Chorus

haste, When I must stand be - fore my Judge And pass the sol - emn test.
test; When I *etc.*

Thou lovely Chief of all my joys,
Thou Ruler of my heart;
How could I bear to hear thy voice
Pronounce the sound: "Depart!"

[1] See FHA, notes on No. 2, for references.

The thunder of that dismal word
Would so torment my ear,
'Twould tear my soul asunder, Lord,
With most tormenting fear.

The text is by Isaac Watts, 1674–1748.

No. 63
GOSPEL POWER, REV 83

Hexatonic, mode 3 b (I II III IV V VI —)

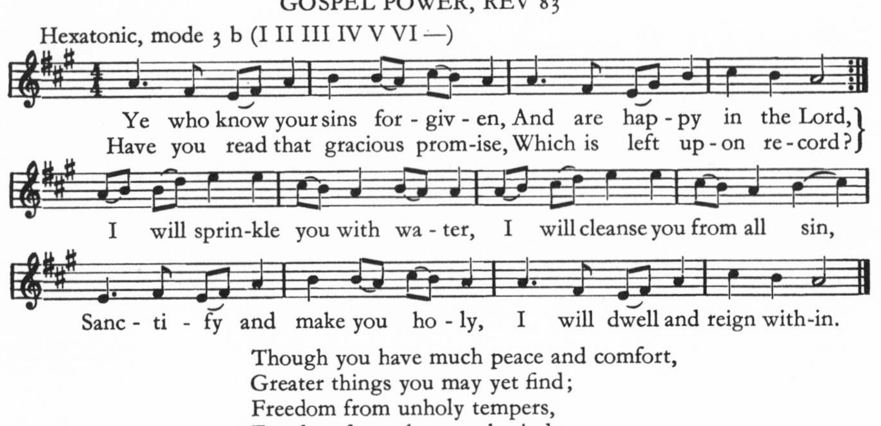
Ye who know your sins for - giv - en, And are hap - py in the Lord,
Have you read that gracious prom-ise, Which is left up - on re - cord?
I will sprin-kle you with wa - ter, I will cleanse you from all sin,
Sanc - ti - fy and make you ho - ly, I will dwell and reign with-in.

Though you have much peace and comfort,
Greater things you may yet find;
Freedom from unholy tempers,
Freedom from the carnal mind.
To procure your perfect freedom,
Jesus suffer'd, groan'd and died;
On the cross the healing fountain
Gushéd from his wounded side.

Seven more stanzas are to be found in the *Revivalist.* The tune is a variant of 'Holy Manna'.[1] Its differences from the latter are to be laid either at the door of the Rev. L. Hartsough, its "arranger", or to variations in the oral tradition.

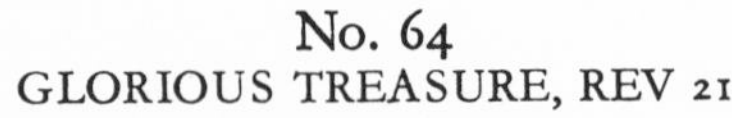

No. 64
GLORIOUS TREASURE, REV 21

Heptatonic ionian, mode 3 (I II III IV V VI VII)

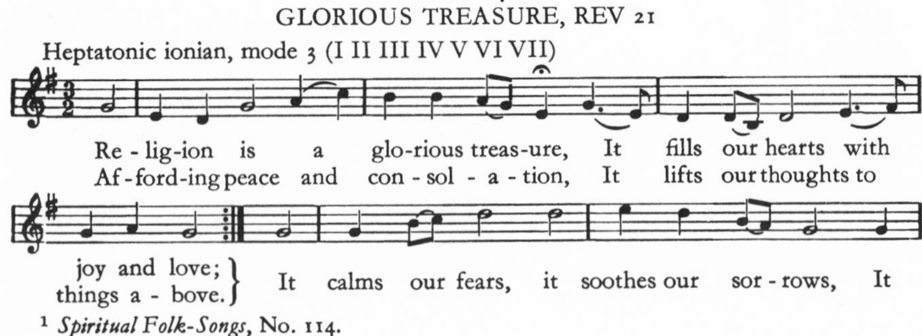
Re - lig-ion is a glo-rious treas-ure, It fills our hearts with joy and love;
Af-ford-ing peace and con - sol - a - tion, It lifts our thoughts to things a - bove.
It calms our fears, it soothes our sor - rows, It

[1] *Spiritual Folk-Songs*, No. 114.

smooths our way o'er life's rough sea; 'Tis mix'd with pa-tience and
ho - ly vir - tue, This heav'n - ly por - tion mine shall be.

My flesh and blood shall be dissolvéd,
And mortal life shall soon be o'er,
And earthly fears and earthly sorrows
Shall vex my heart and eyes no more.
But pure religion abides forever,
And my glad heart shall strengthen'd be,
While endless ages are onward rolling,
This heav'nly portion mine shall be.

There are two more stanzas of the text in the *Revivalist.* The barring of the tune in that songbook was a confused attempt to fit it to common time. I have thus been forced to revise it as above. Another attempt in the same direction was made by Miss Gilchrist, JFSS, viii, 74.

No. 65

NIGHT THOUGHT, CL, ii, 18

Pentatonic, mode 5 (I — 3 IV — 6 7)

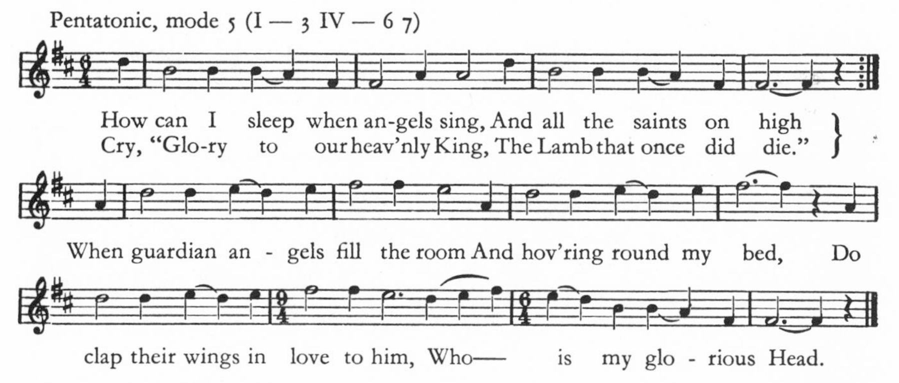
How can I sleep when an-gels sing, And all the saints on high
Cry, "Glo-ry to our heav'nly King, The Lamb that once did die."
When guardian an - gels fill the room And hov'ring round my bed, Do
clap their wings in love to him, Who— is my glo - rious Head.

There are six more stanzas of the text in the *Christian Lyre.* As to the tune Miss Gilchrist states: "It has the character of a Highland Gaelic 'iorraim' (rowing song) — though how it became an American hymn is a puzzle." Her suspicion as to its source may be based on its mode, the fifth, in which numbers of Highland folk-songs are cast, including some of the rowing songs which she mentioned.[1] Be it noted also that 'Night Thought' is one of the *only three tunes* in this volume cast in mode five with its phrygian implications. The others are a variant tune, 'Road to Ruin', and 'Experience'. Another melodic variant here, in a different mode however, is 'Ho Everyone That Thirsts'.

Winston Wilkinson calls my attention to a close melodic relationship of the above to 'Washington',[2] 'Union',[3] and 'The Death of Robin Hood'.[4]

No. 66

FOSTER, SKH 36

Heptatonic aeolian, mode 2 (I II 3 IV V 6 7)

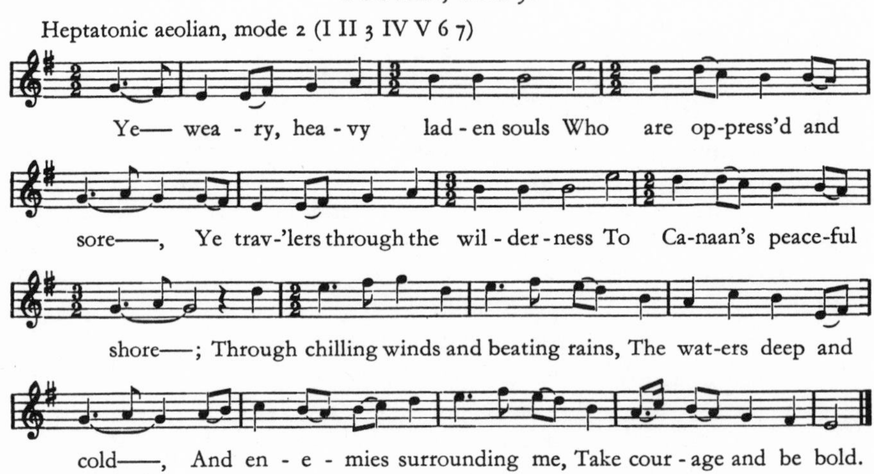
Ye— wea - ry, hea - vy lad - en souls Who are op-press'd and
sore—, Ye trav-'lers through the wil - der - ness To Ca-naan's peace-ful
shore—; Through chilling winds and beating rains, The wat-ers deep and
cold—, And en - e - mies surrounding me, Take cour - age and be bold.

Though storms and huricanes arise,
The desert all around,
And fiery serpents oft appear
Through the enchanted ground.
Dark nights and clouds and gloomy fears
And dragons often roar;
But while the gospel trump we hear
We'll press for Canaan's shore.

[1] See Miss Gilchrist's notes on the modes used in Gaelic melodies, JFSS, iv, 150–153, and Miss Broadwood's additional note, p. 154f.

[2] *Spiritual Folk-Songs*, No. 52, where a secular tune relative is given.

[3] *Ibid.*, No. 39.

[4] Davis, p. 586, No. 30, and Wilkinson's private Ms. collection of folk-songs, vi, 226, and vii, 226.

We're often like the lonesome dove,
Who mourns her absent mate,
From hill to hill, from vale to vale,
Her sorrow to relate.
But Canaan's land is just before,
Sweet spring is coming on;
A few more winds and beating rains,
And winter will be gone.

The text is an interesting collection of wandering couplets, with the resultant confusion in figurative expression. It is hard to follow the hymnster's lead rapidly through the wilderness, the waters deep and cold, the beating rains, the dry desert inhabited by fiery serpents and roaring dragons, and finally to Canaan's shore.[1]

The compiler of the *Supplement to the Kentucky Harmony* ascribed the tune to Wyeth. It is a variant of 'Dying Penitent' in this volume and of 'Separation' in *Spiritual Folk-Songs* where references to related secular tunes are given.

No. 67

HAMILTON, CL, ii, 112

Heptatonic aeolian, mode 2 minorized (I II 3 [III] IV V 6 7 [VII])

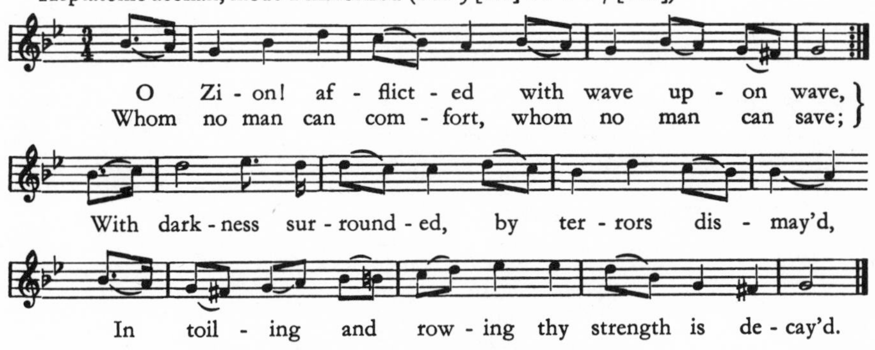
O Zi - on! af - flict - ed with wave up - on wave,
Whom no man can com - fort, whom no man can save;
With dark - ness sur - round - ed, by ter - rors dis - may'd,
In toil - ing and row - ing thy strength is de - cay'd.

Loud roaring the billows now nigh overwhelm,
But skilful the pilot who sits at the helm;
His wisdom conducts thee, his pow'r thee defends,
In safety and quiet thy warfare he ends.

[1] The model upon which the opening stanza above may have been made is the beginning of the hymn by Samuel Deacon (1746–1816)

Ye heavy-laden souls,
With guilt and fear opprest,
Come, for the great Redeemer calls,
And calls to give you rest.

"O fearful! O faithless!" in mercy he cries;
"My promise, my truth, are they light in thine eyes?
Still, still I am with thee, my promise will stand,
Through tempest and tossing, I'll bring thee to land.

"Forget thee, I will not, I cannot, — thy name
Engrav'd on my heart doth forever remain!
The palms of my hands while I look on, I see
The wounds I receivéd, when suffering for thee."

Two more stanzas of the text in the *Christian Lyre*.

No. 68

ERIE, HOC 105

Hexatonic, mode 1 A (I II III IV V VI —)

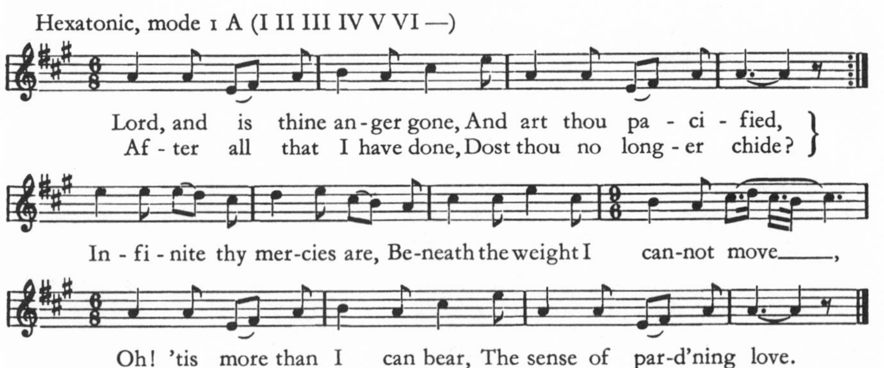
Lord, and is thine an-ger gone, And art thou pa - ci - fied,
Af - ter all that I have done, Dost thou no long - er chide?
In - fi - nite thy mer-cies are, Be-neath the weight I can-not move,
Oh! 'tis more than I can bear, The sense of par-d'ning love.

If I have begun once more,
Thy sweet return to feel;
If even now I find thy power,
Present my soul to heal;
Still and quiet may I lie,
Nor struggle out of thine embrace;
Never more resist or fly
From thy pursuing grace.

To the cross, thine altar, bind
Me with the cords of love;
Freedom let me never find
From thee, my Lord, to move;
That I never, never more
May with my much-loved Master part,
To the posts of mercy's door,
Oh! nail my willing heart.

The tune is a member of the 'Hallelujah' family, a large group of romping tunes which were equally popular in secular and spiritual environment, in the British Isles and America, during the first part of the nineteenth century.[1]

No. 69

HAYDEN, OL 234

Pentatonic, mode 3 (I II III — V VI —)

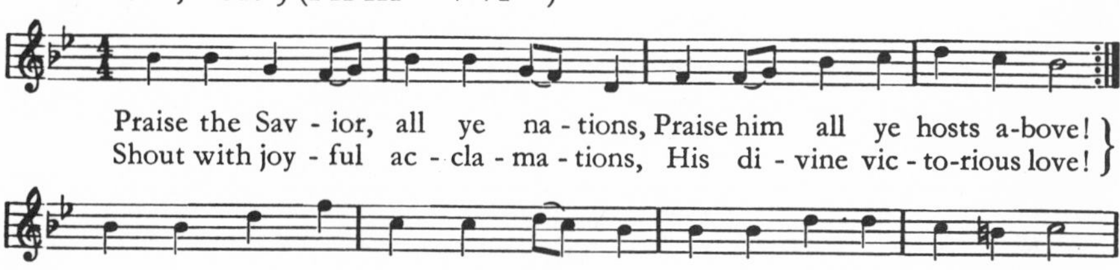
Praise the Sav - ior, all ye na - tions, Praise him all ye hosts a-bove!
Shout with joy - ful ac - cla - ma - tions, His di - vine vic - to-rious love!
Be his king - dom now pro - mot - ed; Let the earth her Monarch know.

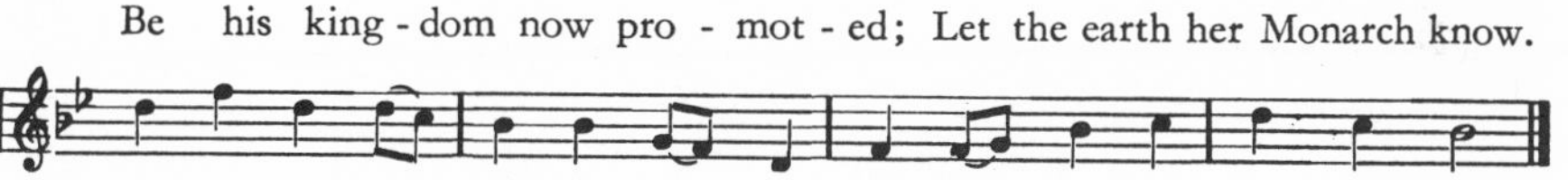
Be my all to him de - vot - ed, To my Lord my all I owe.

See how beauteous on the mountains,
Are the feet whose grand design
Is to guide us to the fountains
That o'erflow with bliss divine! —
Who proclaim the joyful tidings
Of salvation all around;
Disregard the world's deridings,
And in works of love abound.

"Sing this while the collection is being taken up," William Hauser compiler of the *Olive Leaf* suggests. He states that the song is "quoted from [or, as sung by?] Elder Amos S. Hayden," after whom it is named. The tune is a member of the 'I Will Arise' family.

The following incident may shed a light on the infection of the 'I Will Arise' song:[2] My sister, Mrs. Elena Jackson Quillian, listening recently to a "Chinese song" being sung by Mrs. Elizabeth Bryan Leavelle, who was born in China and lived there most of her life, recognized the tune as 'I Will Arise', note for note, though the manner and words were oriental. Inquiring about the song she

[1] References are given in *Spiritual Folk-Songs* under 'Hallelujah', the song for which the group has been named. Add to them 'Wellington', SKH 148, a tune recorded by A. Davisson probably before 1820.

[2] Compare *Spiritual Folk-Songs*, No. 239. To the tune-comparative references given there add 'Hind Horn', Greig-Keith, p. 20f; and FHA, notes on No. 28.

learned that Mrs. Leavelle had first heard it at the funeral of a high Chinese official and that the text had to do with the desire to be with the high Emperor in the celestial regions of joy. This my sister recognized as

> I will arise and go to Jesus,
> He will embrace me in his arms;
> In the arms of my dear Jesus,
> O there are ten thousand charms.

Subsequently Mrs. Leavelle learned from her father, a retired missionary, of the song's probable American provenience, its coming to China with the missionaries from the southern states. It seems obvious to me that the tune's five-tone scale made it all the more acceptable to the orientals.

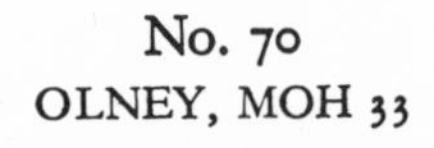

No. 70
OLNEY, MOH 33

Heptatonic ionian, mode 3 (I II III IV V VI VII)

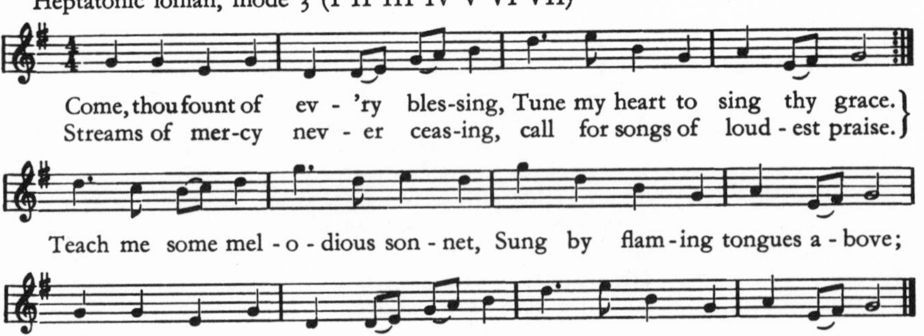
Come, thou fount of ev - 'ry bles-sing, Tune my heart to sing thy grace.
Streams of mer-cy nev - er ceas-ing, call for songs of loud - est praise.
Teach me some mel - o - dious son - net, Sung by flam - ing tongues a - bove;
Praise the mount, O fix me on it, Mount of thy un-chang - ing love.

> Here I raise my Ebenezer;
> Hither by thy grace I've come;
> And I trust by thy good pleasure
> Safely to arrive at home.
> Jesus sought me when a stranger,
> Wandering from the fold of God;
> He, to rescue me from danger,
> Interposed with precious blood.

The poem is by Robert Robinson, 1735–1790. The tune is attributed in the southern books usually to "Chapin", sometimes to "Boyd". It is found in practically all the shape-note song books. In the *Baptist Hymn and Tune Book*, 1857, it is called a "Western Melody".

No. 71
BOUNDLESS MERCY, SWP 27

Pentachordal, mode 3 (I II III — V — —)

Droop-ing souls, no long - er grieve, Heav-en is pro - pi - tious;
If in Christ you do be - lieve, You will find him pre - cious.
Je - sus now is pas - sing by, Calls the mourn - er to him;
Brings sal - va - tion from on high, Now look up and view him.

From his hands, his feet, his side,
Runs the healing lotion;
See the consolating tide,
Boundless as the ocean.
See the healing waters move
For the sick and dying;
Now resolve to gain his love,
Or to perish trying.

For five more stanzas of text and a related tune see 'Drooping Souls'.[1] It may be that the anonymous writer of this widely sung text was influenced by the Charles Wesley hymn which begins

Drooping souls, shake off thy fears.[2]

No. 72
CHRISTIAN VOLUNTEERS, HH 94

Pentatonic, mode 3 (I II III — V VI —)

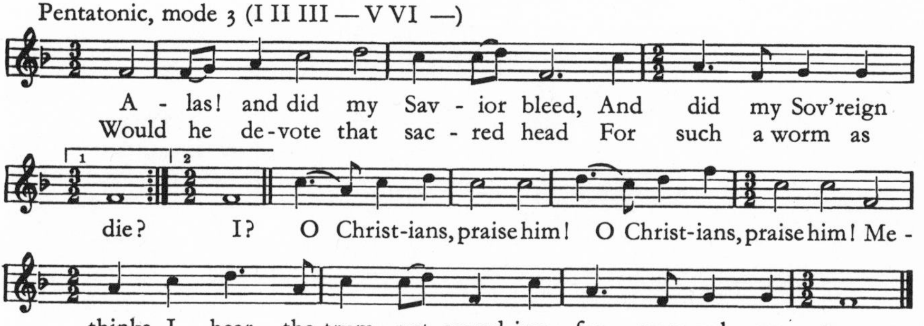
A - las! and did my Sav - ior bleed, And did my Sov'reign
Would he de-vote that sac - red head For such a worm as
1
2
die? I? O Christ-ians, praise him! O Christ-ians, praise him! Me -
thinks I hear the trum - pet sound-ing for more vol - un - teers.

The verse text is by Isaac Watts, 1674–1748. The tune belongs to the 'Roll Jordan' family; references given under 'Glorious Day' in this volume.

[1] *Spiritual Folk-Songs*, No. 116. [2] See *Methodist Hymns*, 1842, p. 46.

No. 73

GLORIOUS DAY, CHH 114

Hexatonic, mode 3 A (I II III — V VI VII)

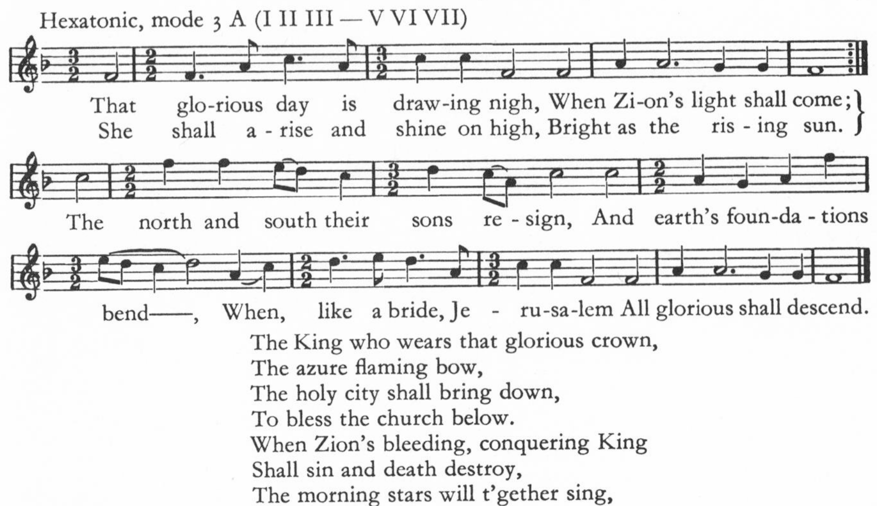
That glo-rious day is draw-ing nigh, When Zi-on's light shall come;
She shall a-rise and shine on high, Bright as the ris-ing sun.
The north and south their sons re-sign, And earth's foun-da-tions
bend——, When, like a bride, Je - ru-sa-lem All glorious shall descend.

The King who wears that glorious crown,
The azure flaming bow,
The holy city shall bring down,
To bless the church below.
When Zion's bleeding, conquering King
Shall sin and death destroy,
The morning stars will t'gether sing,
And Zion shout for joy.

"The melody [is] as I learned it from my dear mother when I was only five years old," William Walker states in his *Christian Harmony*. That would have been in 1814. The tune belongs to the 'Roll Jordan' family, other members of which are 'Sister's Farewell', 'Christian Volunteers', 'Sweet Rivers', 'Away Over Jordan', 'O Christians Praise Him', 'Christian's Comfort', 'Pleasant Hill', and 'Zion's Light', all in this volume.[1]

No. 74

GREENSBOROUGH, GOS 46

Pentatonic, mode 3 (I II III — V VI —)

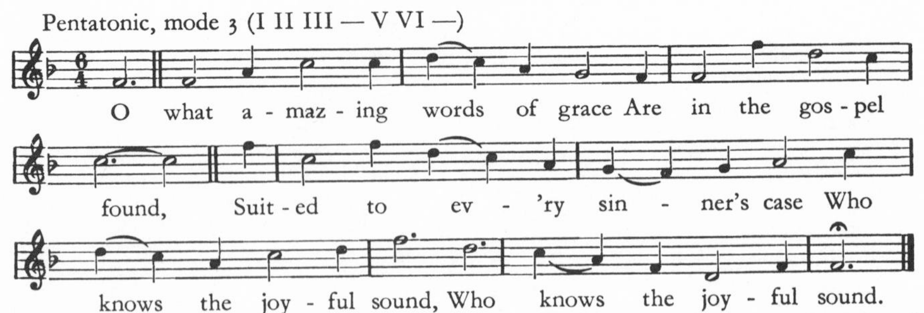
O what a-maz-ing words of grace Are in the gos-pel
found, Suit-ed to ev-'ry sin-ner's case Who
knows the joy-ful sound, Who knows the joy-ful sound.

[1] Further references to related secular and negro songs are given under No. 184 in *Spiritual Folk-Songs*.

Poor sinful, thirsty, fainting souls
Are freely welcome here;
Joy and peace like a river rolls,
Abundant, free and clear; abundant, free and clear.

Come then, with all your wants and wounds,
Your every burden bring;
Here love, unchanging love abounds,
A deep, celestial spring; a deep celestial spring.

Burrage ascribes the text to Samuel Medley, 1738–1799. The name of John Mercer (brother of Jesse Mercer of Georgia, early benefactor of Mercer University which is now at Macon, Georgia) is given in *Good Old Songs* as the composer of the tune. The chorus tune-frame is used also in 'Roll On' in this volume.

No. 75

FELLOWSHIP, CHI 95

Heptatonic aeolian,[1] mode 2 (I II 3 IV [IV ♯] V 6 7 [VII])

Come a-way to the skies, my be-lov ed a - rise, And re-joice in the day thou wast

born. On this fes - ti - val day, come ex-ult - ing a - way, And with sing - -

ing to Sion re - turn———, And with sing-ing to Si-on re - turn.

There are eight stanzas of this obvious parody on some secular birthday song.[2] The text was made by Charles Wesley and is found also with 'Exultation' and 'Christian Fellowship' in this volume. The tune is a variant of the one used today by the Primitive Baptists with 'Exultation'. But the 134 years of singing, between the two recorded variants, have made their relationship hard to recognize at first sight.

[1] The compiler of the *Christian Harmony* has minorized the tune.
[2] The text is given in full in *Methodist Hymns*, 1842, p. 357.

No. 76

LEAD ME TO THE ROCK (A), WHM 162

Hexatonic, mode 3 b (I II III IV V VI —)

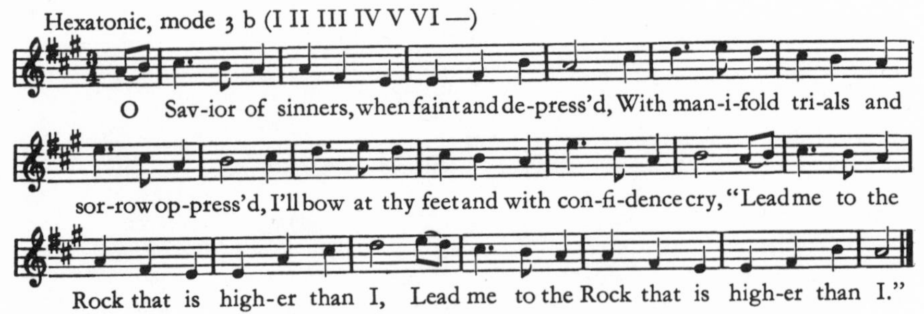
O Sav-ior of sinners, when faint and de-press'd, With man-i-fold tri-als and
sor-row op-press'd, I'll bow at thy feet and with con-fi-dence cry, "Lead me to the
Rock that is high-er than I, Lead me to the Rock that is high-er than I."

When tempted by Satan the Spirit to grieve,
And the service of Christ, my Redeemer, to leave,
I'll claim my relation to Jesus on high —
The Rock of salvation that's higher than I.

When God from my soul shall his presence remove,
To try by his absence the strength of my love,
I'll rest on the promise of Jesus, and try
The pow'r of that Rock which is higher than I.

When sorely afflicted, and ready to faint,
Before my Redeemer I'll spread my complaint;
Mid storms and distresses, my soul shall rely
On Jesus, the Rock that is higher than I.

When weak and encompass'd with numberless foes,
Attempting my comfort and peace to oppose,
I'll look to the Savior of sinners, and cry,
Lead me to the Rock that is higher than I.

When judgments, O Lord, are abroad in the land,
And merited vengeance descends from thy hand;
O'erwhelmed with the sight, for protection I'll fly,
And hide in the Rock that is higher than I.

When summoned by death before God to appear,
By free grace supported I'll yield without fear;
Most gladly I'll venture with Jesus on high,
Christ Jesus , the Rock that is higher than I.

An interesting variant of this text is found under 'Lead Me to the Rock (B)' in this volume. The tune is related to many secular melodies sung in the British Isles and America.[1]

[1] These kindred songs are listed in *Spiritual Folk-Songs* under No. 11. Add also Petrie, No. 1545; and 'I Send You the Precious Treasure', a sort of game song, JIFS, xxi, 44.

No. 77

THERE'S NOTHING TRUE BUT HEAVEN, SAM 228

Pentachordal (I II III IV V — —)

The faith - less world pro - mis - cuous flows, En - rapt in fan - cy's
vis - ion; Al - lur'd by sense, be - guil'd by show, And emp - ty
dreams, and scarce - ly knows There is a bright - er heav - en.

Fine gold will change, and diamonds fade,
Swift wings to wealth are given;
All varying time our forms invades,
The seasons roll, life sinks in shade;
There's nothing lasts but heaven.

Empires decay and nations die,
Our hopes to winds are driven;
The vernal blooms in ruin lie,
Death reigns o'er earth and air and sky;
There's nothing lives but heaven.

Creation's mighty fabric all
Will be to atoms riven;
The sky consume, the planets fall,
Convulsions wreck this earthly ball;
There's nothing firm but heaven.

This world is poor, from shore to shore,
And like a baseless vision,
Their lofty domes and brilliant ore,
Their gems and crowns are vain and poor;
There's nothing rich but heaven.

Adieu to all below, — adieu;
Let life's dull chain be riven;
The charms of Christ have caught my view,
To worlds of light I will pursue,
To live with him in heaven.

The text is a parody of Thomas Moore's three-stanza poem 'Nothing True but Heaven'. The tune is a folk-sung variant of the more arty melody associated with the Moore text in *The Wesleyan Harp*, p. 156.

No. 78

ELYSIAN, OSH 139

Heptatonic ionian, mode 3 (I II III IV V VI VII)

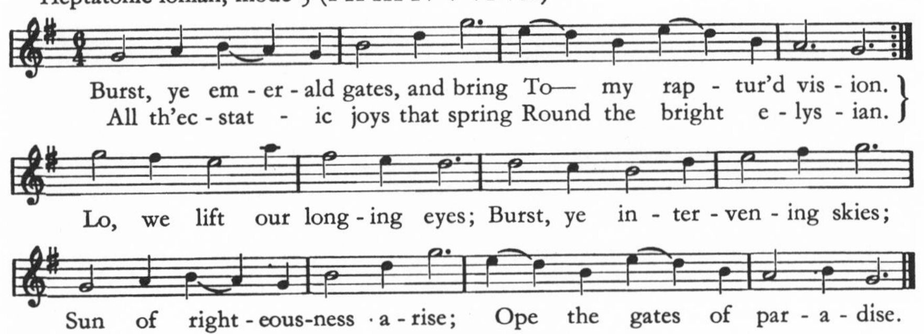
Burst, ye em - er - ald gates, and bring To— my rap - tur'd vis - ion.
All th'ec - stat - ic joys that spring Round the bright e - lys - ian.
Lo, we lift our long - ing eyes; Burst, ye in - ter - ven - ing skies;
Sun of right - eous-ness a - rise; Ope the gates of par - a - dise.

Floods of everlasting light
Freely flash before him;
Myriads with supreme delight
Instantly adore him.
Angel trumps resound his fame,
Lutes of lucid gold proclaim
All the music of his name,
Heaven echoing the theme.

Four and twenty elders rise
From their princely station,
Shout his glorious victories,
Sing the great salvation;
Cast their crowns before his throne,
Cry in reverential tone,
"Glory be to God alone,
Holy, holy, holy One."

No. 79

SUMMER, HOC 122

Heptatonic aeolian, mode 2 (I II 3 IV V 6 7)

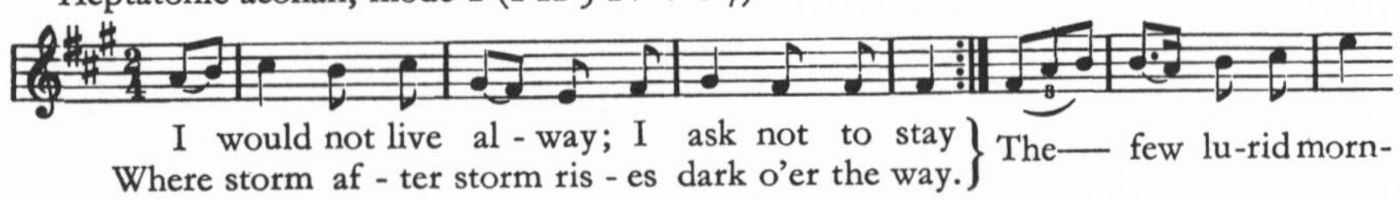
I would not live al - way; I ask not to stay
Where storm af - ter storm ris - es dark o'er the way.
The— few lu-rid morn-

ings that dawn on us here, Are enough for life's woes, full enough for its cheer.

I would not live alway: no — welcome the tomb,
Since Jesus hath lain there, I dread not its gloom;
There, sweet be my rest till he bid me arise,
To hail him in triumph descending the skies.

Who, who would live alway, away from his God,
Away from yon heaven, that blissful abode,
Where the rivers of pleasure flow o'er the bright plains,
And the noontide of glory eternally reigns?

Where the saints of all ages in harmony meet,
Their Savior and brethren transported to greet;
While the anthems of rapture unceasingly roll,
And the smile of the Lord is the feast of the soul.

The text is by William Augustus Mühlenberg (1796–1877).

No. 80

CHARLESTOWN, GOS 255

Hexatonic, mode 3 A (I II III — V VI VII)

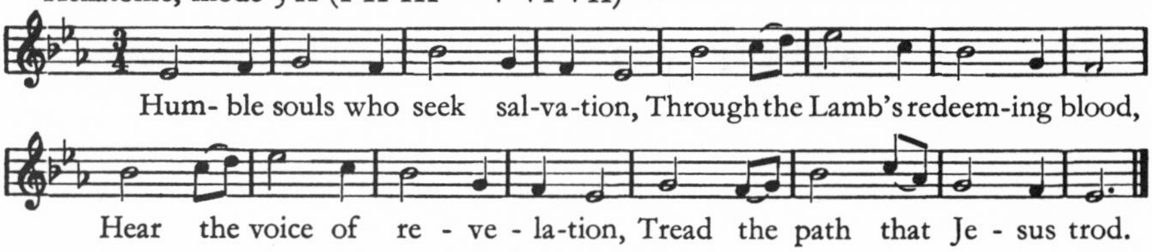

Hum- ble souls who seek sal-va-tion, Through the Lamb's redeem-ing blood,

Hear the voice of re - ve - la-tion, Tread the path that Je - sus trod.

Follow him, your only Savior,
In his mighty name confide;
In the whole of your behavior,
Own him as your sov'reign guide.

Hear, the bless'd Redeemer calls you,
Listen to his gracious voice;
Dread no ill that can befall you,
While you make his ways your choice.

Jesus says, "Let each believer
Be baptizéd in my name."
He himself in Jordan's river
Was immers'd beneath the stream.

Plainly here his footsteps tracing,
Follow him without delay;
Gladly his command embracing,
Lo, your Captain leads the way!

View the rite with understanding,
Jesus' grave before you lies;
Be immers'd at his commanding,
After his example rise.

The text is clearly intended to impress its Baptist singers and hearers with the authenticity of their rite of going down into the water. The tune is found in the shape-note song books generally throughout the first half of the nineteenth century. It belongs to the 'Lord Lovel' family; references given under 'Eden' in this volume.

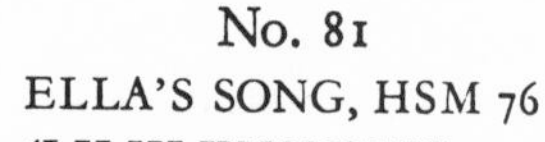

No. 81

ELLA'S SONG, HSM 76

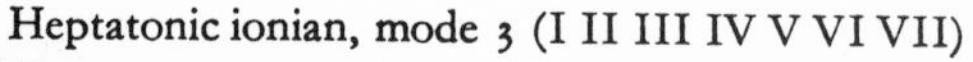

Heptatonic ionian, mode 3 (I II III IV V VI VII)

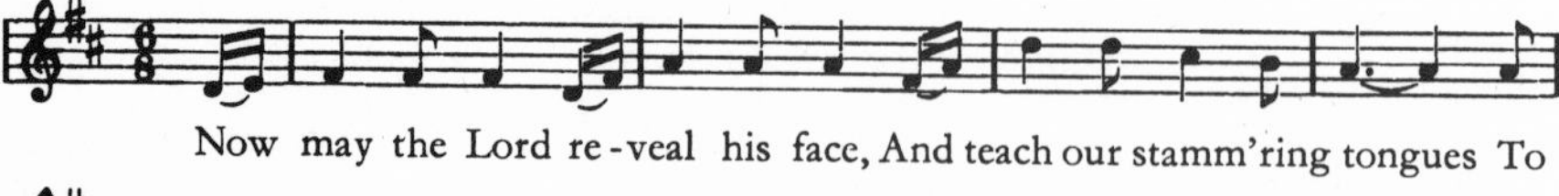
Now may the Lord re-veal his face, And teach our stamm'ring tongues To

make his glo-rious reign of grace, The sub-ject of our songs.

In *Good Old Songs*[1] the hymn has twelve stanzas, most of them on the theme of God's grace. The tune is a variant of that often used with the ancient ballad 'Sir Hugh'.[2]

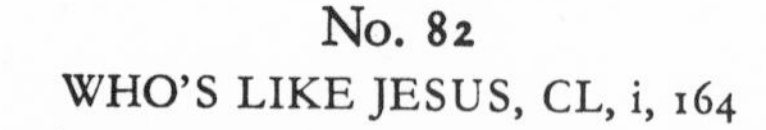

No. 82

WHO'S LIKE JESUS, CL, i, 164

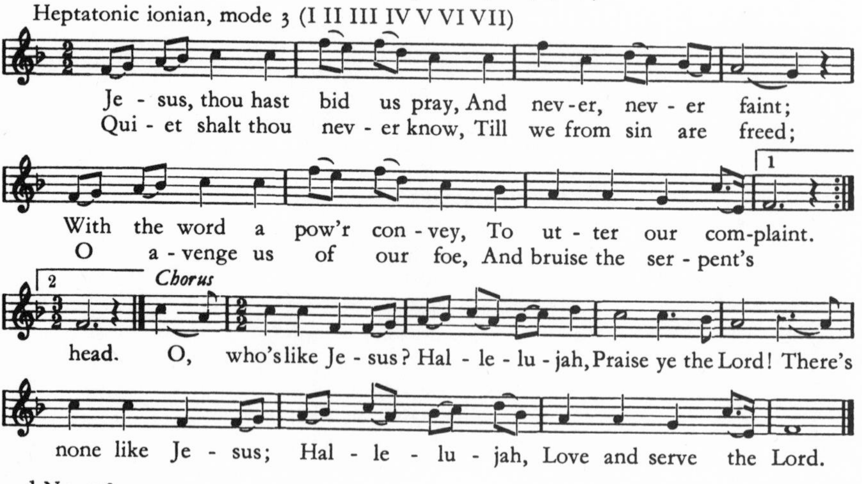
Heptatonic ionian, mode 3 (I II III IV V VI VII)
Je - sus, thou hast bid us pray, And nev-er, nev - er faint;
Qui - et shalt thou nev - er know, Till we from sin are freed;
With the word a pow'r con - vey, To ut - ter our com-plaint.
O a - venge us of our foe, And bruise the ser - pent's
1
2
Chorus
head. O, who's like Je - sus? Hal - le - lu - jah, Praise ye the Lord! There's
none like Je - sus; Hal - le - lu - jah, Love and serve the Lord.

[1] No. 578.
[2] See JAFL, xxxv, 344.

We have now begun to cry,
And we will never end,
Till we find salvation nigh,
And grasp the sinner's Friend.
Day and night we'll speak our wo,
Importunately plead;
O, avenge us of our foe,
And bruise the serpent's head!
Chorus

Speak the word, and we shall be
From all our bands released;
Only thou canst set us free,
By Satan long oppress'd.
Now thy power almighty show,
Arise, thou conquering Seed!
O, avenge us *etc.*

To destroy his work of sin,
Thyself in us reveal;
Manifest thyself within
Our flesh, and fully dwell.
Enter with us here below,
And make us free indeed;
O, avenge us *etc.*

Stronger than the strong man, thou
His fury canst control;
Cast him out, by entering now,
And keep our ransom'd soul.
Satan's kingdom overthrow,
On powers of darkness tread;
O, avenge us *etc.*

To the never-ceasing cries
Of thine elect, attend;
Send deliverance from the skies,
Thy mighty Spirit send.
Though to man thou seemest slow,
And not our cries to heed;
O, avenge us *etc.*

Come, O come, all glorious Lord!
No longer now delay,
With thy Spirit's two-edged sword,
The crooked serpent slay!
Bare thine arm, and give the blow,
Root out the hellish seed;
O, avenge us *etc.*

Jesus, hear thy Spirit's call,
Thy Bride, who bids thee come;
Come, thou righteous Judge of all,
Pronounce the tempter's doom.
Doom him to eternal wo,
For all his angels made;
Now avenge us of our foe,
Forever bruise his head!

The opening melodic phrases of *Spiritual Folk-Songs*, Nos. 161 and 162, are similar to the above.

No. 83

MELINDA, KNH 192

Heptatonic aeolian, mode 4 (I II 3 IV V 6 7)

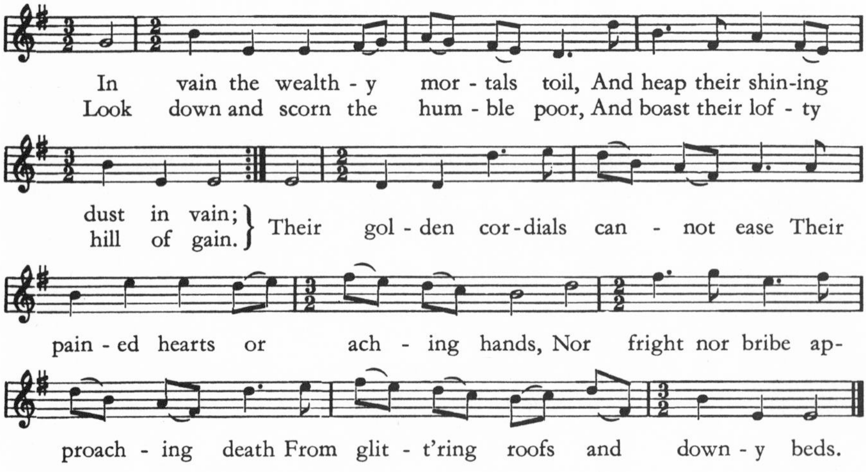

In vain the wealth - y mor - tals toil, And heap their shin-ing
Look down and scorn the hum - ble poor, And boast their lof - ty

dust in vain; } Their gol - den cor-dials can - not ease Their
hill of gain. }

pain - ed hearts or ach - ing hands, Nor fright nor bribe ap-

proach - ing death From glit - t'ring roofs and down - y beds.

In a letter to me Miss Anne G. Gilchrist states: "This [tune] is 'Lady Keith's Lament' — a form of 'Boyne Water' — written on the Battle of the Boyne, in which James II's troops were defeated. Lady Keith declared that she would be Lady Keith again 'the day our King [James] comes o'er the water'." The 'Boyne Water' tune was cast, according to Miss Gilchrist, in the dorian mode with *c*-sharps instead of the *c*-naturals which are seen in the above version. This makes it probable that the *Knoxville Harmony* compiler aeolianized it from an oral dorian form.

No. 84

TEACHER'S FAREWELL, OSH 444

Pentatonic, mode 3 (I II III — V VI —)

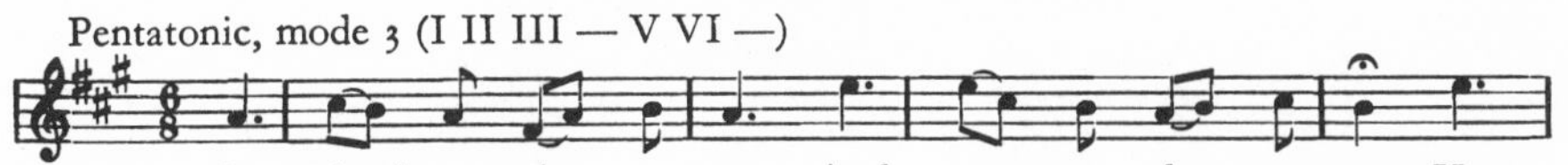
Our school now clos - es out, And we to - day must part; How
Chorus O may we meet in heav'n, The Chris-tian's hap - py home, The
D. C. for Chorus

sad the tho't to part with you, I hope we'll meet a - gain.
house a - bove where all is love, There'll be no part - ing there.

You've been so kind to me;
How can I bear the thought;
To part with you it grieves my heart,
Perhaps to meet no more.

Wherever you may go,
Dear students, think of me;
O pray for me where'er you go,
That we may meet in heaven.

The text is ascribed to Elder Edmund Dumas, Baptist preacher and singing-school master in Georgia. The tune is found also in GOS 177 and in other Baptist tune books. Miss Gilchrist states that it is a variant of 'Sprig of Thyme'.[1] A variant tune in minor is 'Sing to Me of Heaven' in this volume, and one in major is 'Vesper'.[2]

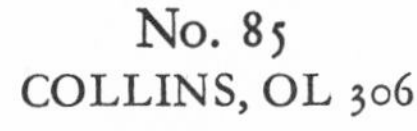

No. 85

COLLINS, OL 306

Pentatonic, mode 3 (I II III — V VI —)

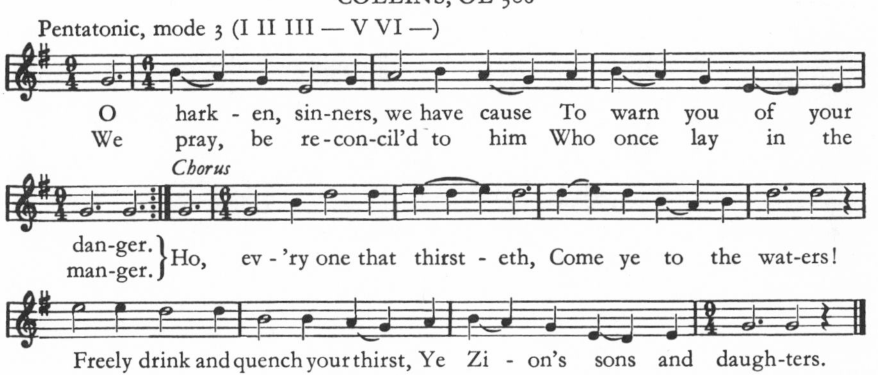
O hark - en, sin-ners, we have cause To warn you of your
We pray, be re-con-cil'd to him Who once lay in the
Chorus
dan-ger.
man-ger.
Ho, ev - 'ry one that thirst - eth, Come ye to the wat-ers!
Freely drink and quench your thirst, Ye Zi - on's sons and daugh-ters.

[1] See JFSS, viii, 69. [2] See *Spiritual Folk-Songs*, No. 55.

That awful God who made the soul,
And all the world around you,
Doth charge you with ten thousand crimes,
But hateth to confound you.
Chorus

O seek his sanctifying grace!
Be wise, do not refuse it;
For if you seek your life to save,
By sin, you're sure to lose it.

In William Hauser's first book of song, the *Hesperian Harp*, 1848, the compiler explained that he named this song after Rev. Charles Collins, president of Emory and Henry College, Virginia. (Hauser attended that institution in 1839.) In the same author's *Olive Leaf*, 1878, he states that he "can't remember how or where I got this air."

No. 86

GOLDEN HILL, MOH 42

Pentatonic, mode 3 (I II III — V VI —)

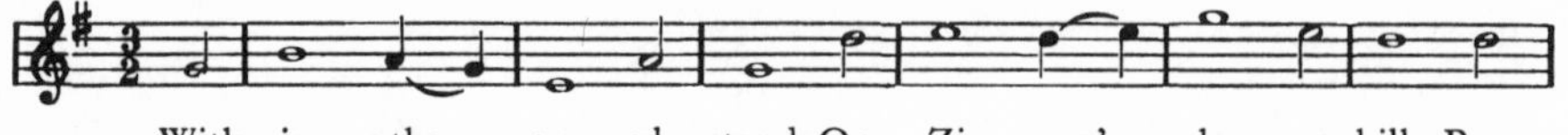
With joy the— peo - ple stand On Zi - on's chos - en hill, Pro-

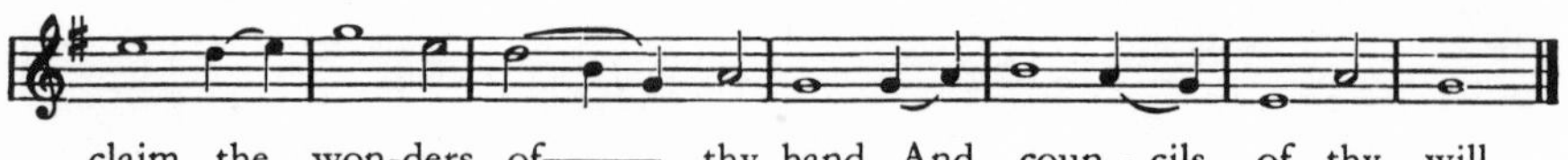
claim the won-ders of——— thy hand, And coun - cils of thy will.

The tune is found in practically all the early ninteenth-century shape-note song books. *The Baptist Hymn and Tune Book*, 1857, calls it a 'Western Melody'. Miss Gilchrist identifies the melody as a variant of 'Sprig of Thyme'. I find it related to 'Mermaid'[1] and 'The Seeds of Love'.[2] It is a member of the 'Lord Lovel' tune family.[3]

[1] See Sharp-Karpeles, i, 291 and 293.
[2] See JFSS, i, 210.
[3] References are given under 'Eden' in this volume.

No. 87

O TURN YE, SWP 87

Hexatonic, mode 3 A (I II III — V VI VII)

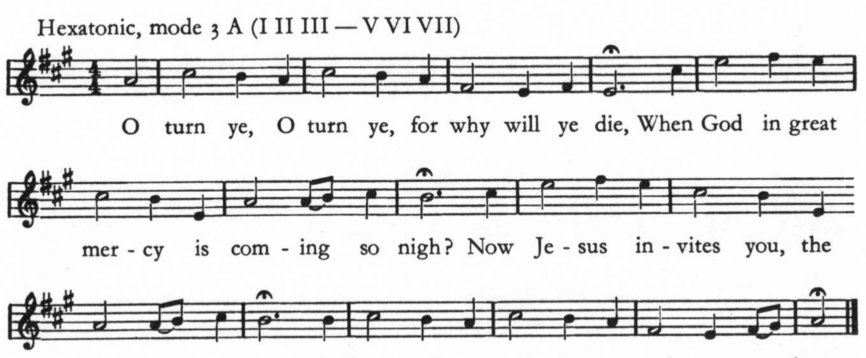
O turn ye, O turn ye, for why will ye die, When God in great
mer - cy is com - ing so nigh? Now Je - sus in - vites you, the
Spi - rit says come, And an - gels are wait - ing to wel-come you home.

How vain the delusion that while you delay,
Your hearts may grow better by staying away;
Come wretched, come starving, come just as you be,
While streams of salvation are flowing so free.

And now Christ is ready your souls to receive,
O how can you question, if you will believe?
If sin is your burden, why will you not come?
'Tis he bids you welcome, he bids you come home.

In riches, in pleasures, what can you obtain,
To soothe your afflictions, or banish your pain?
To bear up your spirit when summon'd to die,
Or waft you to mansions of glory on high?

Why will you be starving, or feeding on air?
There's mercy in Jesus, enough and to spare.
If still thou art doubting, make trial and see,
And prove that his mercy is boundless and free.

Come give us your hand, and the Savior your heart,
And trusting in heaven, we never shall part.
O how can we leave you, why will you not come?
We'll journey together and soon be at home.

The song is found also in CL, i, 40, and LZ 278.

No. 88
SWEET RIVERS, COH 135

Heptatonic ionian, mode 3 (I II III IV V VI VII)

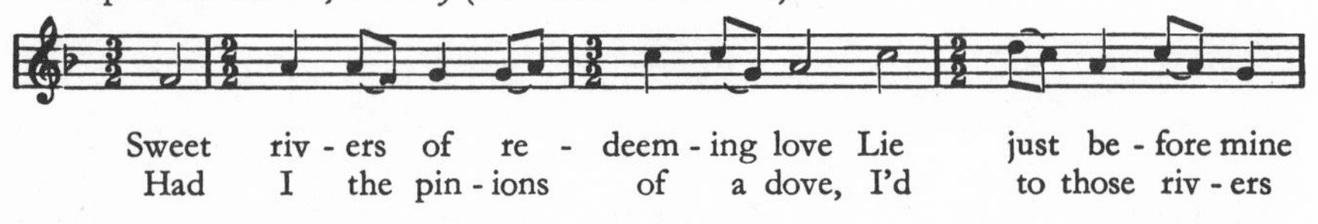
Sweet riv - ers of re - deem - ing love Lie just be - fore mine
Had I the pin - ions of a dove, I'd to those riv - ers

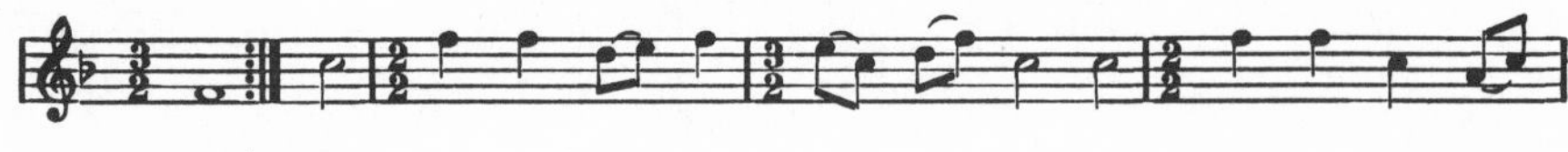

eye, fly. } I'd rise su - per - ior to my pain, With joy out-strip the

wind. I'd cross bold Jor-dan's storm-y main And leave this world be - hind.

While I'm in prison here below,
In anguish, pain and smart,
Ofttimes my troubles I forego,
While love surrounds my heart.
In darkest shadows of the night,
Faith mounts the upper sky;
I then behold my heart's delight,
And could rejoice to die.

I view the monster, death, and smile,
For he has lost his sting;
Though Satan rages all the while,
I still the triumph sing.
My Savior holds me in his arms,
And will not let me go;
I'm so delighted with his charms,
No other good I know.

William Moore, compiler of the *Columbian Harmony*, claimed the song, and subsequent southern rural compilers have allowed his claim to stand. The tune belongs to the large 'Roll Jordan' family; references given under 'Glorious Day' in this volume. 'Pleasant Hill' and 'Zion's Light' in this volume are close variants, though in six-four time.

No. 89

RHODE ISLAND, GOS 394

Hexatonic, mode 2 A (I II 3 IV V — 7)

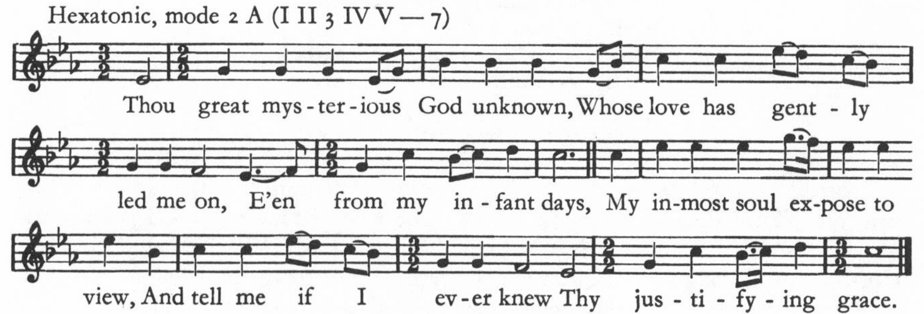
Thou great mys - ter - ious God unknown, Whose love has gent - ly
led me on, E'en from my in - fant days, My in-most soul ex-pose to
view, And tell me if I ev - er knew Thy jus - ti - fy - ing grace.

If I have only known thy fear,
And followed with a heart sincere,
Thy drawings from above,
Now, now the further grace bestow,
And let my sprinkled conscience know
Thy sweet forgiving love.

Short of thy love I would not stop,
A stranger to the gospel hope,
The sense of sins forgiven.
I would not, Lord, my soul deceive,
Without the inward witness live,
That antepast of heaven.

The hymn is by Charles Wesley, 1707–1788. In the *Temperance Song Book* of 1842 (p. 48) the melody is called an "old tune". It appears in many of the southern shape-note song books.

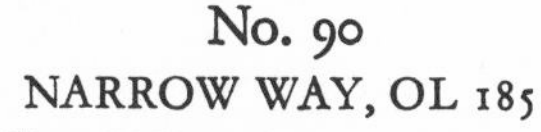

No. 90

NARROW WAY, OL 185

Pentatonic, mode 3 (I II III — V VI —)

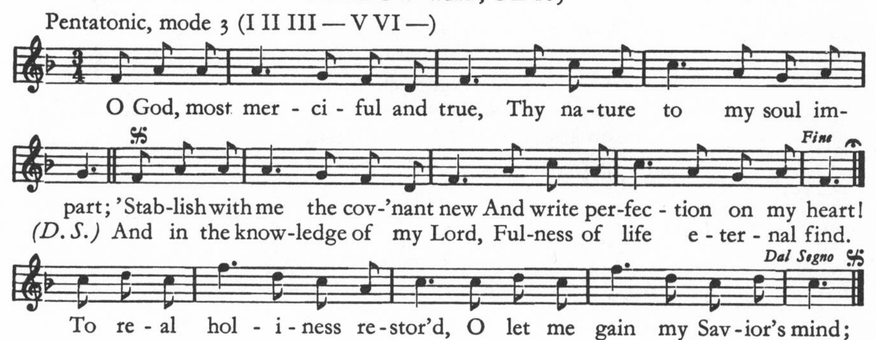
O God, most mer - ci - ful and true, Thy na - ture to my soul im-
Fine
part; 'Stab-lish with me the cov-'nant new And write per-fec - tion on my heart!
(D. S.) And in the know-ledge of my Lord, Ful-ness of life e - ter - nal find.
Dal Segno
To re - al hol - i - ness re - stor'd, O let me gain my Sav - ior's mind;

Remember, Lord, my sins no more,
That them I may no more forget;
But sunk in guiltless shame adore,
With speechless wonder at thy feet!
O'erwhelm'd by thy stupendous grace,
I shall not, in thy presence, move;
But breathe unutterable praise,
And rapturous awe, and silent love.

The text is by Charles Wesley, 1707–1788. The tune is attributed to Rev. John H. White, Forsythe County, N. C. The Reverend White used the various musical phrases belonging to variants of 'The Wife of Usher's Well'.[1] See also 'Horton' and 'Dying Friend' in this volume for more recent borrowings from the same stock-melodic formula which I have called the 'Kedron' family.[2]

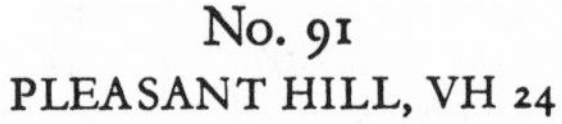

No. 91
PLEASANT HILL, VH 24

Hexatonic, mode 3 A (I II III — V VI VII)

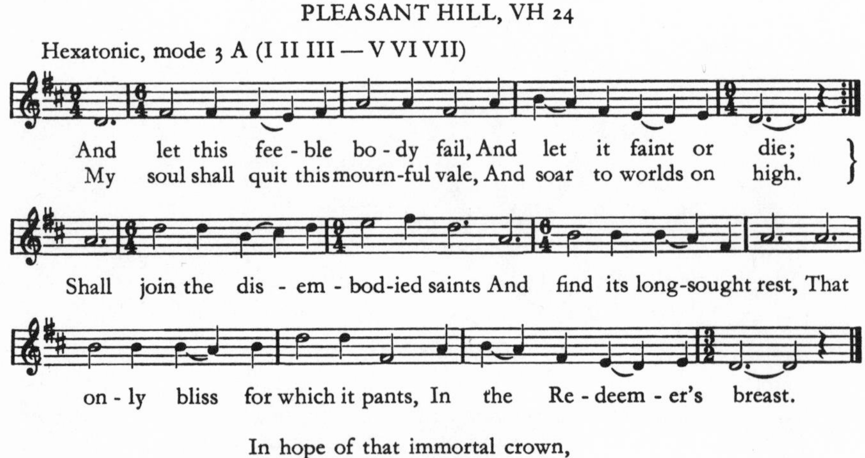
And let this fee - ble bo - dy fail, And let it faint or die;
My soul shall quit this mourn-ful vale, And soar to worlds on high.
Shall join the dis - em - bod-ied saints And find its long-sought rest, That
on - ly bliss for which it pants, In the Re - deem - er's breast.

In hope of that immortal crown,
I now the cross sustain;
And gladly wander up and down,
And smile at toil and pain.
I suffer on my threescore years,
Till my Deliverer come,
And wipe away his servant's tears,
And take his exile home.

[1] See Sharp-Karpeles, i, 150ff.
[2] See 'Distress' in this volume for references.

O what hath Jesus bought for me!
Before my raptured eyes,
Rivers of life divine I see,
And trees of paradise.
I see a world of spirits bright,
Who taste the pleasures there;
They all are robed in spotless white,
And conquering palms they bear.

The text is by Charles Wesley, 1707–1788. In the *Olive Leaf* the "song" (meaning presumably the tune only) is ascribed to "William Nicholson, of Va. and Ohio. Captured by the British at Fort Malden, in the War of 1812." The *Virginia Harmony* (1831) gives merely "Nicholson" as the author. The *Columbian Harmony* (1825) gives the author of the almost identical 'Sweet Rivers' as "Moore". It is a 'Roll Jordan' tune, references to which are given under 'Glorious Day' in this volume.

The following song should be considered in connection with this.

No. 92

ZION'S LIGHT, UVW, No. 163

Hexatonic, mode 3 A (I II III — V VI VII)

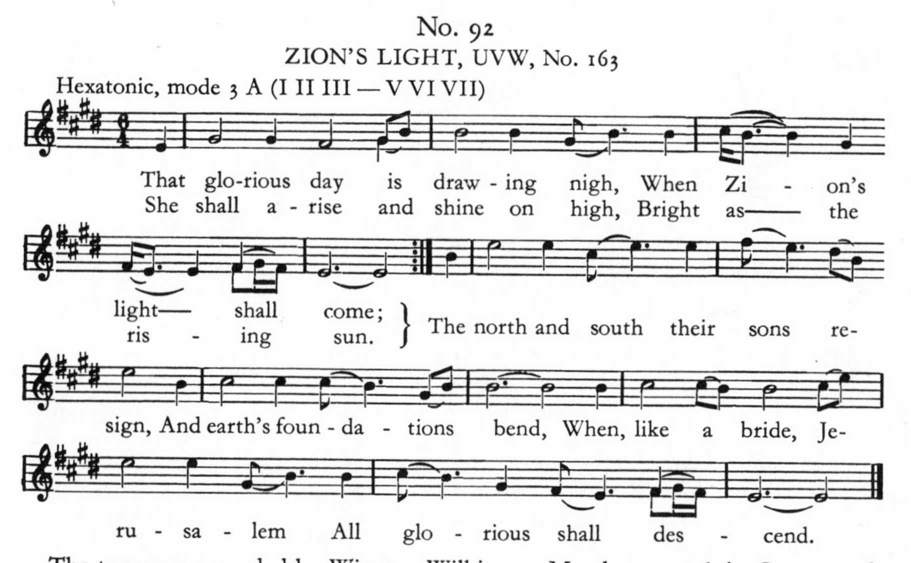
That glo-rious day is draw - ing nigh, When Zi - on's light— shall come;
She shall a - rise and shine on high, Bright as— the ris - ing sun.
The north and south their sons re- sign, And earth's foun - da - tions bend, When, like a bride, Je- ru - sa - lem All glo - rious shall des - cend.

The tune was recorded by Winston Wilkinson, March 12, 1936, in Greenwood, Virginia, from the singing of J. H. Chisholm.[1] Since Mr. Chisholm had forgotten the text, I have supplied the above words from 'Glorious Day' in this volume.

On comparing the tune with that of 'Pleasant Hill', the foregoing song in this volume, it will be seen that the two are practically identical, the only difference

[1] It is No. 163 of the *University of Virginia* (manuscript) *Collection of Folk-Music* and is used here with kind permission.

being that the present song was sung and noted in country style; and that is my chief reason for presenting it here.

Why did not 'Pleasant Hill' show the same country style features? It was recorded in the same state and presumably also from oral tradition, though 105 years before Mr. Chisholm sang his version. My guess is that "Nicholson" or whoever may have been its recorder in 1831 or before was more concerned with the tune's framework and less with the details of "song twisting" (as the country folk call it) than was Mr. Wilkinson. The nature of this twisting is usually the incorporation of the customary vocal graces. In this song the graces are largely of the "Scotch snap" sort of which there are nine instances,[1] the anticipatory scoop,[2] and the little quaver in both cadences.[3] The tune is a member of the 'Roll Jordan' family.[4]

No. 93

LONGING FOR HEAVEN, WHM 106

Heptatonic dorian, mode 2 (I II 3 IV V VI 7 [VII])

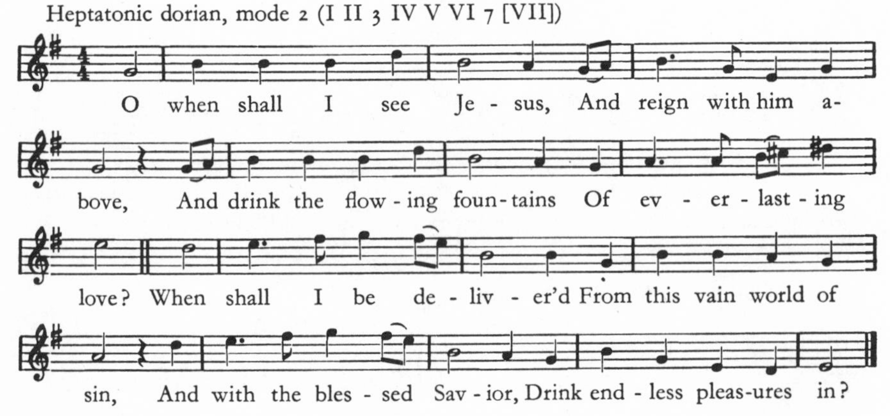
O when shall I see Je - sus, And reign with him a-
bove, And drink the flow - ing foun - tains Of ev - er - last - ing
love? When shall I be de - liv - er'd From this vain world of
sin, And with the bles - sed Sav - ior, Drink end - less pleas-ures in?

The John Leland text — one of the most popular early revival poems — is given in full under 'Faithful Soldier'.[5] The tune is found also in *Social Hymn and Tune Book*, Philadelphia, 1865, and in Ingalls' *Christian Harmony* (1805).[6] Miss Gilchrist calls attention to its melodic relationship to 'Sheffield Apprentice'.[7]

[1] In the second, third, fifth, sixth, nineth, tenth, and eleventh measures.

[2] In the first, seventh, nineth, and tenth measures.

[3] At the end of the third and eleventh measures. Cf. also *White Spirituals*, p. 212.

[4] References given under 'Glorious Day' in this volume.

[5] *Spiritual Folk-Songs*, No. 59. More about Leland under 'Longing for Jesus (A)' in this volume.

[6] P. 59.

[7] Examples in Sharp-Karpeles, ii, 66-68.

No. 94

RESIGNATION, SOH (1854) 38

Pentatonic, mode 3 (I II III — V VI —)

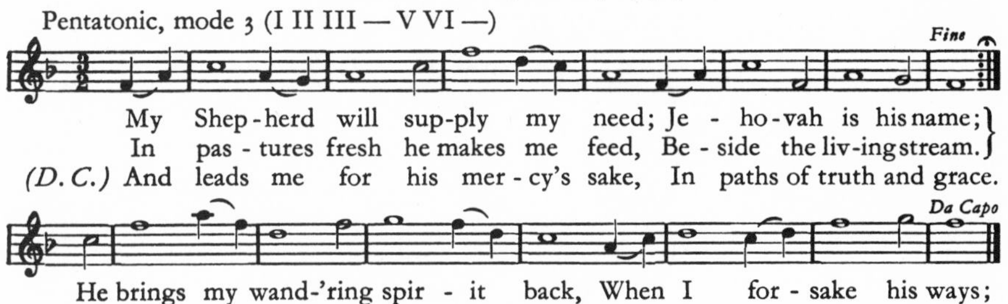
Fine
My Shep-herd will sup-ply my need; Je - ho-vah is his name;
In pas - tures fresh he makes me feed, Be - side the liv-ing stream.
(D. C.) And leads me for his mer - cy's sake, In paths of truth and grace.
Da Capo
He brings my wand-'ring spir - it back, When I for - sake his ways;

When I walk through the shades of death,
Thy presence is my stay;
One word of thy supporting breath
Drives all my fears away.
Thy hand, in sight of all my foes,
Doth still my table spread;
My cup with blessings overflows,
Thine oil anoints my head.

The sure provisions of my God
Attend me all my days;
O may thy house be mine abode,
And all my work be praise!
There would I find a settled rest,
(While others go and come,)
No more a stranger nor a guest;
But like a child at home.

The words are by Isaac Watts, 1674—1748.

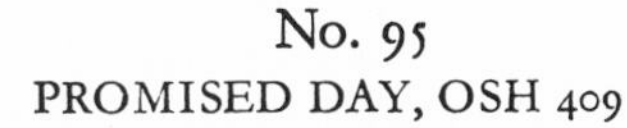

No. 95

PROMISED DAY, OSH 409

Pentatonic, mode 3 (I II III — V VI —)

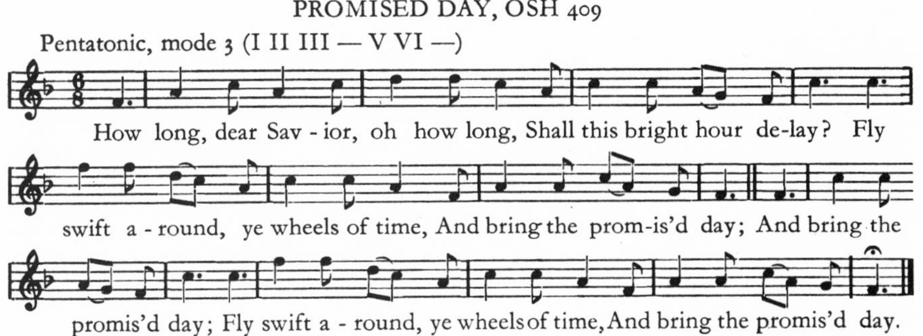
How long, dear Sav - ior, oh how long, Shall this bright hour de-lay? Fly
swift a - round, ye wheels of time, And bring the prom-is'd day; And bring the
promis'd day; Fly swift a - round, ye wheels of time, And bring the promis'd day.

Lo, what a glorious sight appears
To our believing eyes!
The earth and seas are passed away,
And the old rolling skies.
From the third heaven, where God resides,
That holy, happy place,
The New Jerusalem comes down,
Adorned with shining grace.

Attending angels shout for joy,
And the bright armies sing;
Mortals, behold that sacred seat
Of our descending King!
The God of glory down to men
Removes his blest abode;
Men, the dear object of his grace,
And he, the loving God.

The *Sacred Harp* ascribes the text to Isaac Watts. Burrage attributes it to John Leland (1754–1841). The tune is accredited to L. M. Ranford, a Georgia singer of pre-Civil War times. A twentieth-century variant of the tune, in four-four time, is 'Christian's Hope' in *Spiritual Folk-Songs*.

No. 96

LORD OF GLORY, PB 374

Hexatonic, mode 3 A (I II III — V VI VII)

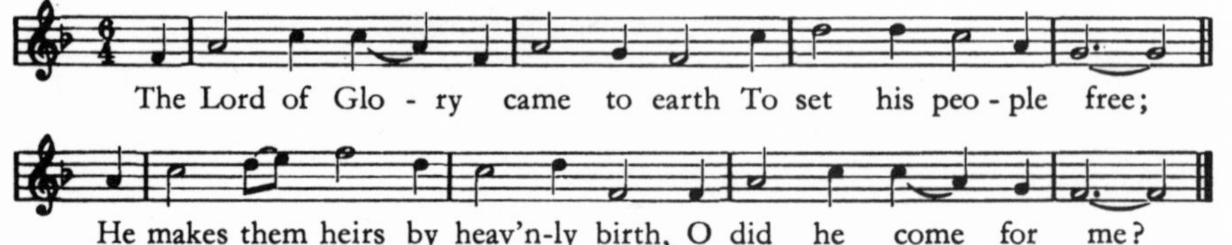
The Lord of Glo - ry came to earth To set his peo - ple free;
He makes them heirs by heav'n-ly birth, O did he come for me?

While here he lived, and bled and died,
And groan'd upon the tree,
To save, redeem and clothe his bride,
O did he die for me?

Then he was laid within the tomb,
As God designed should be;
But he arose up from that gloom ,
O did he rise for me?

Variant tunes are 'St. Columba'[1] and 'Two Brothers'.[2] See also references given under 'Eden' in this volume to the 'Lord Lovel' tune family, of which the above is a member.

[1] In the *Christian Science Hymnal*, No. 339.

[2] See Davis, p. 563, tune A.

No. 97

WATSON, WHM 22

Heptatonic ionian, mode 3 (I II III IV V VI VII)

On Jor-dan's storm - y banks I stand, And cast a wish - ful
eye, To Ca-naan's fair and hap - py land, Where my pos - ses - sions
lie. O, the trans-port-ing rap-turous scene, That ris - es to my
sight! Sweet fields ar - ray'd in liv-ing green, And riv - ers of de - light.

There generous fruits that never fail,
On trees immortal grow;
There rocks and hills and brooks and vale,
With milk and honey flow.
All o'er those wide extended plains,
Shines one eternal day;
There God the Son forever reigns,
And scatters night away.

No chilling winds, or poisonous breath
Can reach that healthful shore;
Sickness and sorrow, pain and death,
Are felt and fear'd no more.
When shall I reach that happy place,
And be forever blest?
When shall I see my Father's face,
And in his bosom rest?

Fill'd with delight, my raptur'd soul
Would here no longer stay;
Though Jordan's waves around me roll,
Fearless I launch away.
There on those high and flowery plains,
Our spirits ne'er shall tire;
But in perpetual, joyful strains,
Redeeming love admire.

The text is by Samuel Stennett, 1727–1795. The tune is practically identical with that of the old Scottish 'The Boatie Rows'[1] which was set by Beethoven. The blackened-face minstrels, too, liked the sprightly melody and the result was the song 'Keeping Marster's Parlor' or 'Kingdom Coming'. My mother, Mrs. Ann Jane Jackson, has given me a version of the ridiculous minstrel text as she heard it sung during Civil War times in Monson, Maine. It begins,

> O darkies hab you seen my marster,
> Wed de mufstache on he face,
> Go long de road some time dis mornin
> Like he gwine to leab de place?

No. 98

GOSPEL POOL (A), OSH 444

Pentatonic, mode 3 (I II III — V VI —)

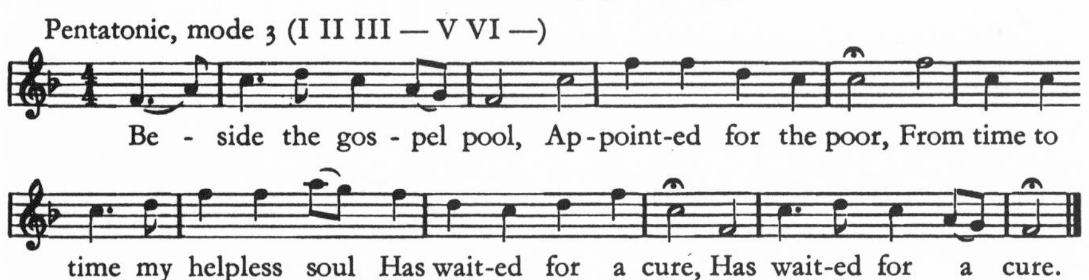
Be - side the gos - pel pool, Ap-point-ed for the poor, From time to
time my helpless soul Has wait-ed for a cure, Has wait-ed for a cure.

The text was taken from *Mercer's Cluster*, a Georgia-made collection of hymns many of which were indigenous to that region. It is given in full under 'Gospel Pool (B)' in this volume. The tune is a member of the 'Lord Lovel' family to which references are given under 'Eden' in this volume.

No. 99

OVERTON, SKH 139

Hexatonic, mode 3 b (I II III IV V VI —)

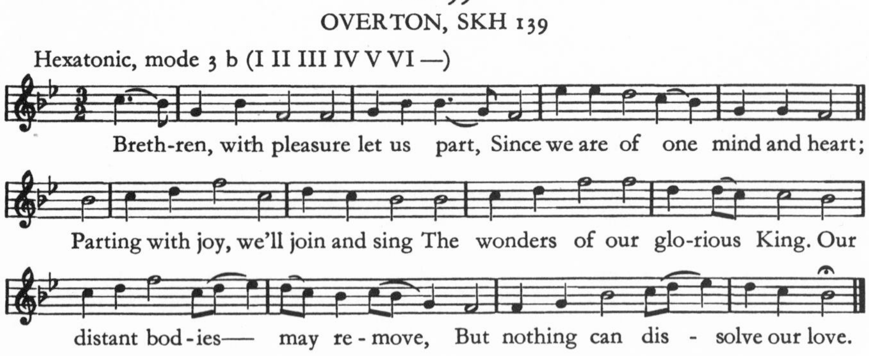
Breth-ren, with pleasure let us part, Since we are of one mind and heart;
Parting with joy, we'll join and sing The wonders of our glo-rious King. Our
distant bod-ies— may re-move, But nothing can dis - solve our love.

[1] See Pittman, Brown and Mackay, *Songs of Scotland*, Boosey and Company, Vol. 1, p. 39.

In vain may earth and hell combine
To quench that love which is divine;
It will not cease with dying breath,
Nor cool when we are cold in death.
Now join'd in love in Jesus' name
We'll part and fly to spread his fame,
That other souls may learn their woe,
And join with us in glory too.

A few more rolling days or years
Will bring a period to our tears;
We soon shall reach that happy shore,
Where parting shall be known no more.
Then shall our eyes behold the Lamb,
The righteous Judge, the great I AM,
And every sense find sweet employ
In that eternal world of joy.

The tune, though claimed by Davisson, compiler of the *Supplement to the Kentucky Harmony*, is a good variant of the old Scottish ballad tune 'Wae's me for Prince Charlie'. The major cadence at the end of this essentially mixolydian melody is possibly due to Davisson's meddling. See 'Mourner's Lamentation'[1] for references to other secular related tunes.

No. 100

INVOCATION, GOS 67

Pentatonic, mode 4 (I II — IV V — 7)

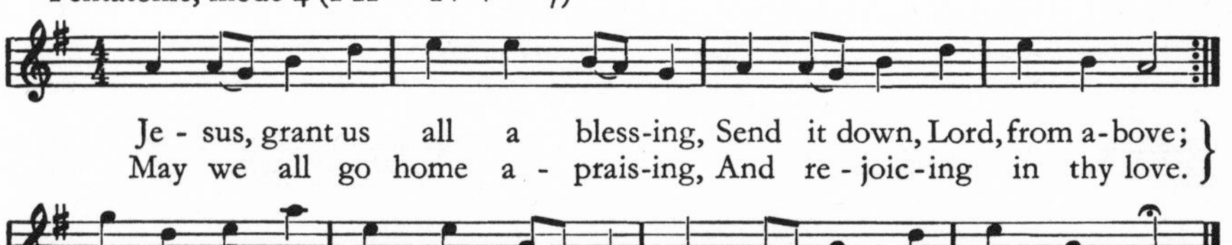
Je - sus, grant us all a bless-ing, Send it down, Lord, from a-bove;
May we all go home a - prais-ing, And re - joic-ing in thy love.
Fare-well breth-ren, Fare-well sis-ters, Till we all shall meet a - gain.

Jesus, pardon all our follies,
Since together we have been;
Make us humble, make us holy,
Cleanse us all from every sin.
Farewell brethren *etc.*

[1] *Spiritual Folk-Songs*, No. 28.

May thy blessing, Lord, go with us
To each ones respective home;
And the presence of our Jesus
Rest upon us, every one.

The tune is a close variant of 'Mount Watson' in *Spiritual Folk-Songs*, No. 90. I have corrected the mistakes — obvious when the tune is compared with its variants — in the *Good Old Songs* version. In all of the variants the dorian mode is implied. Further references are given under 'O Hallelujah', the following song.

No. 101

O HALLELUJAH, UVW, 176

Hexatonic, mode 4 A (I II — IV V VI 7)

a
b
c
O hal - le - lu - jah, how I love my Sav - ior! O hal - le-
8
d
lu - jah, Yes, I—— do. O hal - le - lu - jah, how I love my
e
f
g
a
Sav - ior! Mourn - ers, you can love him too.
b
b
c
(?)
d
d
d
e
f
g
g

This song was recorded by Winston Wilkinson in Evington, Virginia, October 19, 1935, as sung by Mrs. Kit Williamson.[1] It is simply the chorus of the folk-

[1] It is No. 176 in the *University of Virginia* (manuscript) *Collection of Folk-Music*, and is used here by kind permission.

hymn 'Mount Watson' in variant melodic form.[1] Other tune variants are the religious ballad 'Villulia'[2] and the secular ballad 'William Taylor'.[3] The modal implications are dorian.

No. 102

LOCHLEVEN, SAM 154

Heptatonic dorian, mode 2 (I II 3 IV V VI 7)

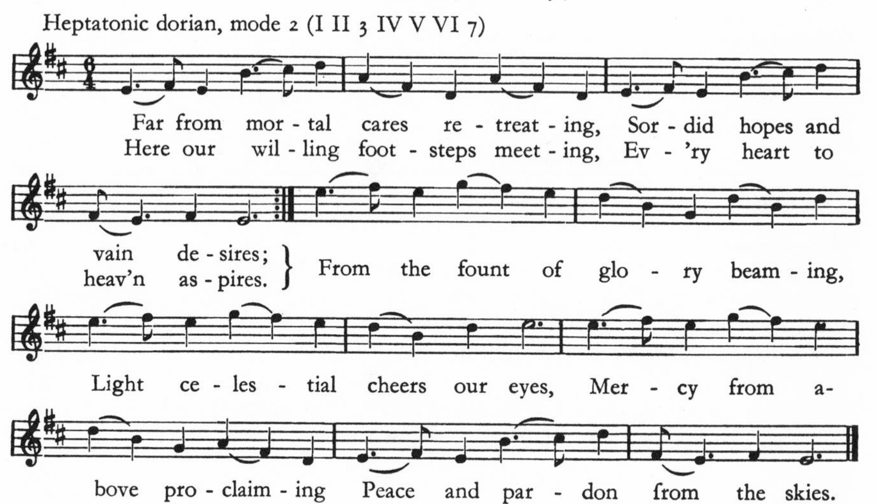
Far from mor - tal cares re - treat - ing, Sor - did hopes and
Here our wil - ling foot - steps meet - ing, Ev - 'ry heart to
vain de - sires;
heav'n as - pires.
From the fount of glo - ry beam - ing,
Light ce - les - tial cheers our eyes, Mer - cy from a-
bove pro - claim - ing Peace and par - don from the skies.

Who may share this great salvation?
Every pure and humble mind;
Every kindred tongue and nation,
From the stains of guilt refin'd.
Blessings all around bestowing,
He withholds his care from none;
Grace and mercy ever flowing
From the fountain of his throne.

Samuel P. Bayard has found a close variant of this tune in Hopekirk, Helen, *Seventy Scottish Songs*, under the title 'Highland Boat Songs'; and another in Smith, R. A., *The Scottish Minstrel* (Edinburgh, 1820—1824) where it is called 'Queen Mary's Escape from Loch-Leven Castle'. I have restored the tune's quite evident dorian character by adding *c*-sharp to the *Sacred Melodeon* editor's key signature.

[1] *Spiritual Folk-Songs*, No. 90. Further references are given.
[2] *Ibid.*, No. 21.
[3] JFSS, v, 68.

No. 103

WINDHAM, UVW 164

Heptatonic dorian, mode 2 (I II 3 IV V VI 7)

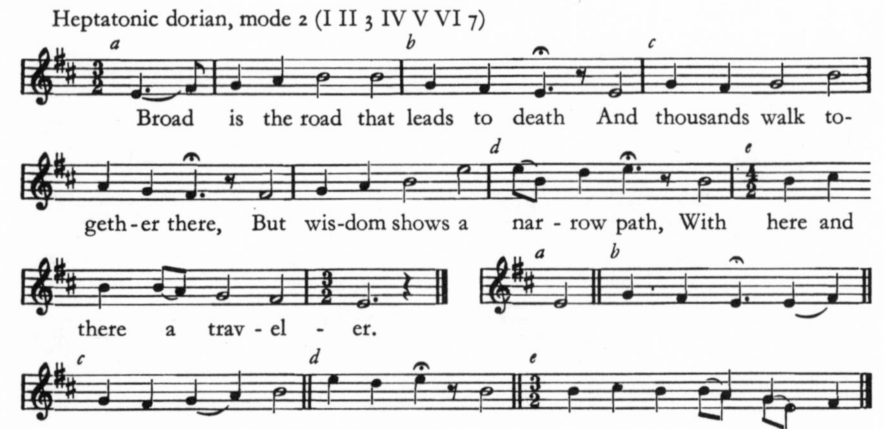
a b c d e
Broad is the road that leads to death And thousands walk to-
geth-er there, But wis-dom shows a nar - row path, With here and
there a trav - el - er.

This song was recorded by Winston Wilkinson in Stanardsville, Virginia, November 9, 1935, as sung by Z. B. Lam. It is No. 164 in the *University of Virginia* (manuscript) *Collection of Folk-Music* and is used here by kind permission.

The text is ascribed to Isaac Watts in most of the shape-note books; the tune to Daniel Read the New England composer and compiler, 1757–1836.[1] The above tune shows interesting variations from the standard hymn-book notation.[2]

No. 104

HUMILIATION, SWP 88

Heptatonic aeolian, mode 2 (I II 3 IV V 6 7)

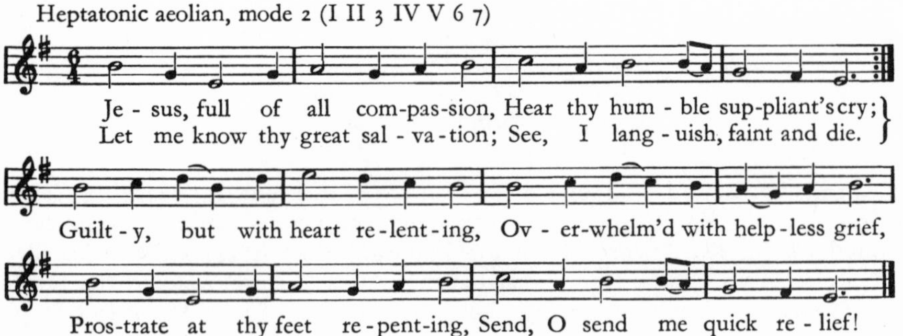
Je - sus, full of all com-pas-sion, Hear thy hum - ble sup-pliant's cry;
Let me know thy great sal - va-tion; See, I lang - uish, faint and die.
Guilt - y, but with heart re-lent-ing, Ov - er-whelm'd with help-less grief,
Pros-trate at thy feet re-pent-ing, Send, O send me quick re - lief!

[1] Frank J. Metcalf sees in this tune a strong resemblance to a German choral; but he does not state which. See *American Writers and Compilers of Sacred Music*, p. 99.

[2] One variation introduced by the folk singers is the dorian mode. The song books all have the tune in a minorized aeolian form.

Whither should a wretch be flying,
But to him who comfort gives?
Whither, from the dread of dying,
But to him who ever lives?
While I view thee, wounded, grieving,
Breathless on the curséd tree,
Fain I'd feel my heart believing,
That thou suffer'dst thus for me.

With thy righteousness and spirit,
I am more than angels blest;
Heir with thee, all things inherit, —
Peace and joy and endless rest.
Without thee, the world possessing,
I should be a wretch undone;
Search through heaven, — the land of blessing,
Seeking good and finding none.

Hear then, blesséd Savior, hear me!
My soul cleaveth to the dust;
Send the Comforter to cheer me;
Lo! in thee I put my trust.
On the word thy blood hath sealéd,
Hangs my everlasting all;
Let thine arm be now revealéd;
Stay, oh stay me, lest I fall.

In the world of endless ruin,
Let it never, Lord, be said,
"Here's a soul that perish'd suing
For the boasted Savior's aid!"
Sav'd — the deed shall spread new glory
Through the shining realms above;
Angels sing the pleasing story,
All enraptur'd with thy love.

No. 105

MESSIAH (A), VH 30

Pentatonic, mode 2 minorized (I — 3 IV V — 7 [VII])

"He comes, he comes to judge the world," A - loud th'arch-an-gel cries!
While thun-der rolls from pole to pole, And lightnings cleave the skies.

Th'af-frighted na-tions hear the sound, And upwards lift their eyes—— The

slum-b'ring ten-ants of the ground, In—— liv - ing ar-mies rise.

Amidst the shouts of num'rous friends,
Of hosts divinely bright,
The Judge in solemn pomp descends,
Arrayed in robes of white.
His head and hairs are white as snow,
His eyes are fiery flame,
A radiant crown adorns his brow,
And Jesus is his name.

Writ on his thigh his name appears,
And scars his vict'ries tell;
Lo! in his hand the Conqueror bears
The keys of death and hell.
So he ascends the judgment seat,
And at his dread command
Myriads of creatures around his feet
In solemn silence stand.

This poetic picture of pomp and pageantry — by Samuel Stennett, 1727–1795 — apparently a re-make of Charles Wesley's 'He comes, he comes, the Judge severe', vanished from the more recent version of this song as it appears in *Good Old Songs*,[1] a version much better suited to the humble and more quietly emotional Primitive Baptists who sing it from that book. There the Savior is reduced to the rejected and despised one in whom "the world no beauty sees, no form nor comliness." He comes, not to judge, but to bring truth, mercy and grace.

[1] No. 106.

The southern shape-note song books ascribe the song to Carrell.[1] The oldest known appearance of the song is, to be sure, the one reproduced here from Carrell's *Virginia Harmony;* but there the compiler laid no claim to it.

The following tune is a variant from Virginia oral tradition.

No. 106

MESSIAH (B), UVW, No. 167

Pentatonic, mode 2 (I — 3 IV V — 7)

When I can read my ti - tle clear To man-sions in the skies;
I'll bid fare-well to ev - 'ry fear, And wipe my wea - ry eyes.
Should earth a - gainst my soul en - gage, And fier - y darts be hurl'd———, Then I can smile at Sa - tan's rage, And face a frown-ing world.
a
b
a
a
b

The familiar text is by Isaac Watts, 1674–1748. The tune is interesting chiefly as a hundred-years-later recording, from oral tradition, of the foregoing song-book tune, 'Messiah (A)', and thus as fine material for comparison. It was noted by Winston Wilkinson, March 12, 1936, in Greenwood, Virginia, as sung by J. H. Chisholm.[2] It differs from its antecedent principally in the modest ornament which Mr. Chisholm sang into it.[3] One should not make the mistake of assuming,

[1] James P. Carrell, 1787–1854, of Lebanon, Virginia. More as to the man and his work in *White Spirituals*, pp. 34–38.

[2] It is No. 167 of the *University of Virginia* (manuscript) *Collection of Folk-Music* and is used here by kind permission.

[3] Compare also 'Zion's Light' in this volume for similar variations between singing and song book.

however, that that ornamentation, not found in the old *Virginia Harmony* variant, was necessarily the individual offering of Mr. Wilkinson's singer. *Certain* ornaments may be the work of individuals; but *ornamentation* is a general and beloved phase of folk-melodism.

No. 107
DISTRESS, OSH 50

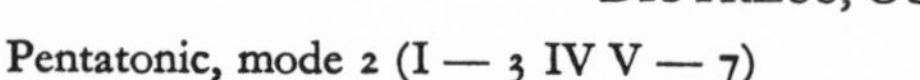
Pentatonic, mode 2 (I — 3 IV V — 7)

So fades the love-ly bloom-ing flow'r, Frail, smiling sol-ace of an hour; So

soon our trans-ient com-forts fly, And pleas-ure on - ly blooms to die.

Is there no kind, no healing art,
To soothe the anguish of the heart?
Spirit of grace, be ever nigh;
Thy comforts are not made to die.

Let gentle patience smile on pain,
Till dying hope revives again,
Hope wipes the tear from sorrows eye,
And faith points upward to the sky.

Anne Steele (1716–1778) is named, in the *Sacred Harp*, as the author of this beautiful poem. The tune is a member of the 'Kedron' family.[1] Other member tunes in this volume are 'Dying Friend' and 'Horton'. 'Suffering Savior', also in this volume, brings in its wake a group of tunes somewhat like the 'Kedron' group but differing rather radically in their third phrase.

I append here a very old Scottish tune which is possibly the prototype of the 'Kedron' formula.

'Laird o' Cockpen'[2]

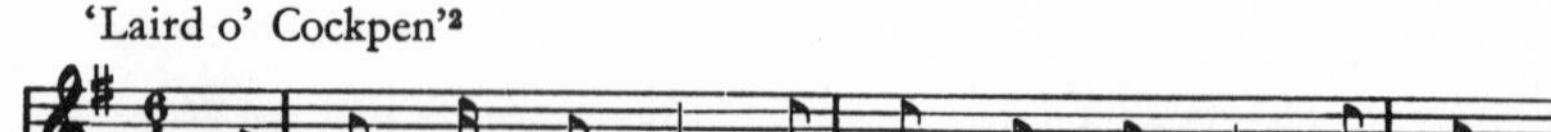

The Laird o' Cock-pen, He's proud a' he's great, His mind is ta'n

[1] See *Spiritual Folk-Songs*, No. 57.
[2] From *Our Familiar Songs*, p. 418.

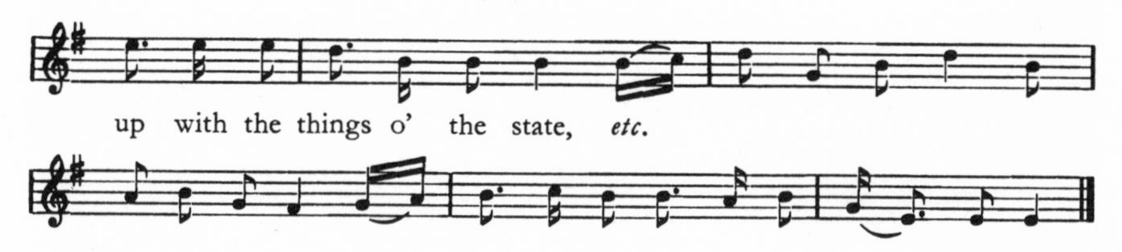
up with the things o' the state, *etc.*

The tune's relationship to 'Distress' will be seen as far less notable than to 'Kedron' itself.

No. 108

EDEN, OSH 154

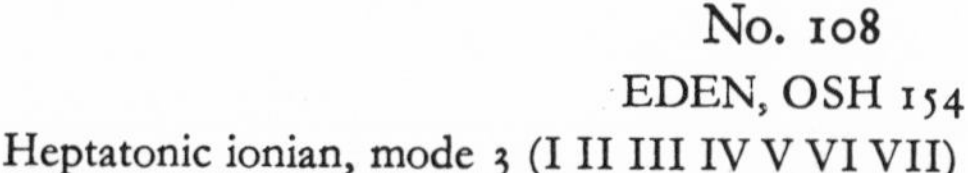

Heptatonic ionian, mode 3 (I II III IV V VI VII)

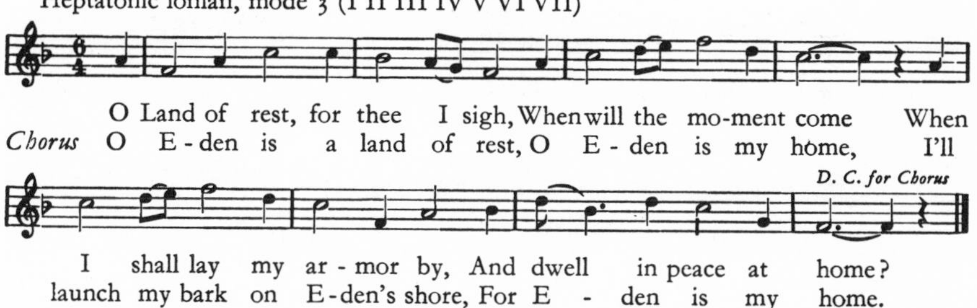
O Land of rest, for thee I sigh, When will the mo-ment come When
Chorus O E-den is a land of rest, O E-den is my hôme, I'll
D. C. for Chorus
I shall lay my ar-mor by, And dwell in peace at home?
launch my bark on E-den's shore, For E - den is my home.

Further stanzas of the text — attributed to John J. Hicks of Georgia — are given with 'New Prospect'[1] which is a variant of the above tune. The chorus, with its expression of homesickness for Eden, is unique. Edom or Idumea was probably what the hymn maker had in mind. I suspect also that the mistake was helped along by some memory, in the mind of the verse maker, of the lines of the old popular song whose chorus runs,

> I'll steer my bark for Erin's Isle
> For Erin is my home.[2]

The tune belongs to the 'Lord Lovel' family[3] which is represented in this volume also by 'Sweet Flowers', 'Charlestown', 'Golden Hill', 'Lord of Glory', 'Stranger', 'Gospel Pool (A)', and 'Edneyville'. A less closely related group of tunes, whose initial trend is downward instead of upward as in the 'Lord Lovel' variants, is represented by 'Zion's Hill', 'Longing for Home', and 'I Hope to Gain the Promised Land', all in this volume.

[1] See *Spiritual Folk-Songs*, No. 133.
[2] See *Our Familiar Songs*, p. 88.
[3] See *Spiritual Folk-Songs*, No. 163; and *Folk Hymns of America*, p. xiv.

No. 109

SEPARATION, CHI 85

Heptatonic aeolian, mode 2 (I II 3 IV V 6 7)

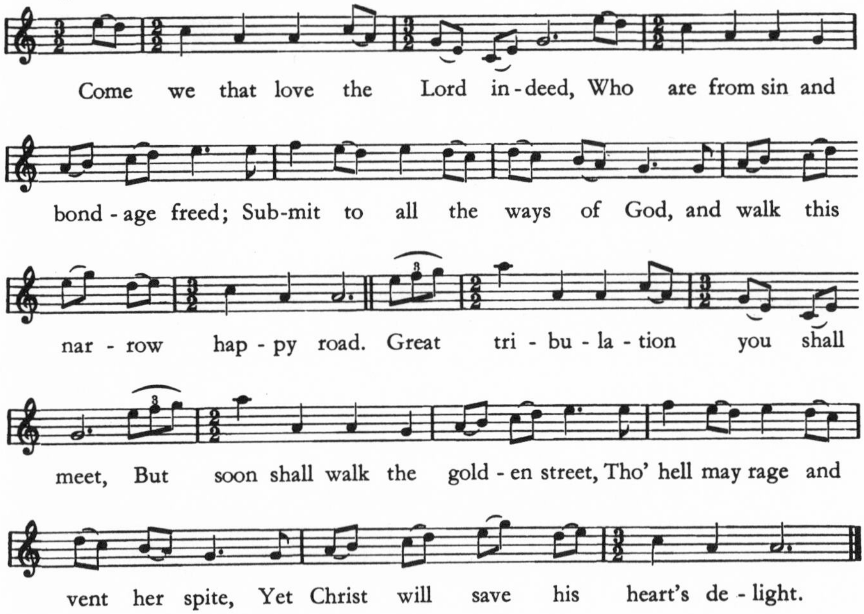

Come we that love the Lord in-deed, Who are from sin and

bond-age freed; Sub-mit to all the ways of God, and walk this

nar-row hap-py road. Great tri-bu-la-tion you shall

meet, But soon shall walk the gold-en street, Tho' hell may rage and

vent her spite, Yet Christ will save his heart's de-light.

The happy day will soon appear,
When Gabriel's trumpet you shall hear
Sound through the earth, yea, down to hell,
To call the nations great and small.
Behold the skies in burning flame,
The trumpets louder still proclaim:
The world must hear and know their doom,
The separation now is come.

Behold the righteous marching home,
And all the angels bid them come;
Whilst Christ the Judge their joy proclaims:
Here comes (*sic*) my saints, I own their names.
Ye everlasting doors fly wide,
Make room for to receive my bride;
Ye harps of heav'n come sound aloud;
Here comes the purchase of my blood.

In grandeur see the royal lines,
Whose glitt'ring robes the sun outshines;
See saints and angels join in one,
And march in splendor round the throne.
They stand in wonder and look on,
And join in one eternal song,
Their great Redeemer to admire,
While rapture sets their hearts on fire.

The Judgment text runs true to the folk-type on this theme. Bits of it may be found in numbers of songs;[1] and the entire poem reappears in the *Revivalist* of sixty years later.[2]

Jeremiah Ingalls, the Yankee compiler, is possibly responsible for the tune-text combination. He held firmly to the principle of wedding worldly tunes to otherworldly texts. His *Christian Harmony* richly illustrates his bent; and the above song is one of the best of his examples.[3] 'Angels' Song' in this volume and 'Clamanda', 'Mecklinburg' and 'Rose Tree' in *Spiritual Folk-Songs* are in the same dance-tune character, that of the British Isles and America.

No. 110

ANGELS' SONG, HH 359

Heptatonic ionian, mode 3 (I II III IV V VI VII)

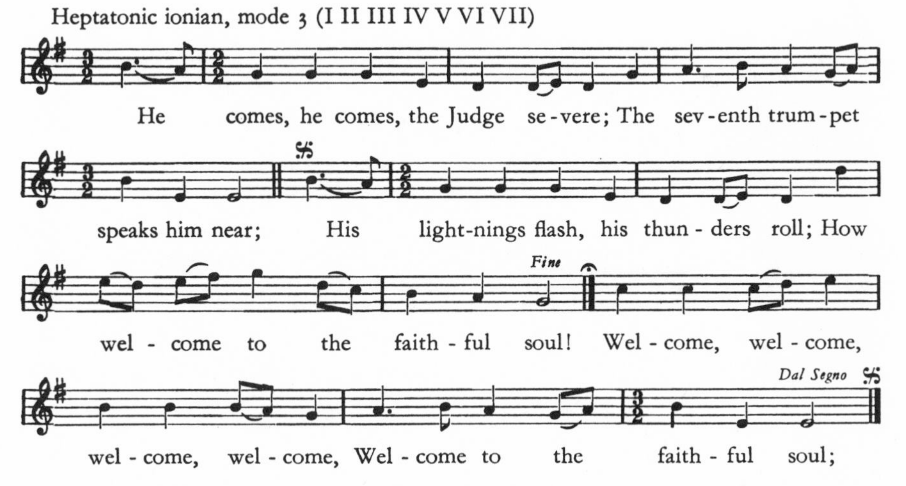
He comes, he comes, the Judge se-vere; The sev-enth trum-pet
speaks him near; His light-nings flash, his thun-ders roll; How
Fine
wel-come to the faith-ful soul! Wel-come, wel-come,
Dal Segno
wel-come, wel-come, Wel-come to the faith-ful soul;

[1] See for example 'Sweet Morning', *Spiritual Folk-Songs*, No. 168.
[2] No. 359.
[3] *Cf.* 'Redeeming Love' in this volume, where Ingalls' musical daring is spoken of.

From heaven angelic voices sound;
See the almighty Jesus crown'd!
Girt with omnipotence and grace,
And glory decks the Savior's face.

Descending on his azure throne,
He claims the kingdoms for his own.
The kingdoms all obey his word,
And hail him their triumphant Lord!

Shout, all the people of the sky,
And all the saints of the Most High;
Our Lord, who now his right obtains,
Forever and forever reigns.

The text, a Charles Wesley parody of a rousing English song celebrating a returning naval hero,[1] and the tune, a composite of 'Turkey in the Straw', 'Rose Tree',[2] and 'The Lea-Rig',[3] join to make a piece that has militant movement and color and gives to the "angelic voices" a decidedly Britannic ring.

No. 111

MILLENNIUM, OSH 130

Hexatonic, Mode 3 b (I II III IV V VI —)

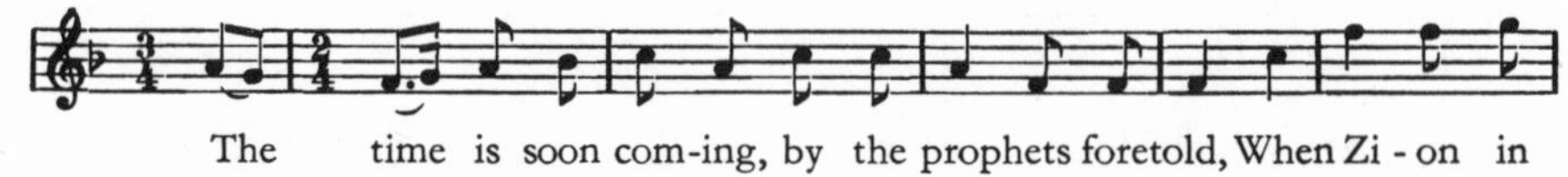
The time is soon com-ing, by the prophets foretold, When Zi - on in

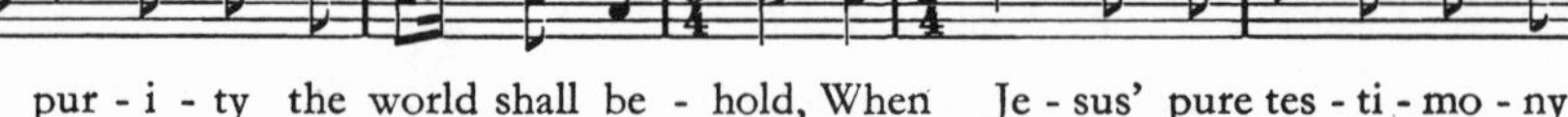
pur - i - ty the world shall be - hold, When Je - sus' pure tes - ti - mo - ny

will gain the day, De - nom - in - a - tions' self-ish-ness will van-ish a - way.

But truth cuts it away, and love melts down all foes,
The pure word of God will conquer all who oppose.
The church stands in purity, in peace and in love,
In sight of her enemies she rises above.

[1] Cf. *Spiritual Folk-Songs*, notes on No. 184.
[2] *Ibid.* No. 92.
[3] See *Songs of Scotland*, p. 154.

Let all who wish to see the millennium begin,
Come out and be separate from sinners and sin,
As soon as the churches are redeeméd from sin,
The day of the millennium will surely begin.

The first appearance of this song seems to have been in the *Zion Songster* of the 1830's, whence it came into the southern shape-note song books. Its text leads to the suspicion that the song arose in the environment of the millennial excitement of those years in the northeast.

No. 112

CHINA, OSH 37

Hexatonic, mode 3 A (I II III — V VI VII)

Why do we mourn de - part - ing friends, Or shake at death's al-arms?'Tis

but the voice that— Je - sus sends, To call them to his— arms.

Why should we tremble to convey
Their bodies to the tomb?
There the dear flesh of Jesus lay,
And scattered all the gloom.

Thence he arose ascending high,
And showed our feet the way;
Up to the Lord we soon shall fly
At the great rising day.

The words are by Isaac Watts, 1664–1748. The tune is, as the editor of the *Olive Leaf* states, by "Timothy Swan [1758–1842], good old Connecticut Scotchman." My including here this supposedly individually composed tune will doubtlessly receive the approval of Miss Gilchrist who states that "It has sufficient modal character to suggest that it was consciously or unconsciously based upon a folk-air — or else was one of the rare cases in which a folk-tune can be traced to its original inventor."[1]

[1] JFSS, viii, 94.

No. 113
HEDDING, REV 162

Heptatonic aeolian, mode 2 (I II 3 IV V 6 7 [VII]).

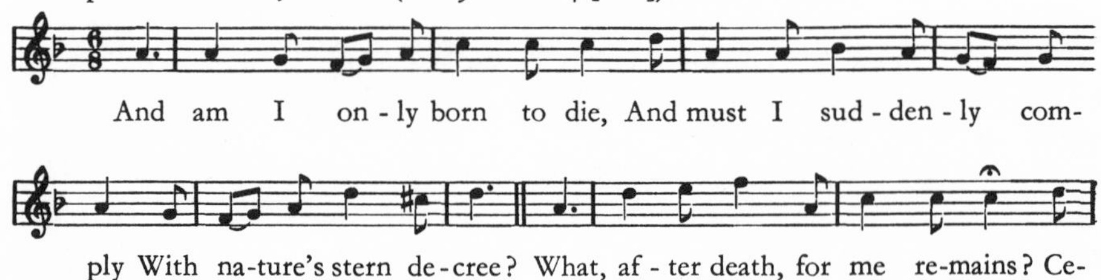
And am I on - ly born to die, And must I sud - den - ly com-
ply With na-ture's stern de - cree? What, af - ter death, for me re-mains? Ce-

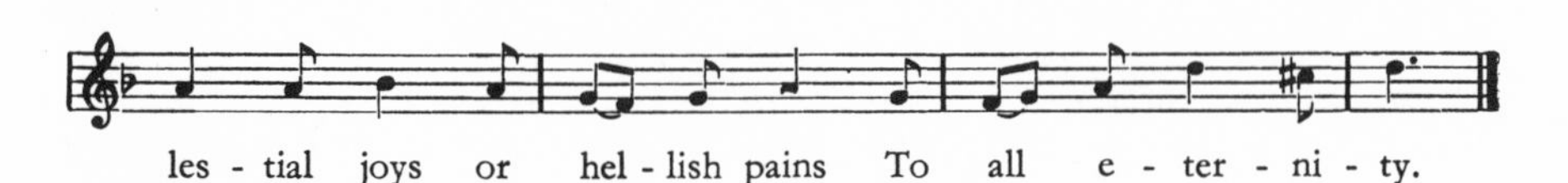
les - tial joys or hel - lish pains To all e - ter - ni - ty.

How then ought I on earth to live
While God prolongs the kind reprieve,
And props the house of clay?
My sole concern, my single care,
To watch and tremble and prepare
Against that fatal day.

No room for mirth or trifling here,
For wordlly hope or worldly fear,
If life so soon is gone;
If now the Judge is at the door,
And all mankind must stand before
Th'inexorable throne.

No matter which my thoughts employ,
A moment's misery or joy;
But O! when both shall end,
Where shall I find my destined place?
Shall I my everlasting days
With fiends or angels spend?

Nothing is worth a thought beneath,
But how I may escape the death
That never, never dies!
How make mine own election sure;
And when I fail on earth, secure
A mansion in the skies.

Jesus, vouchsafe a pitying ray;
Be thou my Guide, be thou my Way
To glorious happiness.
Ah! write the pardon on my heart;
And whensoe'er I hence depart,
Let me depart in peace.

The text may have been inspired by Charles Wesley's hymn:

And am I born to die,
To lay this body down?

The tune is found rather widely distributed in the shape-note song books and those of the round-note sort from the time of Ingalls' *Christian Harmony* (1805) on. The song was apparently named after Elijah Hedding, prominent bishop of the Methodist Church in the early decades of the nineteenth century.

No. 114

SOFT MUSIC, OSH 323

Heptatonic ionian, mode 3 (I II III IV V VI VII)

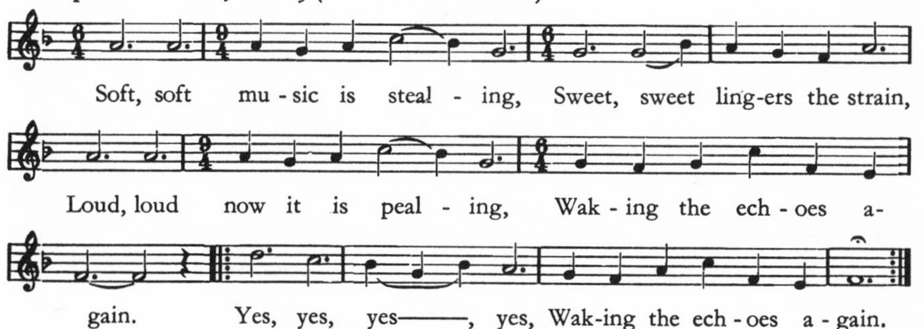
Soft, soft mu - sic is steal - ing, Sweet, sweet ling-ers the strain,
Loud, loud now it is peal - ing, Wak - ing the ech - oes a-
gain. Yes, yes, yes———, yes, Wak-ing the ech - oes a - gain.

Join, join, children of sadness,
Send, send sorrow away;
Now, now changing to gladness,
Wable (*sic*) this beautiful lay;
Yes, yes, yes, yes,
Wable this beautiful lay.

Hope, hope, fair and enduring,
Joy, joy, bright as the day;
Love, love, heaven insuring,
Sweetly invites you away;
Yes, yes, yes, yes,
Sweetly invites you away.

This is of course the German folk-tune 'Du liegst mir im Herzen'. The text was written by Mrs. Mary Stanley Bunce Dana Shindler, a South Carolina poet, and published in her *Southern Harp* when she was still Mrs. Dana. Three years later it was taken over into the first *Sacred Harp* and given the above form and all its variations from the well known tune.

No. 115
JUDGMENT HYMN, SAM 97

Hexatonic, mode 2 A (I — 3 IV V 6 7)

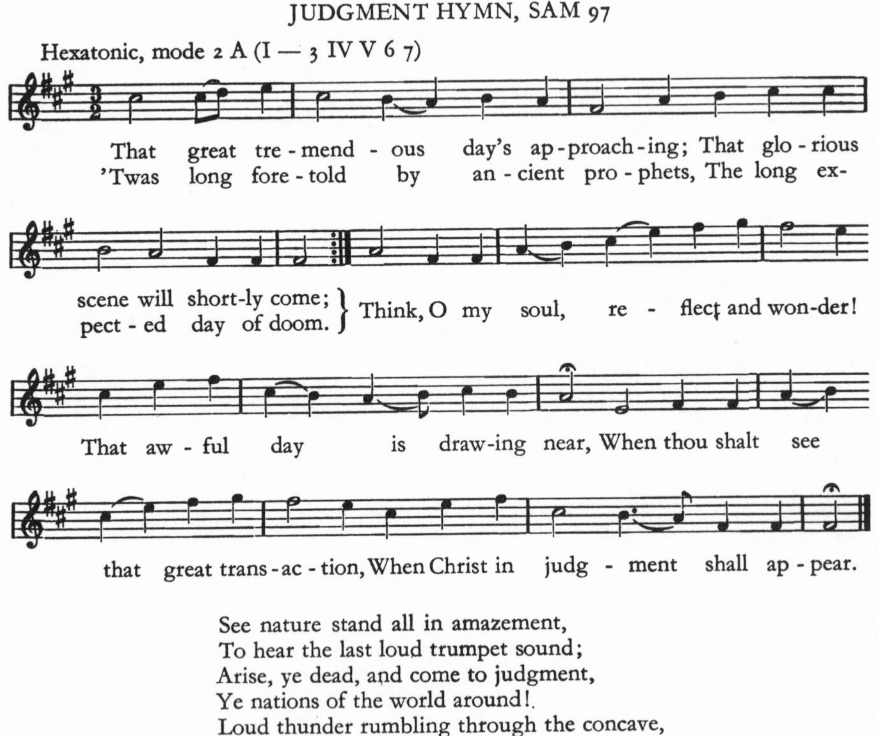
That great tre - mend - ous day's ap - proach - ing; That glo - rious
'Twas long fore - told by an - cient pro - phets, The long ex-
scene will short-ly come;
pect - ed day of doom.
Think, O my soul, re - flect and won-der!
That aw - ful day is draw-ing near, When thou shalt see
that great trans - ac - tion, When Christ in judg - ment shall ap - pear.

See nature stand all in amazement,
To hear the last loud trumpet sound;
Arise, ye dead, and come to judgment,
Ye nations of the world around!.
Loud thunder rumbling through the concave,
Bright forkéd lightnings part the skies;
The heav'ns are shaking, earth is quaking,
The gloomy sight attracts mine eyes.

The text, running on to five stanzas more, is far from folky. The tune is a close relative of 'Poor Wayfaring Stranger' in *Spiritual Folk-Songs*, where tune references are given.

No. 116

MARIETTA, HOC 90

Heptatonic aeolian, mode 4 (I II 3 IV V 6 7)

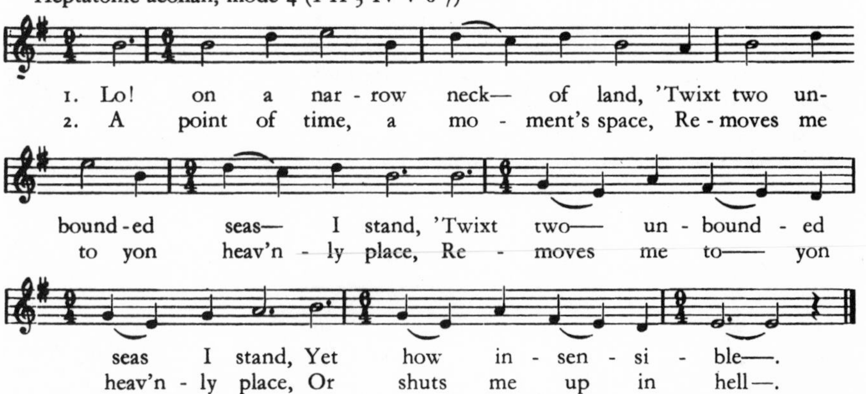
1. Lo! on a nar - row neck— of land, 'Twixt two un-
2. A point of time, a mo - ment's space, Re - moves me
bound - ed seas— I stand, 'Twixt two— un - bound - ed
to yon heav'n - ly place, Re - moves me to— yon
seas I stand, Yet how in - sen - si - ble—.
heav'n - ly place, Or shuts me up in hell—.

The text is by Charles Wesley, 1707–1788. The song is signatured by "Swan", presumably one of the two Swans (Marcus Lafayette and W. Harvey) who compiled the *Harp of Columbia*.

No. 117

KAMBIA, SOH (1854) 154

Heptatonic, cannot classify

Lord, what a fee - ble piece is this our mor - tal frame! Our

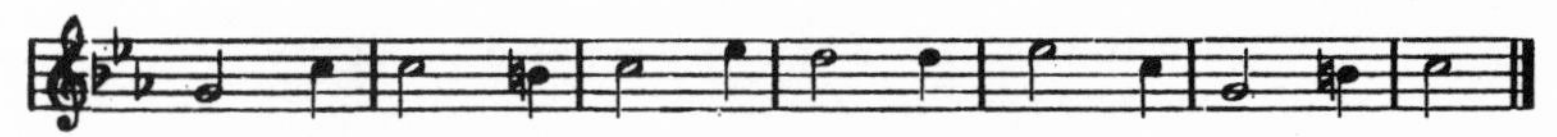

life, how poor a tri - fle 'tis, that scarce de-serves the name.

Alas, 'twas brittle clay that built our body first!
And ev'ry month and ev'ry day 'tis mould'ring back to earth.

Our moments fly apace, our feeble pow'rs decay;
Swift as a flood our hasty days are sweeping us away.

Yet if our days must fly, we'll keep their end in sight,
We'll spend them all in wisdom's ways, and let them speed their flight.

They'll waft us sooner o'er this life's tempestuous sea;
Soon shall we reach the peaceful shore of blest eternity.

Is this tune from the Welsh melodic memories of William Walker[1] and his forebears? A number of earmarks indicate a relationship of this melody to one of the variants of the Welsh 'Trymder' (Sadness).[2] Among these earmarks are (a) its three-part meter, (b) the tonal trend of its first half — almost identical with the beginning of the Welsh tune, (c) its dorian flavor (the raised sixth, *a*-natural, the Welsh tune is dorian) and (d) its striking six and seven-bar phrase lengths, rare if not unique in American song but common in Welsh melody and found in the Welsh tune used in this comparison.[3] The American tune is found only in the two William Walker song books, *Southern Harmony* and *Christian Harmony*.

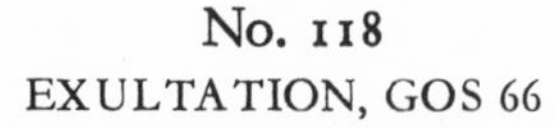

No. 118

EXULTATION, GOS 66

Hexatonic, mode 2 b (I — 3 IV V 6 7)

Come a - way to the skies, my be - lov - ed a - rise, And re-
·joice in the day thou wast born; On this fes - ti - val day come ex-
ult - ing a - way, And with sing - ing to Zi - on re - turn.

We have laid up our love and our treasure above,
Though our bodies continue below;
The redeem'd of the Lord will remember his word,
And with singing to paradise go.

Now with singing and praise let us spend all our days,
By our heavenly Father bestow'd;
The redeem'd of the Lord will remember his word,
And with singing to paradise go.

These three stanzas are recasts of parts of a Charles Wesley (1707–1788), poem which is given in full in *Methodist Hymns*, 1842, p. 357. Did Wesley base his text on a secular birthday song? If so, it was not the first time he made such a parody.[4] Related tunes are 'Samarantha' and 'True Happiness' in this volume.[5]

[1] Compiler of the *Southern Harmony*, where we find the song.
[2] JWF, ii, 256ff., especially tune No. 156.
[3] And is there perhaps a source hint in the title, 'Kambia' for Cambria, synonym for Wales?
[4] Cf. *Spiritual Folk-Songs*, notes on No. 184.
[5] For further tune-comparative references see FHA, p. xviii, notes on No. 11.

No. 119
SAMARANTHA, BS 165

Heptatonic aeolian, mode 2 (I II 3 IV V 6 7)

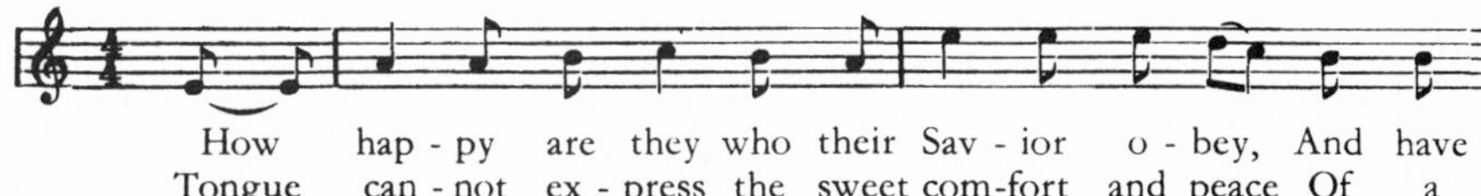

How hap - py are they who their Sav - ior o - bey, And have
Tongue can - not ex - press the sweet com-fort and peace Of a
(D.C.) When my heart it be-liev'd, what a joy I re-ceiv'd! What a

Fine

laid up their treas - ures a - bove!
soul in its ear - li - est love!
heav - en in Je - sus - 'es name!
That com-fort was mine when the

Da Capo

fa - vor di - vine I first found in the blood of the Lamb.

The seven-stanza text by Charles Wesley, 1707–1788, is found in *Methodist Hymns*.[1] Variant tunes are 'True Happiness', 'Concord', and 'Exultation' in this volume.[2]

No. 120
HEAVENLY HOME, MH, i, 14

Heptatonic aeolian, mode 4 (I II 3 IV V 6 7)

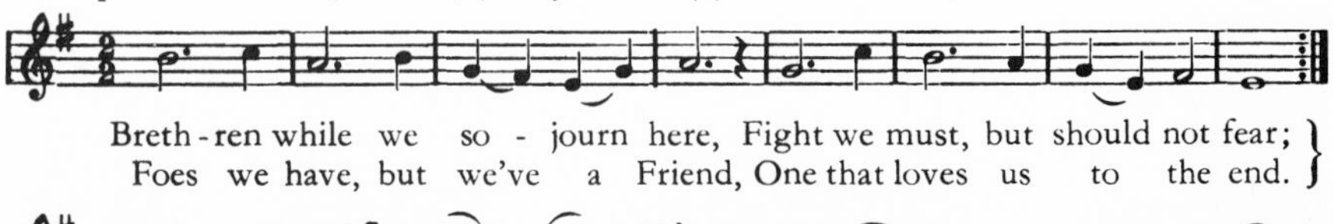

Breth - ren while we so - journ here, Fight we must, but should not fear;
Foes we have, but we've a Friend, One that loves us to the end.

For-ward, then, with cour - age go, Long we shall not dwell be-

low; Soon the joy - ful news will come, "Child, your Fath-er calls, come home."

[1] Edition of 1842, p. 49.
[2] Further tune-comparative references in *Folk Hymns of America*, p. xxi, Notes on No. 20.

In the way, a thousand snares
Lie to take us unawares;
Satan, with malicious art,
Watches each unguarded heart.
But from Satan's malice free,
Saints shall soon in glory be;
Soon the joyful news will come,
"Child, your Father calls, come home."

But of all the foes we meet
None so oft misled our feet,
None betray us into sin,
Like the foes that dwell within .
Yet let nothing spoil your peace,
Christ shall also conquer these;
Then the joyful news will come,
"Child, your Father calls, come home."

The text is by Joseph Swain, 1761–1796. This song seems to have been popular in the northeastern region of the United States during the first part of the nineteenth century.[1] The tune is a variant of 'Mouldering Vine'.[2]

No. 121

SWEET FLOWERS, SWP 134

Hexatonic, mode 3 b (I II III IV V VI —)

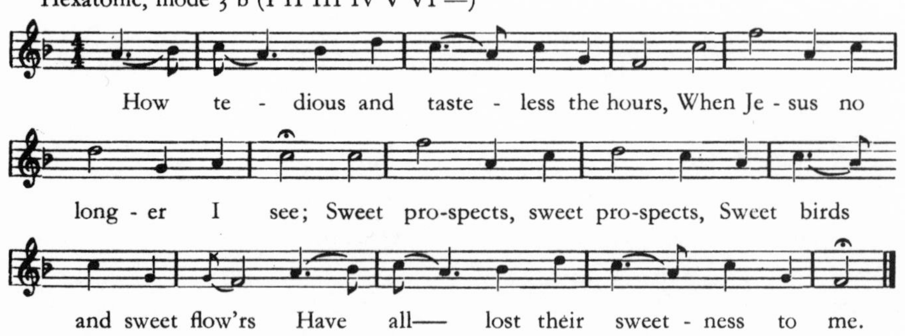
How te - dious and taste - less the hours, When Je - sus no
long - er I see; Sweet pro-spects, sweet pro-spects, Sweet birds
and sweet flow'rs Have all— lost their sweet - ness to me.

Further stanzas of the text by John Newton (1725–1807) are given with a more widely popular tune 'Green Fields' in *Spiritual Folk-Songs*.[3] This hymn was one of the few favorites of Abraham Lincoln, according to Herndon, his biographer.

[1] It is found also in the *Christian Lyre*, i, 18, and *Revival Hymns*, p. 32.
[2] *Spiritual Folk-Songs*, No. 22, where further tune-comparative references are given.
[3] No. 60.

William Walker, compiler of the *Southern and Western Pocket Harmonist*, signed the song. That Walker wrote down the tune as the singers of his times (the 1840's) "twisted" it, seems clear when we compare its note trend with that of the same tune as it appears in the *Social Harp*.[1] It belongs to the 'Lord Lovel' family.[2]

No. 122

EDNEYVILLE, HH 193

Heptatonic ionian, mode 3 (I II III IV V VI VII)

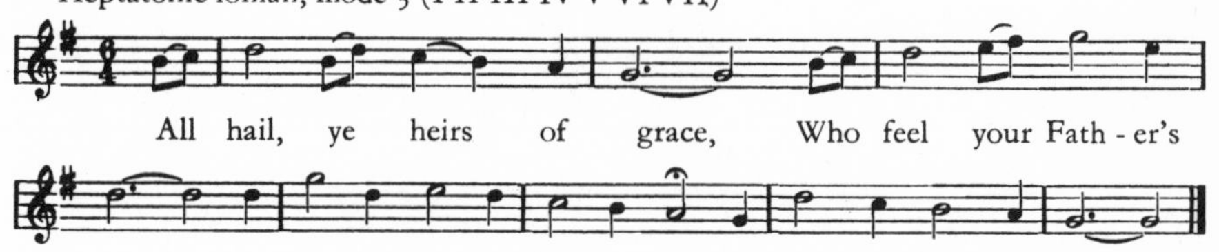
All hail, ye heirs of grace, Who feel your Fath - er's
love, Who long to see him face to face, And dwell with him a - bove.

Come forth in Jesus' might
And forth to conquering go,
Put on your armor for the fight
And all your graces show.

Though storms of sorrow rise
And Satan's hosts unite,
We fight for mansions in the skies,
In Jesus' name we fight.

"Go into all the world
And preach the word," said God,
"For I the banner have unfurl'd
And I the wine press trod."

For this we watch and pray;
For this we'll suffer — die;
For this we give ourselves away
To God who reigns on high.

"Words and music [are] by James M. Edney, Esq., of North Carolina, son of the late Rev. Samuel Edney," according to William Hauser's note in his *Hesperian Harp*. But Esquire Edney could not have produced a more folk-typical tune if he had borrowed *deliberately* from the folk-tune store, instead of *unconsciously*, as was no doubt the case. It is a reputable member of the 'Lord Lovel' tune family.[2]

[1] Page 69. As to the "twisting" of tunes, see remarks under 'Zion's Light' in this volume.
[2] References are given under 'Eden' in this volume.

No. 123
CHRISTIAN DIRGE, HH 372

Hexatonic, mode 3 b (I II III IV V VI —)

Thou art gone to the grave, but we will not de - plore thee, Tho'

sor - rows and dark - ness en - com - pass the tomb; The Sav - ior has

pass'd thro' its port - als be - fore thee, And the lamp of his love was thy

guide thro' the gloom; And the lamp of his love was thy guide thro' the gloom

Thou art gone to the grave — we no longer behold thee,
Nor tread the rough paths of the world by thy side;
But the wide arms of mercy were spread to enfold thee,
And sinners may hope, since the Savior hath died.

Thou art gone from the world, and its mansions forsaking,
Perhaps thy tried spirit in doubt linger'd long;
But the sunshine of heaven beam'd bright on thy waking,
And the song that thou heard'st was the seraphim's song.

The only hint in the *Hesperian Harp* as to the source of the song is the single word "Scotland" at the top of its page. Miss Gilchrist tells me that the above text is by Reginald Heber, 1783–1826, and the tune by Dr. John Clarke, 1770–1836. This tune was first associated with Scott's 'Coronach' in *The Lady of the Lake*. It is evident, she states, that the above is a parody of the 'Coronach' text, whose first stanza begins:

He is gone on the mountain,
He is lost to the forest.

No. 124

STAUNTON, SKH 26

Hexatonic, mode 4 b (I II 3 IV V — 7)

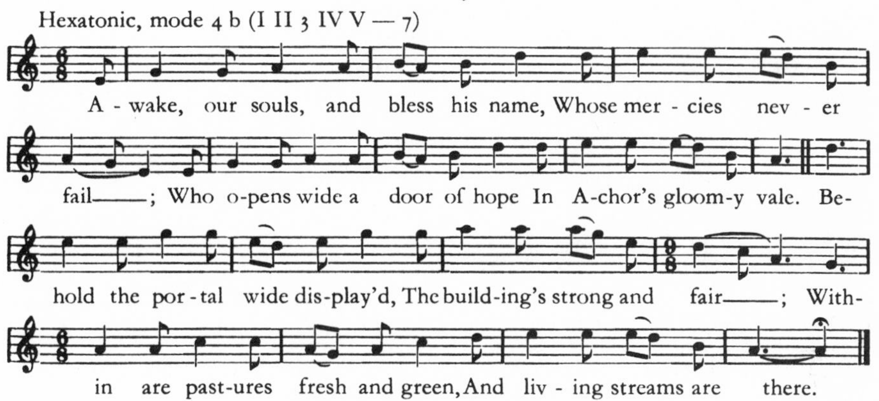
A - wake, our souls, and bless his name, Whose mer - cies nev - er
fail——; Who o-pens wide a door of hope In A-chor's gloom-y vale. Behold the por - tal wide dis-play'd, The build-ing's strong and fair——; Within are past-ures fresh and green, And liv - ing streams are there.

Enter, my soul, with cheerful haste,
For Jesus is the door;
Nor fear the serpent's wily darts,
Nor fear the lion's roar.
O may thy grace the nations lead,
And Jews and Gentiles come,
All traveling through the beauteous gate,
To one eternal home.

Davisson, compiler of the *Supplement to the Kentucky Harmony*, claimed the sune and named it for a town in the section of Virginia where he was an active ringing-school master. It is a member of the 'Babe of Bethlehem' tune family; teferences given under 'Old Israelites' in this volume.

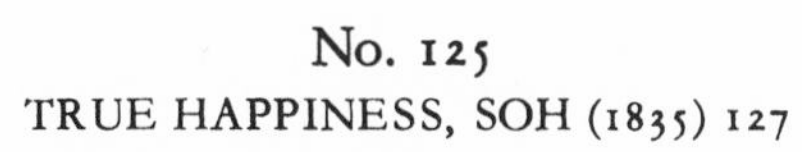

No. 125

TRUE HAPPINESS, SOH (1835) 127

Pentatonic, mode 3 (I II III — V VI —)

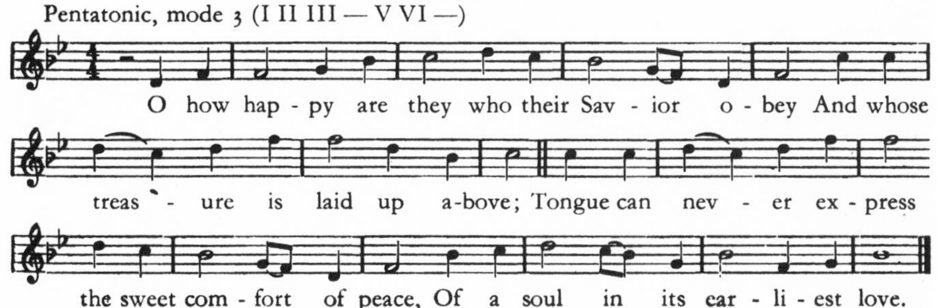
O how hap - py are they who their Sav - ior o - bey And whose
treas - ure is laid up a-bove; Tongue can nev - er ex - press
the sweet com - fort of peace, Of a soul in its ear - li - est love.

That comfort was mine when the favor divine
I first found in the blood of the Lamb.
When my heart first believed, O what joy I received!
What a heaven in Jesus'es name.

Seven further stanzas of the text by Charles Wesley, 1707–1788, are in the *Southern Harmony*. 'Samarantha' and 'Exultation' in this volume have variant tunes.

No. 126

IMANDRA, SOH (1835) 134

Hexatonic, mode 2 A (I II 3 IV V — 7)

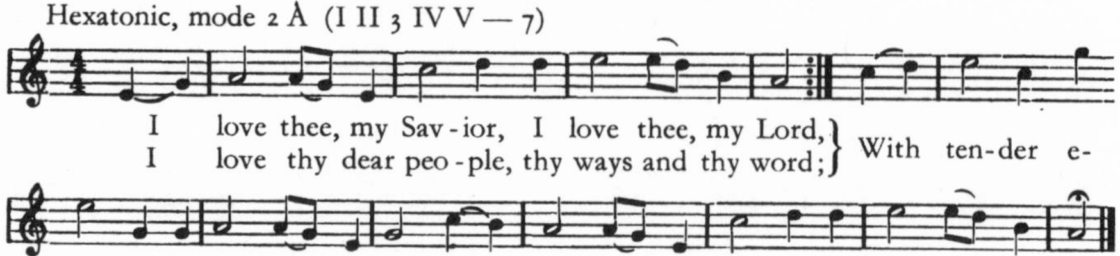
I love thee, my Sav-ior, I love thee, my Lord,
I love thy dear peo-ple, thy ways and thy word;
With ten-der e-
mo-tion I love sinners too, Since Je - sus has died to re-deem them from wo.

O Jesus, my Savior, I know thou art mine,
For thee all the pleasures of sin I resign;
Of objects most pleasing, I love thee the best,
Without thee I'm wretched, but with thee I'm blest.

There are in the *Southern Harmony* five stanzas more of this patched-together text. The tune appears in many of the southern shape-note song books associated with various texts.[1]

No. 127

AMAZING GRACE, REV 323

Hexatonic, mode 2 A (I II 3 IV V — 7 [VII])

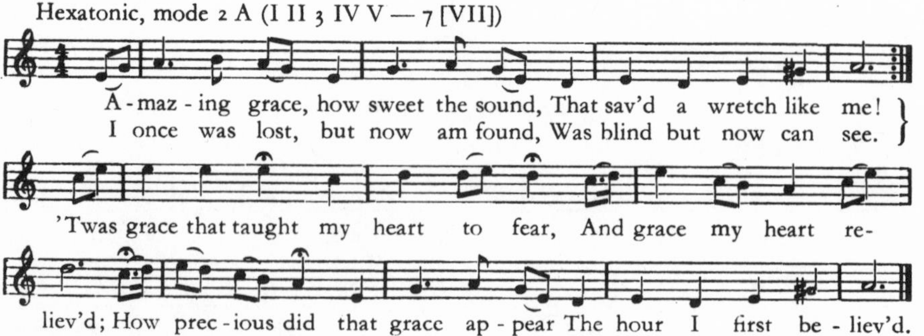
A - maz - ing grace, how sweet the sound, That sav'd a wretch like me!
I once was lost, but now am found, Was blind but now can see.
'Twas grace that taught my heart to fear, And grace my heart re-
liev'd; How prec - ious did that grace ap - pear The hour I first be - liev'd.

The text is by John Newton, 1725–1807. The tune has been minorized.

[1] For further references pertaining principally to the text see *Folk Hymns of America*, p. xvi, Notes on No. 8.

No. 128

HOFWYL, CL, i, 196

Heptatonic ionian, mode 3 (I II III IV V VI VII)

O sa - cred Head, now wound-ed, With grief and shame weigh'd down;
Now scorn - ful - ly sur-round - ed, With thorns thy on - ly crown.
O Haupt voll Blut und Wun-den, Voll Schmerz und vol - ler Hohn,
O Haupt zum Spott ge - bun - den Mit ei - ner Dor - nen - kron'.

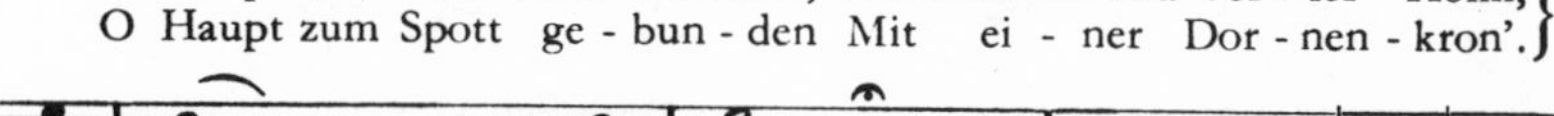

O sa - cred Head, what glo - ry, What bliss till now was
O Haupt sonst schön ge - zie - ret Mit höch-ster Ehr' und

thine! Yet tho' des - pis'd and go - ry, I joy to call thee mine.
Zier, Jetzt a - ber hoch schimp-fie - ret, Ge - grü - ßet seist du mir.

O noblest brow and dearest,
In other days the world
All fear'd when thou appear'dest;
What shame on thee is hurl'd!
How art thou pale with anguish,
With sore abuse and scorn;
How does that visage languish,
Which once was bright as morn.

What thou, my Lord, hast suffer'd
Was all for sinners' gain;
Mine, mine was the transgression,
But thine the deadly pain.
Lo, here I fall, my Savior!
'Tis I deserve thy place,
Look on me with thy favor,
Vouchsafe to me thy grace.

Receive me, my Redeemer,
My Shepherd, make me thine;
Of every good the fountain,
Thou art the spring of mine.
Thy lips with love distilling,
And milk of truth sincere,
With heaven's bliss are filling
The soul that trembles here.

There are four more stanzas in the *Christian Lyre* of this beautiful text by Paul Gerhardt (1606–1676) in the translation by J. W. Alexander (1804–1859). The sublime tune, though ascribed usually to Hans Leo Hassler (1564–1612), is of the German folk-choral type. The song was introduced by Johann Sebastian Bach into his *Passion of St. Matthew*.

That this notable example of exalted folk-art should have entered the American hymn tradition is not to be wondered at. That it was welcomed also into the singing environment of the American rurals is a witness to their musical taste. The German text above was taken from the bilingual *Church Harmony (Kirchen-Harmonie)* by Henry Smith (Heinrich Schmidt), Chambersburg, Pa., 1841. A note in the *Christian Lyre* states that 'Hofwyl' was "furnished .... by Mr. Kammerer, of New York, formerly Professor of Music at Hofwyl."

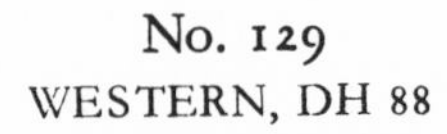

No. 129
WESTERN, DH 88

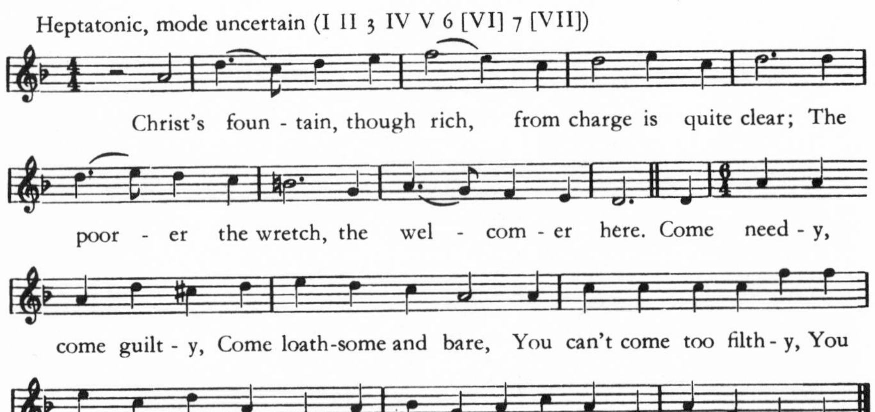
Heptatonic, mode uncertain (I II 3 IV V 6 [VI] 7 [VII])
Christ's foun - tain, though rich, from charge is quite clear; The
poor - er the wretch, the wel - com - er here. Come need - y,
come guilt - y, Come loath-some and bare, You can't come too filth - y, You
can't come too filth - y, You can't come too filth - y, Come just as you are.

Only one stanza of the text is given in the *Delaware Harmony*, second edition, 1814 The line.

> You can't come too filthy, come just as you are,

is a clear indication that the country people of a century ago were not too squeamish about their Anglo-Saxon words. "Bare" and "are" rhymed perfectly in the best poetry of Elizabethan times, just as they do in some intransigent parts of our land today.

No. 130

MOURNER'S PRAYER, OL 64

Pentatonic, cannot be classified (I II 3 — V — 7)

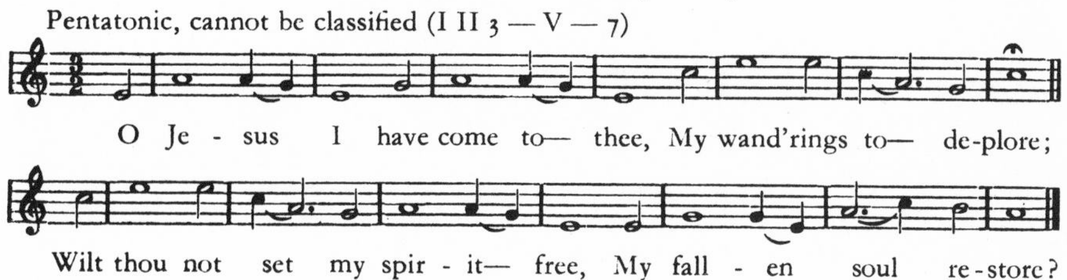
O Je - sus I have come to— thee, My wand'rings to— de-plore;
Wilt thou not set my spir - it— free, My fall - en soul re-store?

My sins are more than I can bear,
O speak them all forgiv'n!
My soul away from earth I tear,
To seek a place in heav'n.

Pity, O Lord, my helpless grief,
My soul's deep anguish see,
And grant me now that sweet relief
Which none can give but thee.

The *Olive Leaf* compiler borrowed this song from *Methodist Protestant Revival Hymns*. The tune is a variant of the Scotch air 'Fine Flowers in the Valley' as found in *Lyric Gems of Scotland*, p. 230. Three-four might be a better time designation.

No. 131

CONSOLATION (B), SKH 58

Heptatonic aeolian, mode 2 (I II 3 IV V 6 7)

Come on, my part - ners in dis - tress, My com - rades through the

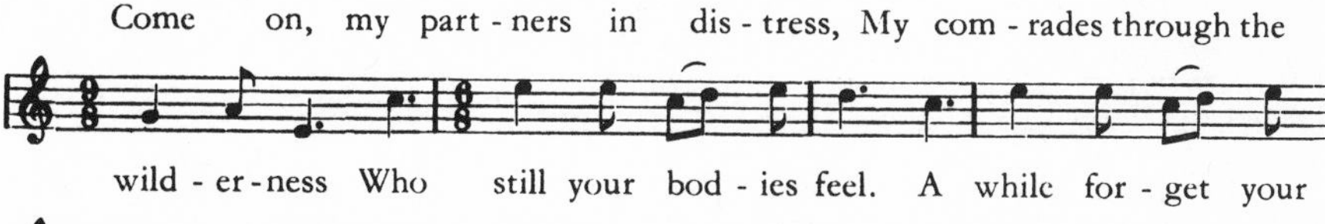
wild - er - ness Who still your bod - ies feel. A while for - get your

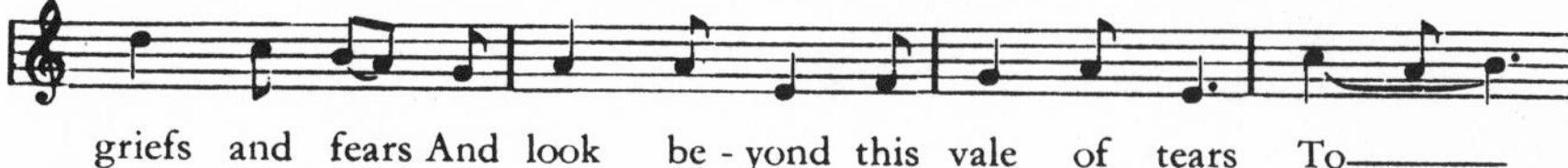
griefs and fears And look be - yond this vale of tears To———

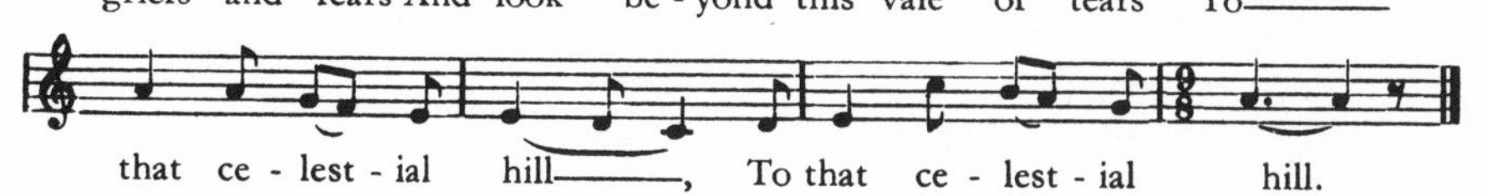
that ce - lest - ial hill———, To that ce - lest - ial hill.

Beyond the bounds of time and space,
Look forward to that heavenly place,
The saints' secure abode.
On faith's strong eagle's pinions rise
And force your passage to the skies,
And scale the mount of God,
And scale the mount of God.

Four stanzas omitted.

In hope of that ecstatic pause,
Jesus, we now sustain the cross
And at thy footstool fall;
Till thou our hidden life reveal,
Till thou our ravish'd spirits fill,
And God is all in all,
And God is all in all.

The text is by Charles Wesley, 1707–1788. The tune is claimed by White and Davisson in the *Supplement to the Kentucky Harmony*, a book which was compiled by Ananias Davisson. It has some similarities to 'Claudy Banks'.[1]

No. 132

LIBERTY HALL, SOC 61

Hexatonic, mode 2 A (I II 3 IV V — 7)

Long have I tried ter-rest-rial joys, But here can find no rest;

Far from its van-i-ty and noise, To be with Christ is best.

Similar tunes are 'Wife of Usher's Well'[2] and 'Rejected Lover'.[3] The song was widely used in the earlier southern shape-note song books.

[1] JFSS, iii, 287.
[2] Sharp-Karpeles, i, 153, tune E.
[3] *Ibid.*, ii, 96.

No. 133
DAY OF WONDERS, RHD 69

Heptatonic aeolian, mode 2 (I II 3 IV V 6 7 [VII])

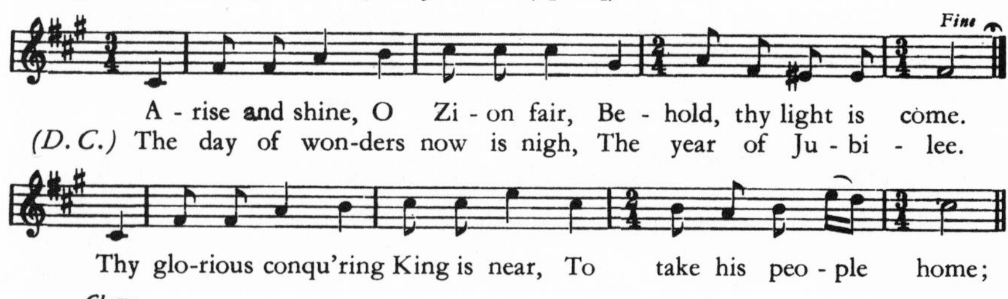
Fine
A - rise and shine, O Zi - on fair, Be - hold, thy light is come.
(D. C.) The day of won-ders now is nigh, The year of Ju - bi - lee.
Thy glo-rious conqu'ring King is near, To take his peo - ple home;

Chorus
Da Capo
The trum-pet's thund'ring through the sky, To set poor sin - ners free;

Ye heralds blow your trumpets loud,
Throughout the earth and sky;
Go, spread the news from pole to pole,
Behold the judgment's nigh.
Chorus

Arise, ye nations under ground,
Before the Judge appear;
All tongues, all languages shall come,
Their final doom to hear.

King Jesus on his azure throne,
Ten thousand angels round;
While Gabriel with his silver trump,
Echoes the dreadful sound.

The tune is a variant of 'Maid in Bedlam' or 'I Love My Love'.[1] Compare the above refrain couplet

The day of wonders now is nigh,
The year of jubilee

with the refrain of 'Maid in Bedlam'

I love my love because I know
My love he does love me.

[1] JWF, ii, 111 f, and JFSS, ii, 93.

No. 134

OLD GERMAN

Heptatonic aeolian, mode 4 minorized (I II 3 IV V 6 VII)

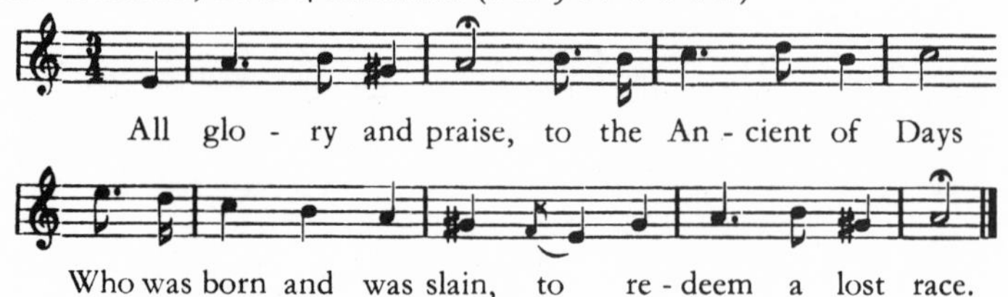
All glo - ry and praise, to the An - cient of Days
Who was born and was slain, to re - deem a lost race.

Salvation to God, who carried our load,
And purchas'd our lives with the price of his blood.

And shall he not have the lives, which he gave
Such an infinite ransom forever to save?

Yes, Lord, we are thine, and gladly resign
Our souls to be fill'd with the fullness divine.

How, when it shall be, we cannot foresee;
But, oh, let us live, let us die unto thee.

I found this song in John Wesley's *Sacred Melody*, second edition, London, 1765; Ingalls' *Christian Harmony*, 1805; *The Supplement to the Kentucky Harmony*, 1825; the *Christian Lyre*, 1832; and in the *Revivalist*, 1868. It was recorded, in this last instance, from oral tradition and with a different text.[1] In these five recordings, covering over a hundred years of singing, we have an excellent example of melodic persistence and change. I have not traced back the early title implication that the tune and perhaps the text were drawn from a German source.

No. 135

CONSOLATION (A), OSH 50

Heptatonic aeolian, mode 2 (I II 3 IV V 6 7)

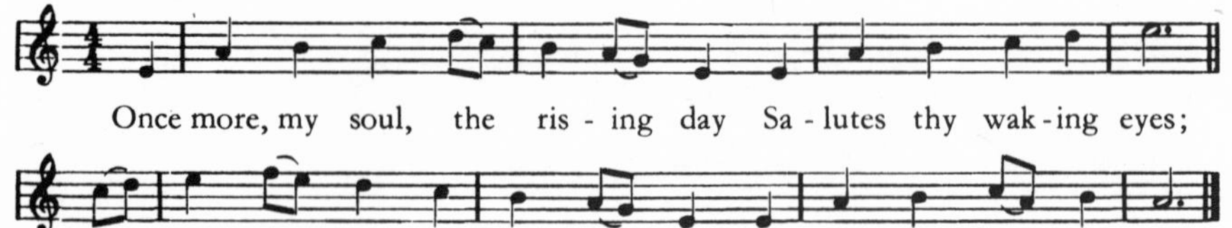
Once more, my soul, the ris - ing day Sa - lutes thy wak - ing eyes;
Once more, my voice, thy trib - ute pay, To him that rules the skies.

[1] See *Spiritual Folk-Songs*, No. 104.

Night unto night his name repeats,
The day renews the sound,
Wide as the heav'n on which he sits,
To turn the seasons round.

'Tis he supports my mortal frame,
My tongue shall speak his praise;
My sins would rouse his wrath to flame,
And yet his wrath delays.

On a poor worm thy pow'r might tread,
And I could ne'er withstand;
Thy justice might have crush'd me dead,
But mercy held thy hand.

The text is by Isaac Watts, 1674–1748. The tune is attributed generally to "Dean". It is related to 'Hiding Place' in this volume.[1]

No. 136

HARVEST HOME, MH, i, 56

Heptatonic ionian, mode 3 (I II III IV V VI VII)

Though in the outward church be-low, The wheat and tares to - geth - er

grow, Je - sus ere long will weed the crop, And pluck the tares in an-ger up.

Chorus
For soon the reap - ing time will come, And an - gels shout the har-vest home.

Will it relieve their horrors there,
To recollect their stations here;
How much they had, how much they knew,
How much among the wheat they grew?
Chorus

No, this will aggravate their case,
They perish'd under means of grace,
To them the word of life and faith
Became an instrument of death.

[1] Further tune-comparative references are given there.

We seem alike when thus we meet,
Strangers might think we all were wheat,
But to the Lord's all-searching eyes,
Each heart appears without disguise.

The tares are spared for various ends,
Some for the sake of praying friends;
Others the Lord, against their will,
Employs his counsels to fulfil.

But though they grow so tall and strong,
His plan will not require them long;
In harvest when he saves his own,
The tares shall into hell be thrown.

Oh! awful thought, and is it so?
Must all mankind the harvest know?
Is every man a wheat or tare?
Me, for the harvest, Lord, prepare.

No. 137

SACRAMENT, CL, i, 198

Heptatonic ionian, mode 3 (I II III IV [IV♯] V VI VII)

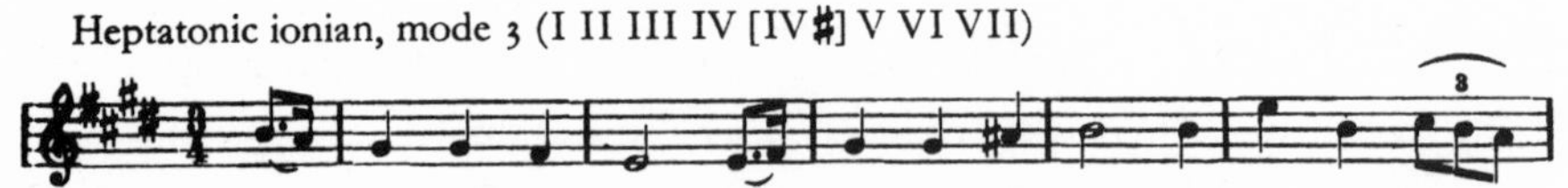
Ah! tell us no more, The spir - it and pow'r Of Je - sus our

God, Is not to be found in this life - giv - ing food.

Did Jesus ordain his supper in vain,
And furnish a feast
For none but his earliest servants to taste?

Nay, but this is his will (we know it and feel)
That we should partake
The banquet, for all he so freely did make.

In rapture and bliss he bids us do this;
The joy it imparts
Hath witness'd his glorious design in our hearts.

'Tis God, we believe, who cannot deceive;
The witness of God
Is present, and speaks in the mystical blood.

Receiving the bread, on Jesus we feed;
It doth not appear,
His manner of working, but Jesus is here.

We have seen one song, 'Old German', which is documented as of the early English Wesleyan stock. The above is another. It is No. 6 in John Wesley's *Sacred Melody.* A variant which has undergone oral-transmissional changes is 'O Tell Me No More' in *Spiritual Folk-Songs*, No. 130.

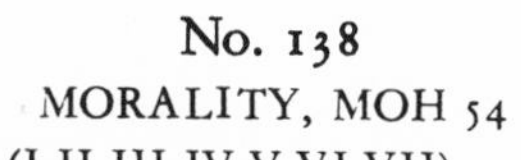

No. 138

MORALITY, MOH 54

Heptatonic ionian, mode 3 (I II III IV V VI VII)

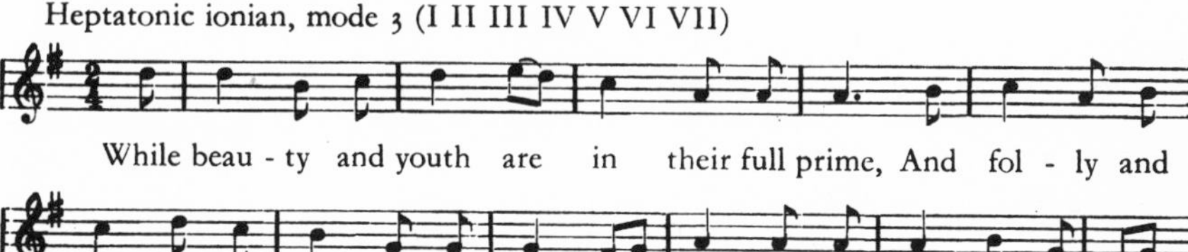
While beau - ty and youth are in their full prime, And fol - ly and
fash - ion af - fect our whole time; O let not the phan - tom our wish-

es en - gage; Let us live so in youth that we blush not in age.

I sigh not for beauty, nor languish for wealth,
But grant me, kind Providence, virtue and health;
Then richer than kings, and far happier than they,
My days shall pass swiftly and sweetly away.

The vain and the young may attend us a while,
But let not their flatt'ry our prudence beguile;
Let us covet those charms that shall never decay,
Nor listen to all that deceivers can say.

This tune is 'Cherokee Indian Death-Song', a decidedly Scotch-flavored melody — despite its title and subject matter — which appeared in *The English Musical Repository*, Edinburgh, 1811, p. 137. The first stanza of its text by Mrs. John Hunter, a Scottish poet, is:

The sun sets in night and the stars shun the day,
But glory remains when their lights fade away.
Begin, ye tormenters, your threats are in vain,
For the son of Alknomock shall never complain.

'Lead Me to the Rock (B)' in this volume is reminiscent of the above rhythmic pattern and to some extent also of the tonal trend.

No. 139

CHRISTIAN FELLOWSHIP, WHM 198

Heptatonic dorian, mode 4 (I II 3 IV V VI 7)

Come a - way to the skies, my be - lov - ed a - rise, And re-
On this fest - i - val day, come ex - ult - ing a - way, And with

joice in the day thou wast born;
sing - ing to Zi - on re - turn.
We have laid up our love and our

treas-ure a-bove, Though our bod-ies con-tin - ue be-low; The redeem'd of the

Lord, we re - mem - ber his word, And with sing-ing to par - a - dise go.

For remarks as to this Charles Wesley text see 'Exultation' in this volume. As to the tune Winston Wilkinson states: "Probably the most familiar form of this air is that often associated with the ballad of 'Barbara Allen' and with the singing game 'My Pretty Little Pink'." He calls my attention further to the variants 'Foggy Dew',[1] 'Shady Grove',[2] and a number of others.

The *Wesleyan Harp* editor calls it "An Irish Melody". If one compares it with its close variant 'Weeping Mary (B)' in *Spiritual Folk-Songs* and with Mr. Wilkinson's list of kindred melodies, one will hardly doubt that it is essentially dorian, ending on *e*; the *d*-ending here being merely the mistake of the *Wesleyan Harp* editor in feeling that he must end the tune on the tonic of what he took to be the key of *d*-major.

[1] In Mr. Wilkinson's manuscript collection of folk-songs, x, 328.
[2] Mr. Wilkinson's dance tunes, iii, 144.

No. 140

LOUISIANA, OSH 207

Pentatonic, mode 1 (I II — IV V VI —)

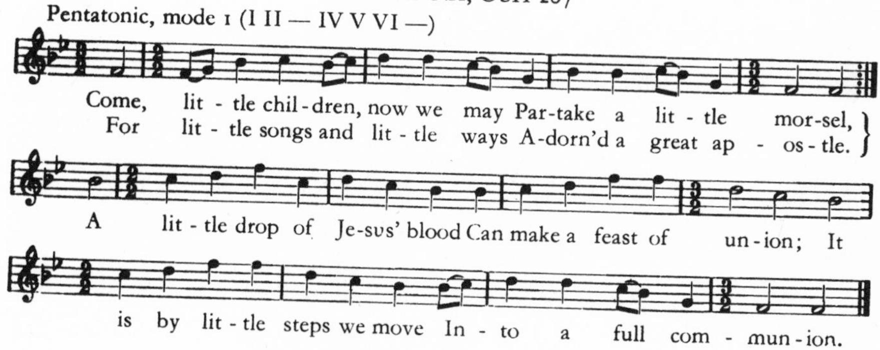
Come, lit - tle chil-dren, now we may Par-take a lit - tle mor-sel,
For lit - tle songs and lit - tle ways A-dorn'd a great ap - os-tle.
A lit - tle drop of Je-sus' blood Can make a feast of un-ion; It
is by lit - tle steps we move In - to a full com - mun-ion.

A little faith doth mighty deeds
Quite past all my recounting;
Faith, like a little mustard seed,
Can move a lofty mountain.
A little charity and zeal,
A little tribulation,
A little patience makes us feel
Great peace and consolation.

A little cross with cheerfulness,
A little selfdenial,
Will serve to make our troubles less,
And bear the greatest trial.
The Spirit, like a little dove,
On Jesus once descended;
To show his meekness and his love,
The emblem was intended.

The title of the little Lamb
Unto our Lord was given,
Such was our Savior's little name,
The Lord of earth and heaven.
A little voice that's small and still
Can rule the whole creation;
A little stone the earth shall fill
And humble every nation.

The song is found apparently only in the shape-note books of the Southeast.[1] Related tunes are 'Flower' and 'Judgment Day (A)' in this volume.[2]

[1] See SOH 62 and CHH 267.

[2] Other variants are Nos. 28, 29, and 30 in *Spiritual Folk-Songs*, where still further tune-comparative references are given.

No. 141

JUDGMENT DAY (A), REV 178

Hexatonic, mode 1 b (I II — IV V VI 7)

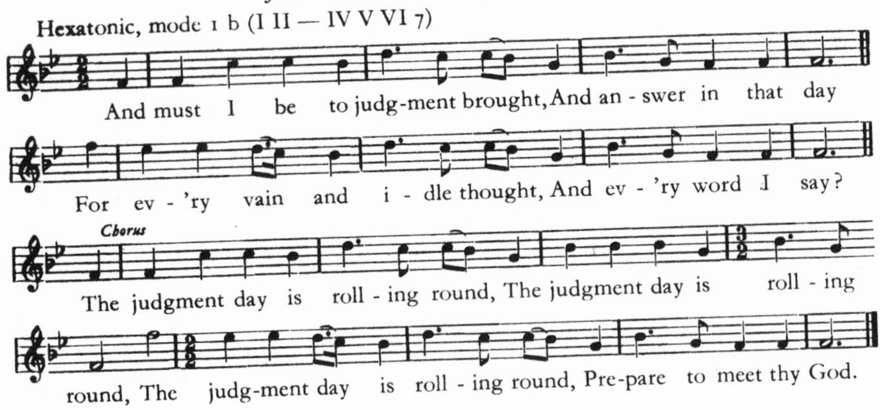
Chorus
And must I be to judg-ment brought, And an - swer in that day
For ev - 'ry vain and i - dle thought, And ev - 'ry word I say?
The judgment day is roll - ing round, The judgment day is roll - ing
round, The judg-ment day is roll - ing round, Pre-pare to meet thy God.

Yes, every secret of my heart
Shall shortly be made known,
And I receive my just desert
For all that I have done.
Chorus

How careful then ought I to live,
With what religious fear,
Who such a strict account must give
For my behavior here.

The text is by Charles Wesley, 1707–1788. Related tunes are given under 'Louisiana' in this volume.

No. 142

CONFIDENCE, SOH (1835) 33

Hexatonic, mode 3 b (I II III IV V VI —)

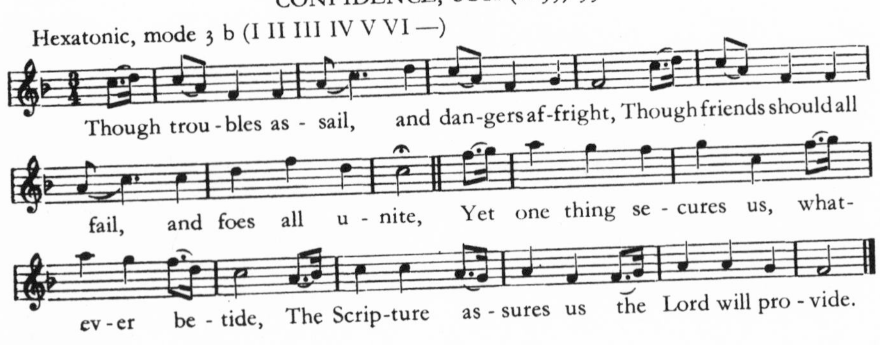
Though trou - bles as - sail, and dan-gers af-fright, Though friends should all
fail, and foes all u - nite, Yet one thing se - cures us, what-
ev - er be - tide, The Scrip-ture as - sures us the Lord will pro - vide.

The birds without barn or storehouse are fed;
From them let us learn to trust for our bread;
His saints, what is fitting shall ne'er be denied,
So long as 'tis written, the Lord will provide.

We may, like the ships, by tempests be toss'd
On perilous deeps, but cannot be lost;
Though Satan enrages the wind and the tide,
The promise engages, the Lord will provide.

When life sinks apace, and death is in view,
This word of his grace shall comfort us through;
No fearing or doubting with Christ on our side,
We hope to die shouting, "the Lord will provide."

Four stanzas more of the text by John Newton (1725–1807) in the *Southern Harmony.*

No. 143

ZION'S SOLDIERS, REV 66

Pentatonic, mode 2 (I — 3 IV V — 7)

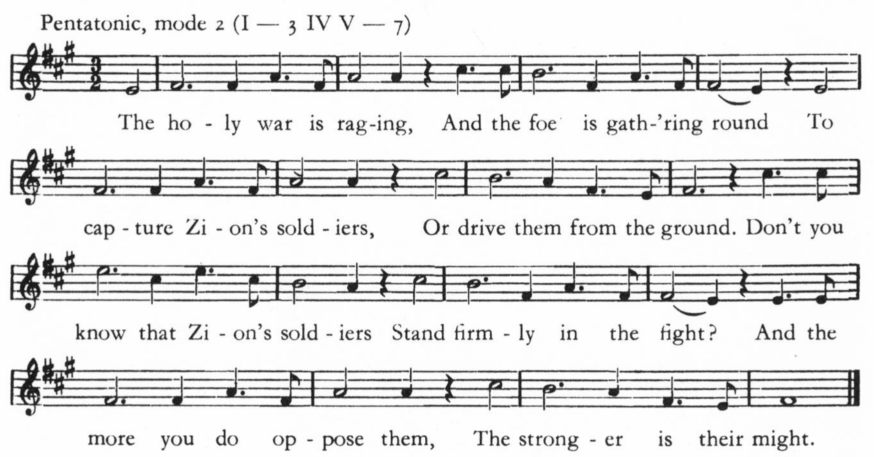
The ho - ly war is rag-ing, And the foe is gath-'ring round To
cap - ture Zi - on's sold - iers, Or drive them from the ground. Don't you
know that Zi - on's sold - iers Stand firm - ly in the fight? And the
more you do op - pose them, The strong - er is their might.

The alien army's moving,
And in terrible array,
With their sword of lying wonders,
They are bound to gain the day.
The foe steps quick and sprightly,
Like a spirit is their tramp;
But the roar of Judah's Lion
Throws terror in their camp.

We see the shining armor
Of the soldiers in the field,
And the holy courage on their brow
Seems to say they will not yield.
We read upon their banners,
In words of living light,
That one can chase a thousand,
And two, ten thousand fight.

I have revised the barring and time designation found in the *Revivalist*, which was impossibly confused.

No. 144

PEACE, REV 25

Pentatonic, mode 2 (I — 3 IV V — 7)

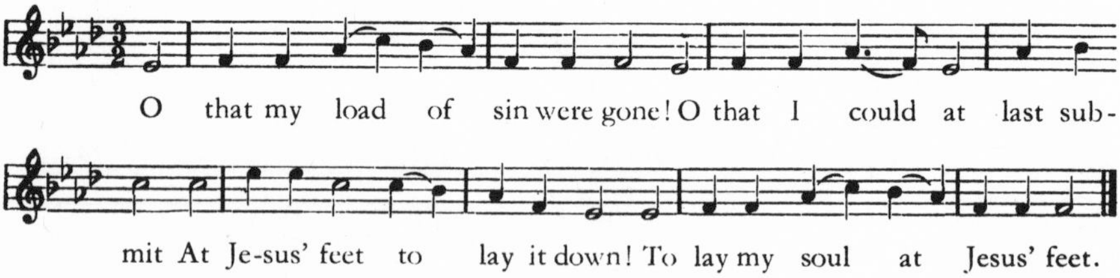

O that my load of sin were gone! O that I could at last submit At Je-sus' feet to lay it down! To lay my soul at Jesus' feet.

Rest for my soul I long to find;
Savior of all, if mine thou art,
Give me thy meek and lowly mind,
And stamp thine image on my heart.

Break off the yoke of inbred sin,
And fully set my spirit free;
I cannot rest till pure within,
Till I am wholly lost in thee.

Fain would I learn of thee, my God,
Thy light and easy burden prove;
The cross all stain'd with hallow'd blood,
The labor of thy dying love.

I would, but thou must give the pow'r;
My heart from every sin release;
Bring near, bring near the joyful hour,
And fill me with thy perfect peace.

Come, Lord, the drooping sinner cheer,
Nor let thy chariot wheels delay;
Appear, in my poor heart appear!
My God, my Savior, come away!

The text is by Charles Wesley, 1707–1788. The tune is built of thematic elements which appear in 'Bourbon'[1] and 'I Will Arise'.[2]

No. 145
HOW FIRM A FOUNDATION, UH 58

Pentatonic, mode 3 (I II III — V VI —)

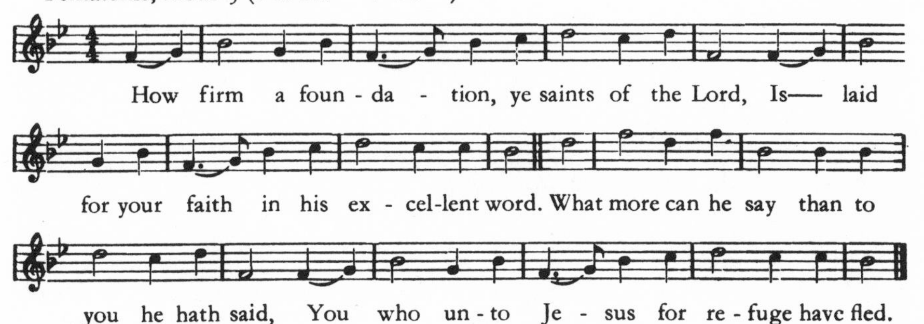
How firm a foun - da - tion, ye saints of the Lord, Is— laid
for your faith in his ex - cel-lent word. What more can he say than to
you he hath said, You who un - to Je - sus for re - fuge have fled.

In every condition, in sickness and health,
In poverty's vale, or abounding in wealth,
At home and abroad, on the land, on the sea,
As thy days may demand, shall their strength ever be.

Fear not, I am with thee, O be not dismay'd,
I, I am thy God, and will still give thee aid;
I'll strengthen thee, help thee, and cause thee to stand,
Upheld by my righteous, omnipotent hand.

The soul that on Jesus doth lean or repose,
I will not, I will not desert to his foes;
That soul, though all hell should endeavor to shake,
I'll never, no never, no never forsake.

For a discussion of the elusive sources of words and tune — the latter source being in the American folk-hymn environment — see McCutchan, p. 340ff. The tune is perhaps the most widely sung of any of the American folk-hymns. A variant is 'O Give Him Glory', in this volume.

[1] *Spiritual Folk-Songs*, No. 109.
[2] *Ibid.*, No. 239, where other tune-comparative references are given.

No. 146

NINETY-THIRD PSALM, OSH 31

Hexatonic, mode 3 A (I II III — V VI VII)

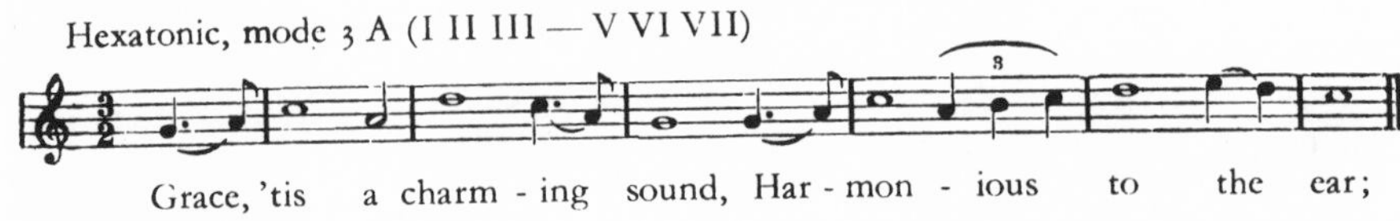
Grace, 'tis a charm - ing sound, Har - mon - ious to the ear;

Heav'n with the ech - o shall re - sound, And all the earth shall hear.

Grace first contrived the way
To save rebellious man;
And all the steps that grace display
Which drew the wondrous plan.

Grace taught my wand'ring feet
To tread the heav'nly road;
And new supplies each hour I meet,
While pressing on to God.

The well known text is by Philip Doddridge, 1702–1751. The tune appears widely in the southern shape-note song books where it is attributed to Chapin or Ingalls. Sometimes it is called a "Western Melody".[1] We need not be concerned with any of these source designations. It is clearly recognisable as an American folk-chorale of impressive native dignity. In considering it, ohne is reminded also of 'How Firm a Foundation' in this volume and 'Harmony Grove', (Grace 'tis a charming sound)[2] which match the above tune in dignified strength, hence in beauty.

No. 147

PROSPECT, OSH 30

Pentatonic, mode 3 (I II III — V VI —)

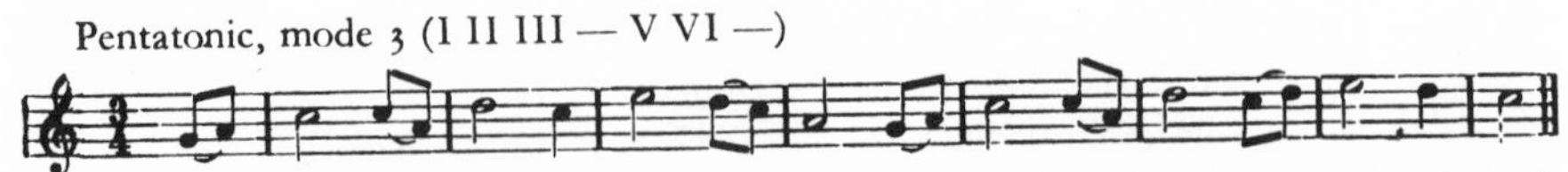
Why should we start and fear to die? What tim-'rous worms we mor-tals are!

Death is the gate to end - less joy, And yet we dread to en - ter there.

[1] For example, in the *Baptist Hymn and Tune Book*, 1857, p. 429.
[2] *Spiritual Folk-Songs*, No. 135.

The pains, the groans, the dying strife,
Fright our approaching souls away;
And we shrink back again to life,
Fond of our prison and our clay.

O if my Lord would come and meet,
My soul would stretch her wings in haste,
Fly fearless through death's iron gate,
Nor feel the terrors as she pass'd.

The poem is by Isaac Watts, 1674–1748. The tune is attributed in the southern shape-note song books to "Graham".

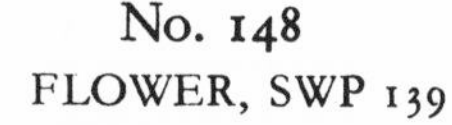

No. 148
FLOWER, SWP 139

Pentatonic, mode 1 (I II — IV V VI —)

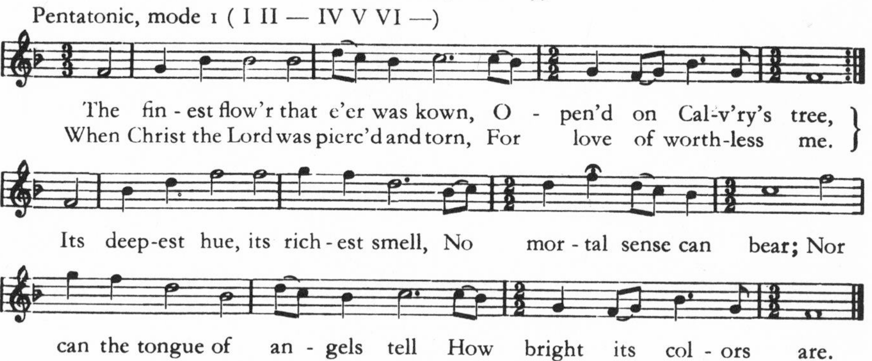
The fin - est flow'r that e'er was kown, O - pen'd on Cal-v'ry's tree,
When Christ the Lord was pierc'd and torn, For love of worth-less me.
Its deep-est hue, its rich - est smell, No mor - tal sense can bear; Nor
can the tongue of an - gels tell How bright its col - ors are.

Earth could not hold so rich a flow'r,
Nor half its beauties show;
Nor could the world and Satan's pow'r
Confine it here below.
On Canaan's banks supremely fair
This flow'r of wonder blooms,
Transplanted to its native air,
And all the shore perfumes.

But not to Canaan's shores confined,
The seeds which from it blow
Take root within the human mind,
And scent the church below.
Love is the sweetest bud that blows,
Its beauty never dies;
On earth among the saints it grows,
And ripens in the skies.

The song is attributed to David Walker. A key signature of two flats would seem more in keeping with the mixolydian implications of the tune. Related melodies are 'Louisiana' and 'Judgment Day (B)' in this volume. See the former for further references.

No. 149

CAROLINA, SWP 15

Hexatonic, mode 2 A (I II 3 IV V — 7)

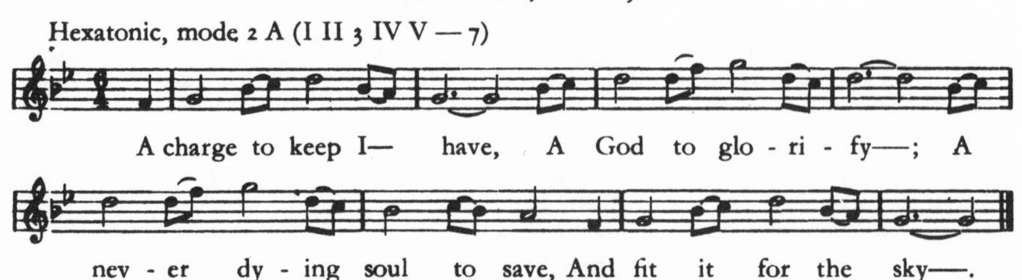
A charge to keep I— have, A God to glo - ri - fy—; A
nev - er dy - ing soul to save, And fit it for the sky—.

To serve the present age,
My calling to fulfil,
O may it all my pow'rs engage,
To do my Master's will.

Arm me with jealous care,
As in thy sight to live;
And O thy servant, Lord, prepare,
A strict account to give.

Help me to watch and pray,
And on thy self rely,
Assured, if I my trust betray,
I shall forever die.

The text is by Charles Wesley, 1707–1788.

No. 150

ROCKINGHAM, SOH (1854) 300

Heptatonic ionian, mode 3 (I II III IV V VI VII)

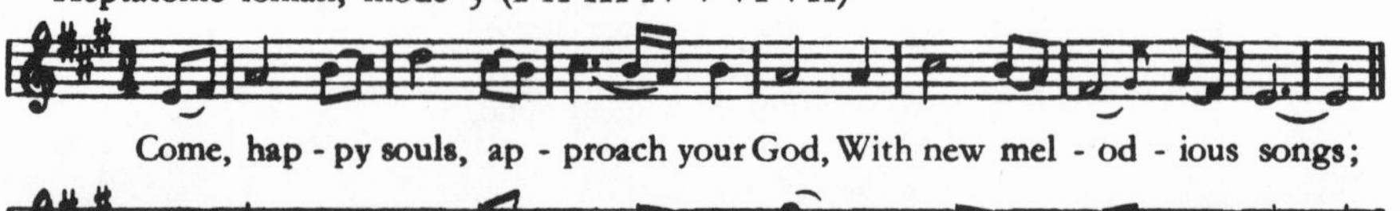
Come, hap - py souls, ap - proach your God, With new mel - od - ious songs;

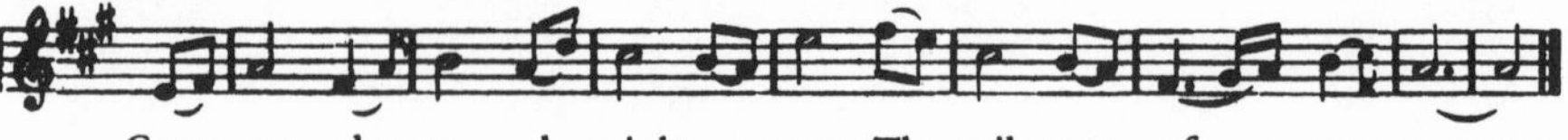

Come, ten - der to al - might - y grace The trib-utes of— your tongues.

So strange, so boundless was the love
That pitied dying men,
The Father sent his equal Son
To give them life again.

Thy hands, dear Jesus, were not arm'd
With a revenging rod;
No hard commission to perform
The vengeance of a God.

But all was mercy, all was mild,
And wrath forsook the throne,
When Christ on the kind errand came,
And brought salvation down.

The text is by Isaac Watts, 1674–1748. The tune is attributed in the southern song books regularly to "Chapin". In putting the tune into notation, William Walker, compiler of the *Southern Harmony*, recorded effectively the folk manner in singing.

No. 151

AVON, BS 60

Hexatonic, mode 3 b (I II III IV V VI —)

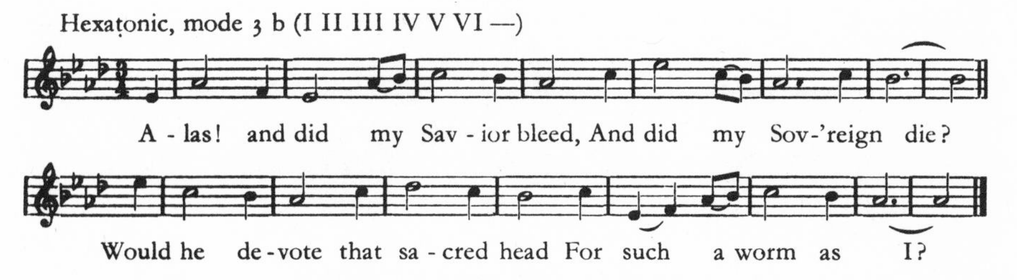
A - las! and did my Sav - ior bleed, And did my Sov-'reign die?
Would he de - vote that sa - cred head For such a worm as I?

Was it for crimes that I had done
He groan'd upon the tree?
Amazing pity! grace unknown!
And love beyond degree!

Well might the sun in darkness hide,
And shut his glories in,
When Christ, the great Creator, died
For man, the creature's sin.

Thus might I hide my blushing face
While his dear cross appears;
Dissolve my heart in thankfulness,
And melt my eyes to tears.

But drops of grief can ne'er repay
The debt of love I owe;
Here, Lord, I give myself away,
'Tis all that I can do.

The text is by Isaac Watts, 1674–1748. The tune, though often attributed to Hugh Wilson, 1764–1824, is "said to have been well known twenty-five years before its appearance in any book of .... tunes," according to McCutchan, No. 70. This would explain the oral-traditional or folk-singing influence which is evident in its structure.

No. 152

KINGWOOD, OSH 66

Pentatonic, cannot be classified (I II III — V — VII)

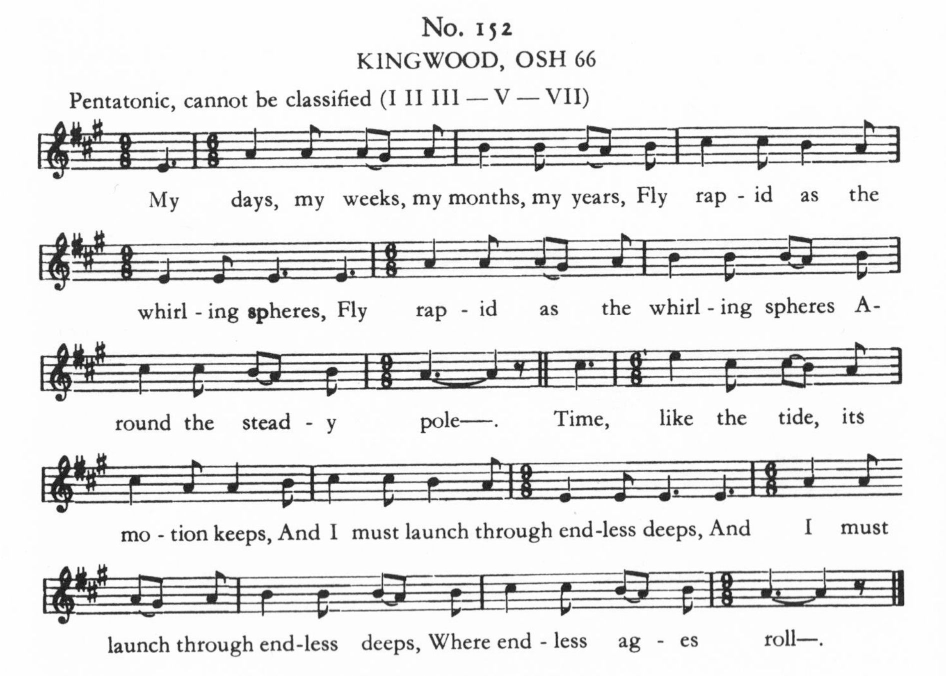
My days, my weeks, my months, my years, Fly rap - id as the
whirl - ing spheres, Fly rap - id as the whirl - ing spheres A-
round the stead - y pole—. Time, like the tide, its
mo - tion keeps, And I must launch through end-less deeps, And I must
launch through end-less deeps, Where end - less ag - es roll—.

The grave is near the cradle seen;
How swift the moments pass between,
And whisper as they fly.
Unthinking man, remember this,
Though fond of sublunary bliss,
That you must groan and die.

My soul, attend the solemn call,
Thine earthly tent must shortly fall,
And thou must take thy flight
Beyond the vast expansive blue,
To sing above as angels do,
Or sing in endless night.

The song is usually attributed, in the southern shape-note song books, to "Humphreys". Was it Joseph Humphreys, co-worker with George Whitefield? 'Lead Me to the Rock (B)' in this volume, is a variant tune.

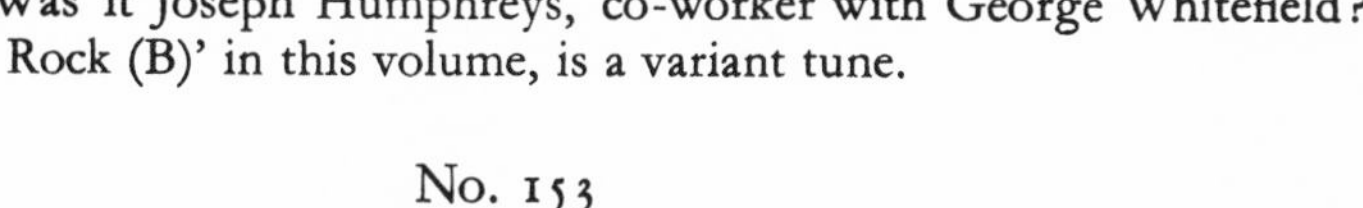

No. 153

LEAD ME TO THE ROCK (B), SOC 233

Hexatonic, cannot be classified, obviously ionian (I II II IV V — VII)

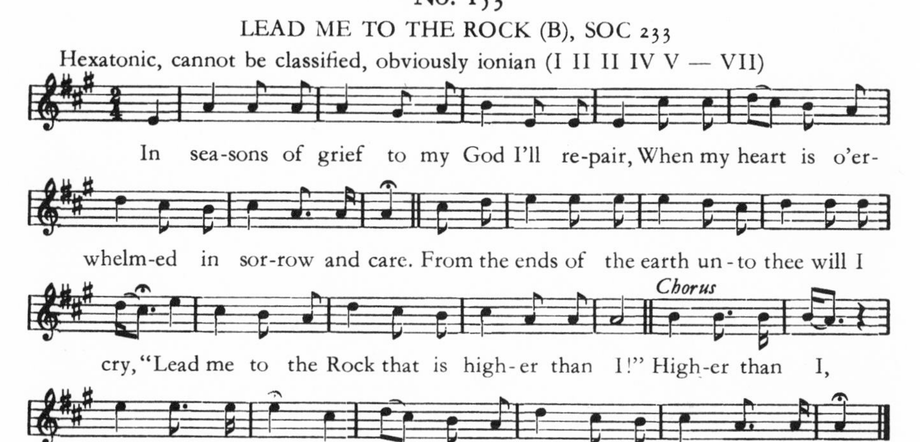
In sea-sons of grief to my God I'll re-pair, When my heart is o'er-
whelm-ed in sor-row and care. From the ends of the earth un-to thee will I
cry, "Lead me to the Rock that is high-er than I!" High-er than I,
Chorus
High - er than I; Lead me to the Rock that is high - er than I.

I furnish the following stanzas found in the *Hesperian Harp*, p. 312.

When Satan, my foe, comes in like a flood,
To drive my poor soul from the fountain so good,
I'll pray to the Savior who kindly did die:
"Lead me to the Rock that is higher than I!"
Chorus

And when I have ended my pilgrimage here,
In Jesus' pure righteousness let me appear:
From the swellings of Jordan to thee I will cry;
"Lead me to the Rock that is higher than I!"

And when the last trumpet shall sound through the skies
And the dead from the dust of the earth shall arise,
With millions I'll join, far above yonder sky,
To praise the great Rock that is higher than I

The text is, I suspect, a reconstruction from faulty memory of the verses used in this volume with 'Lead Me to the Rock (A)'. The tune reminds one of the student songs 'Here's to good old Yale, drink it down, drink it down' and 'The Deitch [deutsch] company is the best company'. 'Morality', a tune in this volume, has tonal and rhythmic similarities.

No. 154

DAY OF JUDGMENT, MH, ii, 28

Heptatonic mixolydian, mode 1 (I II III IV V VI 7)

Oh! the a - maz - ing pomp Of that tre-mend-ous day, When the arch-
an - gel's trump Shall sum - mon us a - way; When Christ to
judg-ment shall des-cend, And ev - ery knee be - fore him bend.

On a refulgent cloud
Jesus, the Judge, appears;
The saints rejoice aloud,
The guilty sinner fears.
On the white throne he takes his seat,
And views the myriads at his feet.

'Midst the vast multitude,
His eye omniscient sees
The purchase of his blood
And dying agonies.
Then calls them forth and bids them stand
With glory crown'd at his right hand.

"Come, souls forever blest,"
He says, "my people come,
Possess the promis'd rest,
Enter your heavenly home;
No more shall aught your peace annoy,
Inherit everlasting joy."

But in what awful sounds
The wicked are address'd!
Heaven with their groans resounds,
As on his left they're placed.
"Depart, ye curs'd," the Judge exclaims,
"To be destroy'd in burning flames!"

Oh! thou eternal God,
Ere this tremendous day,
Cleanse me in Jesus' blood,
Wash all my guilt away.
Then may I join the happy throng,
And praise thee in eternal song.

The colorful poetic picture, so nicely constructed, evidently the work of a poet of no mean gifts, was undoubtedly made for this tune alone. And the tune is of the folky sort; of this there seems no doubt, even though it possesses a deal of individuality. The three-measure length of phrase in the first part is a feature rarely seen in folk-tunes in America.

No. 155

MARSTON, HOC 131

Pentachordal (I II III IV V — —)

O gra-cious Lord of all, Thy lit - tle child-ren see,

And mer - ci - ful - ly call Our wand - 'ring hearts to thee.

O let thy pow'rful grace
Our souls' attention draw,
And on our mem'ries trace
Thy never changing law.

Appropriate to a children's song, this tune clings to that simplicity which is characteristic of what might be called youth-melodism and is widespread in the songs of various western nations. See for example the German student song 'Was kommt dort von der Höh'[1] and 'The Farmer in the Dell'.[2]

[1] Erk-Böhme, iii, 500.
[2] JAFL, xxxi, 158.

No. 156

INNOCENT SOUNDS, CHI 71

Heptatonic ionian, mode 3 (I II III IV V VI VII)

1
En - list - ed in the cause of sin, Why should a good be e - vil?
Mu- sic, a - las, too long has been Press'd to o - bey the

2
de - vil. Drunk-en or lewd or light the lay, Flows to their souls' un-

do - ing, Wid-en'd and strew'd with flowers the way, Down to e - ter-nal ru - in.

Who, on the part of God, will rise,
Innocent sounds recover;
Fly on the prey and seize the prize,
Plunder the carnal lover;
Strip him of every moving strain,
Of every melting measure;
Music in virtue's cause retain,
Risk the holy pleasure.

Come let us try if Jesus' love
Will not as well inspire us;
This is the theme of those above,
This upon earth should fire us.
Try if your hearts are tuned to sing,
Is there a subject greater?
Harmony all its strains may we bring,
Jesus'es name is sweeter.

Jesus the soul of music is,
His is the noblest passion;
Jesus'es name is life and peace,
Happiness and salvation.
Jesus'es name the dead can raise,
Show us our sins forgiven,
Fill us with all the life of his grace,
Carry us up to heaven.

Then let us in his praises join,
Triumph in his salvation,
Glory ascribe to love divine,
Worship and adoration.
Heaven already is begun,
Open'd to each believer,
Only believe, and still sing on,
Heaven is ours forever.

The first American appearance of this song, rationalizing the use of popular secular tunes in the religious environment, seems to have been in Ingalls' *Christian Harmony*, 1805.[1] In subsequent collections it was called 'Wesley's Music'. If the tune really bears out, as it seems to do, the theories of the maker of the text, it must have been plundered "from the carnal lover". But what "drunken or lewd or light" lay it was is unknown, even though it has the 'Barbara Allen' movement and reminds one somewhat of one of its tunes.[2]

No. 157

LONGING FOR JESUS, REV 386

Heptatonic ionian, mode 3 (I II III IV V VI VII)

O when shall I see Je - sus And dwell with him a - bove,
To drink the flow-ing foun - tain Of ev - er - last - ing love?
When shall I be de - liv - er'd From this vain world of
sin, And with my bless - ed Je - sus Drink end - less pleas-ures in.

The text is attributed to John Leland, 1754–1841, colorful Baptist preacher.[3] He was born in Massachusetts and died there, but his itinerant evangelical duties took him for fifteen years of his life (1776–1791) also into Pennsylvania, Virginia and North Carolina. The Leland story that has often been told is about the 1600-pound cheese: From his pulpit in Cheshire, Mass., Leland proposed that a giant cheese be made and presented to the newly elected president, Thomas

[1] *Cf.* 'Redeeming Love' in this volume for more about Ingalls and his book. See also the Illustration on p. 12.
[2] See Sharp-Karpeles, i, 183ff.
[3] See Illustration on p. 210.

Jefferson. Every Democrat who owned a cow was invited to bring all the curds of one day to a cider mill where it was to be made. "No Federal cow was allowed to furnish one drop of milk."

When the cheese was made, Leland offered a prayer and the people sang a hymn to the tune of 'Mear'. In the winter when the ground was covered with snow the bulky present was loaded onto a sleigh and Elder Leland drove it to Washington, 500 miles away. The trip took three weeks. Jefferson listened to Leland's speech of presentation, replied appropriately, had the cheese cut in the presence of the notable gathering and gave Leland a generous slice to take back to Cheshire, that its makers might have a taste.

The above hymn has been far-and-away the most widely sung — in its settings to scores of different tunes — of all the spiritual folk-texts. It was one of the favorites of Abraham Lincoln, according to his biographer, Herndon. It is given in full under 'Faithful Soldier' in *Spiritual Folk-Songs.*

No. 158

GARDEN HYMN, REV 164

Pentatonic, mode 3 (I II III — V VI —)

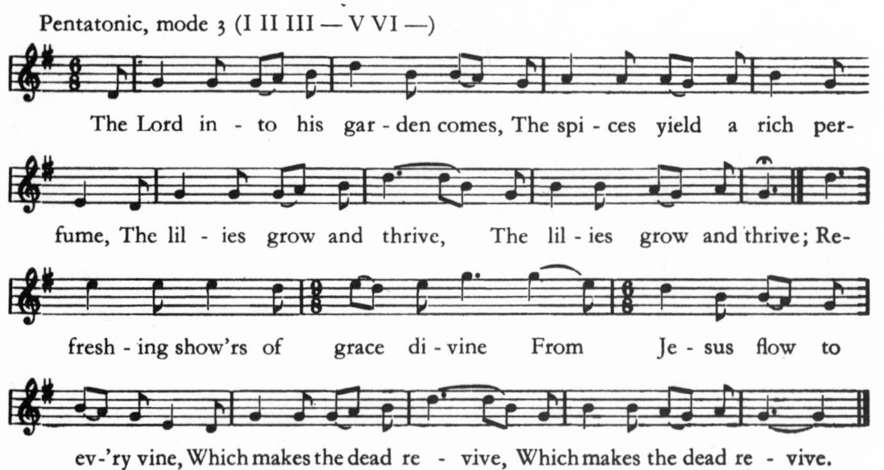
The Lord in - to his gar - den comes, The spi - ces yield a rich per-
fume, The lil - ies grow and thrive, The lil - ies grow and thrive; Re-
fresh - ing show'rs of grace di - vine From Je - sus flow to
ev-'ry vine, Which makes the dead re - vive, Which makes the dead re - vive.

The glorious time is rolling on,
The gracious work is now begun,
My soul a witness is.
I taste and see the pardon free,
For all mankind as well as me,
Who come to Christ may live.

We feel that heav'n is now begun,
It issues from a shining throne,
From Jesus' throne on high.
It comes like floods we can't contain,
We drink, and drink, and drink again,
And yet we still are dry.

Three more stanzas are given in the *Revivalist*. The text alone is found in *Hymns and Spiritual Songs* of the English Primitive Methodists, or "Ranters" as they were called, published about 1821, No. 31.[1]

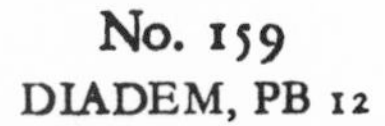

No. 159

DIADEM, PB 12

Hexatonic, mode 3 b (I II III IV V VI —)

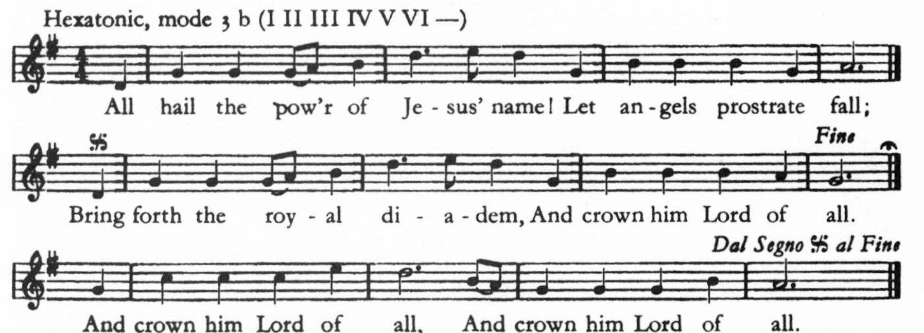
All hail the pow'r of Je - sus' name! Let an - gels prostrate fall;
Fine
Bring forth the roy - al di - a - dem, And crown him Lord of all.
Dal Segno al Fine
And crown him Lord of all, And crown him Lord of all.

Crown him, ye martyrs of our God,
Who from his altar call;
Extol the stem of Jesse's rod,
And crown him Lord of all.

Ye chosen seed of Israel's race,
A remnant weak and small,
Hail him who saves you by his grace,
And crown him Lord of all.

Ye Gentile sinners ne'er forget
The wormwood and the gall;
Go, spread your trophies at his feet,
And crown him Lord of all.

Two more stanzas of the text by Edward Perronet, 1726–1792, are in the *Revivalist*. There are tune resemblances to 'It's of a Pleasant Month of May'[2] and 'The Ploughboy's Dream'.[3]

[1] Tune and text are found also HSM 295 and CHI (1805) 63. Variant tunes are FHA, No. 7, with tune-comparative notes; and *Spiritual Folk-Songs*, No. 132.

[2] JFSS, i, 204. [3] *Ibid.*, ii, 203.

No. 160

GRATITUDE, UHH 16

Hexatonic, mode 3 b (I II III IV V VI —)

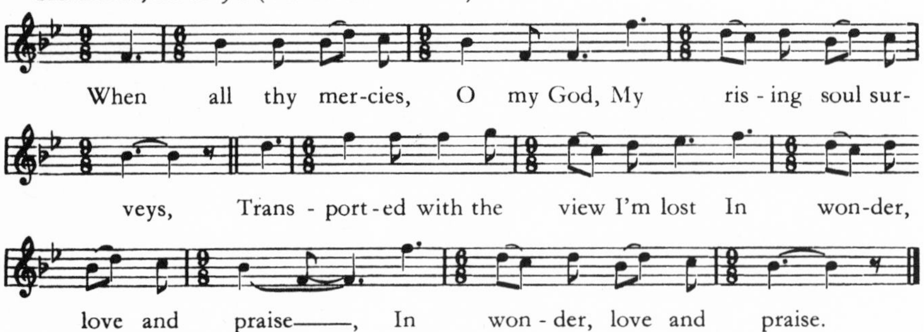
When all thy mer-cies, O my God, My ris - ing soul sur-
veys, Trans - port-ed with the view I'm lost In won-der,
love and praise——, In won - der, love and praise.

Further stanzas of the text by Joseph Addison, the noted English essayist and poet, 1672–1719, are given under 'Tender Care'.[1] Notable in the tune is the perfect alternation between six-eight and nine-eight measures, a feature which might be represented in a less cumbersome manner by uniform measures of fifteen eighth notes.

No. 161

CONCORD, UH 41

Hexatonic, mode 3 b (I II III IV V VI —)

Ye ob - jects of sense and en - joy - ments of time Which
of - ten de-light - ed my heart, I soon shall ex-change you for
views more sub-lime, For the joys that shall nev - er de - part.

Thou lord of the day, and thou queen of the night,
To me ye no longer are known;
I soon shall behold, with increasing delight,
A sun that shall never go down.

[1] *Spiritual Folk-Songs*, No. 121.

Ye wonderful orbs that astonish my eyes,
Your glories recede from my sight;
I soon shall contemplate more beautiful skies,
And stars more resplendently bright.

The text is by Benjamin Francis, 1734–1799. The tune was claimed by William Caldwell, compiler of the *Union Harmony*, and subsequent southern rural compilers who have used the song sustain his claim. That he recorded it from what he called "unwritten" music is probable. The tune, though in a major key, has some resemblance to the aeolian tunes 'Samarantha' and 'Exultation' in this volume.

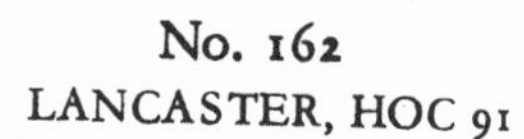

No. 162
LANCASTER, HOC 91

Heptatonic ionian, mode 3 (I II III IV V VI VII)

O glo-rious hope of per - fect love, It lifts me up to
things a-bove, It lifts me up to things a - bove, It
bears on ea - gles' wings; It gives my rav - ish'd
soul a taste, And makes me for some mo - ments feast, And makes me
for some mo - ments feast With Je - sus, priests and kings.

Rejoicing now in earnest hope,
I stand and from the mountain top
See all the land below;
Rivers of milk and honey rise,
And all the fruits of Paradise
In endless plenty grow.

A land of corn and wine and oil,
Favor'd with God's peculiar smile;
With every blessing blest;
There dwells the Lord of righteousness,
And keeps his own in perfect peace
And everlasting rest.

The text is by Charles Wesley, 1707–1788. The tune is related to 'The Mulberry Bush',[1] 'Lazy Mary',[2] and 'Romans and English'[3] — all children's game songs. The Welsh children have songs of similar character in 'The Kind Old Man'[4] and 'Cysga di'.[5] Compare also 'Sunny Bank' in this volume, a closely related tune with a childlike carol text.

No. 163

SOLICITUDE, VSM 31

Heptatonic ionian, mode 3 (I II III IV V VI VII)

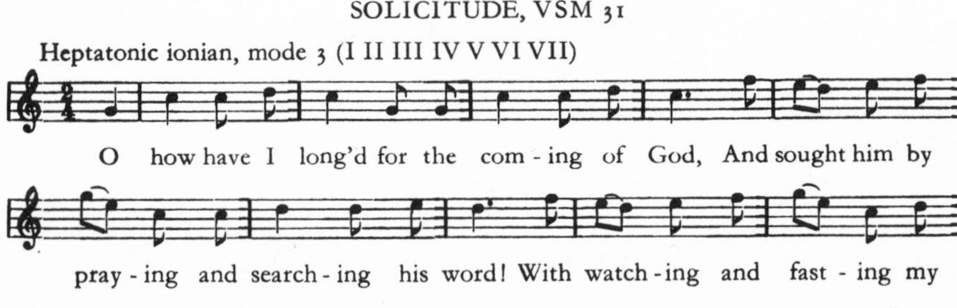
O how have I long'd for the com - ing of God, And sought him by
pray - ing and search - ing his word! With watch - ing and fast - ing my
a
soul was op-press'd, Nor could I give o - ver till Je - sus had bless'd.

For this hymn, whose source I have not found, the Virginia compiler took a secular folk-tune which is still sung in that region. It is 'The Brown Girl' or 'Pretty Polly' which I heard Mrs. Nancy Baldwin sing beautifully at the White Top Folk Festival in Virginia in the summer of 1933. The difference between Mrs. Baldwin's variant and the tune above lies chiefly in the part from *a* on. To make this difference clear I shall give that part of the 'Brown Girl' in a recording, from the same singer, made by Winston Wilkinson.

And her beau - ty were more than her wealth at the best.[6]

[1] Newell, p. 86. [2] JAFL, xxviii, 273. [3] JFSS, iv, 68.
[4] JWF, i, 84. [5] *Ibid.*, iii, 24ff.
[6] From Mr. Wilkinson's manuscript collection of folk-songs, book viii, p. 258. Used here with his kind permission.

A Kentucky variant of 'The Brown Girl' and 'Solicitude' is in Sharp-Karpeles.[1] Related tunes in the British Isles are 'Drink Old England Dry'[2], 'The Earl o' Aboyne',[3] and 'The Yellow Beggar of the League'.[4] Further occurrences of the 'Solicitude' tune, but with different texts, in American collections are Ingalls' *Christian Harmony*, p. 60, and *Southern Harmony* (1835), p. 69.

No. 164

HYMN OF VARIETIES, RHD 53

Heptatonic ionian, mode 3 (I II III IV V VI VII)

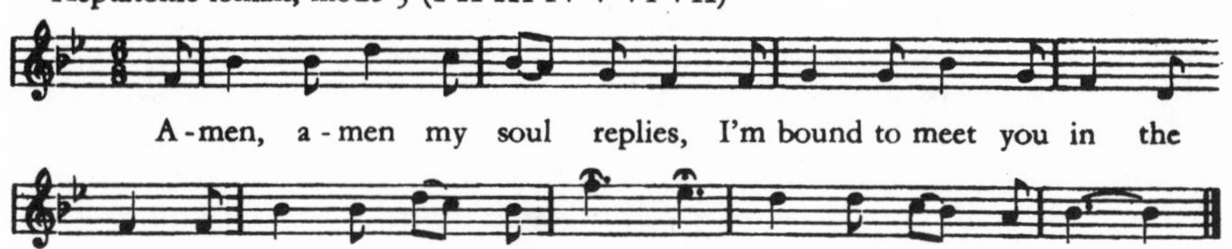
A-men, a-men my soul replies, I'm bound to meet you in the
skies, Where we shall part no more, Where we shall part no more.

Pray on, pray on *(or)* } my brethren now,
Speak on, speak on, }
Before Jehovah's throne we'll bow,
We soon shall meet above, *etc.*

(A verse to be sung after some one has related his trials)

Our conflicts here will soon be o'er,
We then shall meet on Canaan's shore,
And shout redeeming love, *etc.*

(A verse to be sung after one has asked prayers)

O Lord, thy gracious aid impart,
To sanctify and seal his (her) heart
And save his (her) soul in heaven, *etc.*

(A verse to be sung after an exhortation)

O Lord thy quick'ning grace bestow,
To save these souls from guilt and wo,
And bring them home to heaven, *etc.*

(The same)

[1] Vol. i, p. 304. See also JAFL, xxviii, 275.
[2] JDSS, iii, 126.
[3] Greig-Keith, p. 182.
[4] JIFS, xix, 33.

Thy power reveal to bless thy word,
And magnify thy truth, O Lord,
Nor let us hear in vain, *etc.*

In all the song books of rural America this "hymn" seems to be unique. One must not make the mistake of interpreting it as indicating any *formal* practice like those tonal responses which follow sermon and prayer in urban church services. It is probably rather an echo of the *informal precursors* of such practices. To be sure, the early typical revival atmosphere of which this was apparently a part cannot be known. We may however get a fairly clear idea of it if we observe southern country negro practices of the same sort today. There we see the efforts of preachers, pray-ers, exhorters and singers overlapping in time, aim and means. Preachers, pray-ers and exhorters all sing or near-sing; and singers preach and exhort, and all at the same time, sometimes one phase sometimes the other standing out. Assuming that this is a borrowing and a survival, we may picture a similar free-for-all among the white folk of olden times, and we may interpret the above hymn as perhaps a first step away from its confusion.

No. 165

PRIMROSE, OSH 47

Hexatonic, mode 3 b (I II III IV V VI —)

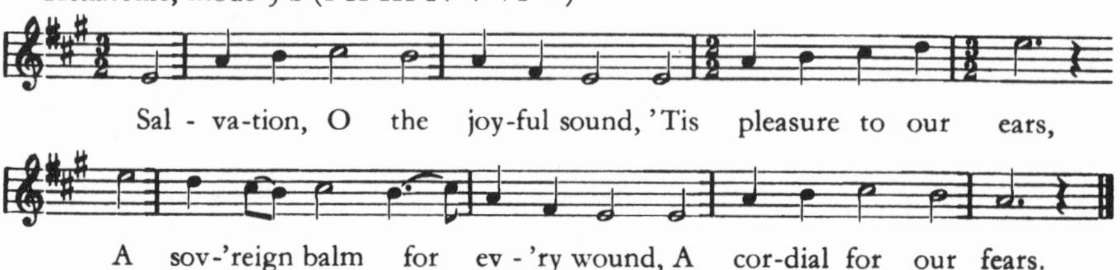
Sal - va-tion, O the joy-ful sound, 'Tis pleasure to our ears,
A sov-'reign balm for ev - 'ry wound, A cor-dial for our fears.

Buried in sorrow and in sin,
At hell's dark door we lay;
But we arise by grace divine,
To see the heav'nly day.

Salvation, let the echo fly
The spacious earth around;
While all the armies of the sky
Conspire to raise the sound.

The poem is by Isaac Watts, 1674–1748. The tune, usually with this text, appears in most of the southern rural song books. It is ascribed most often to the elusive "Chapin",[1] but in some books it is given as an anonymous "Western Melody". It is a variant of 'Harmony Grove';[2] and both these tunes show the melodic framework which reappears in the negro 'Swing Low'. 'Longing for Home' in this volume is a florid treatment of the same melodic pattern.

No. 166

LONGING FOR HOME, CH 95

Pentatonic, mode 3 (I II III — V VI —)

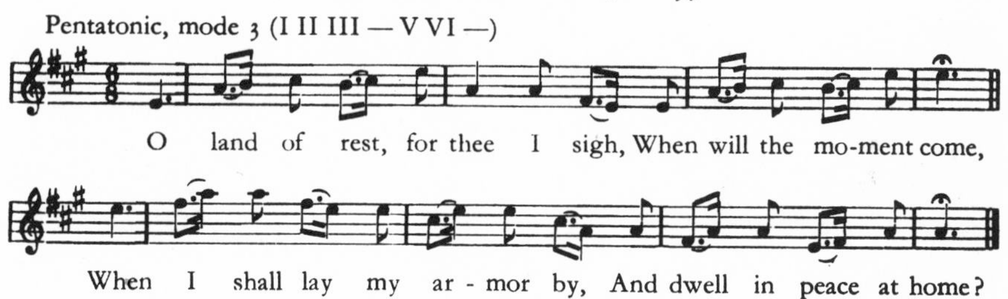
O land of rest, for thee I sigh, When will the mo-ment come,
When I shall lay my ar - mor by, And dwell in peace at home?

No tranquil joys on earth I know,
No peaceful sheltering dome,
This world's a wilderness of woe,
This world is not my home.

To Jesus Christ I fled for rest;
He bade me cease to roam,
And lean for succor on his breast,
And he'd conduct me home.

The second and third stanzas were supplied from *Bible Songs*, No. 373. The source of the text is unknown,[3] excepting for the name "McLain"which is given in *Church Harmony*. The tune is a member of the 'Lord Lovel' family, to which further references are given under 'Eden' in this volume. Annabel Morris Buchanan also gives copious references[4] and a variant of the beautiful tune, her No. 22. In one of her Notes she points out the resemblance between her tune and the negroes' 'Swing Low Sweet Chariot', a resemblance which can be seen clearly in the above tune, and even more clearly in 'Zion's Hill' and 'I hope to Gain the Promised Land' in this volume. The bare skeleton of the tune, stripped of its ornament and left with its straightforward trend, becomes 'Primrose', the foregoing song in this volume.

[1] See 'Vernon' in this volume.
[2] *Spiritual Folk-Songs*, No. 135.
[3] But see 'Eden' in this volume.
[4] FHA, p. xxi.

No. 167

CHRISTIAN'S HOPE, SOH (1835) 74

Hexatonic, mode 3b (I II III IV V VI —)

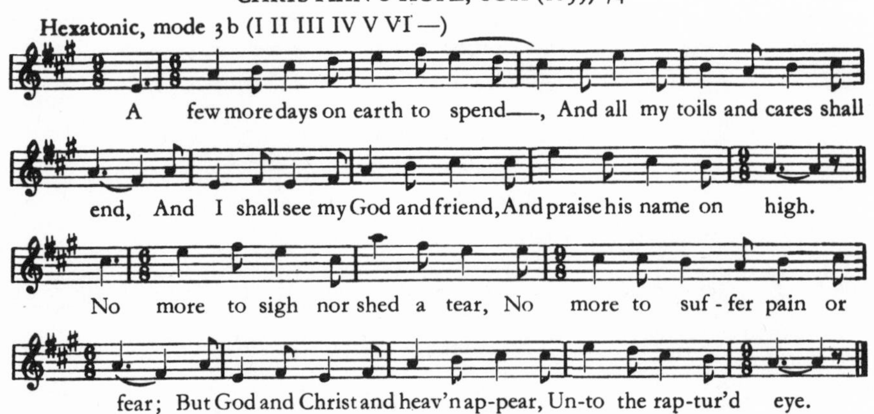
A few more days on earth to spend—, And all my toils and cares shall
end, And I shall see my God and friend, And praise his name on high.
No more to sigh nor shed a tear, No more to suf - fer pain or
fear; But God and Christ and heav'n ap-pear, Un-to the rap-tur'd eye.

Then, O my soul, despond no more;
The storm of life will soon be o'er,
And I shall find the peaceful shore
Of everlasting rest.
O happy day! O joyful hour!
When, freed from earth, my soul shall tow'r
Beyond the reach of Satan's pow'r
To be forever blest.

Three stanzas omitted.

Adieu, ye scenes of noise and show,
And all this region here below,
Where nought but disappointments grow,
A better world's in view.
My Savior calls! I haste away,
I would not here forever stay;
Hail! ye bright realms of endless day,
Vain world, once more adieu!

The text is of the revival-romping sort which, in picturing the end of the world so vivivdly and ecstatically, must have stirred "sinners" powerfully. Many of these iambic-tetrametric rhyme triplets, after being reduced to two lines, went their way, joining other tunes right and left in their function of what we have called "wandering rhyme pairs".[1]

The tune is a corking one! It surprizes and delights one with its variety of phrase structure and its melodic sweep. John Powell has shown his enthusiasm for the air by incorporating it in an operetta which is to appear soon.

[1] *Cf.* 'Satan's Kingdom' in this volume.

No. 168

REEDEMING LOVE, CHI 69

Heptatonic ionian, mode uncertain (I II III IV V VI VII)

O now be - gin thy heav'n - ly theme, Come sing a - loud in
Je - sus' name; Come you who Je - sus' kind - ness prove, Come tri - umph
in re - deem - ing love; Come you, a - las! who - e'er have
been The wil - ling slaves of death and sin; Come now from
bliss no long - er rove, Stop, stop and taste re - deem - ing love.

Come mourning souls, dry up your tears,
And banish all your guilty fears;
And see the guilt secure remov'd,
'Tis cancell'd by redeeming love.

Come welcome all by sin oppress,
Come welcome to his sacred rest;
There's nothing brought him from above,
Nothing but true redeeming love.

'Tis he subdues th'infernal pow'rs,
And his tremendous foes are ours;
Our foes are from his empire drove;
He's mighty in redeeming love.

This song appeared in Jeremiah Ingalls' Vermont song book, the *Christian Harmony*, 1805, and there only, as it seems. Both tune and words are apparently anonymous. The character of the tune is as far from that which is usually considered "spiritual" as one can imagine. We are safe in assuming that Ingalls took it bodily from its proper traditional dance habitat and fitted it to this text; this we assume despite our inability to find any related tune of the worldly sort.[1]

Nor does the tune stand alone in its class in the collection of this Vermonter. There are a number of other melodies filled with a joy of life which is not religious. 'Separation', reproduced in the present volume, is one of them. The conviction is unavoidable, after singing these romping tunes, that Ingalls was a musical dare-devil. It is evident that he was the first in this land to dare put between the covers of a book those capering songs which others had had the courage merely to sing. It is significant that there was no second edition of this probably too early book.[2] Many years elapsed before any New Englander had the temerity to follow his example. The southern songsters were the next to print such tunes; and in the meantine many of Ingalls' best melodies, including the one above, disappeared from singing tradition.

No. 169

CONTRITE HEART, WHM 50

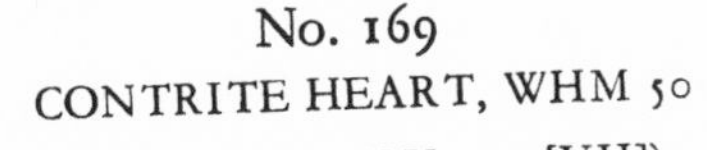

Hexatonic, mode 2 A, minorized (I II 3 IV V — 7 [VII])

O thou whose ten - der mer - cy hears Con - tri - tion's hum-ble
sigh, Whose hand in - dul - gent wipes the tear From ev - 'ry weep - ing
eye, Whose hand in-dul-gent wipes the tear From ev - 'ry weep-ing eye.

See, low before thy throne of grace,
A wretched wanderer mourn,
Hast thou not bid me seek thy face?
Hast thou not said — return?

And shall my guilty fears prevail,
To drive me from thy feet?
O let not this dear refuge fail,
This only safe retreat.

[1] John Powell sees resemblances in the tune to 'Maiden Lane', Sharp's *Country Dances*, Set v, No. 15. Miss Anne G. Gilchrist finds in it phrases of 'Freemason's March' and 'Boyne Water'. But no one has identified it as a whole tune.

[2] See Illustration on page 2 of this volume.

Absent from thee, my guide, my light,
Without one cheering ray,
Through dangers, fears and gloomy night,
How desolate my way!

O shine on this benighted heart,
With beams of mercy shine;
And let thy healing voice impart
A taste of joys divine.

Thy presence only can bestow
Delights which never cloy;
Be this my comfort here below,
And my eternal joy.

The text is ascribed to Anne Steele, 1717–1778, and the tune to "Austin".

No. 170

SOMETIMES A LIGHT SURPRISES, CL, i, 136

Heptatonic aeolian, mode 2 (I II 3 IV V 6 7)

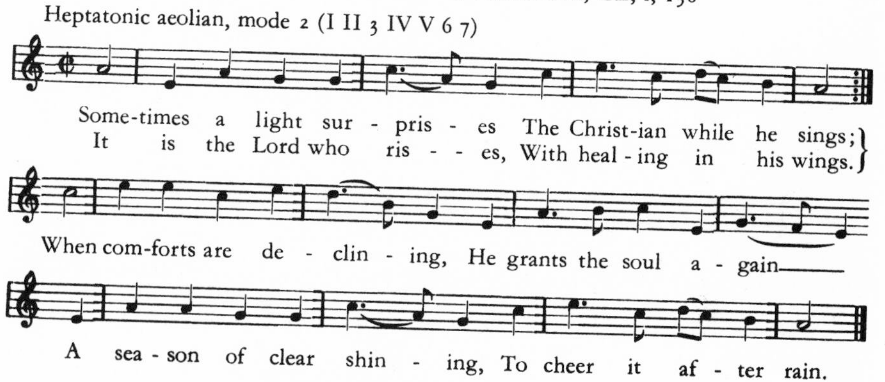
Some-times a light sur - pris - es The Christ-ian while he sings;
It is the Lord who ris - - es, With heal - ing in his wings.
When com-forts are de - clin - ing, He grants the soul a - gain
A sea - son of clear shin - ing, To cheer it af - ter rain.

In holy contemplation,
We sweetly then pursue
The theme of God's salvation,
And find it ever new.
Set free from present sorrow,
We cheerfully can say,
Let the unknown tomorrow
Bring with it what it may.

It can bring with it nothing,
But he will bear us through; —
Who gives the lilies clothing,
Will clothe his people too.

Beneath the spreading heavens,
No creature but is fed;
And he who feeds the ravens
Will give his children bread.

Though vine nor fig-tree, neither
Their wonted fruit shall bear,
Though all the fields should wither,
Nor flocks nor herds be there;
Yet God, the same abiding,
His praise shall tune my voice;
For while in him confiding,
I cannot but rejoice.

The text is by William Cowper, 1731–1800. A variant tune is 'Marion'.[1] Miss Anne G. Gilchrist points out also its relationship to the English traditional tune 'Stormy Winds' which is the same as 'Valiant Lady' and 'Gosterwood', a hymn tune.[2]

No. 171

SWAIN, SKH 146

Hexatonic, mode 4 A (I II — IV V VI 7)

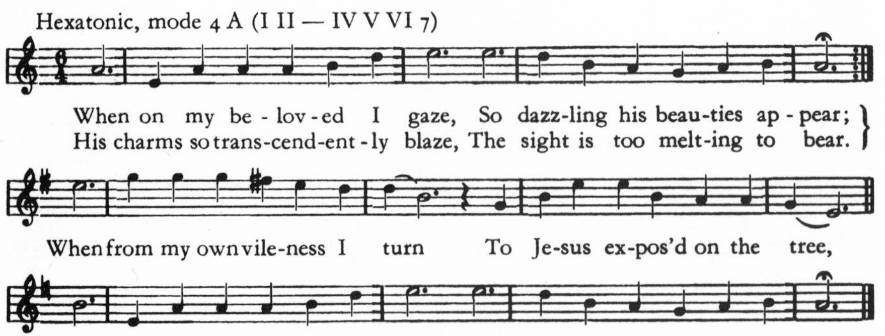
When on my be - lov - ed I gaze, So dazz-ling his beau-ties ap - pear;
His charms so trans-cend-ent - ly blaze, The sight is too melt-ing to bear.
When from my own vile-ness I turn To Je-sus ex-pos'd on the tree,
With shame and with won-der I burn, To think how he suf-fer'd for me.

My sins O how black they appear,
When in that dear bosom they meet;
Those sins were the nail and the spear,
That wounded his hands, side, and feet.
'Twas justice that weav'd for his head
The thorns that encircled it round;
Thy temples, Immanuel, bled,
That mine might with glory be crown'd.

[1] *Spiritual Folk-Songs*, No. 38, where further tune-comparative references are given.
[2] JFSS, viii, 95.

The wonderful love of his heart,
Where he has recorded my name,
On earth can be known but in part,
Heav'n only can bear the full flame.
In rivers of sorrow it flow'd,
And flow'd in those rivers for me;
My sins are all wash'd in his blood,
My soul is both happy and free.

Ananias Davisson, compiler of the *Supplement to the Kentucky Harmony*, signed the tune. He solved the problem — the shape-note book compilers looked on it as such — of fitting this clearly dorian tune into the major-minor mould by modulation; that is, by keying the first and last melodic sentences, from which the disturbing raised sixth was absent, in the natural minor on *a*; and the middle part, in which the raised sixth (*f*-sharp) *did* appear, in the natural key.

No. 172

HAPPY MAN, MH, ii, 32

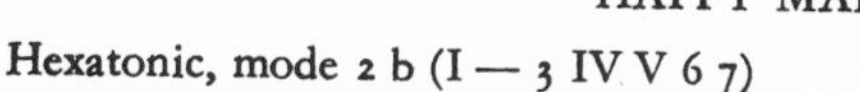
Hexatonic, mode 2 b (I — 3 IV V 6 7)

How hap-py is the man, Who has cho - sen wis-dom's ways, And
(D.C.) In pov-er - ty he's happy, For he knows he has a friend Who

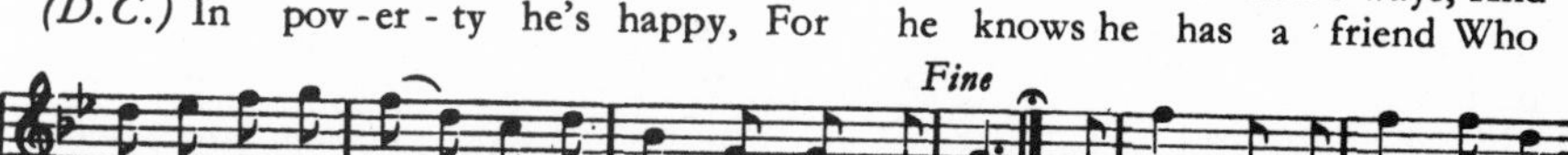
Fine
meas-ur'd out his span To his God in pray'r and praise.
nev-er will for-sake him, And on whom he can de-pend.
His God and his Bi - ble Are

Da Capo al Fine
all that he de-sires; To hol - i-ness of heart and life He con-stant-ly as-pires.

He rises in the morning,
With the lark he tunes his lays,
And offers up a tribute
To his God in prayer and praise;
And then unto his labor
He cheerfully repairs,
In confidence believing
His God will hear his prayers.
Whatever he engages in,
At home or far abroad,
His object is to honor
And to glorify his God.

Three more stanzas are in the *Millennial Harp*. John Powell calls my attention to the tune's relationship to 'Weevily Wheat', a play-party song;[1] and Winston Wilkinson adds the variants, 'Wha'll be King but Charlie,[2] 'The Highland Watch',[3] and 'The American War'.[4] All are, like the one above, excellent tunes. In the *Golden Harp*[5] the tune varies according to the small notes in the first staff above.

No. 173

REPOSE, SOH (1835) 131

Heptatonic aeolian, mode 4 (I II 3 IV V 6 7)

The Lamb ap-pears to wipe our tears, And to com-plete our
glo - ry; Then we shall rest with all the blest, And tell the
love - ly sto - ry. To sit and tell Christ lov'd us
well, And that when we were sin - ners; Heav - en will ring while
saints do sing, "Glo - - ry to the Re - - deem - er."

William Walker's choice of this tune for his hymn of consolation was a happy one, this even though the metrical misfit is evident in some places. Robert Burns was so deeply impressed with the tune's beauty that he embodied it with his lovely lament for his dead loved one, Mary Campbell, and thus gave the world his song 'Highland Mary'. Whittier praised this song in his lines

> Give lettered pomp to teeth of time,
> So 'Bonnie Doon' but tarry;
> Blot out the epics' stately rhyme,
> But spare his 'Highland Mary'.

[1] Winston Wilkinson's manuscript collection of folk-songs, iii, 67. See also Sandburg, p. 161.
[2] Pittman, Brown, and Mackay, Vol. i, p. 198.
[3] *Ibid.*, p. 204.
[4] *Ibid.*, vol. ii, p. 154.
[5] P. 129.

Burns said, "You will see at first glance that it [the poem] suits the air." I give here a part of the Burns tune for purposes of comparison.[1]

etc.

Ye banks and braes, and streams a-round The cas - tle o' Mont-gom-er - y

The Scottish tune has an Irish forebear in 'Catherine Ogie'.[2] The Walker variant above is reminiscent of the 'Babe of Bethlehem' tune formula.[3] Miss Anne G. Gilchrist calls attention to a related tune in *Richard Weaver's* (English Primitive Methodist) *Tune Book* associated with a 'Good Old Way' text. Another beautiful one is 'Edenton'[4] whose text begins:

> Keep silent, all created things,
> And wait your Maker's nod.

No. 174

CONFIDENCE IN GOD, SWP 91

Hexatonic, mode 2 A (I II 3 IV V — 7)

Be - gone, un - be - lief! my Sav - ior is near, And for my re-

lief will sure - ly ap - pear; By prayer let me wres - tle, and

he will per - form; With Christ in the ves - sel, I smile at the storm.

The fuller text, with a different tune, is 'Be Gone Unbelief', *Spiritual Folk-Songs*, No. 117. The following song has a variant tune.

[1] Found in *Our Familiar Songs*, p. 359. See also *Lyric Gems of Scotland*, p. 118.
[2] JIFS, ii, 22.
[3] See 'Old Israelites' in this volume.
[4] *Supplement to the Kentucky Harmony*, p. 136.

No. 175

CHILD OF GRACE, KNH 74

Hexatonic, mode 2 A (I II 3 IV V — 7)

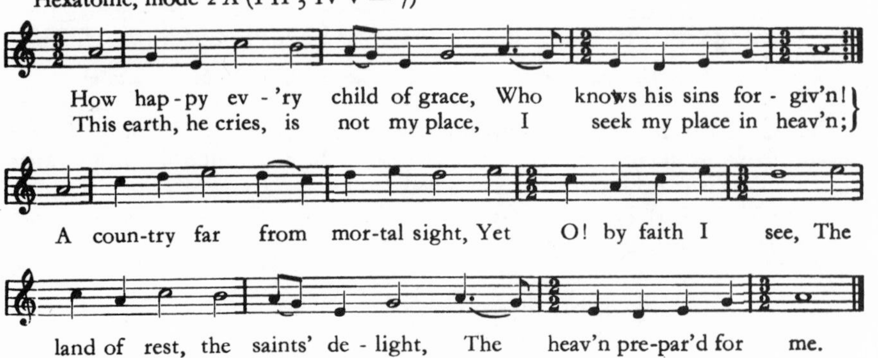
How hap-py ev - 'ry child of grace, Who knows his sins for - giv'n!
This earth, he cries, is not my place, I seek my place in heav'n;
A coun-try far from mor-tal sight, Yet O! by faith I see, The
land of rest, the saints' de - light, The heav'n pre-par'd for me.

O what a blessed hope is ours!
While here on earth we stay,
We more than taste the heavenly powers,
And antedate that day.
We feel the resurrection near,
Our life in Christ conceal'd,
And with his glorious presence here
Our earthen vessels fill'd.

O would he more of heav'n bestow!
And let the vessels break;
And let our ransom'd spirits go,
To grasp the God we seek;
In rapt'rous awe on him to gaze,
Who bought the sight for me,
And shout and wonder at his grace
To all eternity.

The author of the text is Charles Wesley, 1707–1788. The tonal trend is of that typical sort, a tune idiom, which led many of the southern rural song book compilers honestly to claim this tune as their own. This particular form of the tune was claimed for example by John B. Jackson in his *Knoxville Harmony* and by E. J. King, co-compiler of the earliest *Sacred Harp*. The preceding song here has a variant tune.

No. 176

SALVATION, UVW 161

Heptatonic dorian, mode 2 (I II 3 IV V VI 7)

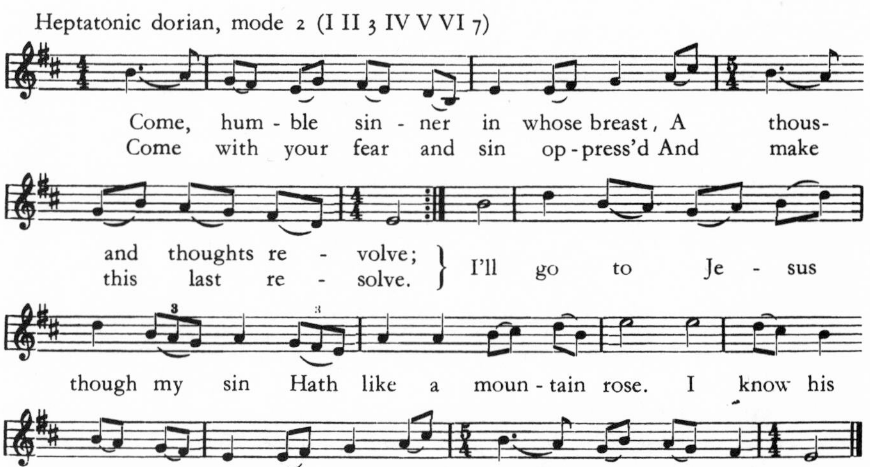
Come, hum - ble sin - ner in whose breast, A thous-
Come with your fear and sin op - press'd And make
and thoughts re - volve;
this last re - solve.
I'll go to Je - sus
though my sin Hath like a moun - tain rose. I know his
courts, I'll en - ter in, What - ev - er may op - pose.

The song was recorded by Winston Wilkinson in Standardsville, Virginia, November 9, 1935, from the singing of Z. B. Lam. It is No. 161 of the *University of Virginia* (manuscript) *Collection of Folk-Music* and is used here by kind permission.

The rest of the text by Edmund Jones, 1722–1765, is given under 'Lover of the Lord' in this volume. The tune is a variant of 'Salvation (B)' in *Spiritual Folk-Songs*. A comparison of the two tunes shows interesting disparities between the oral tradition, as represented by the above air, and the tune-book version of a century ago. One of those differences is in mode; the above being dorian, and the song-book tune aeolian, possibly aeolianized by its compiler.

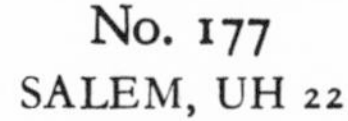

No. 177

SALEM, UH 22

Heptatonic aeolian, mode 4 (I II 3 IV V 6 7)

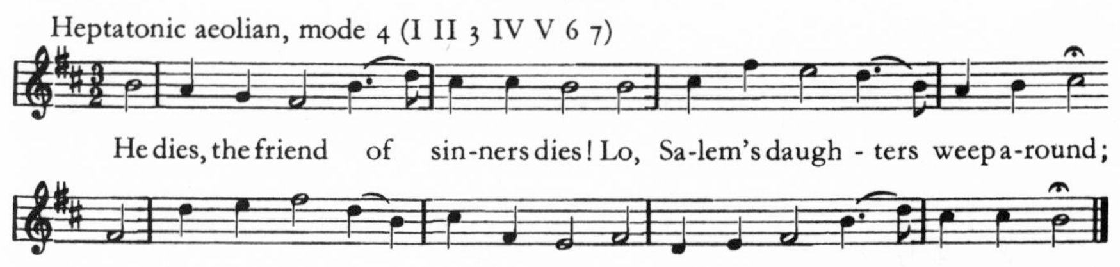
He dies, the friend of sin-ners dies! Lo, Sa-lem's daugh - ters weep a-round;
A sol-emn dark - ness veils the skies, A sud-den trem-bling shakes the ground.

Here's love and grief beyond degree —
The Prince of glory dies for men;
But lo! what sudden joys we see!
Jesus, the dead, revives again.
The rising King forsakes his tomb,
Up to his Father's court he flies;
Cherubic legions guard him home,
And shout him welcome to the skies.

Break off your tears, ye saints, and tell
How high your great Deliv'rer reigns;
Sing how he spoiled the hosts of hell,
And led the monster Death in chains.
Say, "Live forever, wondrous King!
Born to redeem, and strong to save;"
Then ask the monster, "Where's thy sting?"
And "Where's thy vict'ry, boasting grave?"

The text is by Isaac Watts, 1674–1748. The tune is ascribed in the southern rural books to "Bovelle". Related tunes are 'A Brisk Young Sailor'[1] and an 'ancient Herefordshire tune' in the *Episcopal Hymnal* (Hutchins).[2]

No. 178

ARISE MY SOUL, GOS 664

Heptatonic aeolian, mode 4 (I II 3 IV V 6 7)

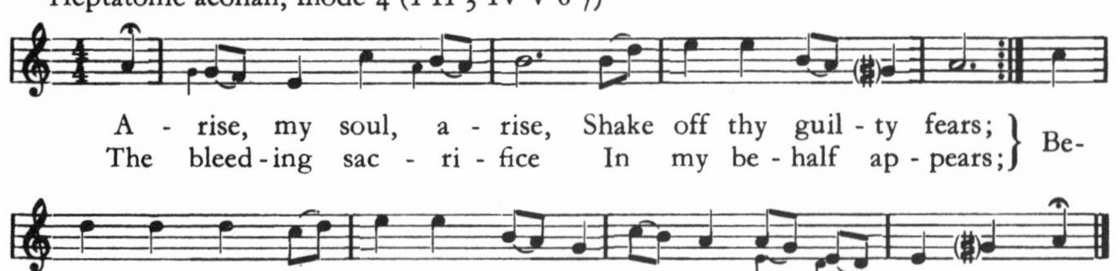
A - rise, my soul, a - rise, Shake off thy guil - ty fears;
The bleed - ing sac - ri - fice In my be - half ap - pears;
Be-
fore the throne my Sure - ty stands, My name is writ - ten on his hands.

He ever lives above,
For me to intercede;
His all-redeeming love,
His precious blood to plead;
His blood atoned for all our race,
And sprinkles now the throne of grace.

[1] Sharp, *One Hundred English Folksongs*, No. 94.
[2] No. 652.

Five bleeding wounds he bears,
Receiv'd on Calvary,
Now pour effectual prayers,
And strongly plead for me;
Forgive him, O forgive, they cry,
Nor let that ransom'd sinner die!

The Father hears him pray,
The dear annointed One;
He will not turn away
The pleading of his Son;
His spirit answers to the blood,
And tells me I am born of God.

My God is reconcil'd,
His pard'ning voice I hear;
He owns me for his child,
I can no longer fear;
With confidence I now draw nigh,
And Father, Abba, Father cry.

I have supplied the second and fifth stanzas of this text (by Charles Wesley, 1707–1788) from *Methodist Hymns*, 1842, p. 165. The tune with different text appeared in variant form in the *Golden Harp*.[1] I have indicated the melodic variations of that New York State tune (features which point to the tampering of an editor) by small notes and the parenthesized sharp in the end cadence. It would seem that the Georgia editor of the *Sacred Harp*, on the other hand, was content to give the tune in its folk-sung form.

No. 179

EUREKA, OSH 378

Pentatonic, mode 2 (I — 3 IV V — 7)

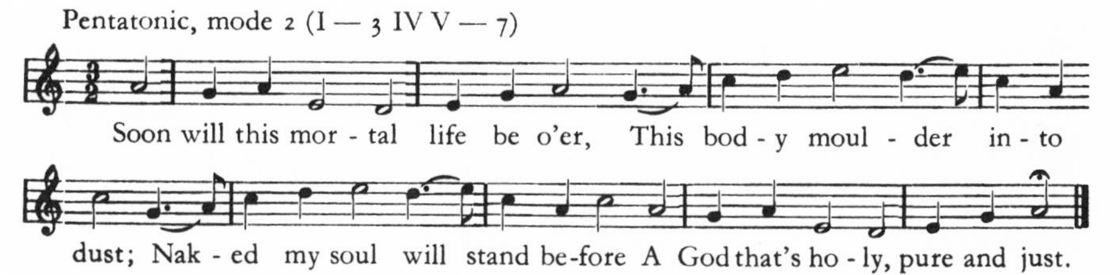
Soon will this mor - tal life be o'er, This bod - y moul - der in - to
dust; Nak - ed my soul will stand be-fore A God that's ho - ly, pure and just.

Its standing doom of bliss or woe,
Will from the Great I Am receive;
Up to the realms of glory go,
Or in hell's torments ever live.

[1] Auburn, N. Y., 1855, p. 138.

Without an int'rest in the blood
Of Jesus shed on Calvary,
We can't escape his vengeful rod,
Howe'er so mortal here we be.

Away then, all selfrighteousness!
My soul from nature's sleep arise;
Be justified by faith through grace,
And claim a mansion in the skies.

Perfection's height may I ascend,
And feel my soul dissolv'd in love;
That when below my days shall end,
Angels may waft my soul above.

The compiler of the *Sacred Harp* borrowed this text from *Campmeeting Songs*, p. 204. J. P. Rees, Georgia singing-master, is given credit for the tune.

No. 180

BABEL'S STREAMS, OSH 126

Heptatonic aeolian, mode 2 (I II 3 IV V 6 7)

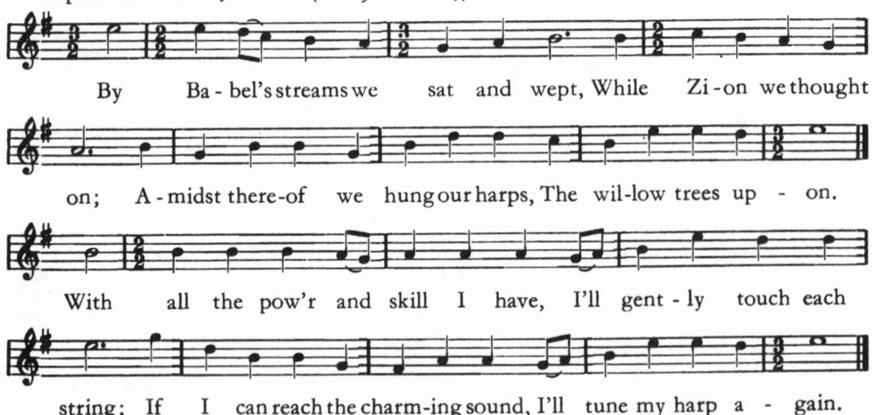
By Ba - bel's streams we sat and wept, While Zi - on we thought
on; A - midst there-of we hung our harps, The wil-low trees up - on.
With all the pow'r and skill I have, I'll gent - ly touch each
string; If I can reach the charm-ing sound, I'll tune my harp a - gain.

This song has been in the *Sacred Harp* since its first edition in 1844. The editor of the 1911 edition states that it "is one of the oldest melodies," and that "It is strongly claimed that the music and the words came from the Welsh musicians." The opening quatrain of the text, based on the 137th Psalm, and the opening notes of the tune bear some resemblance to those parts of the version of the same Psalm found in Day's *Psalter*, 1583.

No. 181

SCHOOL HYMN, REV 269

Hexatonic, mode 2 A (I II 3 IV V — 7 [VII])

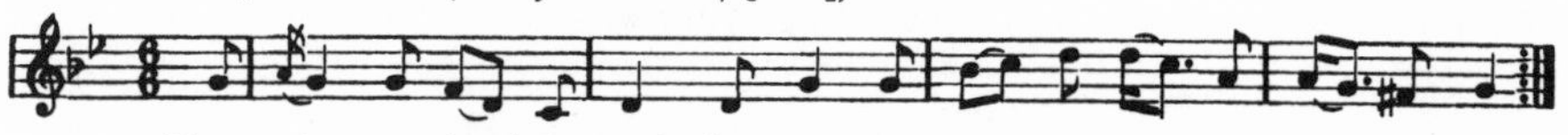
There is a school on earth be-gun, In-struc-ted by the ho-ly one;
He calls his pu-pils there to prove The great-ness of re-deem-ing love.

Then come, dear friends, wher-e'er you be, Say, will you go to school with me? Christ

Je-sus is my Master's name; Come deaf and dumb, come blind and lame.

The school book is the scriptures true;
Our lessons are forever new;
The scholars, too, are all agreed;
O! 'tis a blesséd school indeed.
'Tis here the blind may learn to see,
Then come, ye blind, the school is free;
And here the lame may learn to walk,
The dumb may also learn to talk.

'Tis here the deaf may learn to hear,
Then come, ye deaf, and lend an ear
Unto my Master's pleasant voice;
He'll make your mourning souls rejoice.
He learns the swearing man to pray,
Come, ye profane, without delay;
He'll change your tongues to speak his name,
And spread abroad the Savior's fame.

Now brethern, you who are at school,
Attention pay to every rule;
Here may you learn the happy art
Of loving God with all the heart.
Our mortal frames must shortly die,
Then we shall lay our school books by;
We'll reign with Master Jesus then,
Glory to God, glory, amen.

The text is ascribed to E. B. Sherwood. In a more indigenous version of the words, appearing a half century earlier in an anonymous *Hymns and Spiritual*

Songs booklet, we read that "My master learns the blind to see" and that he "learns the deaf to hear". Its last stanza opens with

> Come brethren dear who are at school,
> Let not the Christian play the fool,
> 'Tis best for all to mind their book,
> Who have their sinful ways forsook.

The tune belongs to the 'Lazarus' group. For further references see 'Lazarus and Dives' in this volume.

No. 182

STAR IN THE EAST, SOH (1835) 16

Heptatonic aeolian, mode 2 (I II 3 IV V 6 7)

Hail the blest morn, see the great Me-di - a - tor Down from the re-gions of
Shep-herds, go wor-ship the babe in the man - ger! Lo, for his guard the bright

Chorus

glo - ry des-cend! / an - gels at - tend. } Bright-est and best of the sons of the morn-ing,

Dawn on our dark-ness and lend us thine aid. Star in the east, the ho-

ri - zon a - dorn - ing, Guide where our in - fant Re-deem-er was laid.

> Cold on his cradle the dew-drops are shining;
> Low lies his bed, with the beasts of the stall;
> Angels adore him, in slumbers reclining,
> Wise men and shepherds before him do fall.
> *Chorus*

> Say, shall we yield him, in costly devotion,
> Odors of Eden, and off'rings divine,
> Gems from the mountain, and pearls from the ocean,
> Myrrh from the forest, and gold from the mine?

The text is an altered form of that by Reginald Heber, 1783–1863. The tune is related to 'Fiducia', the following song.

No. 183

FIDUCIA, SOH (1835) 92

Hexatonic, mode 2 A (I II 3 IV V — 7)

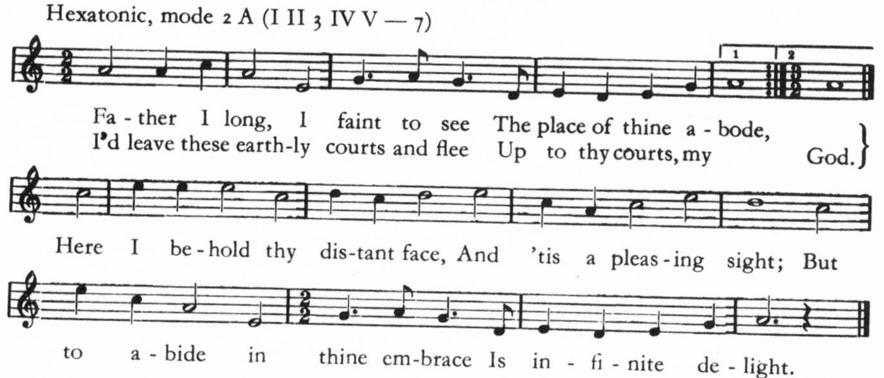
Fa - ther I long, I faint to see The place of thine a - bode,
I'd leave these earth-ly courts and flee Up to thy courts, my God.
Here I be - hold thy dis-tant face, And 'tis a pleas - ing sight; But
to a - bide in thine em-brace Is in - fi - nite de - light.

The text is by Isaac Watts, 1674–1748. The maker of the tune is given as "Robertson" in some books, "J. Robertson" in others. 'Star of the East', the preceding song in this volume, has a variant tune.

No. 184

SUFFERING SAVIOR, CL, i, 42

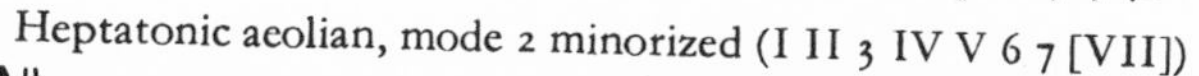

Heptatonic aeolian, mode 2 minorized (I II 3 IV V 6 7 [VII])

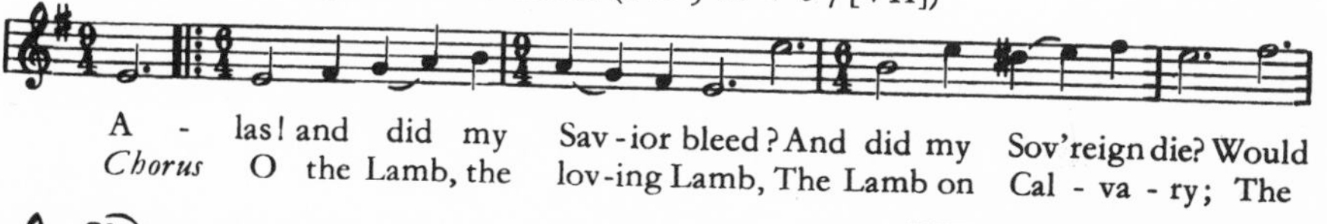
A - las! and did my Sav - ior bleed? And did my Sov'reign die? Would
Chorus O the Lamb, the lov-ing Lamb, The Lamb on Cal - va - ry; The

he de-vote that sa - cred head For such a wretch as I?
Lamb that was slain, that liv-eth a-gain, To in - ter - cede for me.

The text by Isaac Watts, 1674–1748, is given in fuller form under 'Avon'. The tune is related to 'Edgefield' in *Spiritual Folk-Songs*.[1] *The Christian Lyre*, where this song was found, is, it will be remembered, a book used largely in the Northeast. The same tune in the Georgia *Hesperian Harp* is in the pure aeolian mode; — another instance of modal persistence in the South and the abandonment of the modes in the books of the same period in the North. The tune formula

[1] No. 149.

was widely used in the early part of the nineteenth century. Winston Wilkinson has assembled a number of spiritual and secular variants to be used in his forthcoming *Purcell Collection.*[1]

Miss Anne G. Gilchrist assigns the tune to the first half of the eighteenth century and thinks it may have been composed as a psalm tune by Dr. Maurice Greene, 1696–1755.[2] The 'Suffering Savior' tune and its variants approach the 'Kedron' melodic family,[3] differing radically only in the third phrase.

No. 185

GOSPEL POOL (B), CL, i, 82

Hexatonic, apparently aeolian but seventh lacking, mode 2 (I II 3 IV V 6 —)

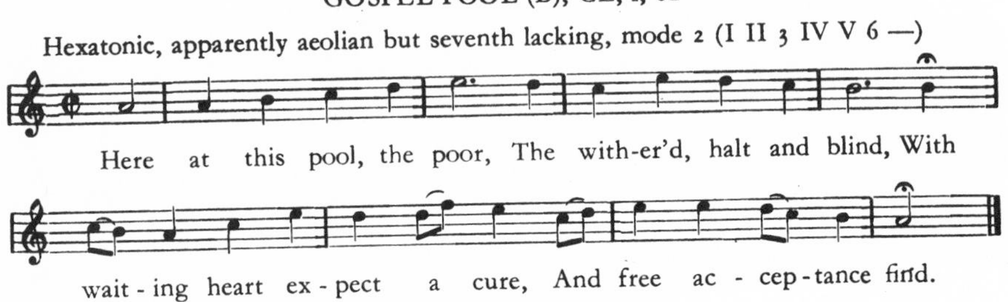
Here at this pool, the poor, The with-er'd, halt and blind, With
wait - ing heart ex - pect a cure, And free ac - cep - tance find.

Here streams of virtue flow,
To heal a sin-sick soul;
To wash the filthy white as snow,
And make the wounded whole.

The dumb break forth in praise,
The blind their sight receive;
The cripple run in wisdom's ways,
The dead revive and live.

Not bound to case or time,
These waters always move;
Sinners, in every age and clime,
Their vital influence prove.

Yet numbers near them lie,
Who meet with no relief;
With life in view they pine and die
In hopeless unbelief.

[1] The title of the book is not yet definitely decided upon.
[2] JFSS, iii, 45 f.
[3] See 'Distress' in this volume.

'Tis strange they will not bathe,
And yet frequent the pool;
But none can have a saving faith,
While love of sin bears rule.

Their conscience sin has seal'd,
And stupefied their thought;
For were they willing to be heal'd,
The cure would soon be wrought.

Dear Savior, interpose,
Their stubborn will constrain;
Or else to them the waters flow,
And grace is preach'd in vain.

The tune is similar to 'America' in this volume.

No. 186

SOLITUDE IN THE GROVE, MOH 45

Hexatonic, mode 4 a (I II — IV V 6 7)

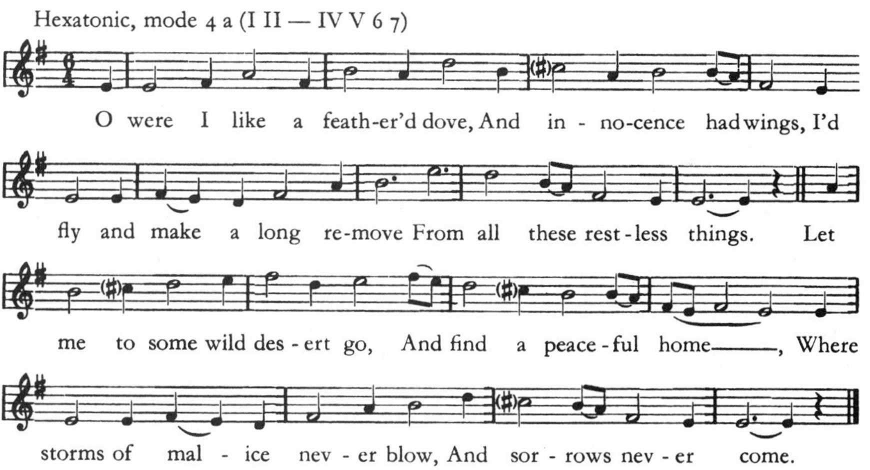
O were I like a feath-er'd dove, And in - no-cence had wings, I'd
fly and make a long re-move From all these rest-less things. Let
me to some wild des - ert go, And find a peace-ful home——, Where
storms of mal - ice nev - er blow, And sor - rows nev - er come.

The tune appears also in the *Kentucky Harmony* where it is claimed by the compiler, Ananias Davisson. It is clearly of dorian character; thus the *c*'s of the *Missouri Harmony* should be *c*-sharps as I have suggested above. The song appears widely in the early shape-note books. The metrical misfit of words and tune is quite evident.

No. 187

AMERICA, CH 35

Hexatonic, mode 2 A minorized (I II 3 IV V — 7 [VII])

And must this bod - y die, This mor - tal frame de - cay? And must these

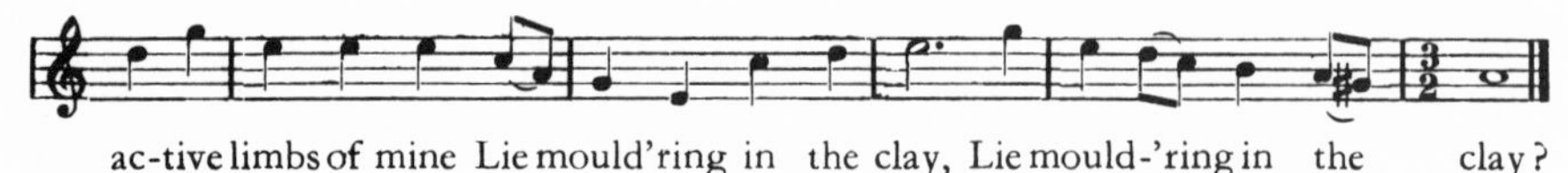
ac-tive limbs of mine Lie mould'ring in the clay, Lie mould-'ring in the clay?

Corruption, earth, and worms
Shall but refine this flesh,
Till my triumphant spirit comes
To put it on afresh,
To put it on afresh.

God my Redeemer lives,
And always from the skies
Looks down and watches all my dust,
Till he shall bid it rise,
Till he shall bid it rise.

The text is by Isaac Watts, 1674–1748. The tune is similar to 'Gospel Pool (B)' in this volume.

No. 188

FIGHT ON, OSH 385

Hexatonic, mode 2 A (I II 3 IV V — 7)

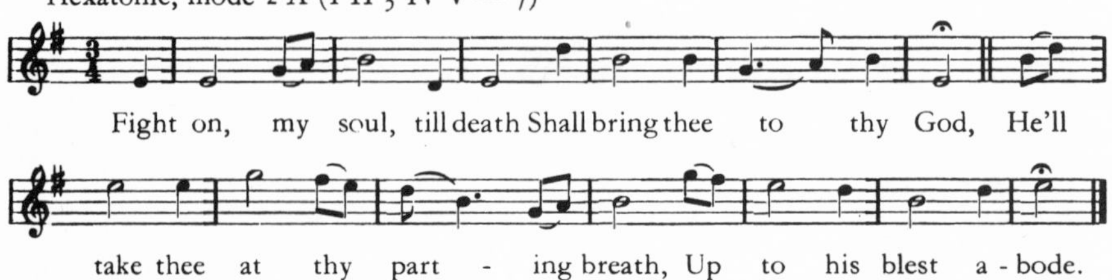
Fight on, my soul, till death Shall bring thee to thy God, He'll
take thee at thy part - ing breath, Up to his blest a - bode.

The tune is ascribed in the *Original Sacred Harp* to J. P. Rees who was active in country singing circles in Georgia before the Civil War.

No. 189

ZION'S SECURITY, HOC 30

Pentatonic, mode 2 (I — 3 IV V — 7)

Glo-rious things of thee are spok - en, Zi - on, cit - y of our God; }
He whose word can not be brok-en, Form'd thee for his own a-bode. } On the

Rock of A - ges found-ed, What can shake thy sure re-pose? With sal-

va - tion's walls sur - round - ed, Thou may'st smile at all thy foes.

See the streams of living waters,
Springing from eternal love,
Well supply thy sons and daughters,
And all fear of want remove.
Who can faint while such a river
Ever flows their thirst t'assuage!
Grace which, like the Lord, the giver,
Never fails from age to age.

Round each habitation hovering,
See the cloud and fire appear,
For a glory and a covering,
Showing that the Lord is near.
Thus deriving from their banner
Light by night, and shade by day;
Safe they feed upon the manna,
Which he gives them when they pray.

The text is by John Newton, 1725–1807. An interesting variant of the tune, changed to a major key, is 'Invitation', *Spiritual Folk-Songs*, No. 63.

No. 190

JUST AS I AM, OL 232

Hexatonic, mode 2 A (I II 3 IV V — 7)

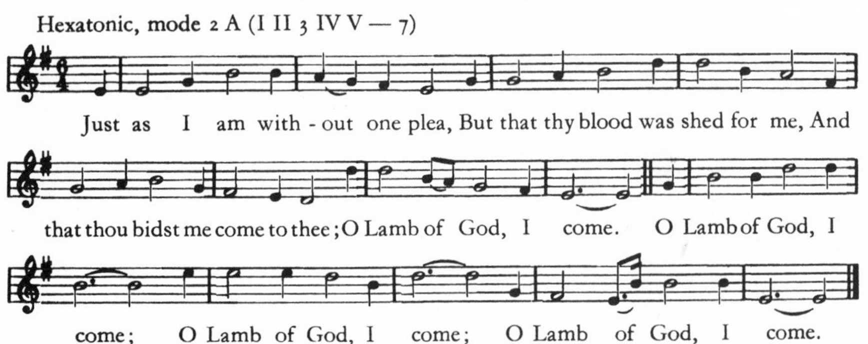
Just as I am with - out one plea, But that thy blood was shed for me, And
that thou bidst me come to thee; O Lamb of God, I come. O Lamb of God, I
come; O Lamb of God, I come; O Lamb of God, I come.

The well-known poem is by Charlotte Elliott, 1789–1871. William Hauser, compiler of the *Olive Leaf*, claims the tune and dates it May 19, 1874. I find in the melody some reminders of the old psalm tune 'Martyr's' as to the source of which Carleton Sprague Smith informs me, "It occurs apparently first in *The CL Psalmes of David in Prose and Meeter, and with their whole usuall tunes* etc., Edinburgh, 1615, as one of the *xii common tunes* which appeared in this edition of the *Scottish Book of Common Order*. Ravencroft's *Psalter* of 1621 classes it as a Scotch tune in triple time. In all the old books the tune is in the dorian mode." We may thus have here a psalm-tune of folk orign.

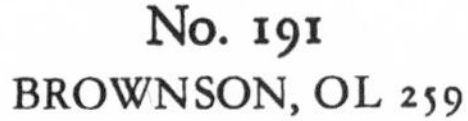

No. 191

BROWNSON, OL 259

Hexatonic, mode 4 A (I II — IV V VI 7 [VII])

Bless - ing, hon - or, thanks and praise Pay we, grac - ious God, to thee;
Thou in thine a - bun-dant grace Giv - est us the vic - to ry.

True and faith - ful to thy word, Thou hast glo - ri - fied thy Son,

Je - sus Christ, our dy - ing Lord, He for us the fight hath won.

Lo! the pris'ner is released,
Lighten'd of his fleshly load;
Where the weary are at rest,
He is gather'd unto God.
Lo! the pain of life is past,
All his warfare now is o'er;
Death and hell behind are cast,
Grief and suffering are no more.

Yes, the Christian's course is run,
Ended is the glorious strife;
Fought the fight, the victory won,
Death is swallow'd up in life.
Borne by angels on their wings,
Far from earth the spirit flies;
Finds his God, and sits and sings,
Triumphing in Paradise.

The text is by Charles Wesley, 1707–1788. William Hauser, compiler of the *Olive Leaf*, states: "Air learned of some unknown ladies, at Mount Vernon Camp Meeting, Davidson Co., N. C., about 1830." It is a member of the 'Babe of Bethlehem' tune family; references given under 'Old Israelites' in this volume.

While Hauser felt it necessary to provide this essentially dorian tune with a leading tone, *e*-sharp, still he preserved its characteristic raised sixth, *d*-sharp, by means of accidentals.

No. 192

CHILDREN OF THE HEAVENLY KING, SOH (1835) 6

Hexatonic, mode 2 A (I II 3 IV V — 7)

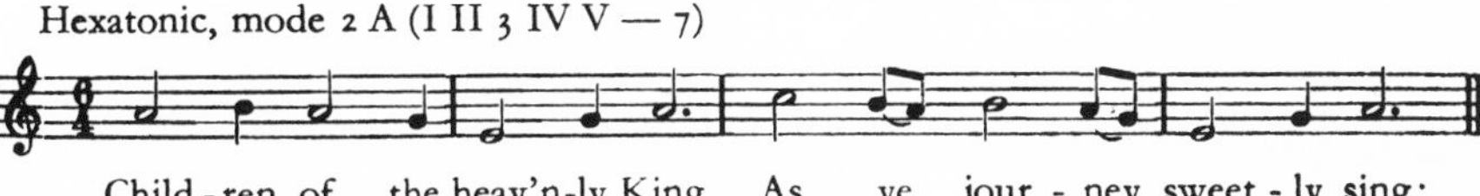
Child-ren of the heav'n-ly King, As ye jour - ney sweet - ly sing;

tr
Sing your Sav - ior's wor-thiest praise, Glor-ious in his works and ways.

Ye are trav'ling home to God,
In the way the fathers trod;
They are happy now, and ye
Soon their happiness shall see.

O ye banish'd seed, be glad!
Christ our Advocate is made
Us to save, our flesh assumes,
Brother to our souls becomes.

The text is by John Cennick, 1718–1755. The tune is ascribed in the southern song books to Freeman Price.

No. 193

TIME IS PASSING, *Shaker Music*, p. 27

Heptatonic aeolian, mode 4 (I II 3 IV V 6 7)

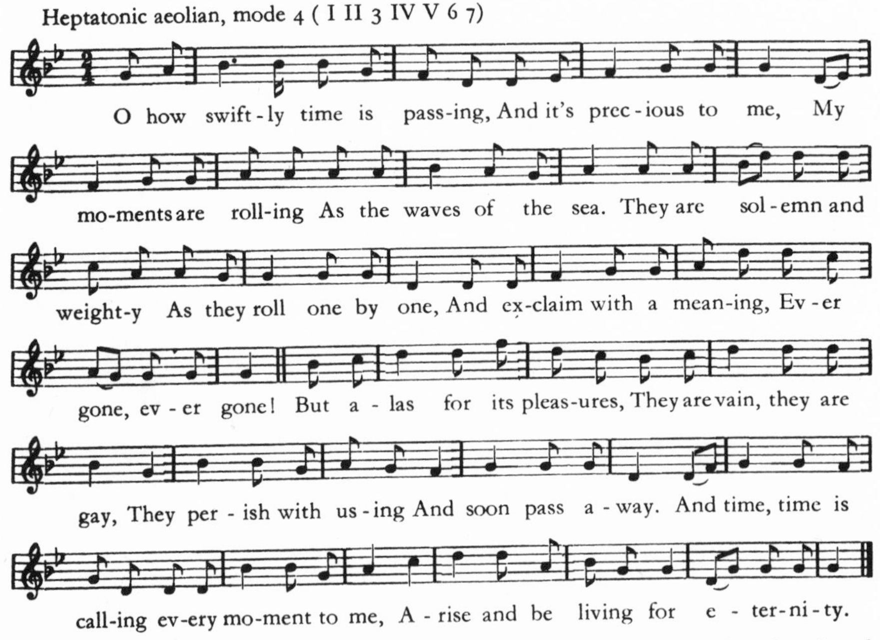
O how swift-ly time is pass-ing, And it's prec-ious to me, My
mo-ments are roll-ing As the waves of the sea. They are sol-emn and
weight-y As they roll one by one, And ex-claim with a mean-ing, Ev-er
gone, ev-er gone! But a-las for its pleas-ures, They are vain, they are
gay, They per-ish with us-ing And soon pass a-way. And time, time is
call-ing ev-ery mo-ment to me, A-rise and be living for e-ter-ni-ty.

At the top left of the page on which this song appears in *Shaker Music* is printed "South Union, Ky.", the name of the Shaker colony where this song presumably was "received". The Shakers did not "compose" their songs.[1]

The tune sounds old and Celtic-folky. I see melodic, rhythmic and textual influence from the 'Captain Kidd' stanzaic pattern in the repeated rhythmic motif ♪ ♫| ♩ ♪ ♫| ♩ associated with such phrases as "as the waves of the sea", "they are vain, they are gay", and "ever gone, ever gone". Compare with the song 'You Shall See' in this volume.

[1] *Cf.* 'South Union' in this volume.

No. 194

FINDLAY, CH (Supplement) 27

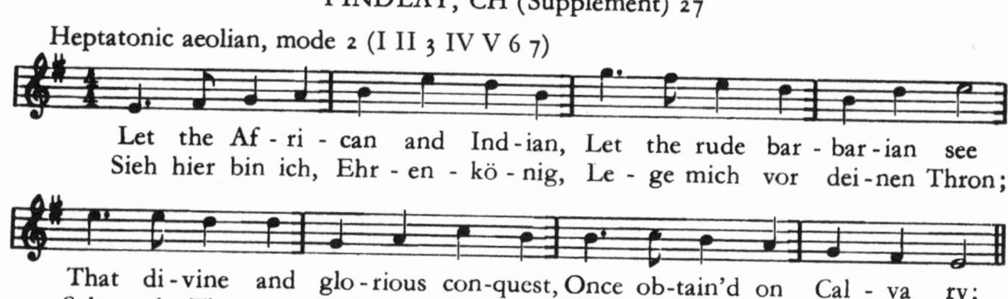
Heptatonic aeolian, mode 2 (I II 3 IV V 6 7)
Let the Af - ri - can and Ind - ian, Let the rude bar - bar - ian see
Sieh hier bin ich, Ehr - en - kö - nig, Le - ge mich vor dei - nen Thron;
That di - vine and glo - rious con-quest, Once ob-tain'd on Cal - va ry;
Schwa-che Thrä-nen, kind - lich Seh - nen Bring ich dir, du Men-schen-sohn;

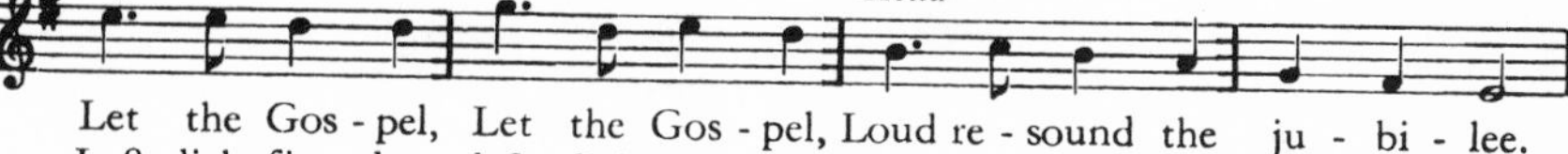
Soft
Loud
Let the Gos - pel, Let the Gos - pel, Loud re - sound the ju - bi - lee.
Laß dich fin - den, laß dich fin - den, Von mir, der ich Asch und Thon.

Only the above stanzas are given in this bilingual song book, *Church Harmony (Kirchen-Harmonie)*, for the Pennsylvania singers. It will be noticed that the German is not a translation of the English hymn.

No. 195

FAIRFIELD (A), HH 62

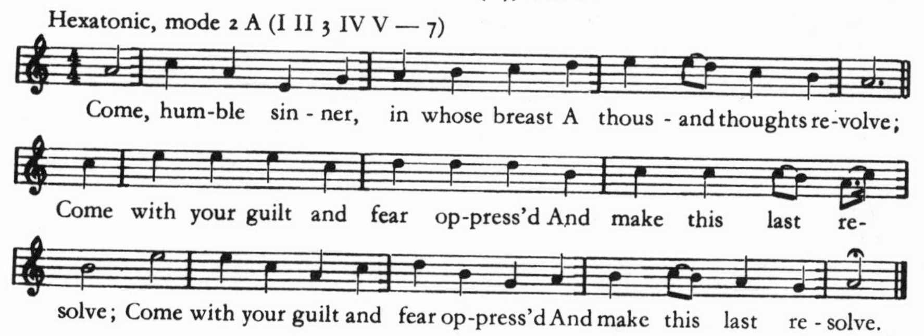
Hexatonic, mode 2 A (I II 3 IV V — 7)
Come, hum-ble sin - ner, in whose breast A thous - and thoughts re-volve;
Come with your guilt and fear op-press'd And make this last re-
solve; Come with your guilt and fear op-press'd And make this last re - solve.

Further stanzas of the text by Edmund Jones, 1722–1765, are given under 'Salvation (B)' in *Spiritual Folk-Songs.* The tune is attributed in the southern song books usually to "Hitchcock". Its last four measures are practically identical with those of 'The True Penitent' which is ascribed to William Billings in Ingalls' *Christian Harmony* of 1805.

The following song is a variant of this but recorded from present day oral-traditional singing.

No. 196

FAIRFIELD (B), UVW, No. 162

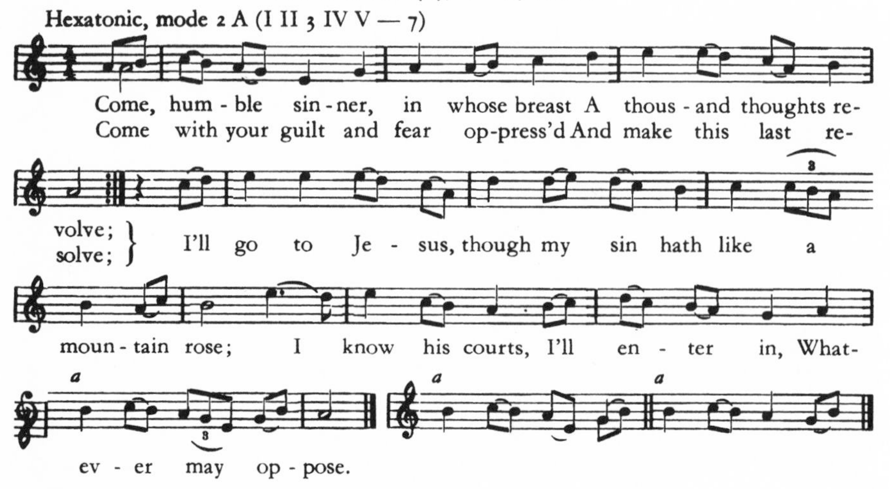
Hexatonic, mode 2 A (I II 3 IV V — 7)
Come, hum - ble sin - ner, in whose breast A thous - and thoughts re-
Come with your guilt and fear op-press'd And make this last re-
volve;
solve;
I'll go to Je - sus, though my sin hath like a
moun - tain rose; I know his courts, I'll en - ter in, What-
ev - er may op - pose.

This variant of the preceding song was recorded by Winston Wilkinson in tanardsville, Virginia, November 9, 1935, as sung by Z. B. Lam.[1]

No. 197

SWEET PROSPECT (A), OSH 65

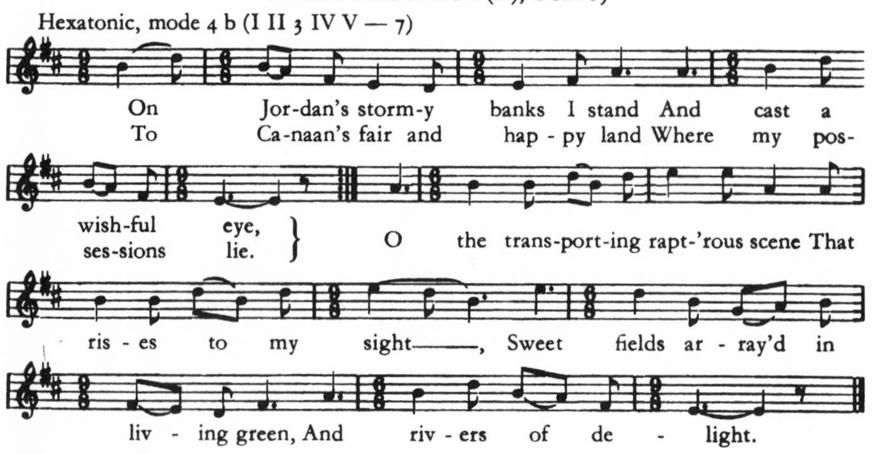
Hexatonic, mode 4 b (I II 3 IV V — 7)
On Jor-dan's storm-y banks I stand And cast a
To Ca-naan's fair and hap - py land Where my pos-
wish-ful eye,
ses-sions lie.
O the trans-port-ing rapt-'rous scene That
ris - es to my sight——, Sweet fields ar - ray'd in
liv - ing green, And riv - ers of de - light.

[1] It is No. 162 in the *University of Virginia* (manuscript) *Collection of Folk-Music*, and is used here by kind permission.

For a continuation of the text (by Samuel Stennett, 1727–1795) see 'Jordan' in *Spiritual Folk-Songs*.[1] The tune is ascribed to William Walker of Spartanburg, South Carolina. A close variant is 'Melody'[2] which, in filling out the gap of the sixth step in the scale with a *c*-sharp, fixes the natural mode of this tune as dorian. An interesting melodic forebear is 'Knoxville'.[3] A recent variant recording from oral tradition is the following song.

No. 198

SWEET PROSPECT (B), UVW, No. 168

Heptatonic dorian, mode 4 (I II 3 IV V VI 7)

On— Jor-dan's storm - y banks I stand *etc.*
a
a

This variant of the foregoing song in this volume was recorded by Winston Wilkinson in Greenwood, Virginia, March 12, 1936, as sung by J. H. Chisholm.[4] I interpret the *g*-sharps toward the end of the tune as mixolydian influence.

[1] No. 86.
[2] *Primitive Baptist Hymn and Tune Book*, No. 313.
[3] *Supplement to the Kentucky Harmony*, p. 59.
[4] It is No. 168 of the *University of Virginia* (manuscript) *Collection of Folk-Music*, and is used here by kind permission.

No. 199

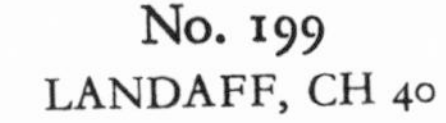

LANDAFF, CH 40

Heptatonic aeolian, mode 2 (I II 3 IV V 6 7 [VII])

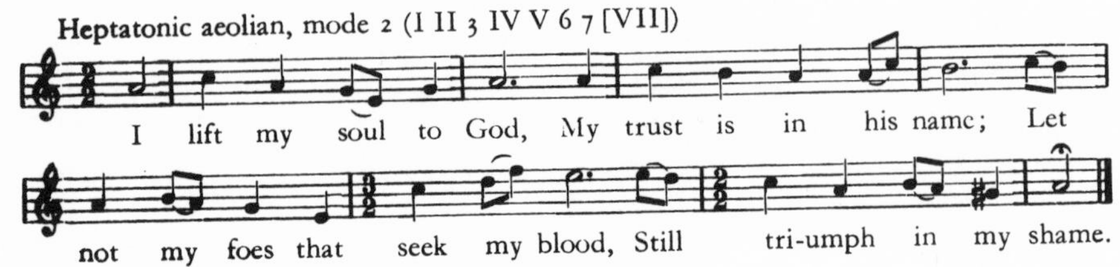
I lift my soul to God, My trust is in his name; Let
not my foes that seek my blood, Still tri-umph in my shame.

Sin and the pow'rs of hell
Persuade me to despair;
Lord, make me know thy cov'nant well,
That I may 'scape the snare.

From gleams of dawning light
Till evening shades arise,
For thy salvation, Lord, I wait
With ever-longing eyes.

Remember all thy grace,
And lead me in the truth;
Forgive the sins of riper days,
And follies of my youth.

The text is Isaac Watts' version of the twenty-fifth psalm. The tune is ascribed to "Findlay".

No. 200

I LOVE THE LORD, SOC 61

Pentatonic, mode 2 (I — 3 IV V — 7)

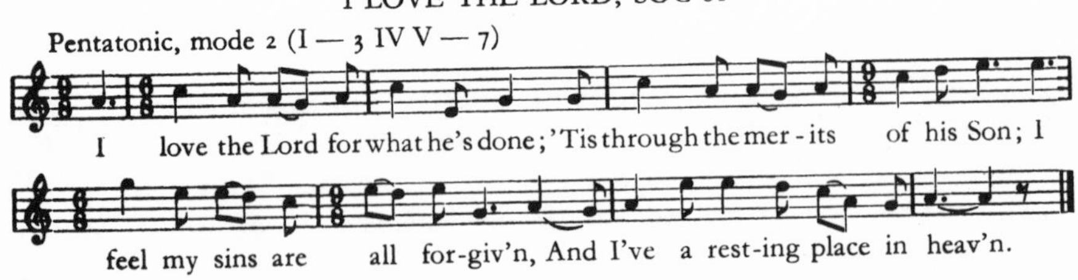
I love the Lord for what he's done; 'Tis through the mer-its of his Son; I
feel my sins are all for-giv'n, And I've a rest-ing place in heav'n.

The song is claimed by John G. McCurry, compiler of the *Social Harp*, and is dated 1842. The tune is a distant though unmistakable member of the 'I Will Arise' family.[1]

[1] For related tune references see *Spiritual Folk-Songs*, No. 239; *Folk Hymns of America*, notes on No 28; and 'Hayden' in this volume.

No. 201

SONG OF TEXAS, GOS 538

Hexatonic, mode 2 A (I II 3 IV V — 7)

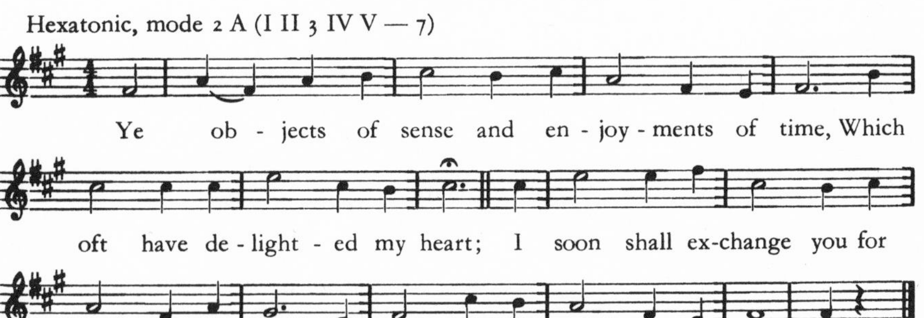
Ye ob - jects of sense and en - joy - ments of time, Which
oft have de - light - ed my heart; I soon shall ex-change you for
views more sub - lime, For joys that shall nev - er de - part.

Further stanzas of the text by Benjamin Francis, 1934–1799, are given under 'Concord' in this volume. The editor of *Good Old Songs* found this tune in the 1850 edition of the *Sacred Harp* where it was associated with a secular text beginning:

> Away here in Texas, the bright Sunny South,
> The cold storms of winter defy;
> The dark, lurid clouds that envelope the North,
> Scarce darken our beautiful sky.

No. 202

TIME FLIES, OL 63

Hexatonic, mode 2 A minorized (I II 3 IV V — 7 [VII])

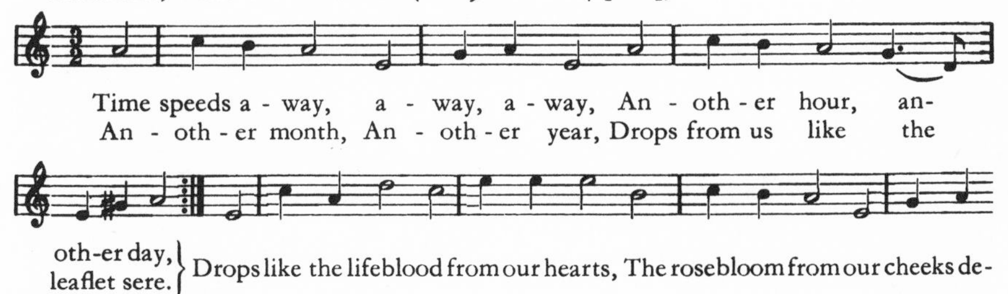
Time speeds a - way, a - way, a - way, An - oth - er hour, an-
An - oth - er month, An - oth - er year, Drops from us like the
oth-er day, leaflet sere. Drops like the lifeblood from our hearts, The rosebloom from our cheeks de-
parts, The tress-es from our tem-ples fall; The eye grows dim and strange to all.

Time speeds away, away, away,
Like torrents in a summer day;
He undermines the stately tower,
Uproots the tree, and snaps the flower;
And sweeps from our distracted breast,
The friends that loved, the friends that bless'd;
And leaves us weeping on the shore,
To which they can return no more.

Time speeds away, away, away;
No eagle through the sky of day,
No wind along the hills can flee
So swiftly or so smooth as he;
Like fiery steed, from stage to stage,
He bears us on from youth to age;
Then plunges in the fearful sea
Of fathomless eternity.

"As sung by Rev. Charles Augustus Moore, of Georgia," William Hauser compiler of the *Olive Leaf* states.

No. 203

SHEPHERD, SWP 72

Heptatonic aeolian, mode 2 (I II 3 IV V 6 7)

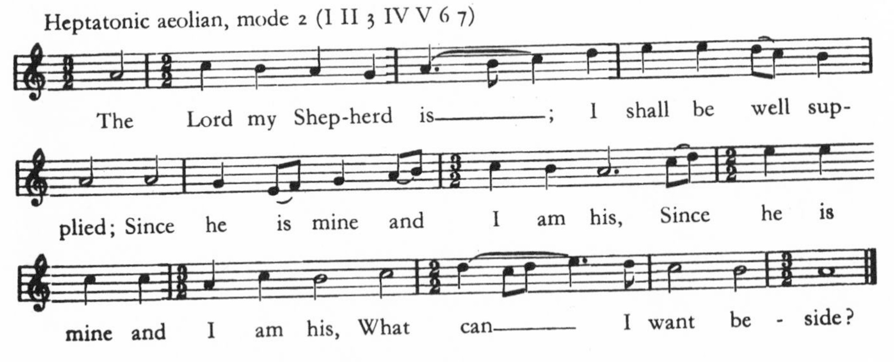
The Lord my Shep-herd is——; I shall be well sup-
plied; Since he is mine and I am his, Since he is
mine and I am his, What can—— I want be - side?

He leads me to the place
Where heavenly pasture grows,
Where living waters gently pass,
And full salvation flows.

If e'er I go astray,
He doth my soul reclaim,
And guides me in his own right way,
For his most holy name.

While he affords his aid,
I cannot yield to fear;
Though I should walk through death's dark shade,
My Shepherd's with me there.

Amid surrounding foes,
Thou dost my table spread;
My cup with blessings overflows,
And joy exalts my head.

The bounties of thy love
Shall crown my following days;
Nor from thy house will I remove,
Nor cease to speak thy praise.

The text is Isaac Watts' version of the twenty-third psalm. The tune opens much like 'Fairfield' in this volume.

No. 204

HANOVER, OSH 46

Heptatonic aeolian, mode 2 (I II 3 IV V 6 7)

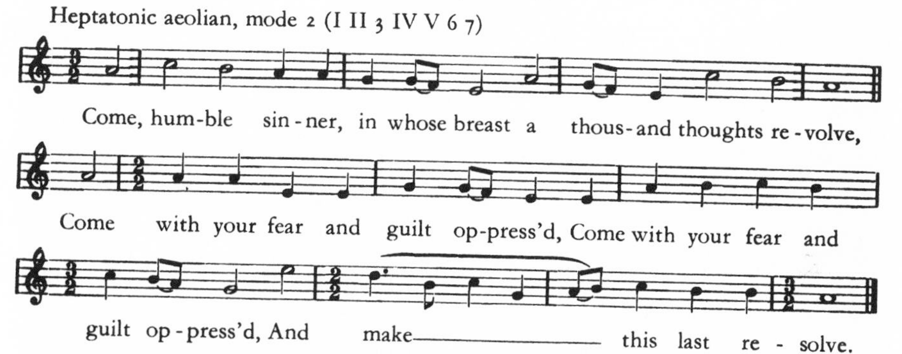
Come, hum-ble sin-ner, in whose breast a thous-and thoughts re-volve,
Come with your fear and guilt op-press'd, Come with your fear and
guilt op-press'd, And make this last re - solve.

The following stanzas are supplied from Tillett and Nutter, p. 138.

I'll go to Jesus, though my sins
Like mountains round me close;
I know his courts, I'll enter in,
Whatever may oppose.

Prostrate I'll lie before his throne,
And there my guilt confess;
I'll tell him I'm a wretch undone
Without his sovereign grace.

Perhaps he will admit my plea,
Perhaps will hear my prayer;
But if I perish, I will pray,
And perish only there.

I can but perish if I go;
I am resolved to try;
For if I stay away, I know
I must forever die.

The text is by Edmund Jones, 1722–1765. The southern shape-note song books have used regularly instead of Jones' phrase,

Like mountains round me close,

the more indigenous,

Hath like a mountain rose.

No. 205

SING TO ME OF HEAVEN, GOS 21

Hexatonic, mode 2 A (I II 3 IV V — 7)

O sing to me of heav'n, When I am call'd to die;
(Cho.) There'll be no sor - row there, There'll be no sor - row there,
Sing songs of ho - ly ec - sta - cy, To waft my soul on high.
In heav'n a - bove where all is love, There'll be no sor - row there.

When cold and sluggish drops
Roll off my marble brow,
Break forth in songs of joyfulness,
Let heav'n begin below.
Chorus

When the last moments come,
O watch my dying face
To catch the bright seraphic gleam
Which o'er my features plays.

The text is by Mrs. Mary Stanley Bunce Dana Shindler, a hymn writer of South Carolina, 1810–1883. The tune is ascribed in the *Original Sacred Harp* to John Massengale of Georgia, elsewhere to C. R. Dunbar. Miss Anne G. Gilchrist finds it related to 'Sprig of Thyme'.[1] A majorized version of the tune is 'Teacher's Farewell' in this volume.

[1] JFSS, viii, 69.

No. 206

SOPHRONIA, SOH (1835) 35

Heptatonic aeolian, mode 2 (I II 3 IV V 6 7)

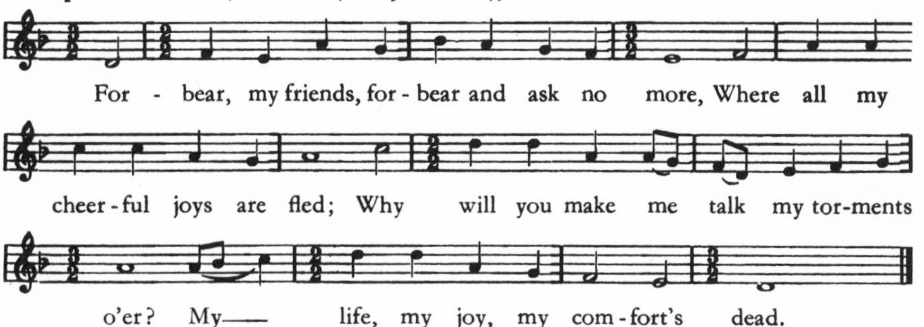
For - bear, my friends, for - bear and ask no more, Where all my
cheer - ful joys are fled; Why will you make me talk my tor-ments
o'er? My—— life, my joy, my com - fort's dead.

The text is an eighteenth-century lament because

Lovely Sophronia sleeps in death.

I find five more stanzas of this text in Mintz, David B. *Hymns and Spiritual Songs*, Newbern, North Carolina, No. xiii.

No. 207

PLEASANT GROVE, OSH 107

Heptatonic aeolian, mode 2 (I II 3 IV V 6 7)

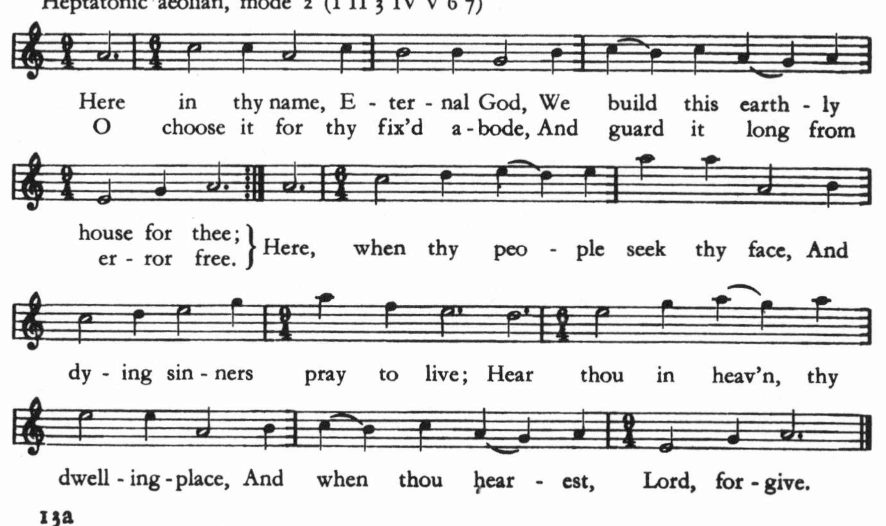
Here in thy name, E - ter - nal God, We build this earth - ly
O choose it for thy fix'd a - bode, And guard it long from
house for thee;
er - ror free.
Here, when thy peo - ple seek thy face, And
dy - ing sin - ners pray to live; Hear thou in heav'n, thy
dwell - ing - place, And when thou hear - est, Lord, for - give.

Here, when thy messengers proclaim
The blessed gospel of thy Son,
Still, by the pow'r of his great name,
Be mighty signs and wonders done.
When children's voices raise the song,
Hosanna! to their heavenly King,
Let heaven with earth the strain prolong;
Hosanna! let the angels sing.

The text is attributed in the *Original Sacred Harp* to James Montgomery, 1771–1854.

No. 208

RED HILL, HH 110

Hexatonic, mode 2 A (I II 3 IV V — 7)

Be-hold the Sav-ior of man-kind, Nail'd to the shame - ful tree!

How vast the love that him in-clin'd To bleed and die for thee.

Hark! how he groans while nature shakes,
And earth's strong pillars bend!
The temple's veil in sunder breaks,
The solid marbles rend.

Two stanzas added from Tillett and Nutter, p. 79.

"'Tis done, the precious ransom's paid!
Receive my soul!" he cries;
See where he bows his sacred head!
He bows his head and dies!

But soon he'll break death's envious chain,
And in full glory shine;
O Lamb of God, was ever pain,
Was ever love like thine?

The text is by Samuel Wesley, 1662–1735. The tune is related to 'Cross of Christ' in *Spiritual Folk-Songs*, to 'House Carpenter' and a number of other secular melodies.[1]

[1] Some of them are listed in *Spiritual Folk-Songs* under No. 91.

No. 209

SOLITUDE, VSM 20

Heptatonic aeolian, mode 2 (I II 3 IV V 6 7)

Come lead me to some lone - ly shade, Where tur-tles mourn their loves;

Tall shad - ows were for lov - ers made, And grief be-comes the groves.

No. 210

AMANDA, FH 4

Hexatonic, mode 2 A (I II 3 IV V — 7)

Death, like an ov - - er - flow - ing stream, Sweeps
us a - way——, our life's a dream, An emp - ty tale——, a
morn - ing flow'r, Cut down and with - - er'd in an hour.

In the *Federal Harmony*, 1790, the song is ascribed to "Morgan". It is found also in *The New Jersey Harmony* (1787) without ascription and in *The Missouri Harmony*, p. 46.

No. 211
OTTERBEIN, CH 195

Heptatonic aeolian, mode 2 (I II 3 IV V 6 7)

Thou man of grief——, re - mem - ber me; Thou
ne - ver canst thy - self for - get Thy last ex - pir - ing
ag - o - ny, Thy faint - ing pangs and blood - y sweat.

The full text of six stanzas by Charles Wesley, 1707–1788, is in *Methodist Hymns*.[1] The tune is clearly a variant of that found in *David's Harp*, London, n. d., p. 48, where it is marked "author unknown".

No. 212
CHANGING SEASONS, SKH 19

Heptatonic aeolian, mode 2 (I II 3 IV V 6 7)

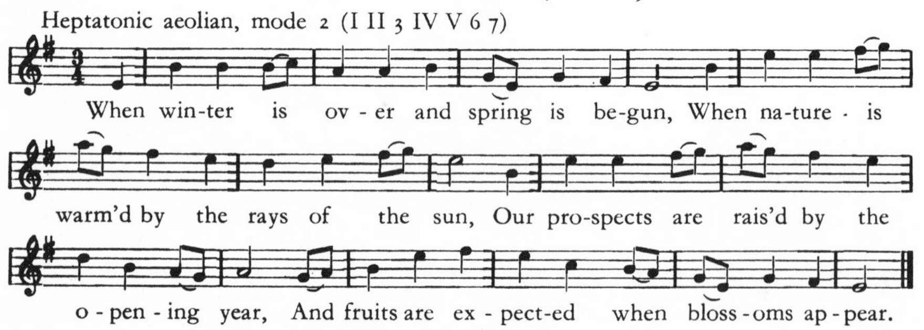
When win-ter is ov - er and spring is be-gun, When na-ture - is
warm'd by the rays of the sun, Our pro-spects are rais'd by the
o - pen - ing year, And fruits are ex - pect-ed when bloss - oms ap - pear.

Our fond expectations thus bear us away,
While beautiful prospects our eyes still survey;
But sudden, a dreadful and untimely frost
Restores winter's gloom and our hopes are all lost.

Just so in a season when conscience awakes,
Calls loudly to sinners their crimes to forsake;
'Tis then that with pleasing emotions we trace
The tears of the mourner adorning each face.

But O, in the midst of this pleasing delight,
We look for the fruit, but it's snatch'd from the sight;
Some fatal temptation conviction destroys,
And cuts off the hope which had promis'd us joys.

[1] Edition of 1842, p. 51.

Eighty-Eight
Revival Spiritual Songs

CAMP MEETING SCENE — from Charles Pitman's *Sweet Singer of Israel*, 1837.

Shout on, children, shout, you're free,
For Christ has bought your liberty.

Millennial Harp, Boston, 1843.

ELDER JOHN LELAND, 1754–1841, noted Baptist preacher of 8000 sermons in New England and Virginia, maker of a 1600-pound cheese for

REV. JOHN LELAND.

President Thomas Jefferson, and writer of 'O When Shall I See Jesus', the most widely sung folk-hymn. See song No. 157.

"BLACKWOOD TOWN CAMP MEETING" — from *Camp Meeting Chorister*, 1830.

I pitch my tent on this camp ground
And give old Satan another round.

Social Harp, 1855.

No. 213

ZION'S WALLS, SOC 137

Pentatonic, mode 3 (I II III — V VI —)

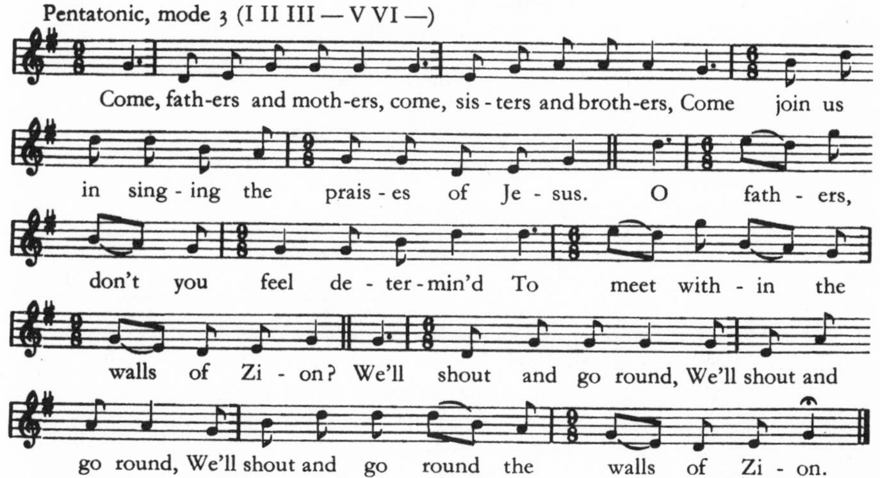
Come, fath-ers and moth-ers, come, sis - ters and broth-ers, Come join us
in sing - ing the prais - es of Je - sus. O fath - ers,
don't you feel de - ter - min'd To meet with - in the
walls of Zi - on? We'll shout and go round, We'll shout and
go round, We'll shout and go round the walls of Zi - on.

I have been forced to change the very faulty notation of the editor of the *Social Harp*. My alterations touch however merely the rhythm. I have left the pitch and relative length of the notes unchanged.

This is the only recording, as far as I know, of this revival spiritual song. A variant of the tune with different words is 'Christian Warfare' in this volume. John G. McCurry, compiler of the *Social Harp*, signatured the song and dated it 1853.

No. 214

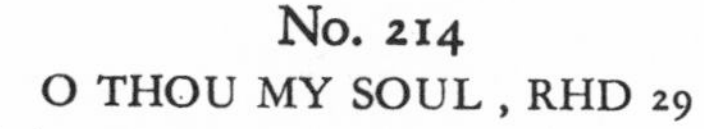

O THOU MY SOUL, RHD 29

Heptatonic dorian, Mode 4 (I II 3 IV V VI 7)

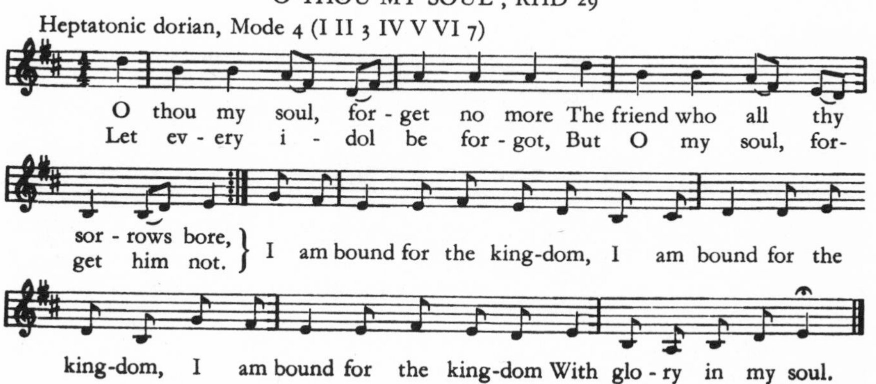
O thou my soul, for - get no more The friend who all thy
Let ev - ery i - dol be for - got, But O my soul, for-
sor - rows bore,
get him not.
I am bound for the king-dom, I am bound for the
king-dom, I am bound for the king-dom With glo - ry in my soul.

Renounce thy works and ways of grief
And fly to this divine relief,
Nor him forget who left his throne,
And for thy life gave up his own.

Infinite truth and mercy shine
In him, and he himself is thine;
And canst thou then, with sin beset,
Such charms, such matchless charms forget?

Oh no! — till life itself depart,
His name shall cheer and warm my heart;
And lisping this, from earth I'll rise
And join the chorus of the skies.

The theme of the chorus text is used with various verse texts. The tune is a variant of 'Holy War'[1] which is also in the dorian mode. These two variant tunes, the above from the New England region and 'Holy War' from South Carolina, recorded only four years apart, testify to the broad territory covered at that time, the 1840's, by the revival spiritual songs.

Winston Wilkinson finds this melody a leveled-off relative of the Cork reel 'Take Her Out and Air Her'.[2]

No. 215

HO EVERY ONE THAT THIRSTS, REV 52

Hexatonic, mode 4 b (I II 3 IV V — 7 [VII])

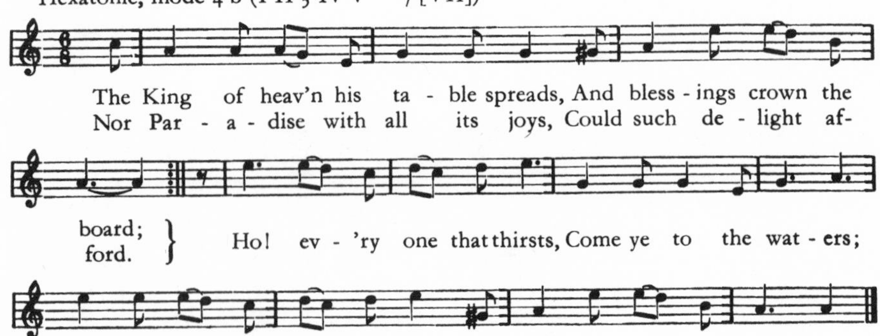
The King of heav'n his ta - ble spreads, And bless - ings crown the board;
Nor Par - a - dise with all its joys, Could such de - light af- ford.
Ho! ev - 'ry one that thirsts, Come ye to the wat - ers;
Free - ly drink and quench your thirst, With Zi - on's sons and daughters.

[1] *Spiritual Folk-Songs*, No. 212.
[2] Petrie, No. 397.

Pardon and peace to dying men,
And endless life are given,
Through the rich blood that Jesus shed,
To raise our souls to heaven.
Ho! every one *etc.*

Millions of souls, in glory now,
Were fed and feasted here;
And millions more still on the way,
Around the board appear.

All things are ready, come away,
Nor weak excuses frame;
Crowd to your places at the feast,
And bless the Founder's name.

The text is by Philip Doddridge, 1702–1751. The raised seventh in the *Revivalist* tune is doubtlessly the work of the arranger of what is essentially a dorian tune. 'Paralytic' in *Spiritual Folk-Songs* and 'Night Thought' and 'Road to Ruin' in this volume are related melodies.

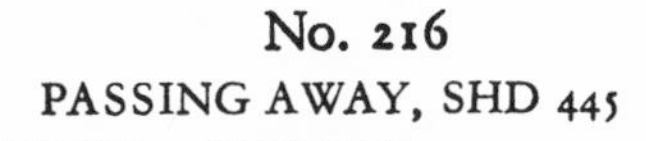

No. 216

PASSING AWAY, SHD 445

Hexatonic, mode 3 A (I II III — V VI VII)

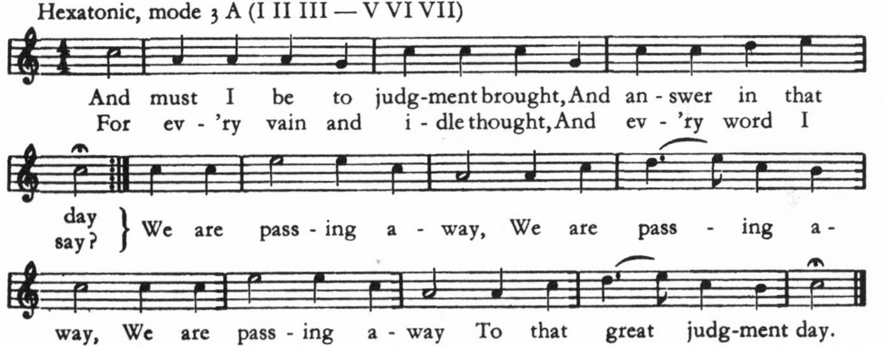
And must I be to judg-ment brought, And an - swer in that
For ev - 'ry vain and i - dle thought, And ev - 'ry word I
day / say? } We are pass - ing a - way, We are pass - ing a -
way, We are pass - ing a - way To that great judg-ment day.

Yes, every secret of my heart
Shall shortly be made known;
And I receive my just desert
For all that I have done.
We are passing *etc.*

How careful then ought I to be,
With what religious fear,
Who such a strict account must give
For my behavior here.

The text is by Charles Wesley, 1707–1788. The tune is accredited to John A. Watson of Alabama and dated December, 1872. The song was lifted from Walker's *Christian Harmony* and inserted in the Denson Revision of the *Original Sacred Harp*, 1936. 'We'll Pass Over Jordan', in this volume has a variant chorus tune.

No. 217

TILL THE WARFARE IS OVER, OSH 76

Tetratonic, mode 3 (I — III — V VI —)

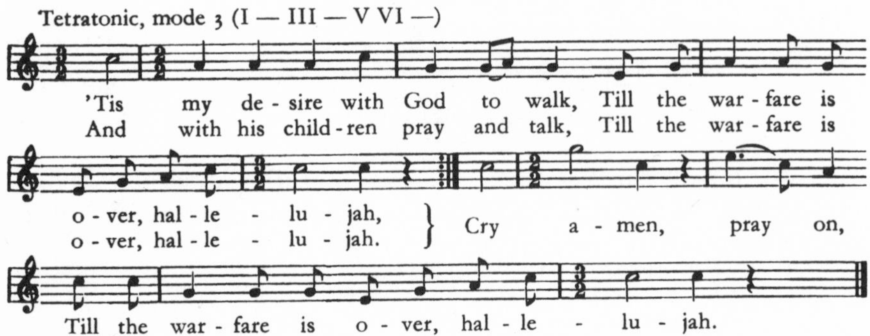
'Tis my de - sire with God to walk, Till the war - fare is
And with his child - ren pray and talk, Till the war - fare is
o - ver, hal - le - lu - jah,
o - ver, hal - le - lu - jah.
Cry a - men, pray on,
Till the war - fare is o - ver, hal - le - lu - jah.

The compiler of the *Sacred Harp* found the text in the *Baptist Harmony*.[1] Variant tunes are 'Warfare' in *Spiritual Folk-Songs*,[2] 'Peace Be Still'[3] and various tunes used with the secular ballad 'Little Musgrave and Lady Barnard'.[4]

No. 218

OLD CHURCHYARD (B), MH, ii, 24

Heptatonic mixolydian, mode 1[5] (I II III IV V VI 7)

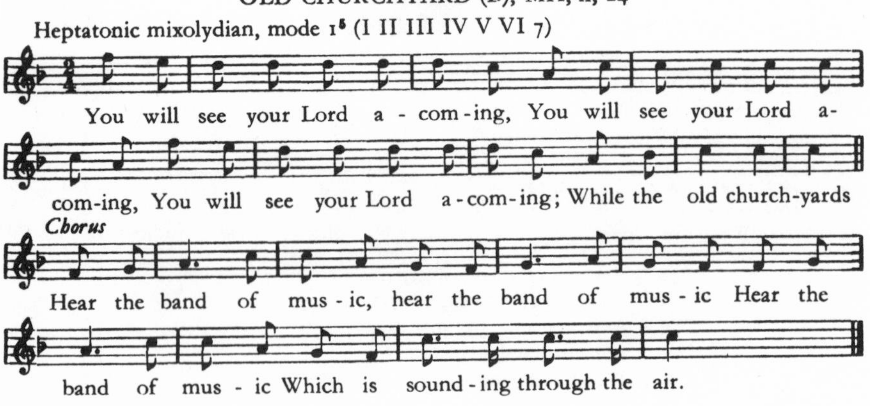
You will see your Lord a - com - ing, You will see your Lord a-
com - ing, You will see your Lord a - com - ing; While the old church-yards
Chorus
Hear the band of mus - ic, hear the band of mus - ic Hear the
band of mus - ic Which is sound - ing through the air.

[1] P. 479. [2] No. 243. [3] *Shaker Music*, p. 63.

[4] For example, Sharp-Karpeles, i, 161, tune A; and 181, tune N.

[5] It may be looked on rather as an ionian "circular" tune with the final unique trumpet — like passage "sounding through the air" on the fift of its scale.

Gabriel sounds his mighty trumpet, *(three times)*
Through the old churchyards,
While the band of music, *(three times)*
Shall be sounding through the air.

He'll awake all the nations,
From the old churchyards,
While the band *etc.*

There will be a mighty wailing,
At the old churchyards,
While the band *etc.*

O sinnner, you will tremble,
At the old churchyards, *etc.*

You will flee to rocks and mountains,
From the old churchyards.

You will see the saints arising,
From the old churchyards.

Angels bear them to the Savior,
From the old churchyards.

Then we'll shout our sufferings over,
From the old churchyards.

This New England revival spiritual song is found elsewhere only in Mason's *Harp of the South*, a northern book despite its title,[1] where the text varies a little. The first part of the above tune is nearly the same as the chorus part of 'Holy War',[2] and of 'O Thou My Soul' in this volume. 'Resurrection Morning' in this volume is a variant tune and has the same Last Day subject matter and the same type of movement but, surprisingly, no textual overlapping with the above despite the fact that both texts are made up of wandering lines.

There is a record of this song's having been sung at a Millerite (Second Adventist) baptism in eastern New York state in 1843[3]. The prominent "churchyard" theme made the song appropriate to meetings in the cemeteries before the time of the predicted coming of Christ. According to Sears, "Many [of the Millerites] sought the graveyards where friends were buried, so as to join them as they arose

[1] P. 294.
[2] *Spiritual Folk-Songs*, No. 212.
[3] Sears, p. 136.

from their earthly resting places and ascend with them."[1] And Sears records that on such occasions they sang precisely the "old Millerite song" under present consideration.[2]

After such prophetic warnings as those in the above stanzas pointing to the Second Coming, which the Millerites timed for 1843, and after that event failed to take place, an alteration of the text became imperative. In the New Hampshire *Pilgrims' Songster* of 1853 we find the same song with the stanza:

We have felt the Advent Glory,
While the vision "seemed to tarry",
When we comforted each other
With the words of holy writ.

And another song in the same booklet shows how the Millennial folk postponed the Advent:

O praise the Lord, we do not fear
To tell the world he'll come next year.
In eighteen hundred fifty- four
The saints will shout their sufferings o'er.

Winston Wilkinson notes the relationship of the tune to an Irish reel 'Take Her Out and Air Her'. He was not able to document the precise variant, but points out a less close relationship to the tune in Petrie, No. 397.

The same tune was used in the young Total Abstinence crusade in the 1840's with a text whose opening stanza was

The tetotalers are coming, *three times*
With the cold water pledge.
Chorus
We're a band of freemen, *three times*
And we'll sound it through the land.[3]

[1] *Ibid.*, p. 181.
[2] *Ibid.*, p. 183.
[3] *Ohio Harmonist*, p. 196. Here is told how the movement got its first push "on the glorious eighth of April, 1841" when the "Immortal Six reformed inebriates" of Baltimore (William K. Mitchell, tailor; J. F. Hoss, carpenter; D. Anderson, blacksmith; George Steers, wheelwright; J. McCurley, coachmaker; and Arch Campbell, silver-plater) met and founded the Washington Total Abstinence Society. The wide spread and intensity of this movement is indicated by the prevalence of temperance songs in the country song books of the period both in the southern and the north central states. The songs were made of tunes which were then popular, largely folk-tunes, with temperance text parodies like the one above.

No. 219

WE'LL JOIN HEART AND HAND, OSH 333

Heptatonic ionian, mode 3 (I II III IV V VI VII)

1
2

Come, thou fount of ev-'ry bless-ing, Tune my heart to sing thy grace;
Streams of mer-cy nev-er ceas-ing, Call for songs of loud-est praise.

Chorus

Bless the Lord, O my soul, Praise the Lord, O my broth-er, Shout and sing, O my

sis-ter, Give him glo-ry, O my fath-er, And re-joice, O my mother, And we'll

trav-el on to-geth-er, And we'll join heart and hands for Ca-naan.

The familiar verse text is by Robert Robinson, 1735–1790. The chorus brings a remarkable grouping of revival shouts. The *Sacred Harp* announced the song as the product of the book's compiler, B. F. White, and the Reverend R. E. Brown of Barbour County, Alabama.

No. 220

LIFT UP YOUR HEADS, RHD 27

Heptatonic, aeolian, mode 2 (I II 3 IV V 6 7)

Lift up your heads, Im-man-uel's friends; O glo-ry hal-le hal-le-lu-jah!
And taste the pleas-ures Je-sus sends; O glo-ry hal-le hal-le-lu-jah!

Let no-thing cause you to de-lay,
But hast-en on the good old way, } O glo-ry hal-le hal-le-lu-jah!

Our conflicts here, though great they be,
Shall not prevent our victory;
If we but watch, and strive, and pray,
Like soldiers in the good old way.

O good old way, how sweet thou art!
May none of us from thee depart,
But may our actions always say,
We're marching in the good old way.

Then far beyond this mortal shore,
We'll meet with those who've gone before,
And shout to think we've gained the day,
By marching in the good old way.

The anonymous text was widely sung in American revival circles during the early decades of the nineteenth century. It appeared also among the Primitive Methodists in England.[1] Tonally and textually related are 'Good Old Way (A)' and 'Good Old Way (B)' in *Spiritual Folk-Songs*.[2] The trend of the tune points to a dorian antecedent.

No. 221

CHRISTIAN BAND, MH, ii, 30

Hexatonic, mode 3 A (I II III — V VI VII)

Here is a band of breth-ren dear, I will be in this band, hal-le-lu - jah;
Their lead - er tells them not to fear, I will be in this band, hal-le-lu - jah;

Chorus
I will be in this band, hal-le-lu - jah, In the Second Advent band, hal-le-lu - jah!

As I was walking out one day,
I will be in this band, hallelujah!
And thinking about this good old way,
I will be in this band, hallelujah!

"There was a voice which reached my soul,
Fear not, I make the wounded whole."

My dungeon shook, my chains fell off,
My soul unfettered went aloft.

I little thought he was so nigh,
He spoke and made me smile and cry.

Now bless the Lord, I can proclaim,
That Jesus has done all things well.

[1] See the Ranters' *Hymns and Spiritual Songs*, printed in England about 1820, No. 17.
[2] Nos. 72 and 169 respectively, where further references are given.

O shout on, children, shout, you're free,
For Christ has bought your liberty.

O bless the Lord, we need not fear,
For Daniel says he'll come this year.

Both prophets and apostles too,
Their writings show this doctrine true.

The text is a Second Adventist make-over of verses which were familiar in revival circles.[1] The last two stanzas may well have been added by the Adventists themselves in 1843 or 1844, the time when Christ was to have appeared again. The chorus text was widely popular.[2]

No. 222

JUDGMENT DAY IS COMING, REV 70

Pentatonic, mode 3 (I II III — V VI —)

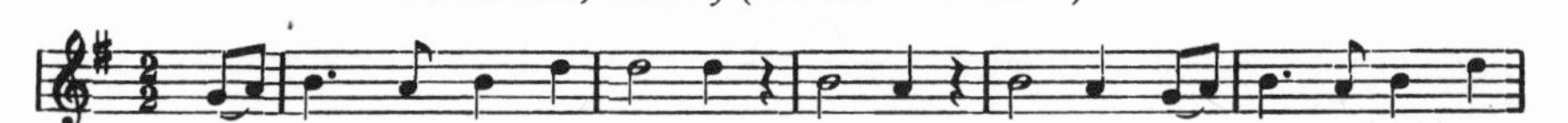

The judg-ment day is com-ing, com-ing, com-ing, The judgment day is

Chorus

coming, Oh that great day. Let us take the wings of the morning And fly a-way to

Je - sus; Let us take the wings of the morn-ing, And shout the ju - bi - lee.

2. I see the Judge descending, *etc.*
3. I see the dead arising.
4. I see the world assembled.
5. I hear the sentence uttered.
6. I hear the wicked wailing, *etc.*
   For they took not the wings *etc.*
7. I hear the righteous shouting, *etc.*
   For they took the wings *etc.*

The words of the chorus are found, in variant form, also in 'Wings of the Morning' and 'Had I Wings' in *Spiritual Folk-Songs.*[3]

[1] See 'Band Hymn' in this volume.
[2] See *Spiritual Folk-Songs*, Nos. 181 and 220.
[3] Nos. 179 and 197 respectively.

No. 223

WE'LL WAIT TILL JESUS COMES, BS 122

Pentatonic, mode 3 (I II III — V VI —)

O land of rest, for thee I sigh, When will the moment come, When I shall

Chorus

lay my arm-or by, And dwell in peace at home? We'll wait till Jesus comes, We'll

wait till Je-sus comes; We'll wait till Je - sus comes, And we'll be gath-er'd home.

Further stanzas of the text are given under 'New Prospect'.[1] Similar tunes are Stephen Foster's 'Hard Times Come Again No More' and its parody, 'Hard Crackers'.[2]

No. 224

BEAUTIFUL MORNING, REV 357

Pentatonic, mode 2 (I — 3 IV V — 7 [VII])

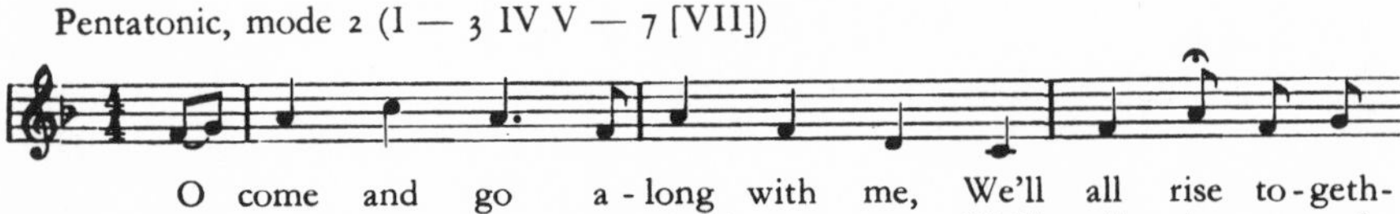

O come and go a - long with me, We'll all rise to - geth-
I'm bound fair Ca - naan's land to see, We'll all rise to - geth-

Chorus

er in the morn - ing; } In the morn - ing, what a beau - ti - ful morn - ing
er in the morn - ing. }

that will be When we all rise to - geth - er in the morn - ing.

[1] *Spiritual Folk-Songs*, No. 133.
[2] Dolph, p. 320.

I'll join with those who're gone before, we'll *etc.*
Where sin and sorrow are no more, we'll *etc.*

A few more rolling years at most
Will land my soul on Canaan's coast.

Oh! what a happy time 'twill be,
When I my friends in heaven shall see.

There we may tell our sufferings o'er,
When we shall reach that happy shore.

Oh! what a happy company!
May I be there that sight to see.

Tune and words are variants of those found as 'Sweet Morning' in *Spiritual Folk-Songs.*

No. 225

WHEN YOU ARRIVE, REV 336

Heptatonic ionian, mode 3 (I II III IV V VI VII)

O tell me no more Of this world's vain store,
A count-ry I've found Where true joys a - bound,
The time for such tri - fles With me now is o'er. Then
To dwell I'm de - ter-min'd On that hap - py ground. When
you'll give him glo - ry, And I'll give him glo - ry, We will
you ar-rive, when I ar-rive, When they ar-rive, when we all ar-rive,
shout and give him glo - ry, When we all ar - rive at home.

The verse text is a part of John Gambold's translation of 'Ach! sagt mir nichts von eiteln Schätzen' by Benjamin Schmolch (1672–1769), a hymnist of the German pietistic movement. The tune is that international one attached in German, for example, to 'O das ist ein' Fliege an der Wand' and to 'O du lieber Augustin'.[1]

[1] See Erk-Böhme, ii, 250.

No. 226

ZION'S HILL, REV 420

Pentatonic, mode 3 (I II III — V VI —)

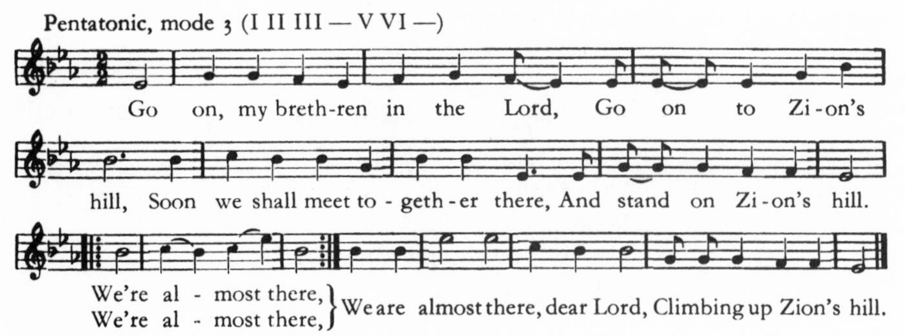
Go on, my breth-ren in the Lord, Go on to Zi-on's
hill, Soon we shall meet to-geth-er there, And stand on Zi-on's hill.
We're al - most there,
We're al - most there,
We are almost there, dear Lord, Climbing up Zion's hill.

I have some friends before me gone,
They've gone to Zion's hill,
And I'm resolved to travel on
Till I reach Zion's hill.

A little longer here below,
Climbing up Zion's hill,
And then to glory I shall go,
And stand on Zion's hill.

Amen, amen, my soul replies,
Climbing up Zion's hill,
I'm bound to meet you in the skies,.
And stand on Zion's hill.

Now here's my heart and here's my hand,
Climbing up Zion's hill;
I'll meet you in that heavenly land,
And stand on Zion's hill.

The text, not found elsewhere, may have been inspired by Charles Wesley's

Our souls are in his mighty hand,
And he shall keep them still,
And you and I shall surely stand
With him on Zion's hill.

McDowell found a variant of this song recently in the Tennessee foothills of the Cumberland Mountains.[1] The tune is related to 'Swing Low Sweet Chariot', the variant made famous by negro singers. Another negro variant of 'Zion's Hill', both tune and words, is 'Climbing up Zion's Hill', BB 56. The tune is a member of the 'Lord Lovel' family; references given under 'Eden' in this volume.

[1] *Songs of the Old Camp Ground*, p. 40.

No. 227

CONTENTION, OL 30

Heptatonic ionian, mode 3 (I II III IV V VI VII)

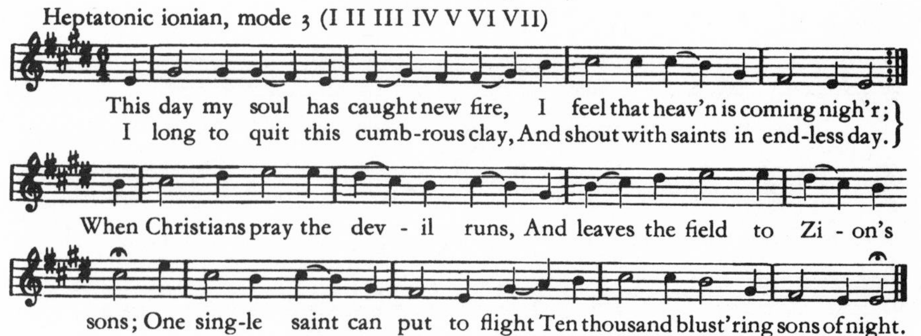
This day my soul has caught new fire, I feel that heav'n is coming nigh'r;
I long to quit this cumb-rous clay, And shout with saints in end-less day.
When Christians pray the dev - il runs, And leaves the field to Zi - on's
sons; One sing-le saint can put to flight Ten thousand blust'ring sons of night.

The troops of hell are mustering round,
But Zion still is gaining ground.
The hottest fire is now begun,
Come, stand the fight till it is won.
Some foes are wounded, others fell;
Fight and save the rest from hell.
Ye little Sampsons, up and try,
And fight old Satan till you die.

When Israel, come to Jericho,
Began to pray, to shout and blow,
The tow'ring walls came tumbling down
Like thunder, flat upon the ground.
See Gideon marching out to fight;
He had no weapon but his light;
He took his pitcher and his lamp,
And stormed with ease the Midian camp.

Our God who conquers death and sin,
Will smile and say, "My saints, come in!
You've fought through many a battle sore,
But now you'll reign forevermore."
All glory! glory to the Lamb!
Through all my soul I feel the flame.
O when my soul shall hence remove,
I'll shout and sing with those above.

The text overlaps largely that of 'Shout Old Satan's Kingdom Down' and 'Satan's Kingdom' in this volume. See the latter for further references. Although this song appears in one of the most recent of the shape-note song books, the *Olive Leaf*, 1878, the song is old. The editor of that book states that the text was furnished by "Rev. Samuel Hauser, this Editor's uncle, 1810". And the tune, he states, was from James Seaton, 1824.

No. 228

AWAY OVER JORDAN, REV 255

Hexatonic, mode 3 b (I II III IV V VI —)

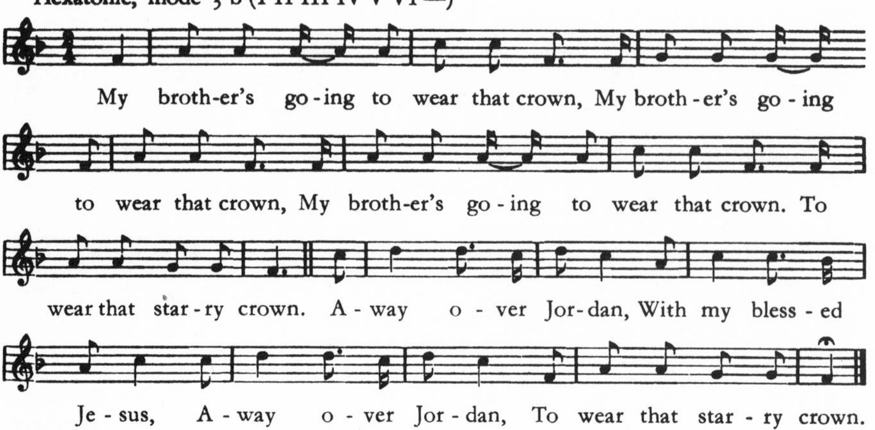
My broth-er's go-ing to wear that crown, My broth-er's go-ing
to wear that crown, My broth-er's go-ing to wear that crown. To
wear that star-ry crown. A-way o-ver Jor-dan, With my bless-ed
Je-sus, A-way o-ver Jor-dan, To wear that star-ry crown.

2. You must live right to wear that crown, *etc.*
3. John Wesley's gone to wear that crown, *etc.*
4. My father's gone to wear that crown.
5. My mother's gone to wear that crown.

The source of this song and of its variant, 'Resurrected' in *Spiritual Folk-Songs* is possibly 'Sister's Farewell' in this volume. All are members of the 'Roll Jordan' tune family.[1]

No. 229

BAND HYMN, REV 416

Hexatonic, mode 3 b (I II III IV V VI —)

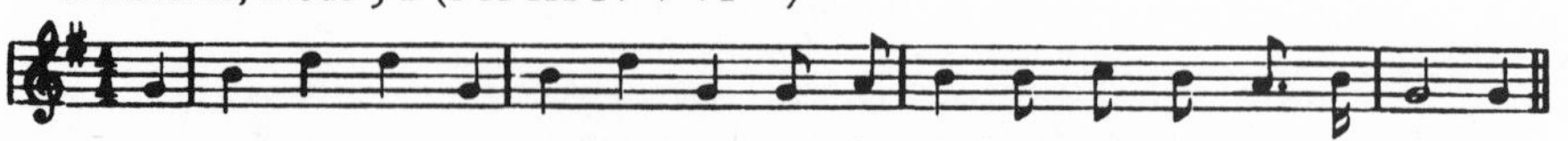

O, we're a band of breth-ren dear, I be-long to this band, hal-le-lu-jah!
Who live as pil-grim stran-gers here, I be-long to this band, hal-le-lu-jah!

Chorus

Hal-le-lu-jah, hal-le-lu-jah, I be-long to this band, hal-le-lu-jah!

[1] References are given under 'Glorious Day' in this volume.

The prophets and apostles too
Did belong *etc.*
And all God's children here below
Do belong *etc.*
Chorus

King David on his throne of state
Did belong *etc.*
And Laz'rus at the rich man's gate
Did belong *etc.*

The Jews and Gentiles, free and bond,
May belong *etc.*
The rich and poor the world around
May belong *etc.*

I hope to meet my brethren there,
They belong *etc.*
Who often join'd with me in prayer,
They belong *etc.*

The tune and the words of the chorus are found also with 'Ragan' and 'Jester' in *Spiritual Folk-Songs.*[1] A variant song in this volume is 'Christian Band'.

No. 230

MARY BLAIN, UHP 148

Hexatonic, mode 3 b (I II III IV V VI —)

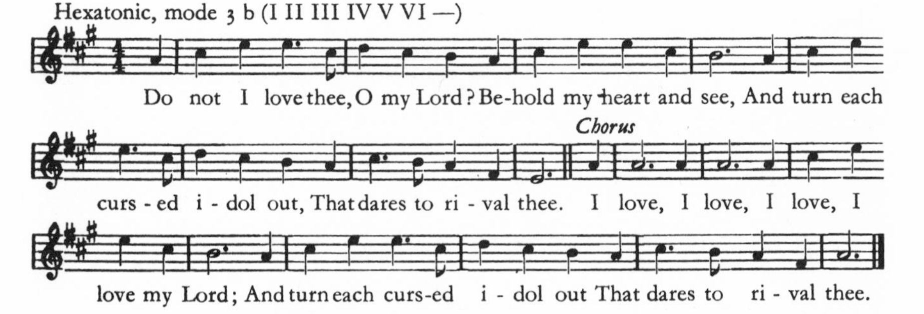
Do not I love thee, O my Lord? Be-hold my heart and see, And turn each
Chorus
curs - ed i - dol out, That dares to ri - val thee. I love, I love, I love, I
love my Lord; And turn each curs-ed i - dol out That dares to ri - val thee.

Do not I love thee from my soul?
Then let me nothing love;
Dead be my heart to every joy
When Jesus cannot move.
Chorus

Thou know'st I love thee, dearest Lord,
But O I long to soar
Far from the sphere of mortal joys
And learn to love thee more.

[1] Nos. 181 and 220 respectively.

The verse text is by Philip Doddridge, 1702–1751. An editor's note in the *Union Harp* states that "The air of 'Mary Blain' is an old melody of ante-bellum [Civil War] days. The notes [presumably the harmonic parts] were first applied to it by Henry F. Chandler [a Georgian] in 1854."

In that same year 'The New Mary Blane' appeared in *The Singer's Companion*, New York, 1854, p. 37. There it has a similar tune with pseudo-negroid word-twistings and looks like pure black-face minstrel stuff; this despite the publisher's note that the song "is supposed to be an original Plantation Melody, arranged and partly composed by E. P. Christy." G. L. Kittredge has given many other versions, text only, of 'Mary Blane'.[1] The oldest of these is from 1846, a song whose composer was given as William Bennett. Subsequent versions are make-overs, all in negro dialect as that dialect was conceived in the North and stylized for minstrel purposes. The song appears to have been immensely popular for a number of years following 1846.

No. 231

COME AND TASTE, SOH (1854) 105

Hexatonic, mode 3 A (I II III — V VI VII)

Come and taste, a - long with me, Con - sol - a - tion run-ning free,
Con - sol - a - tion run - ning free, And I will give him glo - ry.
Chorus
'Tis re - lig - ion we be - lieve, O glo - ry hal - le - lu - jah!
Soon it will land our souls up yon-der; Glo - ry hal - le - lu - jah!

From our Father's wealthy throne,
Sweeter than the honey-comb,
Sweeter than the honey-comb,
And I will *etc.*

Wherefore should I feast alone?
Two are better far than one, *etc.*.

[1] JAFL, xxxix, 200ff.

All that come with free good-will
Make the banquet sweeter still.

Now I go to Mercy's door,
Asking for a little more.

Jesus gives a double share,
Calling me his chosen heir.

Goodness, running like a stream
Through the New Jerusalem.

By a constant breaking forth,
Sweetens earth and heaven both.

Saints and angels sing aloud,
To behold the shining crowd.

Coming in at Mercy's door,
Making still the number more.

Heaven's here, and heaven's there,
Comfort flowing everywhere.

And I boldly do profess
That my soul hath got a taste.

Now I'll go rejoicing home
From the banquet of perfume.

Finding manna on the road,
Dropping from the throne of God.

O return, ye sons of grace,
Turn and see God's smiling face.

Hark, he calls backsliders home,
Then from him no longer roam.

Burrage attributes the text to John Leland, 1754–1841. The tune and, strangely enough, the text also have gone over in somewhat altered form into the play-party environment. Botkin finds the text

Consolation running free, *(three times)*
Come, my love, and go with me.[1]

I assume the borrowing direction as being from the spiritual to the play-party, rather than the other way around, not only because of the textual evidence. This assumption agrees also with the general custom of playing children and youth of borrowing scraps from ballads and popular ditties to satisfy the modest song demands of the play-party and other forms of games.

[1] *The American Play-Party Song*, p. 173.

No. 232

O CHRISTIANS PRAISE HIM, GOS 290

Hexatonic, mode 3 b (I II III IV V VI —)

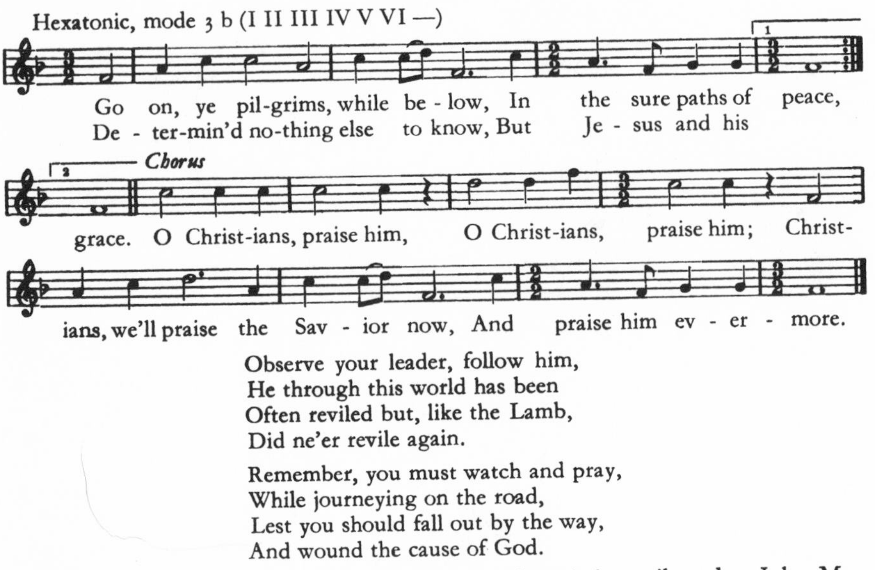
Chorus
Go on, ye pil-grims, while be - low, In the sure paths of peace,
De - ter-min'd no-thing else to know, But Je - sus and his
grace. O Christ-ians, praise him, O Christ-ians, praise him; Christ-
ians, we'll praise the Sav - ior now, And praise him ev - er - more.

Observe your leader, follow him,
He through this world has been
Often reviled but, like the Lamb,
Did ne'er revile again.

Remember, you must watch and pray,
While journeying on the road,
Lest you should fall out by the way,
And wound the cause of God.

The song is found also in the *Sacred Harp* where it is attributed to John Massengale and dated "about 1850". The tune is a member of the 'Roll Jordan' family.[1]

No. 233

WEEPING MARY, *White Spirituals*, p. 257

Heptatonic ionian, mode 3 (I II III IV V VI VII)

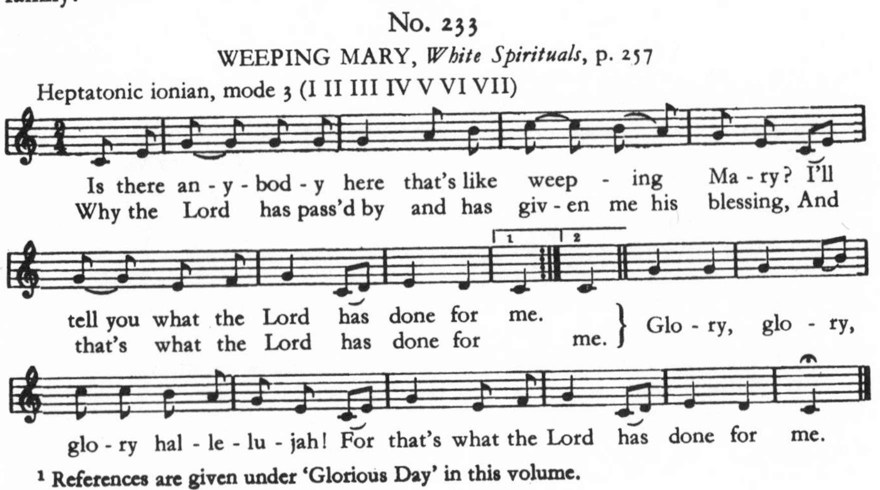
Is there an - y - bod - y here that's like weep - ing Ma - ry? I'll
Why the Lord has pass'd by and has giv - en me his blessing, And
tell you what the Lord has done for me.
that's what the Lord has done for me.
Glo - ry, glo - ry,
glo - ry hal - le - lu - jah! For that's what the Lord has done for me.

[1] References are given under 'Glorious Day' in this volume.

This text was published first by Louise Pound.[1] It had come down as a tradition in her family from the 1820's when it had been heard in a New York state Methodist "protracted meeting". The tune, from the same source, was recorded for me by Miss Pound and I published it in *White Spirituals*.[2] Other variants of the tune are in the minor modes.[3]

No. 234

CHRISTIAN'S COMFORT, SOC 81

Hexatonic, mode 3 b (I II III IV V VI —)

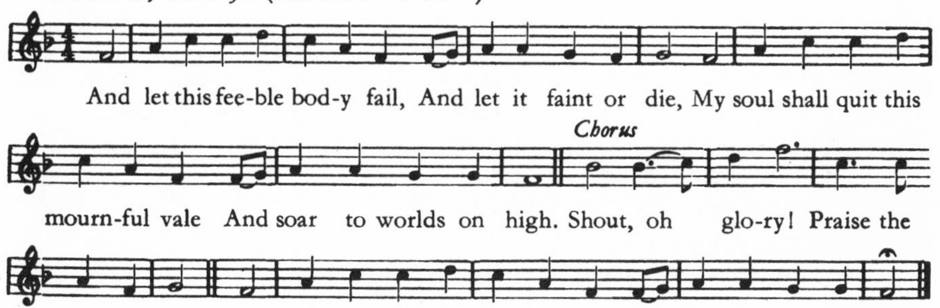

And let this fee-ble bod-y fail, And let it faint or die, My soul shall quit this
Chorus
mourn-ful vale And soar to worlds on high. Shout, oh glo-ry! Praise the
Lord on high. I hope to die while prais-ing God, Then dwell a-bove the sky.

Further stanzas of the text by Charles Wesley, 1707–1788, are given under 'Pleasant Hill' in this volume. The tune is of course a direct borrowing of Stephen Foster's 'Susanna Don't you Cry'. The borrower was presumably William C. Davis, Georgia singing-school master, whose name appears on the page with the song in the *Social Harp*. The song was dated 1852, a year when the Foster minstrel tune was in its first wave of popularity. 'Christian's Comfort' is thus an interesting example of the interplay between folk-song and popular song. An ancestor tune had been taken by Foster, consciously or otherwise, from its revival setting, altered slightly, provided with a comic text, and placed in an environment in which it spread like wild-fire. In the course of this spread it came back to the people, the folk, and despite its smell of burnt cork was welcomed with open arms, shorn of its negroid nonsense, provided with a suitable spiritual text, and re-introduced into the same revivalistic circles from which its tonal forebear had been taken.

And as to authorship claims? Foster had called it his own and gave no credit to the revival folk. Then Davis claimed it and gave no credit to Foster or the

[1] *Modern Language Notes*, xxxiii, 442ff.

[2] P. 256.

[3] Among such variants are those in *White Spirituals*, p. 255ff.; JFSS, viii, 66; 'Susanna', JWF, ii, 174ff.; and 'Where Art Thou Going', JWF, ii, 223, and iii, 76.

minstrel folk. This would seem to be about tit for tat, and correct, for it did belong to both men and both folks.[1] The tune is a member of the 'Roll Jordan' family.[2]

No. 235

'TIS A WONDER, OSH 437

Hexatonic, mode 3 b (I II III IV V VI —)

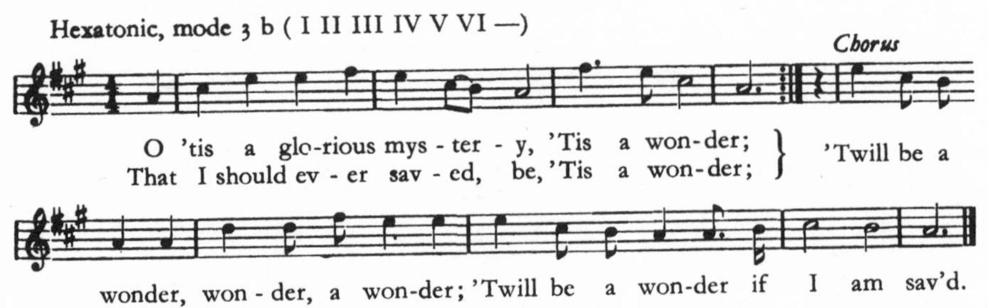
Chorus
O 'tis a glo-rious mys - ter - y, 'Tis a won-der;
That I should ev - er sav - ed, be, 'Tis a won-der;
'Twill be a
wonder, won - der, a won-der; 'Twill be a won-der if I am sav'd.

The song was recorded for the *Sacred Harp* in 1857. For textual and less noteworthy melodic similarities see a song by the same title in *Spiritual Folk-Songs*.

No. 236

STRUGGLE ON, OSH 400

Hexatonic, mode 3 A (I II III — V VI VII)

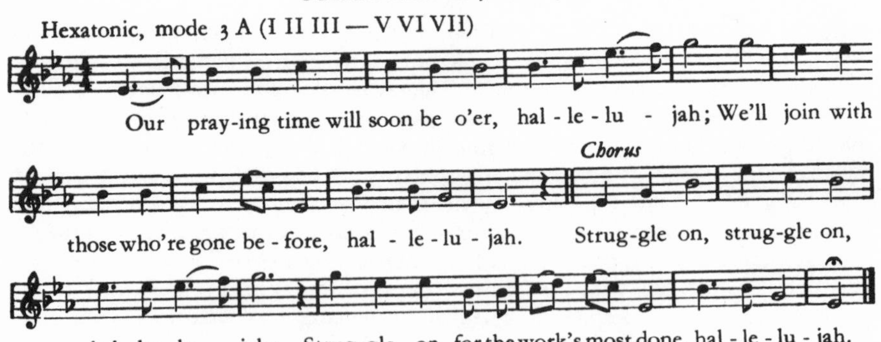
Our pray-ing time will soon be o'er, hal - le - lu - jah; We'll join with
Chorus
those who're gone be - fore, hal - le - lu - jah. Strug-gle on, strug-gle on,
hal - le - lu - jah; Strug-gle on, for the work's most done, hal - le - lu - jah.

To love and bless and praise the name, hallelujah.,
Of Jesus Christ, the bleeding Lamb, hallelujah.

This tune was inserted in the *Sacred Harp*, 1859 edition, and signed by H. S. Rees. It stems perhaps from 'Royal Proclamation'.[3]

[1] Compare in this connection my article in the *Musical Quarterly*, xxii, 156ff.
[2] References are given under 'Glorious Day' in this volume.
[3] *Spiritual Folk-Songs*, No. 84.

No. 237

YEAR OF JUBILEE, SOC 105

Heptatonic aeolian, mode 4 (I II 3 IV V 6 7)

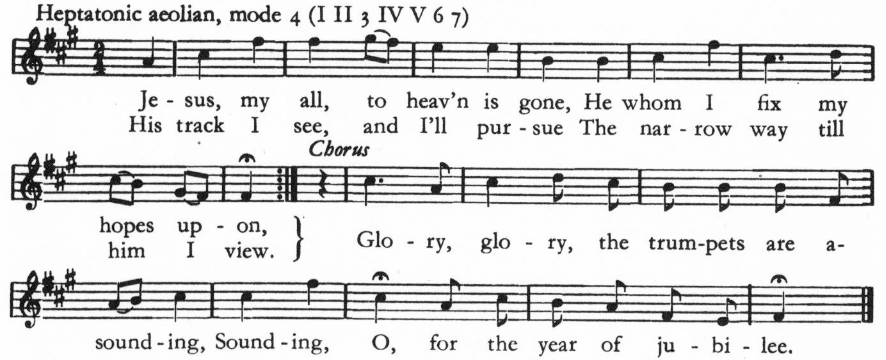
Chorus
Je - sus, my all, to heav'n is gone, He whom I fix my
His track I see, and I'll pur - sue The nar - row way till
hopes up - on,
him I view.
Glo - ry, glo - ry, the trum-pets are a-
sound - ing, Sound - ing, O, for the year of ju - bi - lee.

Further stanzas of the text by John Cennick, 1718–1755, are given under 'River of Jordan'.[1] The song is attributed in the *Social Harp* to J. A. Wade and is dated 1854. The tune is related to 'Heaven Born Soldiers'.[2]

No. 238

PART NO MORE, HOC 75

Pentatonic, mode 1 (I II — IV V VI —)

A - wake our souls, a - way our fears! When we get to
A - wake and run the heav'n - ly race! When we get to
1
2
Chorus
heav - en we will part no more;
heav - en we will part no more.
Fare you well, O
fare you well! When we get to heav-en we will part no more.

Let every trembling thought be gone;
When we get *etc.*
And put a cheerful courage on;
When we get *etc.*
Fare you well, *etc.*

The basic text is by Isaac Watts, 1674–1748.

[1] *Spiritual Folk-Songs*, No. 189.

[2] *Ibid.*, No. 195, where further tune-comparative references are given.

No. 239
GO ON, SOC 20

Pentatonic, mode 3 (I II III — V VI —)

O may I worth - y prove to see The saints in
full pros - per - i - ty.
Chorus
Go on, go on, we'll
soon meet a - gain On the bright fron - tiers of glo - ry.

For the fuller text see 'Exhilaration' in *Spiritual Folk-Songs*. It looks as though the recorders of the tune, J. A. and J. F. Wade, had switched the two halves from their normal order, placing first what seems more suitable as a second part. An alteration according to this suggestion would give the resulting tune the character of mode one, with mixolydian implication.

No. 240
SATAN'S KINGDOM, RHD 62

Pentatonic, mode 3 (I II III — V VI —)

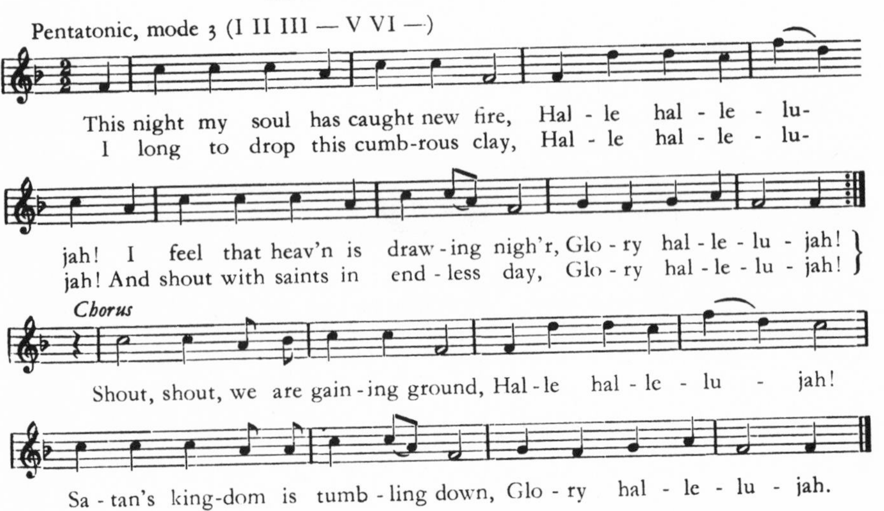
This night my soul has caught new fire, Hal - le hal - le - lu-
I long to drop this cumb-rous clay, Hal - le hal - le - lu-
jah! I feel that heav'n is draw - ing nigh'r, Glo - ry hal - le - lu - jah!
jah! And shout with saints in end - less day, Glo - ry hal - le - lu - jah!
Chorus
Shout, shout, we are gain - ing ground, Hal - le hal - le - lu - jah!
Sa - tan's king-dom is tumb - ling down, Glo - ry hal - le - lu - jah.

When Christians pray the devil runs
And leaves the fields to Zion's sons;
One praying soul will put to flight
Ten thousand blust'ring sons of night.
Chorus

Ye little Sampsons, up and fight,
Put the Philistian host to flight;
The troops of hell are must'ring round,
But Zion's sons, maintain your ground.

The heavenly flame is now begun
And soon the vict'ry will be won.
Some foes are wounded, others fell,
The Lord is saving souls from hell.

When Israel came to Jericho,
Began to pray and shout and blow,
The tottering walls came tumbling down,
The noise like thunder shook the ground.

See Gideon marching out to fight,
He had no weapon but a light,
He took his pitcher and his lamp
And storm'd with ease the Midian camp.

The Hebrews in a dreadful flame
Found Zion's King was still the same;
Young David's weapon seem'd but dull,
Yet broke Goliath's brazen skull.

Saint Paul and Silas bound in jail,
Would pray and sing in spite of hell;
They made the prison loudly ring,
Although opposed by hell's dark king.

Behold what giants great and tall,
And Christ's dear lambs but few and small;
But Jesus, Jesus is their friend,
He'll help them fight unto the end.

Our conflicts here will soon be past,
When Satan into hell is cast;
Then we shall lay our armor by
And shout the vict'ry through the sky.

Our Lord who conquered death and sin,
Will smiling say, "My saints come in,
You've often fought in battles sore,
And now shall reign forever more.

"Come wear the crown and let your tongues
Unite with angels in their songs,
You now are free from toil and pains,
Let victory sound in endless strains."

All glory, glory to the Lamb,
Bless, O my soul, his wondrous name.
On angel's wings I soon shall rise
And shout his glories in the skies.

To God the Father, God the Son,
To God the Spirit, three in one,
Be honor praise and glory given,
By all on earth and all in heaven.

Three songs are both textually and melodically related to this early New England spiritual. They are 'Shout Old Satan's Kingdom Down' in this volume, and 'Shout On Pray On' and 'I'm Going Home'.[1] The text above, like that of its variant songs,[2] is merely an accumulation of independent distichs and quatrains of the "wandering" sort. It was from texts of this sort that the negroes drew most heavily.

A compiler's note in *Revival Hymns* sheds light on the age of the song. "This hymn and the original melody," he says, "which have been so useful in revival seasons for more than half a century, and which, it is believed, have never before been published together, were lately procured after considerable search, from the diary of an aged servant of Christ, bearing the date of 1810." The half century of use, stretching back from the time, 1842, when this note appeared in *Revival Hymns*, would bring the New England use of the song back to the 1790's, before the western-born camp meetings began to help in the spread of the revival spiritual songs.[3]

[1] *Spiritual Folk-Songs*, No. 166 and No. 183 respectively.
[2] 'Contention' in this volume has much the same text.
[3] The first page of 'Satan's Kingdom' as it appears in *Revival Hymns* is reproduced on the frontispiece of this work.

No. 241

OTHER SIDE OF JORDAN, OSH 486

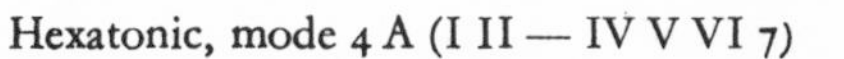

Hexatonic, mode 4 A (I II — IV V VI 7)

On Jor-dan's storm-y banks I stand And cast a wish-ful eye, On the
To Ca-naan's fair and hap-py land Where my pos-ses-sions lie, On the

Chorus

oth-er side of Jor-dan, hal-le-lu-jah. } On the oth-er side of
oth-er side of Jor-dan, hal-le-lu-jah. }

Jor-dan, hal-le-lu-jah, On the oth-er side of Jor-dan, hal-le-lu-jah.

Further stanzas of the text by Samuel Stennett, 1727–1795, are given under 'Jordan' in *Spiritual Folk-Songs*. The song appeared in the 1844 *Sacred Harp* as recorded by J. T. White, relative of the compiler.

It is interesting to note that in the earlier editions of the *Sacred Harp* the *f*'s were not sharped. The tune was thus made over, like so many other dorian airs, into the aeolian form. The song was excluded from the 1869 edition and not taken in again until 1911 when G. B. Daniels, one of the then revisers, restored the song to its dorian character by sharping the *f*'s in accordance with the way they had undoubtedly been sung all along, and as they are still sung, according to my repeated observations at country *Sacred Harp* singings.

No. 242

WAY OVER IN THE HEAVENS

Heptatonic mixolydian, mode 3 (I II III IV V VI 7 [VII]).

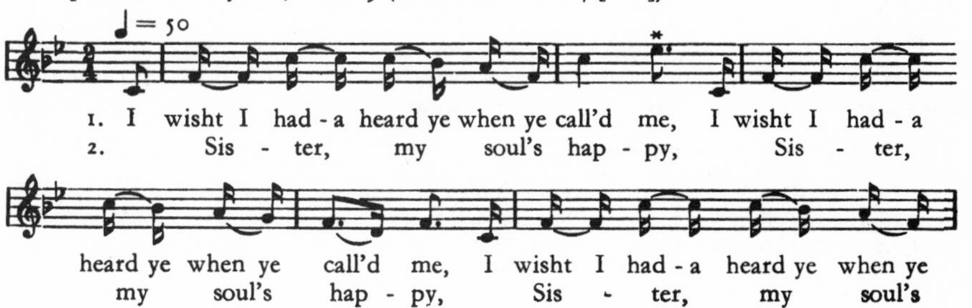

♩ = 50
1. I wisht I had-a heard ye when ye call'd me, I wisht I had-a
2. Sis-ter, my soul's hap-py, Sis-ter,
heard ye when ye call'd me, I wisht I had-a heard ye when ye
my soul's hap-py, Sis-ter, my soul's

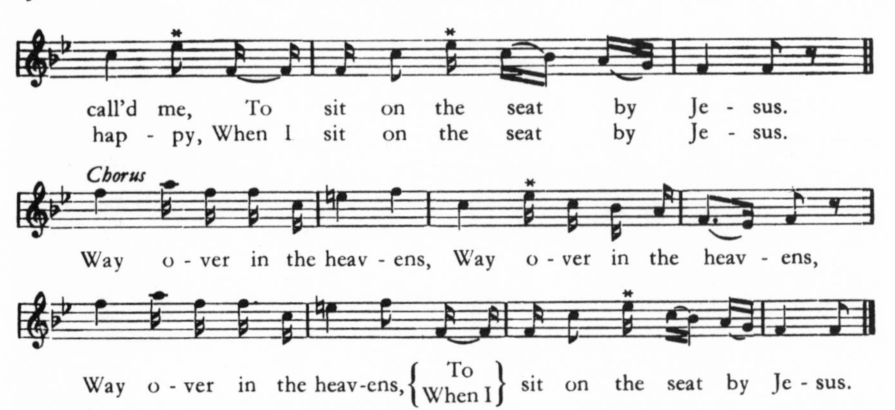
call'd me, To sit on the seat by Je - sus.
hap - py, When I sit on the seat by Je - sus.
Chorus
Way o - ver in the heav - ens, Way o - ver in the heav - ens,
Way o - ver in the heav-ens, To When I sit on the seat by Je - sus.

The song was recorded by the author from the singing of Dr. Sam L. Clark of the Vanderbilt Medical School, Nashville, Tennessee, August 10, 1938. He had learned it from the singing of his mother, Mrs. Martin Clark, and her father, William Giles Lillard, in their family circle. Mr. Lillard had heard and learned it at camp meetings around Murphreesboro, Tennessee, during his youth before the Civil War.

The only other recording of this song known to me is that made recently by L. L. McDowell in a section of Tennessee not far from where Dr. Clark found his song.[1] Mr. McDowell's variant has the two following stanzas:

> I have a mother in the heavens, *(three times)*
> Sitting on a seat with Jesus.
> *Chorus*
> Away up in the heavens, *(three times)*
> Sitting on a seat with Jesus.
>
> Won't you be glad when he calls you? *(three times)*
> Sitting on a seat with Jesus.

The *e*-flats in the above tune (marked by an asterisk) were sung actually and invariably as neutral tones half way between *e*-flat and *e*-natural and became thus the most strangely beautiful feature of the tune.[2]

[1] See *Songs of the Old Camp Ground*, p. 32.

[2] This neutral seventh was noticed and recorded also in Ireland, in a dorian tune; see JIFS. xvi, 97. The singer "never varied". Compare also Sharp *(English Folk-Song, Some Conclusions*, p. 72) as to this phenomenon among English folk-singers.

No. 243

TO THE LAND, SOC 34

Heptatonic mixolydian, mode 1 (I II III IV V VI 7)

Je - - sus my all to heav'n is gone, Where there's
He whom I fix my hopes up - on, Where there's
Chorus To the land, to the land, to the land I am bound, Where there's

Fine *a*

no more storm-y clouds a - ris - ing; }
no more storm-y clouds a - ris - ing. } His track I see, and
no more storm-y clouds a - ris - ing.

I'll pur-sue, Where there's no more storm-y clouds a - ris - ing, The nar-row

D. C. for Chorus

way till him I view, Where there's no more storm-y clouds a - ris - ing.

The basic text is by John Cennick, 1718–1755. Close textual relationship and a melodic kinship of less note may be seen in 'To That Land', the next song in this volume. The second part of the tune, from *a* on, is a building-block[1] in our folk-melodism, one which recurs with remarkable uniformity in many songs. In this volume it is to be found in 'Overton' and 'Louisiana'; in *Spiritual Folk-Songs* in 'Address For All'. Winston Wilkinson points to its occurrence in 'Lady Isabel and the Elf-Knight',[2] 'The Bailiff's Daughter of Islington',[3] and 'Clyde's Water'.[4] I add also 'Sweet William and Lady Margery'.[5]

[1] Some use the German *Baustein* as the technical term for these recurrent tune parts.
[2] In his manuscript collection of folk-songs, iii, 42.
[3] Greig-Keith, p. 84, No. 41, tune 1d.
[4] *Ibid.*, p. 159, No. 67, tune 2b.
[5] Wyman and Brockway, p. 94.

No. 244

TO THAT LAND, REV 61

Heptatonic dorian, mixolydian influence, mode 4 (I II 3 [III] IV V VI 7)

A lit - tle long - er here be - low, Where these dark
Then home to glo - ry we shall go, Where no dark
storm - y clouds a - rise,
storm - y clouds a - rise.
Chorus
To that land, to that land——,
To that land I'm bound, Where no dark storm-y clouds a - rise.

If you get there before I do, *etc.*
Look out for me, I'm coming too, *etc.*

I have some friends before me gone,
And I'm resolved to travel on.

I'll praise God while he lends me breath,
And hope to praise him after death.

And when we land on that blest shore,
We'll shout and sing forever more.

How happy is the pilgrim's lot —
How free from every anxious thought.

Yonder's my house and portion fair;
My treasure and my heart are there.

These stanzaic couplets are of the "wandering" sort. The fourth, 'I'll praise God' etc., for example, wandered all the way from Isaac Watts, first being borrowed and revised by Charles Wesley, according to McCutchan, No. 513.

John Powell calls attention to the tune's relationship to 'The Low Lowlands of Holland'[1] and 'The Rambling Sailor'.[2] Close textual relationship and melodic kinship of less note may be seen in 'To the Land', the preceding song in this volume.

[1] Sharp, *One Hundred English Folksongs*, No. 23.
[2] *Ibid.*, No. 43.

No. 245

LOVER OF THE LORD, OL 119

Pentachordal (I II III IV V — —)

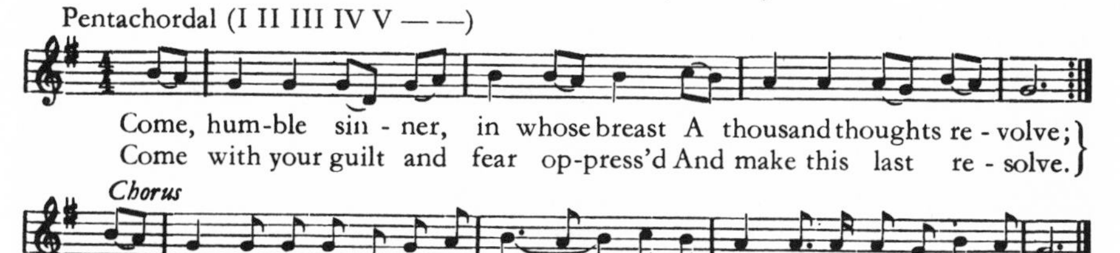
Come, hum-ble sin - ner, in whose breast A thousand thoughts re - volve;
Come with your guilt and fear op-press'd And make this last re - solve.
Chorus
O you must be a lov-er of the Lord——, Or you can't get to heaven when you die.

I'll go to Jesus, though my sin
Hath like a mountain rose;
I know his courts, I'll enter in,
Whatever may oppose.
Chorus

Prostrate I lie before his throne,
And there my guilt confess,
I'll tell him I'm a wretch undone,
Without his sovereign grace.

Further stanzas of the text by Edmund Jones, 1722–1765, are given under 'Hanover' in this volume. The chorus text and the tune, products of the Gospel Hymn era, called forth many parodies. Among them is

O you must be a lover of the landlady's daughter,
Or you can't have a second piece of pie.

No. 246

ONE MORE RIVER, REV 366

Hexatonic, mode 3 A (I II III — V VI VII)

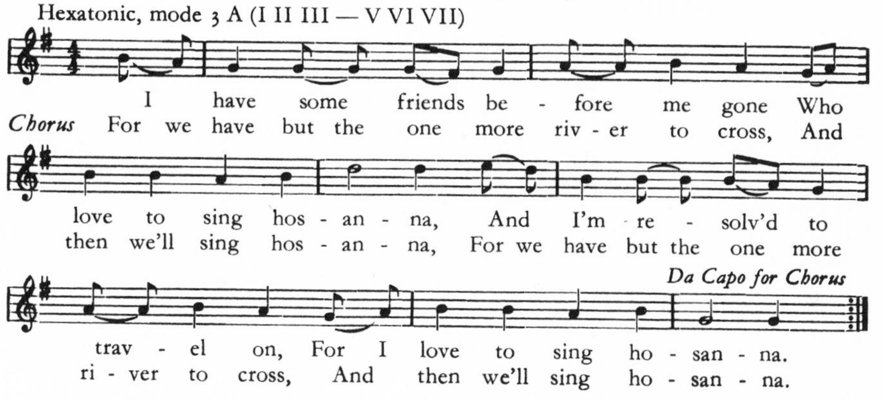
I have some friends be - fore me gone Who
Chorus For we have but the one more riv - er to cross, And
love to sing hos - an - na, And I'm re - solv'd to
then we'll sing hos - an - na, For we have but the one more
Da Capo for Chorus
trav - el on, For I love to sing ho - san - na.
ri - ver to cross, And then we'll sing ho - san - na.

Ten thousand in their endless home
All love to sing hosanna,
And we are to the margin come,
And love to sing hosanna.
Chorus

One family we dwell in him,
We love to sing hosanna,
Though now divided by the stream,
We love to sing hosanna.

One army of the living God,
We love to sing hosanna,
Part of the host have cross'd the flood
Who love to sing hosanna.

Amen, amen, my soul replies,
I love to sing hosanna,
I'm bound to meet you in the skies
Where we will sing hosanna.

The song is constructed of melodic and textual bits which pervaded the revival atmosphere. The "one more river" theme appears again in 'Victoria' in *Spiritual Folk-Songs*[1] and in the negro refrain

And I haint but one more river to cross.[2]

The burnt-cork entertainers, too, were unable to resist its infection. In Shaw's *Popular Songs and Ballads*[3] we find, as the first of fourteen stanzas

Ole Noah, once he built de ark
Dar's one more ribber for to cross,
He patched it up wid hick'ry bark
Dar's one more ribber for to cross.
One more ribber,
And dat ole ribber am Jordan,
One more ribber,
Dar's one more ribber to cross.

[1] No. 229.
[2] *Slave Songs*, p. 5.
[3] Published about 1881; the book's pages are unnumbered.

No. 247

OUR BONDAGE IT SHALL END, OSH 489

Hexatonic, mode 3 A (I II III — V VI VII)

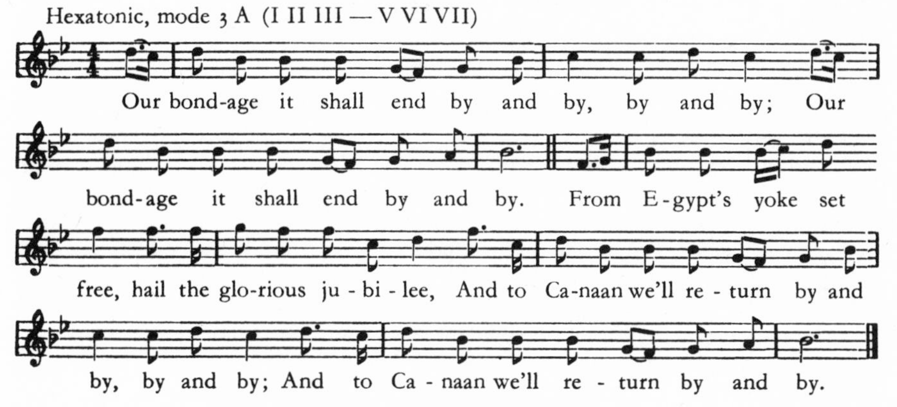
Our bond-age it shall end by and by, by and by; Our
bond-age it shall end by and by. From E-gypt's yoke set
free, hail the glo-rious ju-bi-lee, And to Ca-naan we'll re-turn by and
by, by and by; And to Ca-naan we'll re-turn by and by.

Our deliv'rer he shall come by and by *etc.*
And our sorrows have an end
With our three score years and ten,
And vast glory crown the day by and by *etc.*

Though our enemies are strong, we'll go on *etc.*
Though our hearts dissolve with fear,
Lo, Si-na-ie's *(sic)* God is near,
While the fiery pillar moves we'll go on *etc.*

This song is built on the rhythmic pattern of the 'Captain Kidd' stanza which is discussed under 'You Shall See' in this volume. See references given there to rhythmic and tonal likenesses which tend to cling to the various tunes of the 'Captain Kidd' group.

No. 248

ROUSSEAU'S DREAM, PB 110

Hexatonic mode 3 b (I II III IV V VI —)

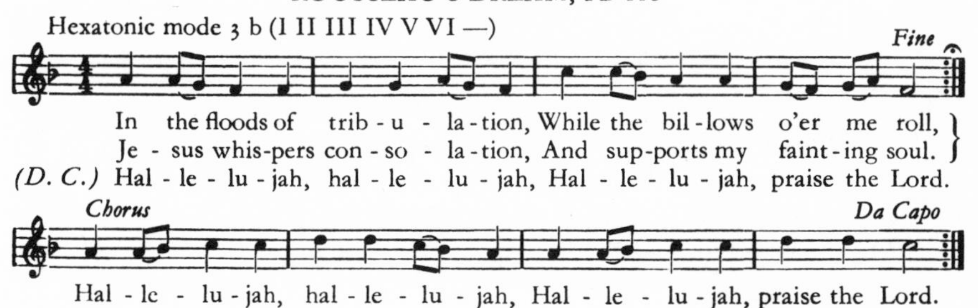
Fine
In the floods of trib-u-la-tion, While the bil-lows o'er me roll,
Je-sus whis-pers con-so-la-tion, And sup-ports my faint-ing soul.
(D. C.) Hal-le-lu-jah, hal-le-lu-jah, Hal-le-lu-jah, praise the Lord.
Chorus
Da Capo
Hal-le-lu-jah, hal-le-lu-jah, Hal-le-lu-jah, praise the Lord.

Wearing there a weight of glory,
Still the path I ne'er forget,
But exulting cry, it led me
To my blessed Savior's feet.
Hallelujah *etc.*

The text is borrowed from the *Sacred Harp.* Samuel Pearce, 1766–1799, is its author. The tune is ascribed generally to Jean Jacques Rousseau. This source assumption has been debated, with Lightwood[1] on the negative, and Metcalf[2] and McCutchan[3] on the affirmative side. If one examines the antecedent Rousseau melody (reproduced by McCutchan) from which the above tune is supposed to have been taken, one may see that the noted French author was merely strolling along in those simplest melodic paths which the folk singers, especially the children, like to follow.

I think therefore that those who take the Rousseau side are imputing a borrowing or an influence where there is merely a basic but accidental *international similarity in tonal trend,* one which the Apostle of Nature followed. Some other tunes which follow this trend more or less faithfully but independently are 'Babylon is Fallen', 'Pleading Savior' and 'Nettleton' in *Spiritual Folk-Songs,*[4] 'Nancy of Yarmouth',[5] and 'Behold There Dawned'.[6] Scarbrough has a good negro parody of the above song, 'Go Tell Aunt Tabbie',[7] one of the many versions sung by Americans generally.

No. 249

HE WAS FOUND WORTHY, SOG 100

Pentatonic, mode 3 (I II III — V VI —)

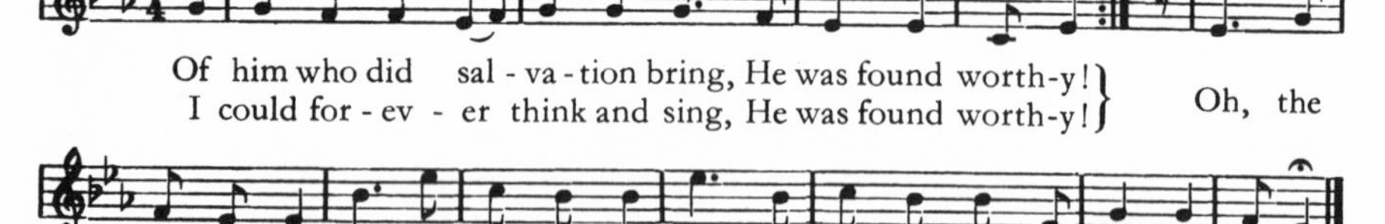
Chorus
Of him who did sal - va - tion bring, He was found worth-y!
I could for - ev - er think and sing, He was found worth-y!
Oh, the
bleeding Lamb, Oh, the bleeding Lamb, Oh, the bleeding Lamb, He was found worthy.

Further stanzas are given under 'At the Fountain' in this volume. See McCutchan[8] for the ancient source of this basic text which came into English from Latin by way of German. The revival refrain and chorus seem to erase its antiquity.

[1] *Hymn-Tunes and Their Story,* p. 366.
[2] *Stories of Hymn Tunes,* p. 81.
[3] *Our Hymnody,* No. 187.
[4] Nos. 192, 100, and 101 respectively.
[5] JFSS, iv, 37.
[6] JWF, ii, 182ff.
[7] *On the Trail of Negro Folk-Songs,* p. 196.
[8] *Our Hymnody,* p. 236.

No. 250

I WENT DOWN TO THE VALLEY, UVW 181

Pentatonic, mode 2 (I — 3 IV V — 7)

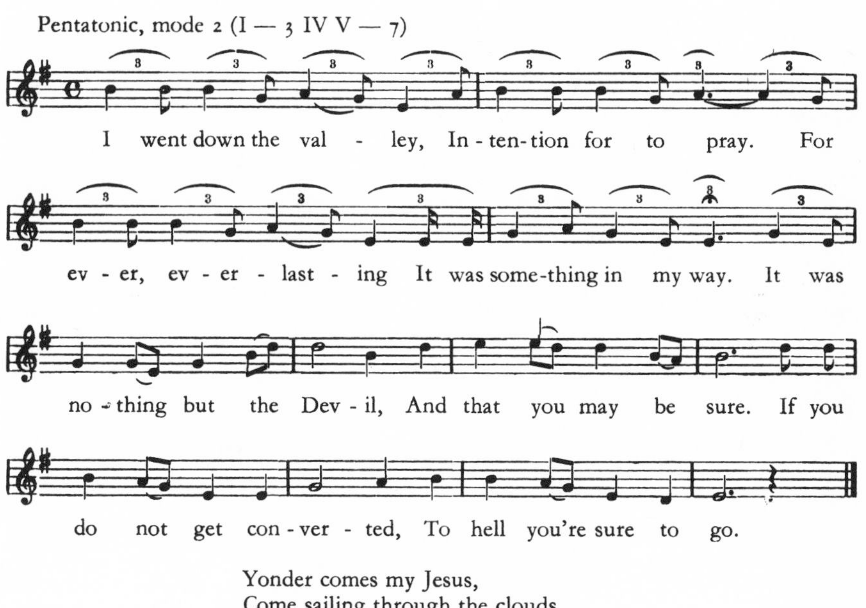

I went down the val - ley, In - ten- tion for to pray. For
ev - er, ev - er - last - ing It was some-thing in my way. It was
no - thing but the Dev - il, And that you may be sure. If you
do not get con - ver - ted, To hell you're sure to go.

Yonder comes my Jesus,
Come sailing through the clouds,
Heavy loaded with bright angels,
Ten thousand by his side.[1]

This song was recorded by Winston Wilkinson in Harriston, Virginia, October 17, 1935, from the singing of Mrs. Lucy McAllister. It is No. 181 in the *University of Virginia* (manuscript) *Collection of Folk-Music* and is used here by kind permission.

The text is related to that of a song by the same title in *Spiritual Folk-Songs* where further references are given, also to songs sung by negroes. Most of the tune seems unique in its trend. The last four measures however represent a standard closing formula which is astoundingly widespread.[2]

[1] The earliest known form of this wandering stanza, found in a camp-meeting 'songster' of 1817 is

Don't you see my Jesus coming?
Don't you see him in yonder cloud?
With ten thousand angels round him,
See how they do my Jesus crowd!

[2] Many references are given under 'Pilgrim' in *Spiritual Folk-Songs.*

No. 251
JUDGMENT-SEAT, CH 273

Heptatonic aeolian, mode 2 minorized (I II 3 IV [IV♯] V 6 7 [VII])

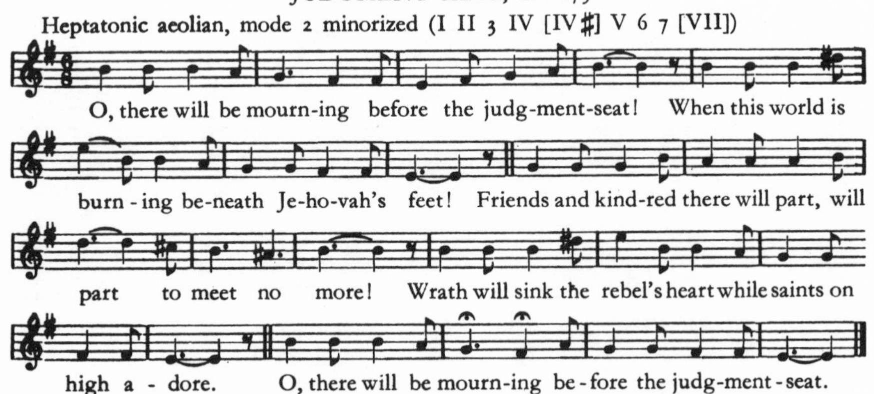
O, there will be mourn-ing before the judg-ment-seat! When this world is
burn - ing be-neath Je-ho-vah's feet! Friends and kind-red there will part, will
part to meet no more! Wrath will sink the rebel's heart while saints on
high a - dore. O, there will be mourn-ing be - fore the judg-ment - seat.

O, there will be mourning before the judgment-seat,
When the trumpet's warning the sinner's ear shall greet!
Friends and kindred *etc.*

O, there will be mourning before the judgment-seat,
When, from dust returning, the lost their doom shall meet!
Friends and kindred *etc.*

The first appearance of this song in the above form was in *Spiritual Songs for Social Worship* compiled by Thomas Hastings and Lowell Mason (rev. ed., Boston, 1834); and it was from that book that the compiler of *Church Harmony* borrowed it. The modulation observable in the tune is what one might well expect from a Lowell Mason, though not from folk singers.[1]

No. 252
WE'LL PASS OVER JORDAN, SWP 172

Hexatonic, mode 3 A (I II III — V VI VII)

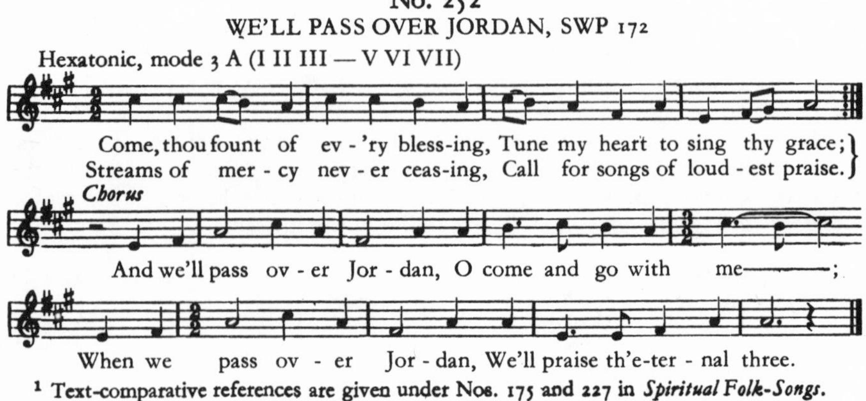
Come, thou fount of ev - 'ry bless-ing, Tune my heart to sing thy grace;
Streams of mer - cy nev - er ceas-ing, Call for songs of loud - est praise.
Chorus
And we'll pass ov - er Jor - dan, O come and go with me———;
When we pass ov - er Jor - dan, We'll praise th'e-ter - nal three.

[1] Text-comparative references are given under Nos. 175 and 227 in *Spiritual Folk-Songs.*

The fuller text by Robert Robinson, 1735–1790, is given under 'Olney' in this volume. A variant tune and text is in the *Lute of Zion*[1] and Mason's *Harp of the South*.[2] The chorus of 'Passing Away' in this volume is a variant of the above chorus.

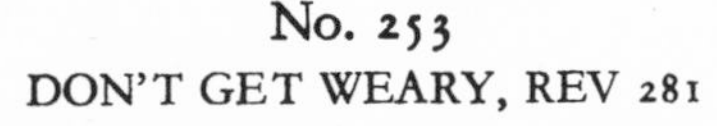

No. 253
DON'T GET WEARY, REV 281

Hexatonic, mode 3 b (I II III IV V VI —)

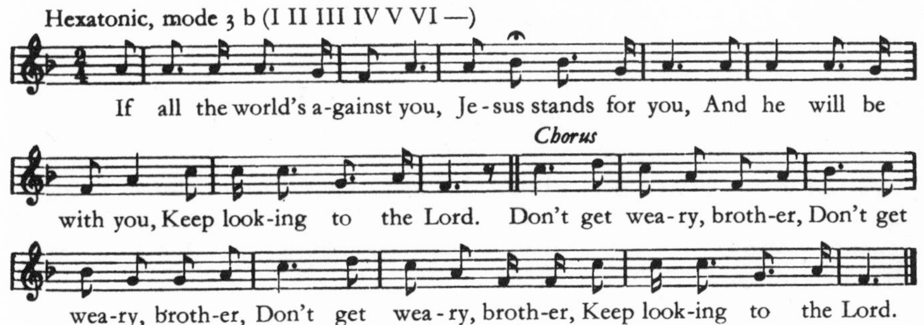
If all the world's a-gainst you, Je-sus stands for you, And he will be
with you, Keep look-ing to the Lord.
Chorus
Don't get wea-ry, broth-er, Don't get
wea-ry, broth-er, Don't get wea-ry, broth-er, Keep look-ing to the Lord.

I have included this spiritual here not because of its intrinsic value as a song, for it has none. I merely wanted readers to see the sole record anywhere among white folks' books — and this one in the Northeast!! — of a chorus ditty which was probably so widely sung that it did not *need* to be written down. In this it was like "For he's a jolly good fellow"' or "We won't go home until morning". Its ubiquity is indicated by two Virginia recordings of negro versions from the same period.[3]

I have made a number of metrical corrections of what seems to be one of the *Revivalist* editor's worst tune recordings. He indicates that the tune goes on with exhortations to sister, mourner and others not to get weary.

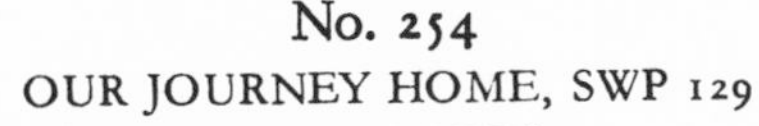

No. 254
OUR JOURNEY HOME, SWP 129

Heptatonic ionian, mode 3 (I II III IV V VI VII)

We shall see a light ap-pear, By and by when he comes; We shall
see a light ap-pear when he comes.
Slow
Ride on, Je-sus,
O ride on!
Tempo primo
We are on our jour-ney home, hal-le-lu-jah!

[1] P. 282. [2] P. 295. [3] See Dett, p. 114, and *Slave Songs*, No. 98.

2. We shall see him as he is
   By and by when he comes *etc.*

3. We shall all with Christ appear *etc.*

4. We shall have a mighty shout.

5. Then the earth shall be all cleansed.

6. We shall shout above the fire.

7. We shall walk the golden streets.

Variant songs are 'Advent Triumph'[1] and 'Jesus Reigns'.[2] Negro adoptions of the "ride on Jesus" motif are in Dett.[3] The 'Captain Kidd' stanzaic pattern[4] seems to have been intended here, though truncated by the inorganic chorus intrusion.

No. 255

NOT TOO LATE, SWP 108

Pentatonic, mode 3 (I II III — V VI —)

Come, ye sin-ners, poor and wretched, Weak and wound-ed, sick and sore;

Je-sus read-y stands to save you, Full of pit - y, love and pow'r. Pray on,

mourners, O hal - le hal - le - lu - jah, Pray on, mourn-ers, it's not too late.

The text — widely popular for nearly two hundred years — is by Joseph Hart, 1712–1768, and is given more fully in *Spiritual Folk-Songs*, No. 239. The first part of the tune was made of the last part of the 'Holy Manna' melody.[5] The chorus is constructed on a rhythmic pattern which has in our own times interesting ramifications both in the British Isles and in America. It will be seen for example in the following:

[1] *Millennial Harp*, ii, 52.
[2] In the *Wesleyan Psalmodist*.
[3] Pp. 148 and 194.
[4] *Cf.* 'You Shall See' in this volume.
[5] *Spiritual Folk-Songs*, No. 114.

Oh, turn sinner turn, may the Lord help you turn,
Oh, turn sinner turn, why *will you die.*[1]

Shule a-mog, sack a lacky, shule a-mog-a-lay,
Sweet William a-mourning a-*mongst the rush.*[2]

O run, nigger, run, for the patrol will get you,
(*elsewhere* — the pat - ty - rol - ler get you)
O run, nigger, run, for it's *almost day.*[3]

The words or syllables in italics show where the three drum-like accents make a hefty finish.

No. 256

I'M HAPPY, SOC 62

Hexatonic, mode 2 A (I II 3 IV V — 7)

Fare - well, vain world, I'm go - ing home, My Sav - ior smiles and
Sweet an - gels beck - on me a - way, To sing God's praise in
Chorus I'm hap - py now and I hope to be, Come, all my friends and

D. C. for Chorus
bids me come; I'm hap - py, I'm hap - py, May the Lord con-tin - ue with me.
end-less day; I'm hap - py, I'm hap - py, May the Lord con-tin - ue with me.
go with me; I'm hap - py, I'm hap - py, May the Lord con-tin - ue with me.

John G. McCurry, compiler of the *Social Harp*, claims the song and dates it 1855. The text is given more fully under 'Golden Harp'.[4] It is anonymous and is one of the most widely sung folk-texts during pre-Civil War decades in revival circles. A possible source of inspiration for its maker was Charles Wesley's

Vain delusive world, adieu,
With all of creature-good.

[1] *Ibid.*, No. 157. See also Nos. 192 and 195.

[2] From Lancashire, JFSS, v, 180. Other variants of this one-time sensible Gaelic are found in England and Scotland are given in JFSS, iii, 29, and Greig-Keith, p. 203. That the rigamarole migrated to America is indicated by the lines in Hudson, *Folk Tunes from Mississippi* No. 32.

Shule, shule, a shule go crule,
Shule go shack, and a shule go crule,
Laugh like a doe, like a dill, a mack, a sail,
Still a mack a vallian, *lan - - do.*

For further references see Belden, *Ballads and Songs*, p. 281 f.

[3] SS, p. 89. "Run nigger, run" is possibly an echo from the popular minstrel song of the 1830's, "Jim Along Josey", whose corresponding refrain ran

Hey get along, get along Josey,
Hey get along, get along Joe.

Spiritual Folk-Songs, No. 152.

The tune type is represented by 'The Wife of Usher's Well',[1] 'The Rejected Lover',[2] and 'When the Stormy Winds Do Blow'.[3]

No. 257

PASSAGE TO HEAVEN, SOC 51

Heptatonic aeolian, mode 4 (I II 3 IV V 6 7)

Hail, scenes of fe - li - ci - ty, trans - port and joy, When hat - red and

pas - sion shall cease to an - noy; Rich bless - ings of grace from a-

bove shall be giv'n, And life on - ly serve as a pass - age to heav'n.

As a pass-age to heav'n, And life on - ly serve as a pass-age to heav'n.

The song is signed by John G. McCurry and dated 1853. Related tunes are 'Rejected Lover',[4] and 'Daily Growing'.[5]

No. 258

JUBILEE (A), REV 355

Hexatonic, mode 4 b (I II 3 IV V — 7 [VII])

What heav'n - ly mus - ic do I hear, Sal - va - tion sound-ing

free! Ye souls in bond-age, lend an ear: This is the ju - bi - lee!

Further stanzas of the text are given under the variant 'This Is the Jubilee', the following song. Other related tunes are 'Leander',[6] 'Jerusalem',[7] 'Jubilee',[8] and 'Pensive Dove'.[9]

[1] Sharp-Karpeles, i, 153, tune E.
[2] *Ibid.*, ii, 95.
[3] JFSS, iii, 249.
[4] Sharp-Karpeles, ii, 98.
[5] Sturgis and Hughes, No. 1.
[6] *Spiritual Folk-Songs*, No. 107.
[7] *Christian Lyre*, i, 76.
[8] *ChristianHarmony*, Ingalls, p. 62.
[9] *Folk Hymns of America*, No. 9.

No. 259

THIS IS THE JUBILEE, OL 113

Hexatonic, mode 2 A minorized (I II 3 IV [IV ♯] V — 7 [VII])

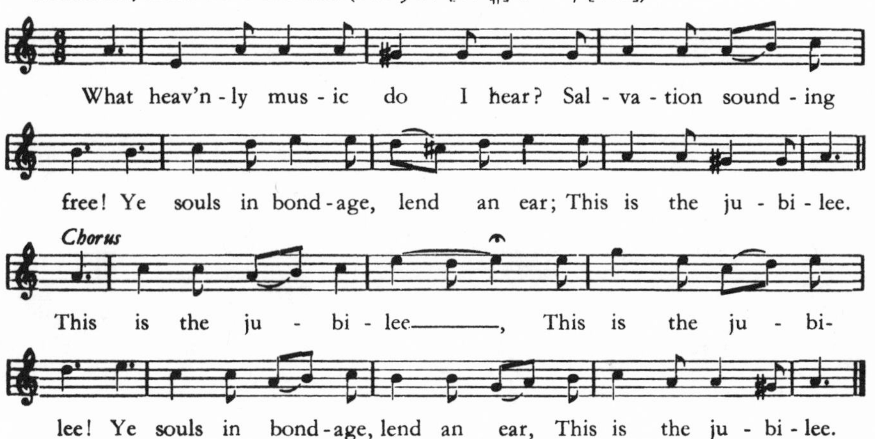
What heav'n - ly mus - ic do I hear? Sal - va - tion sound - ing
free! Ye souls in bond - age, lend an ear; This is the ju - bi - lee.
Chorus
This is the ju - bi - lee——, This is the ju - bi-
lee! Ye souls in bond - age, lend an ear, This is the ju - bi - lee.

How sweetly do the tidings roll,
All round, from sea to sea!
From land to land, from pole to pole —
This is the jubilee!
Chorus

Good news, good news to Adam's race;
Let Christians all agree
To sing redeeming love and grace —
This is the jubilee!

The gospel sounds the sweet release
To all in misery;
And bids them welcome home to peace —
This is the jubilee!

Jesus is on the mercy-seat;
Before him bend the knee.
Let heaven and earth his praise repeat —
This is the jubilee.

Come, ye redeem'd, your tribute bring,
With songs of harmony;
While on the road to Canaan, sing:
This is the jubilee.

William Hauser, compiler of the *Olive Leaf*, drew the body of this song from the *American Vocalist* and claims authorship of the chorus. The tune had been current for at least two generations when Hauser adopted it in 1878.[1]

No. 260

WILL YOU GO (A), OSH 97

Heptatonic aeolian, mode 2 (I II 3 IV V 6 7)

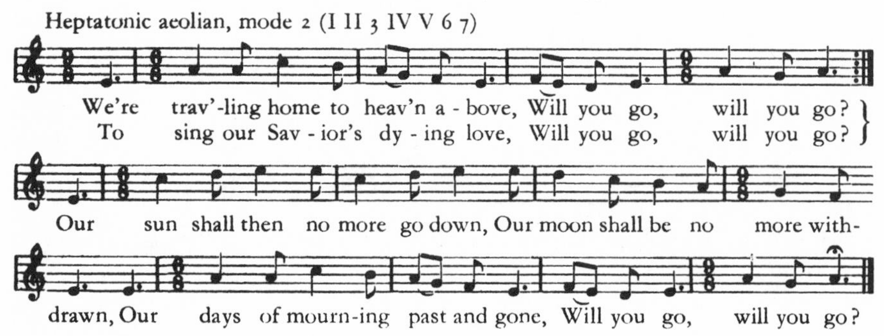
We're trav'-ling home to heav'n a - bove, Will you go, will you go?
To sing our Sav - ior's dy - ing love, Will you go, will you go?
Our sun shall then no more go down, Our moon shall be no more with-
drawn, Our days of mourn-ing past and gone, Will you go, will you go?

I have been unable to verify the *Sacred Harp* editor's statement that Richard Jinkes was the author of this song. A variant, tune and words, is 'We're Traveling Home'.[2] 'Will You Go (B)' in this volume is a variant text with a different tune.

No. 261

I HOPE TO GAIN THE PROMISED LAND, SOC 35

Hexatonic, mode 3 b (I II III IV V VI —)

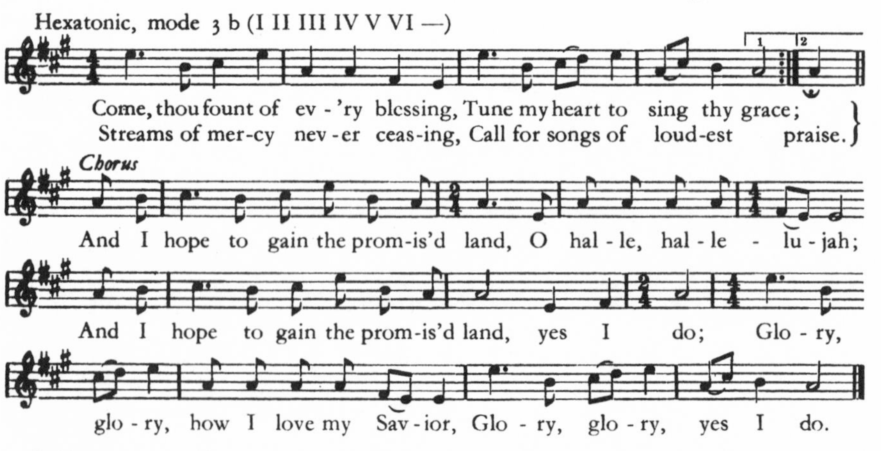
Come, thou fount of ev - 'ry blessing, Tune my heart to sing thy grace;
Streams of mer-cy nev - er ceas-ing, Call for songs of loud-est praise.
Chorus
And I hope to gain the prom-is'd land, O hal - le, hal - le - lu - jah;
And I hope to gain the prom-is'd land, yes I do; Glo - ry,
glo - ry, how I love my Sav - ior, Glo - ry, glo - ry, yes I do.

[1] *Cf.* references under its variant, 'Jubilee (A)', the preceding song in this volume.

[2] *Richard Weaver's Tune Book*, English Primitive Methodist. See also JFSS, viii, 80.

The song is signed by John G. McCurry, compiler of the *Social Harp*, and dated 1849. Further stanzas of the text, by Robert Robinson, 1735–1790, are given under 'Olney' in this volume. The tune reminds one of the negro 'Swing Low Sweet Chariot' and is related to 'Longing for Home' and 'Zion's Hill' in this volume and 'Land of Rest' in *Folk Hymns of America*.

No. 262

FREE GRACE, REV 196

Heptatonic ionian, mode 3 (I II III IV V VI VII)

Come, sin-ners to the gos-pel feast, Let ev-'ry soul be Je-sus' guest; You
need not one be left be-hind, For God hath bid-den all mankind, Through
grace, free grace, Through grace, free grace, To all the Jews and Gen-tile race.

The text by Charles Wesley, 1707–1788, is given in full in *Methodist Hymns*.[1]

No. 263

I WISH YOU WELL, RHD 45

Pentachordal (I II III IV V — —)

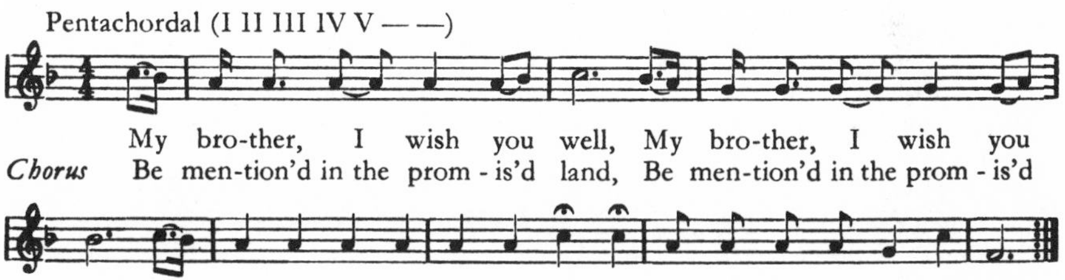
My bro-ther, I wish you well, My bro-ther, I wish you
Chorus Be men-tion'd in the prom-is'd land, Be men-tion'd in the prom-is'd
well, When my Lord calls, I trust I shall be men-tion'd in the prom-is'd land.
land, When my Lord calls, I trust I shall be men-tion'd in the prom-is'd land.

Subsequent stanzas are made by transferring the wellwishing to sister, father, mother, neighbors, young converts, poor sinners and the like. Compare with this early New England version the recent Tennessee recording of the same song in Richardson and Spaeth, p. 69.

[1] Edition of 1842, p. 9.

No. 264

WHEN WE GET TO HEAVEN, SOC 20

Pentatonic, mode 1 (I II — IV V VI —)

1
2
Child-ren of the heav'nly King, When we get to heav'n we will part no more;
As ye jour-ney sweet-ly sing, When we get to heav'n we will part no more.

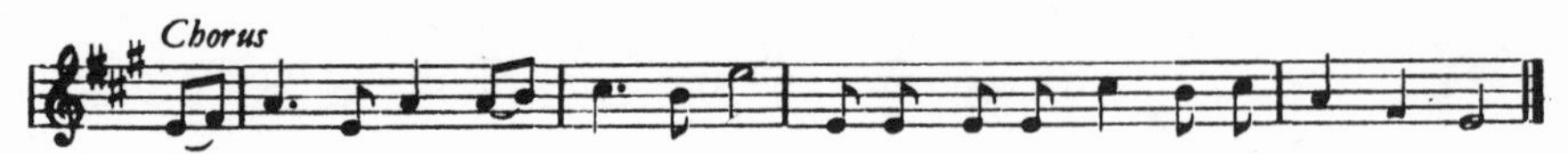
Chorus
Friends, fare ye well, friends, fare ye well, When we get to heav'n we will part no more.

Further stanzas of the text by John Cennick, 1718–1755, are given under 'Children of the Heavenly King'. 'Happy Children' immediately following is a variant song.

No. 265

HAPPY CHILDREN, SOC 33

Pentatonic, mode 1 (I II — IV V VI —)

1
2
Child-ren of the heav'n-ly King, As ye jour - ney let us sing;
Sing your Savior's worthy praise, Glo-rious in his works and ways.

Chorus
I want to get as hap-py as I well can be, Lord, send sal - va - tion down.

John G. McCurry, compiler of the *Social Harp*, signed the song and dated it 1853. The fuller text by John Cennick, 1718–1755, is given under 'Children of the Heavenly King' in this volume. The foregoing song has a variant tune.

No. 266

I'M ALMOST DONE TRAVELING, SHD 294

Pentatonic, mode 3 (I II III — V VI —)

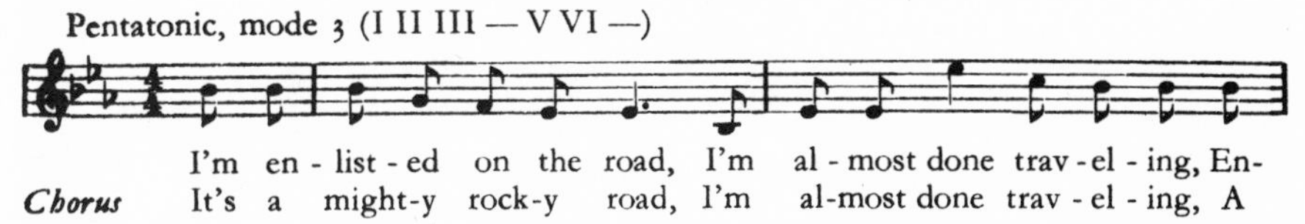
I'm en - list - ed on the road, I'm al - most done trav - el - ing, En-
Chorus It's a might-y rock-y road, I'm al-most done trav - el - ing, A

list-ed on the road, I'm al-most done travel-ing, En-list-ed on the road, I'm
might-y rock - y road, I'm al-most done travel-ing A migh-ty rock-y road, I'm

Fine
al-most done trav - el - ing, I'm bound to go where Je - sus is. My
al-most done trav - el - ing, I'm bound to go where Je - sus is.

soul shall as - cend where Je - sus is, To en - joy the peace-ful home of

Da Capo for Chorus
rest, I'm bound to go where Je - sus is, And be there for - ev - er blest.

Further stanzas read "I've a mother on the road," a "father" and so on. J. C. Brown, an Alabama *Sacred Harp* leader, furnished the song, presumably from oral tradition, to the compilers of the 1936 edition of that book. The song is dated 1935, which was just before Mr. Brown's death.

No. 267

MARINER'S HYMN, MH, ii, 39,

Tetratonic (I II III — V — —)

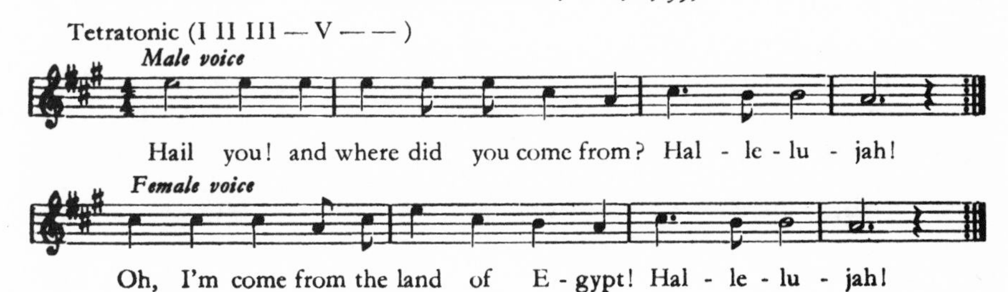
Male voice
Hail you! and where did you come from? Hal - le - lu - jah!
Female voice
Oh, I'm come from the land of E - gypt! Hal - le - lu - jah!

Hail you! and where are you bound for?
Hallelujah!
Oh, I'm bound for the land of Canaan,
Hallelujah!

Hail you! and what is your cargo?
Oh, religion is my cargo.

Hail you! and what is your compass?
Oh, the Bible is my compass.

Hail you! and who is your pilot?
Oh, God's Spirit is my pilot.

Hail you! and who is your captain?
Oh, King Jesus is my captain.

Hail you! where is your harbor?
Oh, God's kingdom is my harbor.

For a discussion of this type of "dialog" song see 'Calvary or Gethsemane' in this volume.

No. 268

BOUND FOR CANAAN, OSH 82

Heptatonic mixolydian, mode 1 (I II III IV V VI 7)

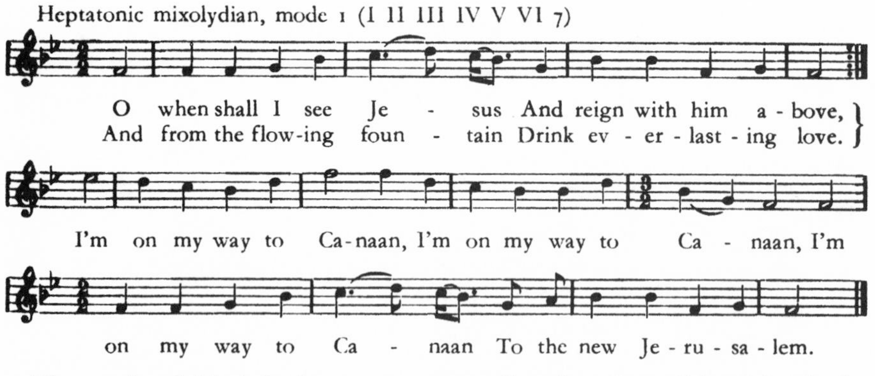
O when shall I see Je - sus And reign with him a - bove,
And from the flow-ing foun - tain Drink ev - er - last - ing love.
I'm on my way to Ca-naan, I'm on my way to Ca - naan, I'm
on my way to Ca - naan To the new Je - ru - sa - lem.

The words of this infectious song are attributed to Rev. John Leland, the New England preacher who was active for a number of years in the Southeast.[1] Further stanzas are given under 'Faithful Soldier' in *Spiritual Folk-Songs*. The tune is in most of the southern shape-note song books. It belongs to the 'Hallelujah' family.[2] Stephen Foster's 'Bring Back my Brother to Me' and 'Don't Be

[1] More about Leland under 'Longing For Jesus'.
[2] See *Spiritual Folk-Songs*, No. 59.

Idle' aremelodically related.[1] The notes in the second full measure from the beginning and in the third measure from the end differ from the *Sacred Harp* notation but are in accord with the actual traditional way the *Sacred Harp* singers intone the song, as I have repeatedly observed.

No. 269

JUDGMENT DAY (B), RHD 47

Heptatonic dorian, mode 4 (I II 3 IV V VI 7)

Will you prom-ise me, my broth-er, To help me now to pray? O
hal - le, O hal - le, hal - le - lu - jah! Will you help me to pray, Till I
pray my life a - way? O hal - le, O hal - le, hal - le - lu - jah!

Will you promise me, my sister,
To help me now to pray? O halle *etc.*
Will you help me pray
Till I pray my life away? *etc.*

The judgment day is coming,
That great and awful day,
O my soul, praise God,
I have trusted in his word.

Go Gabriel, with your trumpet,
And blow a mighty blow,
'Tis the judgment come,
Go call the nations home.

Poor sinners they are crying,
The earth is all on fire,
O my soul, praise God,
I have trusted in his word.

Some call on falling mountains,
Some cry out, Lord, O Lord,
But I call on the King,
The great King Immanuel.

[1] See *The Musical Quarterly*, xxii, 167f.

Some are coming from the east,
Some coming from the west,
On the left the goats,
But the sheep are on the right.

Come to glory, all ye ransom'd,
And praise your mighty King,
But depart from me,
Ye who would not savéd be.

This text and tune seem to be uniquely recorded in *Revival Hymns*. I find no trace of them elsewhere. The tune is one of the few whose dorian character remained unaltered in the American song books.

No. 270

RESURRECTION MORNING, OL 311

Hexatonic, mode 3 A (I II III — V VI VII)

In the res - ur - rec-tion morn-ing We shall see the Sav - ior
com - ing, And the Christ-ians will be shout - ing In the king - dom
of the Lord.
Chorus
Are your lamps all burn - ing? Are your lamps all
burn-ing? Are your lamps all burn-ing? Are your ves-sels fill'd with oil?

Now we feel the Advent glory,
While the Savior seems to tarry,
We will comfort one another,
And be trusting in his name.
Are your garments ready? *(three times)*
For the marriage of the Lamb?

We are all a band of strangers,
Trav'ling through a world of dangers;
But King Jesus leads us onward,
And we'll conquer every foe.
Come and join our army, *(three times)*
And defend the Savior's cause.

In the midst of opposition
We will keep the same position,
And be waiting for the promise,
For the breaking of the day.
Then we'll have deliv'rance, *(three times)*
Who've enlisted for the war.

By faith we can discover
Our warfare'll soon be over,
Then we'll gladly hail each other
Upon Canaan's happy shore.
When we pass over Jordan, *(three times)*
We will live to die no more.

O ye saints of God, take courage!
Ye shall soon be free from bondage,
For the Savior heads the army,
And you'll surely gain the day.
When we gain the vict'ry, *(three times)*
We will lay our armor by.

Come then, all ye valiant soldiers,
And be armed with truth and courage;
We must conquer every nation
Who oppose this holy war.
Let us die in the army, *(three times)*
And we'll reign above the sky.

In the days of earth's dominion
Christ has promised us a kingdom;
'Tis not left to other nations,
And shall never be destroyed.
It shall stand forever, *(three times)*
And the saints possess the land.

We will keep the ark in motion
While we're sailing o'er the ocean;
And we'll keep ourselves all ready
To proclaim the heav'nly King.
When we meet the Savior, *(three times)*
Then how happy we shall be!

William Hauser, editor of the Georgia *Olive Leaf*, comments that this song is "irregular but soul-stirring". It is so closely related to the New England Millerite song 'Old Churchyard (B)' in this volume, that one wonders if the Yankee preachers of the second coming of Christ found recruits also in the Southeast. The first quatrain of the second stanza above would seem to date the text at some time during the Great Disappointment of the Second Adventists early in the 1840's. For further relationship references see 'Old Churchyard (B)'.

No. 271
CLIMBIN' UP JACOB'S LADDER

Hexatonic, mode 3 b (1 II III IV V VI —)

Lively
I'm a-climb-in' up Ja-cob's lad - der, And I won't be troub-led an - y
more; I'm a - climb - in' up Ja - cob's lad - der, Lord, And I
Chorus
won't be troub-led an - y more. And I won't be troub-led an - y
more, And I won't be troub-led an - y more; As soon as my
feet strikes Zi - on's walls, Lord, I won't be troub-led an - y more.

The text was published in Josiah H. Combs', *Folk-Songs du Midi des États Unis*, p. 224, as sung by the author's mother, Mrs. John W. Combs, Hindman, Knott County, Kentucky. Subsequent stanzas are formed from the lines, "Goin' to meet my father (mother, brother, sister, etc.) in the kingdom."

The tune is as sung by Professor Combs (from his memory of his mother's singing) and as notated by Professor Keith Mixson. I am indebted to these gentlemen for permission to use tune and text here.

In *Folk-Songs du Midi* the author stated that it was a song of the negroes. In reply to my request for information as to source, he wrote me; "I believe the whites borrowed this song from the negroes in my country, possibly before the Civil War. . . . There is no iron-clad evidence that the song is of negro origin. I listed it as such because it seems to have the hall-marks of a negro song, with its 'incremental repetitions', etc."

Since there are many scores of songs, as shown by the present collection and by *Spiritual Folk-Songs*, which exhibit similar incremental repetition and are without any doubt a part of the white man's tradition, it would seem that the validity of Professor Combs' supposition as to negro source, tenable once, is now weakened.

No. 272
YOU SHALL SEE

Heptatonic ionian, mode 3 (I II III IV V VI VII)

Some said I'd soon give o'er, You shall see, you shall see; Some
said I'd soon give o'er, you shall see. Some time has pass'd a - way Since
I be - gan to pray; I love the Lord to - day, Bless his
name, bless his name; I love the Lord to - day, bless his name.

This spiritual folk-song was recorded by the author, January 14, 1938, from the singing of A. M. Harris of Vanderbilt University. Professor Harris' story of its source follows: "I heard this song many times, around the year 1880, in the week-day meetings of the Methodist church in Mystic, now New Mystic, Connecticut, — a church which had been founded by George Whitefield — sung by Israel (Uncle Is'rel) Dewey, a faithful attendant at these weekly meetings. Uncle Is'rel would begin the tune, the others joining in at the beginning of the second phrase, 'you shall see'. He had learned the song from his parents who had been members of the earlier congregation of this same church. It was his favorite tune." Professor Harris stated that he had known four or five stanzas of the text, but had forgotten all but this one.

Miss Gilchrist has an English variant of the song in her article often cited in this volume.[1] From her song I supply — with her kind permission and that of her publishers — the first four stanzas.

Come, ye that fear the Lord,
Unto me, unto me, *etc.*
I've something good to say
About the narrow way,
For Christ the other day
Sav'd my soul, sav'd my soul, *etc.*

He gave me first to see
What I was, what I was, *etc.*
He gave me first to see
My guilt and misery,
And then he set me free,
Bless his name, bless his name, *etc.*

[1] JFSS, viii, 78.

My old companions said
He's undone, he's undone, *etc.*
My old companions said
He's surely going mad,
But Jesus makes me glad,
Bless his name, bless his name, *etc.*

Oh, if they did but know
What I feel, what I feel, *etc.*
Had they but eyes to see
Their guilt and misery,
They'd be as mad as me,
I believe, I believe, *etc.*

Miss Gilchrist's fifth stanza varies only slightly from the one sung by Professor Harris. The only American recording of this song, other than the Harris version here, was apparently that in the *Golden Harp*[1] entitled 'The Narrow Way' from which I draw two more stanzas:

O had I angel's wings,
I would fly, I would fly, *etc.*
Had I the wings of Noah's dove,
I'd soon fly home above,
To greet the God of love —
Bless his name, bless his name, *etc.*

O could I hear it said
From the Lord, from the Lord, *etc.*
O could I hear it said,
My warfare's at an end,
My soul would shout and sing:
O farewell, O farewell, *etc.*

The stanzaic form is that of 'Captain Kidd'.[2] Miss Gilchrist who has studied this pattern carefully writes me: "I think the Captain Kidd tune, in its various forms including the Scottish 'My luve's in Germanie, send him hame', is really descended from the sixteenth-century tune to which

My luve is lyand (lying) seik,
Send him joy, send him joy

(a song title in the *Complaynt of Scotland*, 1549) would be sung. The tune 'My luve's in Germanie' has been used over and over again, and it is no wonder if, in 400 years' (postulated) use, it should be found in many variants of the original — for there must have been an original; the metre is so distinctive.

[1] Auburn, New York, p. 52.
[2] Discussed briefly in *Spiritual Folk-Songs*, under No. 142.

"The pious parody (in the *Gude and Godlie Ballatis*, 1567) of the lost sixteenth century secular song," Miss Gilchrist states further, "evidently substitutes a divine for an earthly lover. The first verse runs:

All my lufe, leif (leave) me not,
Leif me not, leif me not,
All my lufe, leif me not
This myne allone.
With ane burding (burden) on my bak,
I may not beir it, I am sa (sae) waik,
Lufe, this burding fra (frae) me tak,
Or ellis I am gone (else I am gone) *etc.*

The last two lines may have been repeated in the same way as some of the 'Captain Kidd' versions."

In this volume the pattern under discussion is found also in 'Our Bondage It Shall End'. It is truncated in 'Our Journey Home'; and its lines are a bit lengthened in 'Mercy's Free'.[1]

No. 273

AT THE FOUNTAIN, REV 469

Hexatonic, mode 3 b (I II III IV V VI —)

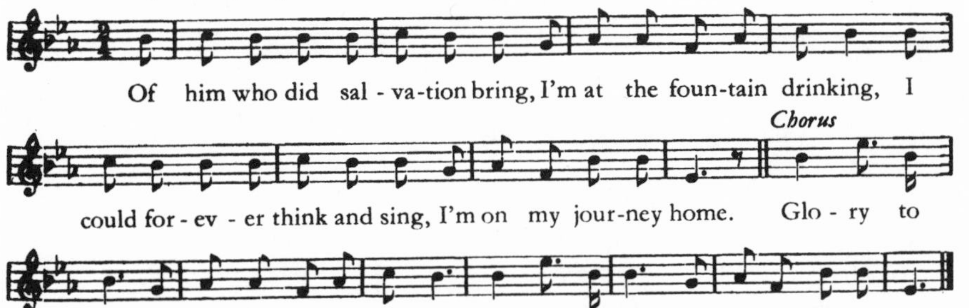
Of him who did sal - va-tion bring, I'm at the foun-tain drinking, I
Chorus
could for - ev - er think and sing, I'm on my jour-ney home. Glo - ry to
God, I'm at the fountain drinking, Glo-ry to God, I'm on my journey home.

Ask but his grace, and lo! 'Tis giv'n,
I'm at the fountain drinking,
Ask and he turns your hell to heav'n,
I'm on my journey home.

Though sin and sorrow wound my soul,
Jesus, thy balm will make it whole.

[1] Further English and Welsh examples are cited, JWF, iii, 44ff.

Let all the world fall down and know,
That none but God such love can show.

Where'er I am, where'er I move,
I meet the object of my love.

Insatiate to this spring I fly,
I drink and yet am ever dry.

The early Latin hymn from which the kernel of the above text came is ascribed to Bernard of Clairvaux. It was translated into German by Anthony Wilhelm Boehm and into English (from the German) by John C. Jacobi.[1] The tune is a variant of 'My Bible Leads to Glory'.[2]

No. 274

NONE BUT THE RIGHTEOUS, REV 426

Hexatonic, mode 3 A (I II III — V VI VII)

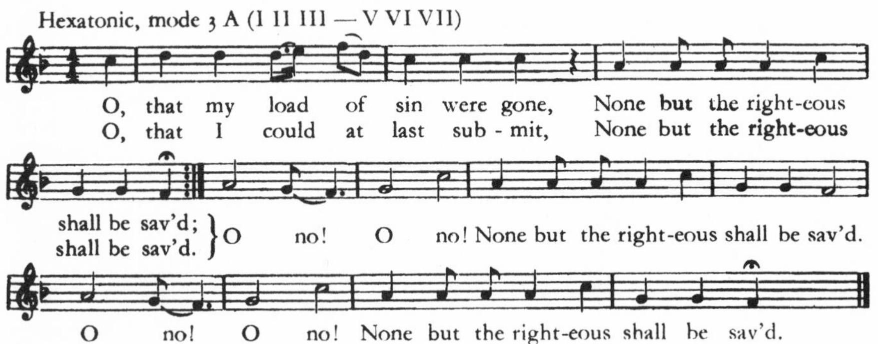
O, that my load of sin were gone, None but the right-eous
O, that I could at last sub - mit, None but the right-eous
shall be sav'd;
shall be sav'd.
O no! O no! None but the right-eous shall be sav'd.
O no! O no! None but the right-eous shall be sav'd.

The text is by Charles Wesley, 1707–1788.

No. 275

POOR SINNERS COME TO JESUS, OSH 176

Hexatonic, mode 2 b (I — 3 IV V 6 7)

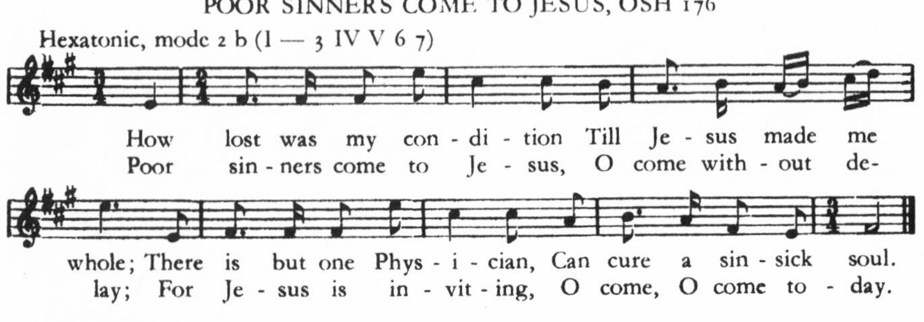
How lost was my con - di - tion Till Je - sus made me
Poor sin - ners come to Je - sus, O come with - out de-
whole; There is but one Phys - i - cian, Can cure a sin - sick soul.
lay; For Je - sus is in - vit - ing, O come, O come to - day.

[1] See McCutchan, No. 188.
[2] *Spiritual Folk-Songs*, No. 233.

Further stanzas of the verse text by John Newton, 1725–1807, are given with 'Good Physician' in *Spiritual Folk-Songs*. The infectious alliterative "sin-sick soul" appeared in Charles Wesley's couplet

> Savior of the sin-sick soul,
> Give me faith to make me whole.[1]

From this hymn of the earliest times of Methodism it spread apparently to Newton and into the atmosphere of the rural folk-hymn singers in America. Then the negroes took it up:

> Brudder George is a-gwine to glory,
> Take car' de sin-sick soul.[2]

Related tunes are 'On the Way to Canaan' in this volume, 'Banks of Sweet Dundee',[3] 'Pinery Boy',[4] 'Virginian Lover',[5] and 'The Green Bed'.[6]

No. 276

I HAVE A HOME, HOC 68

Hexatonic, mode 1 b (1 II — IV V VI 7)

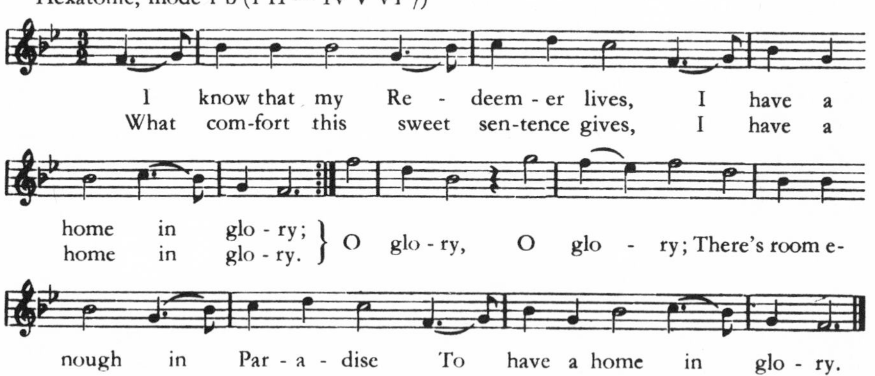
I know that my Re - deem - er lives, I have a
What com-fort this sweet sen-tence gives, I have a
home in glo - ry;
home in glo - ry.
O glo - ry, O glo - ry; There's room e-
nough in Par - a - dise To have a home in glo - ry.

The core of the text is by Samuel Medley, 1738–1799. The tune, all but its middle part, is clearly suggestive of 'Mourner's Lamentation' and 'Wae's me for Prince Charlie'.[7] John Powell calls attention to its likeness to a favorite 'Barbara Allen' tune.[8]

[1] *Methodist Hymns*, 1842, p. 279.
[2] *Slave Songs*, p. 49.
[3] Sharp-Karpeles, i, 399.
[4] Shoemaker, p. 262.
[5] Sharp-Karpeles, ii, 150.
[6] JFSS, v, 68.
[7] See *Spiritual Folk-Songs*, No. 28.
[8] As seen for example in Smith and Rufty, p. 30.

It is by reason of the mixolydian nature of the tune and its relatives that I have given it the key of two flats; this in absence of any key designation in the *Harp of Columbia*.[1]

No. 277

O GIVE HIM GLORY, REV 301

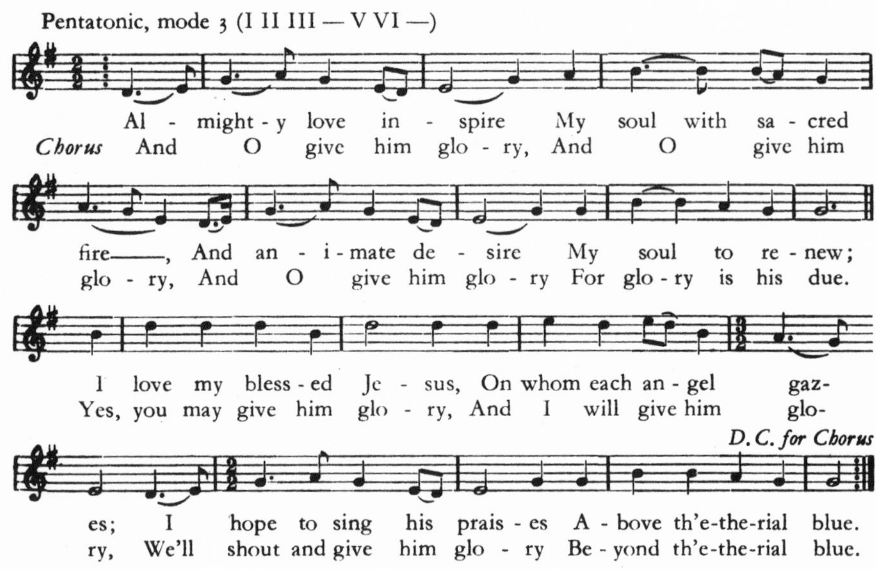
Pentatonic, mode 3 (I II III — V VI —)
Al - might - y love in - spire My soul with sa - cred
Chorus And O give him glo - ry, And O give him
fire——, And an - i - mate de - sire My soul to re - new;
glo - ry, And O give him glo - ry For glo - ry is his due.
I love my bless - ed Je - sus, On whom each an - gel gaz-
Yes, you may give him glo - ry, And I will give him glo-
D.C. for Chorus
es; I hope to sing his prais - es A - bove th'e-the-rial blue.
ry, We'll shout and give him glo - ry Be - yond th'e-the-rial blue.

In him I have believéd,
He has my soul retrievéd,
From sin he has redeeméd
My soul which was dead;
And now I love my Savior,
For I am in his favor,
And hope with him forever
The golden streets to tread.

In hopes of seeing Jesus,
When all my conflict ceases,
To him my love increases,
To worship and adore;

[1] The compilers of the "Old" *Harp of Columbia* discarded all key signatures leaving the singer to determine a song's key by the staff position and the note-head shape of its final. The songs affected by this unique simplification were taken over into *The New Harp of Columbia* unaltered.

Come then, my blesséd Savior,
Vouchsafe to me thy favor,
To dwell with thee forever,
When time shall be no more.

The tune is a variant of the widely sung 'How Firm a Foundation' in this volume.

No. 278

SHOUT OLD SATAN'S KINGDOM DOWN, OL 31

Hexatonic, mode 3 b (I II III IV V VI —)

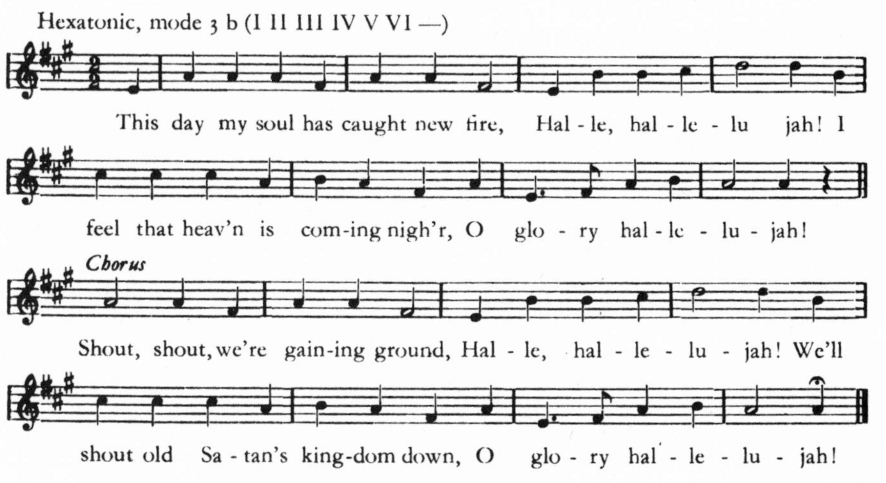
This day my soul has caught new fire, Hal - le, hal - le - lu jah! I
feel that heav'n is com-ing nigh'r, O glo - ry hal - le - lu - jah!
Chorus
Shout, shout, we're gain-ing ground, Hal - le, hal - le - lu - jah! We'll
shout old Sa - tan's king-dom down, O glo - ry hal - le - lu - jah!

The troops of hell are mustering round,
But Zion still is gaining ground.

We soon shall quit this cumbrous clay,
And shout and sing in endless day.

"You've fought through many a battle sore,
But now you'll reign forever more."

All glory, glory to the Lamb!
Through all my soul I feel the flame.

I have omitted all the stanzas from above which are duplicated in 'Satan's Kingdom' a variant in this volume. William Hauser, compiler of the *Olive Leaf*, states that he "learned this tune when a child." He was born in 1812. The song is related also to 'Few Days' and 'I'm Going Home' in *Spiritual Folk-Songs*.

No. 279

LAND FOR ME, OL 17

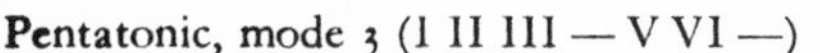
Pentatonic, mode 3 (I II III — V VI —)

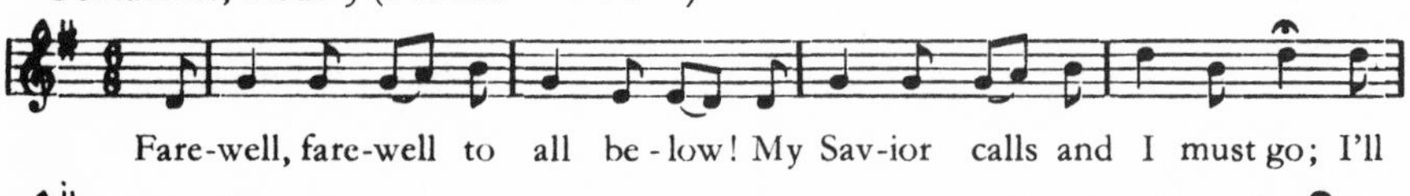
Fare-well, fare-well to all be-low! My Sav-ior calls and I must go; I'll

launch my bark up-on the sea, This land is not the land for me.

I find the winding path of sin
A rugged way to travel in;
Beyond the swelling waves, I see
The land the Savior bought for me.

Farewell, my friends, I cannot stay;
The land I seek is far away.
Where Christ is not, I would not be;
This land is not the land for me.

This is a variant of 'Roll On', the next song in this volume, and of 'Something New' in *Spiritual Folk-Songs*.

No. 280

ROLL ON, OSH 275

Hexatonic, mode 3 A (I II III — V VI VII)
Why should we start and fear to die? What tim'-rous
Death is the gate of end-less joy, And yet we
worms we mor-tals are!
dread to en-ter there.
Roll on, roll on, sweet mo-ments,
roll on, And let the poor pil-grim go home, go home.

Further stanzas of the text by Isaac Watts, 1674–1748, are given under 'Prospect' in this volume. The song was recorded in its above form by Cynthia

Bass, a pre-Civil War song leader in Georgia. The tune is related to 'Land for Me', the preceding song in this volume, 'Something New' in *Spiritual Folk-Songs*, and 'Little Wee Croodin' Doo' which is a Scottish nursery form of 'Lord Randal'.[1]

No. 281

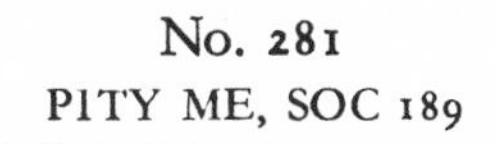
PITY ME, SOC 189

Hexatonic, mode 3 b (I II III IV V VI —)

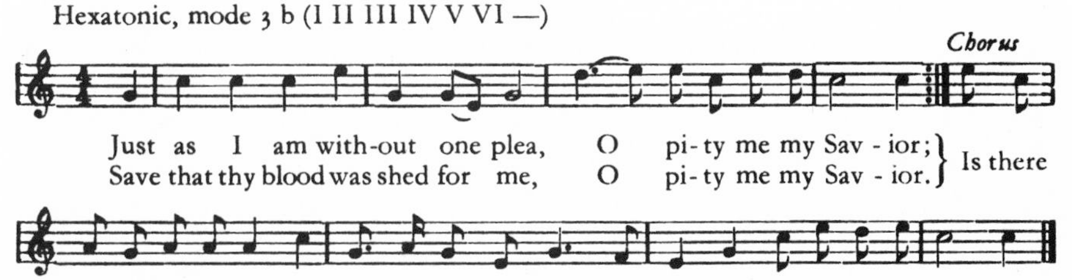
Chorus
Just as I am with-out one plea, O pi-ty me my Sav - ior;
Save that thy blood was shed for me, O pi-ty me my Sav - ior.
Is there
an-y mer-cy here? O pi - ty me, my Lord, And I'll sing hal - le, ha - le - lu - jah.

The basic text is by Charlotte Elliott, 1789–1871. Further stanzas are given under 'Just as I Am' in this volume.

No. 282

WILL YOU GO (B), BS 81

Pentachordal (I II III IV V — —)

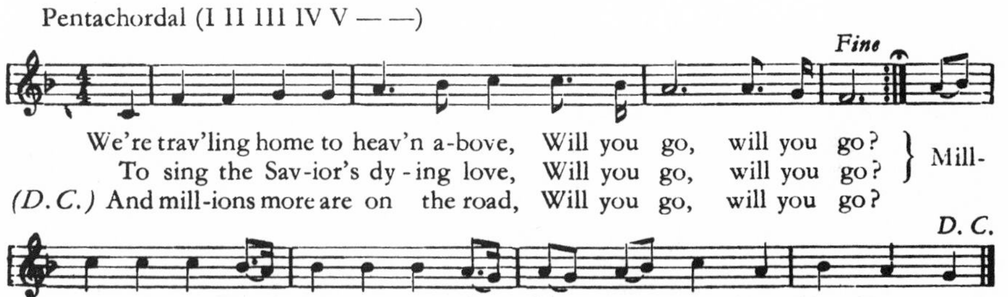
Fine
We're trav'ling home to heav'n a-bove, Will you go, will you go?
To sing the Sav-ior's dy - ing love, Will you go, will you go?
(D.C.) And mill-ions more are on the road, Will you go, will you go?
Mill-
D. C.
ions have reach'd that blest a-bode, An - oint - ed kings and priests of God,

We're going to see the bleeding Lamb,
Will you go, *etc.*
In rapturous strains to praise his name,
Will you go, *etc.*
The crown of life we there shall wear,
The conqueror's palms our hands shall bear,
And all the joys of heav'n we'll share,
Will you go, *etc.*

[1] JFSS, v, 117.

We're going to join the heav'nly choir,
To raise our voice and tune the lyre,
There saints and angels gladly sing
Hosanna to their God and King,
And make the heavenly arches ring.

'Will You Go (A)' in this volume is a variant text and different tune.

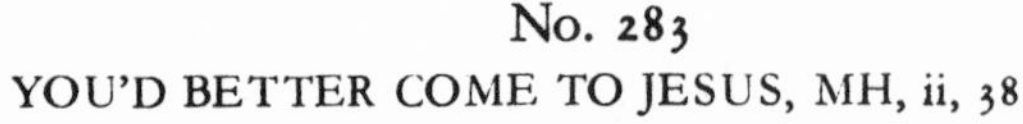

No. 283

YOU'D BETTER COME TO JESUS, MH, ii, 38

Hexatonic, mode 3 b (I II III IV V VI —)

You'd bet - ter come to Je - sus, to Je - sus, You'd bet - ter come to
Chorus
Je - sus in this our day. So come poor sin - ner, You
can't stand his ire, You can't stand his ire in that great day.

2. You need a hope of mercy, *etc.*
3. You'd better be a-praying.
4. You'd better get religion.
5. Come try a bleeding Savior.
6. He offers you salvation.
7. Come, give your hearts to Jesus.
8. You'll see the Judge descending.
9. You'll hear the trumpet sounding.
10. You'll see the dead arising.
11. You'll hear the thunders roaring.
12. You'll see the world a-burning,
13. You'll hear the sinners crying.
14. You'll hear the saints a-shouting.
15. The saints will shine in glory.

The *Millennial Harp* used this song twice, under different titles. Its second occurrence, where it is called 'Entreaty', brings the following additional stanzas.

16. Christians are rejoicing.
17. Angels are a-shouting.
18. Converts are a-praising.
19. The bride she is a-calling.

The supply seems to have been endless.

Winston Wilkinson calls my attention to the striking resemblance between the above tune and 'I Will Give You the Keys of Heaven'.[1] Related songs follow this.

No. 284

JUDGMENT DAY (C), UVW 179

Hexatonic, mode 4 b (I II III IV V — 7)

Fath-er, where shall I run to? Fath-er, where shall I run to? Fath-er,
where shall I run to, In that great day? O I can't stand the fi - re, O I
(neutral)
can't stand the fi - re, O I can't stand the fi - re In that great day.
(pron. fi-er)
a
b
c

The song was recorded by Winston Wilkinson, October 16, 1935, in Harriston, Virginia, as sung by Nathaniel Melhorn Morris. It is No. 179 in the *University of Virginia* (manuscript) *Collection of Folk-Music* and is used here by kind permission.

The song as a whole reminds one of 'Great Day' in *Spiritual Folk-Songs*, while its chorus tune is a variant of that of the foregoing song and of 'O Thou my Soul' in this volume.

No. 285

LAST TRUMPET, MH, ii, 40

Hexatonic, mode 2 A (I II 3 IV V — 7)

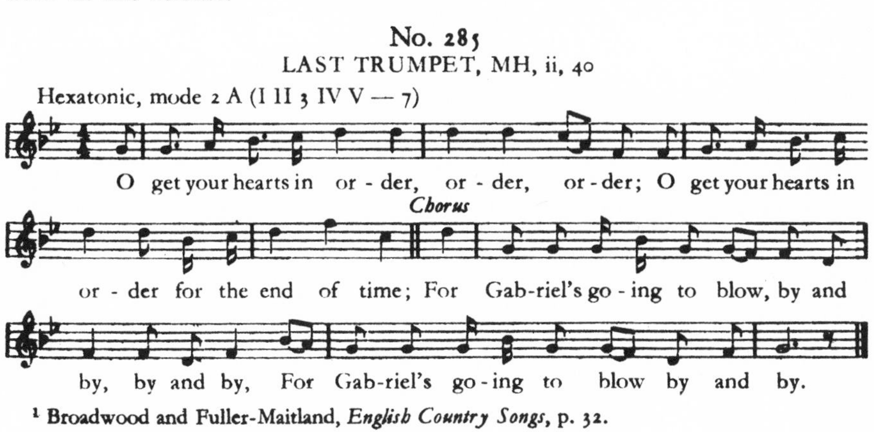
O get your hearts in or - der, or - der, or - der; O get your hearts in
or - der for the end of time; For Gab-riel's go - ing to blow, by and
Chorus
by, by and by, For Gab-riel's go - ing to blow by and by.

[1] Broadwood and Fuller-Maitland, *English Country Songs*, p. 32.

2. He'll encompass land and ocean, *etc.*
   He'll encompass land and ocean at the end of time;
   Chorus
3. You will see the graves a-bursting, *etc.*
4. You will see this world on fire.
5. There will be an awful shaking.
6. How will you stand it, sinner?
7. You will wish you were forgiven.
8. But saints will not be frightened.
9. They'll rise and meet their Jesus.
10. He will lead them to his kingdom.
11. Then the warfare will be ended.
12. We will shout above the fire.

This is a New England 'Judgment Day' song, one of quite a good-sized breed. It is related, especially in its chorus to the two preceding songs here.

No. 286

JUBILEE (B), MH, ii, 14

Heptatonic ionian, mode 3 (I II III IV V VI VII)

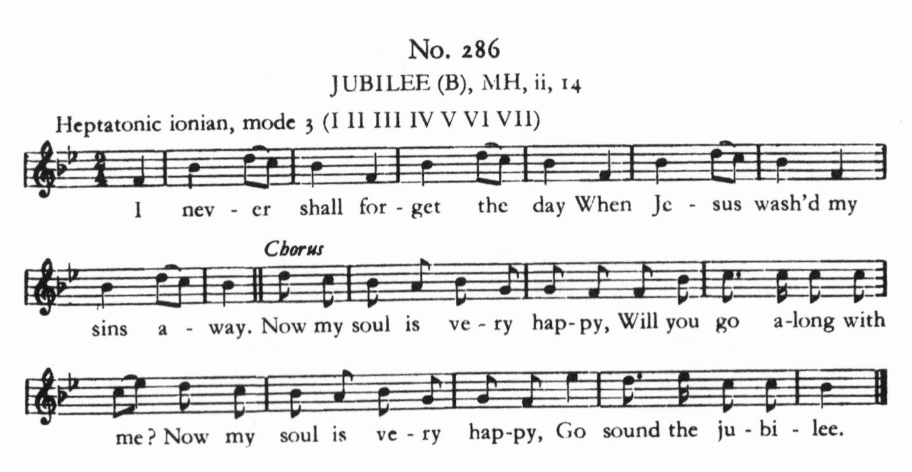
I nev - er shall for - get the day When Je - sus wash'd my
Chorus
sins a - way. Now my soul is ve - ry hap- py, Will you go a-long with
me? Now my soul is ve - ry hap-py, Go sound the ju - bi - lee.

I'm happy in this house of clay,
But what is this to perfect day?
There's a better day a-coming,
Will you go along with me?
There's a better day a-coming,
Go sound the jubilee.

Though sinners persecute me here,
Through Jesus Christ I'll persevere;
Christ will ruin Satan's kingdom —
Will you go along with me?
Christ will ruin Satan's kingdom,
Go sound the jubilee.

A little longer here below,
Then home to glory we shall go;
I am on my way to glory,
Will you go along with me?
I am on my way to glory,
Go sound the jubilee.

Come on, come on, my brethren dear,
We soon shall meet together there;
Then we'll join the saints in glory,
Will you go along with me?
Then we'll join the saints in glory,
Go sound the jubilee.

The Music Division of the Library of Congress has recently acquired a white-man-made broadside of pre-Civil War times bearing a parody of this old revival spiritual song entitled 'I'm Sold and Going to Georgia'. It was found in London and was made and used for anti-slavery propaganda.

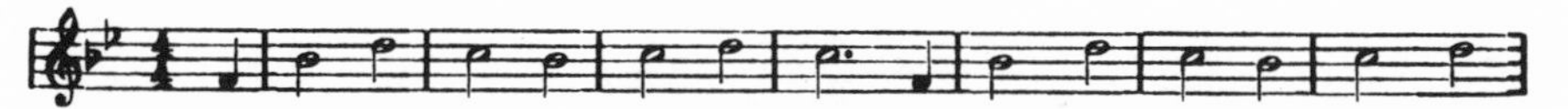
O when shall we poor souls be free? When shall these slav-'ry chains be

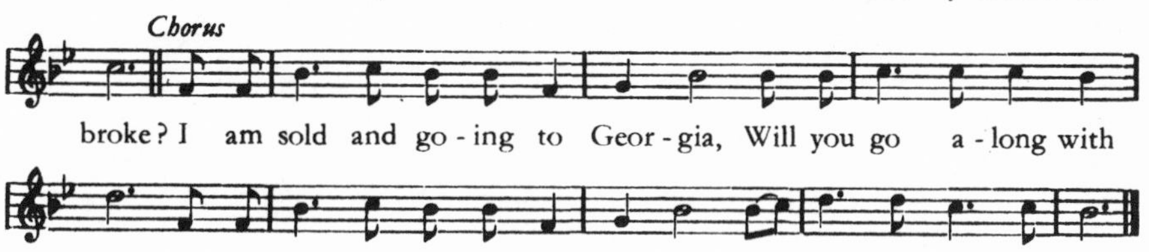
Chorus
broke? I am sold and go-ing to Geor-gia, Will you go a-long with
me? I am sold and go-ing to Geor-gia, Go sound the ju-bi-lee.

I left my wife and child behind,
They'll never see my face again;
Chorus

I'm bound to yonder great rice swamp
Where my poor bones will find a grave!

Farewell, my friends, I leave you all,
I'm sold but I have done no fault.

This explanation follows: "This song is usually sung by the chained gangs who are on their way, being driven from Maryland, Virginia and Kentucky to the more southern states for sale. The last line of each verse is the chorus, and gives a most impressive effect when sung — as it often is — by 100 or 150 voices echoing the plaintive grief of their hearts. This last line is intended as an appeal to all who have it in their power to aid in bringing about the jubilee of emancipation. — J. W. C. Pennington, D. D."

I have reproduced this song and its maker's comment as an early though typical example of the deceits, now transparent, of emancipation propaganda. There is little possibility that this was either a negro-made or negro-sung ditty. Such deceptions were essentially the same as those practiced by the burnt-cork minstrels, though less obvious and more altruistic. Both led those hearers who had no more reliable sources of information to form distorted concepts of the actual lyrism of the black man.

No. 287

RENOWN, CHI 109

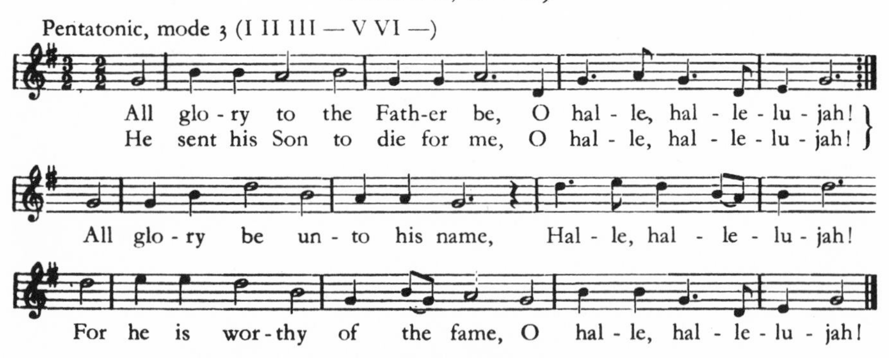
Pentatonic, mode 3 (I II III — V VI —)
All glo - ry to the Fath-er be, O hal - le, hal - le - lu - jah!
He sent his Son to die for me, O hal - le, hal - le - lu - jah!
All glo - ry be un - to his name, Hal - le, hal - le - lu - jah!
For he is wor - thy of the fame, O hal - le, hal - le - lu - jah!

I long to be in realms above, O halle, *etc.*
Where there is nought but praise and love, O halle, *etc.*
I long in Jesus to be wed, Halle, *etc.*
And on his breast recline my head, O halle, *etc.*

Come, come poor sinners, come away,
Why from your Jesus will you stray?
Come, come poor sinners, come behold,
His face is brighter than the gold.

Come, come poor sinners, come and see
Your mangled Savior on the tree!
He groan'd and died for you and me,
That happy, happy we might be.

Farewell, vain world, I bid adieu,
For only Jesus I'll pursue;
My Jesus took me by the hand
And brought me to the promis'd land.

The anonymous text is of the post-Revolutionary vintage. Its stanzas, all drawn from the 'wandering' stock, don't make sense as a hymn. The song's worth lies merely in its strength as a *sung* revival spiritual.

I have corrected the barring of the tune in the *Christian Harmony*.

No. 288

LOVELY MORNING, MH, ii, 7

Hexatonic, mode 3 b (I II III IV V VI —)

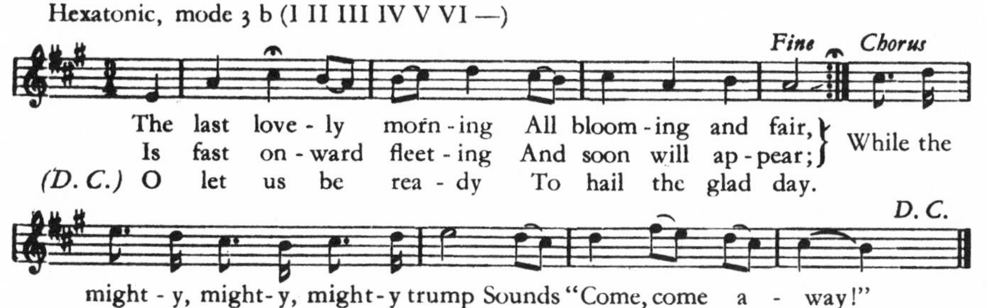
Fine
Chorus
The last love - ly morn - ing All bloom - ing and fair,
Is fast on - ward fleet - ing And soon will ap - pear;
While the
(D. C.) O let us be rea - dy To hail the glad day.
D. C.
might - y, might - y, might - y trump Sounds "Come, come a - way!"

And when that bright morning
In splendor shall dawn,
Our tears shall be ended,
Our sorrows all gone;
While the mighty *etc.*

The Bridegroom from glory
To earth shall descend;
Ten thousand bright angels
Around him attend.

The graves will be open'd,
The dead will arise,
And with the Redeemer
Mount up to the skies.

The saints then immortal
In glory shall reign!
The Bride with the Bridegroom
Forever remain.

I have corrected a faulty barring in the first section of the tune. The melody is based on 'Afton Water' a Scottish air.[1]

[1] See *Our Familiar Songs*, p. 322.

No. 289

WHAT A HAPPY TIME, OSH 377

Hexatonic, mode 3 b (I II III IV V VI —)

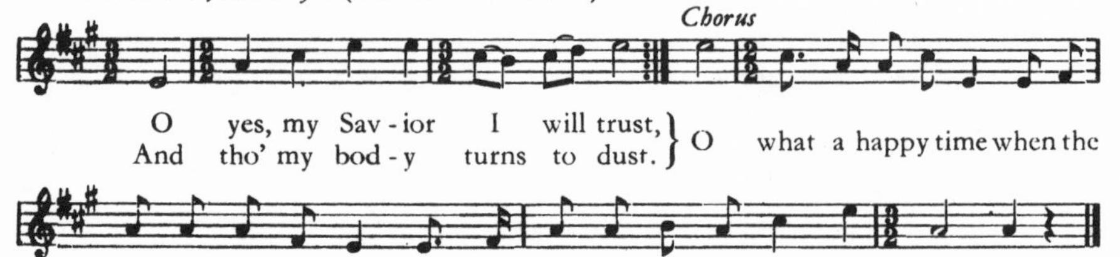
Chorus
O yes, my Sav-ior I will trust,
And tho' my bod-y turns to dust.
O what a happy time when the
Christ-ians all get home, And we'll shout and praise the Lamb in glo-ry.

My spirit will fly out and sing
Eternal praises to my King.
O what—*etc.*

To these two verses the compiler of the *Sacred Harp* assumed apparently that the singers would be able to add others at will from the same ever-flowing source, the remembered and easy-to-make rhyme pairs of the revival environment.[1]

No. 290

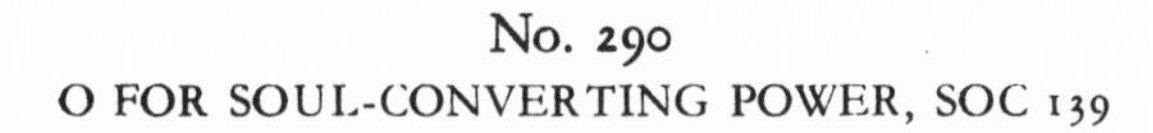

O FOR SOUL-CONVERTING POWER, SOC 139

Heptatonic ionian, mode 3 (I II III IV V VI VII)

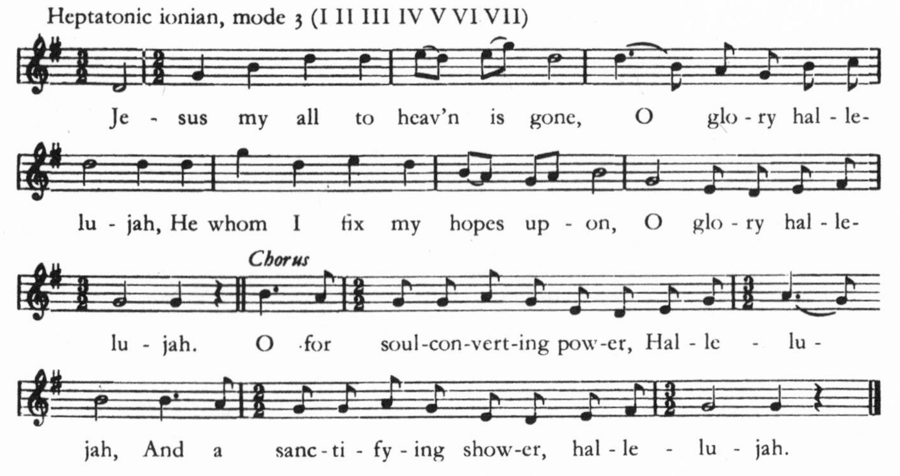
Je-sus my all to heav'n is gone, O glo-ry hal-le-
lu-jah, He whom I fix my hopes up-on, O glo-ry hal-le-
Chorus
lu-jah. O for soul-con-vert-ing pow-er, Hal-le-lu-
jah, And a sanc-ti-fy-ing show-er, hal-le-lu-jah.

[1] See them for example in 'Jubilee (B)', 'Land for Me', 'I'm Happy', 'Free Grace' etc. in this volume.

The song is claimed by John G. McCurry, compiler of the *Social Harp*, and dated 1845. Further stanzas of the text by John Cennick, 1718–1755, are given under 'River of Jordan' in *Spiritual Folk-Songs*; and the tune is a variant of 'Old Ship of Zion' also in that volume.

No. 291

MERCY'S FREE, OSH 337

Pentatonic, mode 3 (I II III — V VI —)

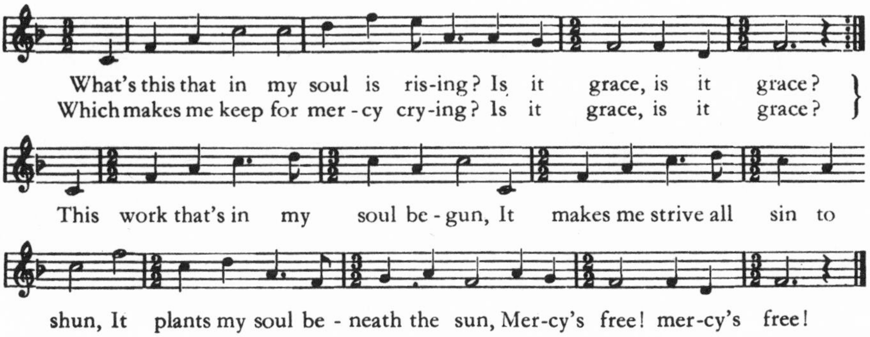

What's this that in my soul is ris-ing? Is it grace, is it grace?
Which makes me keep for mer-cy cry-ing? Is it grace, is it grace?

This work that's in my soul be-gun, It makes me strive all sin to

shun, It plants my soul be-neath the sun, Mer-cy's free! mer-cy's free!

Great God of love, I can but wonder,
Though I've no price at all to tender,
Though mercy's free, our God is just,
And if a soul should e'er be lost,
This will torment the sinner most,
Mercy's free, mercy's free.

This truth through all our life shall cheer us,
And through the vale of death shall bear us;
And when to Jordan's bank we come,
And 'cross the raging billows roam,
We'll sing when safely landed home,
Mercy's free, mercy's free.

In the 1850 edition of the *Sacred Harp* the tune is attributed to Leonard Breedlove, a well known singer and leader in fasola circles at that time. This peculiar type of stanza, along with some textual features, reappears in 'All Is Well'.[1] The stanzaic pattern of both songs is probably influenced by the 'Captain Kidd' formula which is discussed under 'You Shall See' in this volume.

[1] *Spiritual Folk-Songs*, No. 58.

No. 292

IN THE WILDERNESS, REV 65

Heptatonic ionian, mode 3 (I II III IV V VI VII)

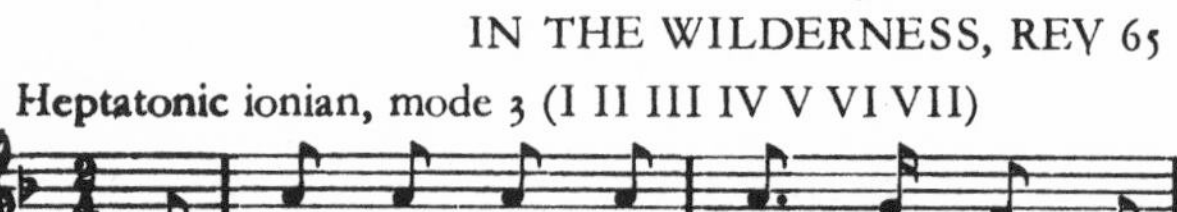
I have a home a - bove———, From sin and sor - row

free———, A man-sion which e - ter - nal love De-sign'd and form'd for

Chorus
me. We'll camp a while in the wild-er-ness, We'll camp a while in the wild-er-

ness, We'll camp a while in the wild-er-ness, And then we're go - ing home.

My Father's gracious hand
Has built this sweet abode;
From everlasting it was planned,
My dwelling place with God.
Chorus

My Savior's precious blood
Has made my title sure;
He passéd death's dark raging flood
To make my rest secure.

Loved ones are gone before
Whose pilgrim days are done;
I soon shall greet them on that shore
Where parting is unknown.
Last chorus
To camp no more in the wilderness *(three times)*
Where parting is unknown.

The verse text is ascribed to Horace Waters. The corresponding part of the tune reminds one of the individually composed Gospel Hymns. Features of that musically weak style are the ubiquitous jump of a sixth at the start and the recurrent series of one and the same tone. The chorus however is more folky in tone and word. The "in the wilderness" phrase pervaded the revival atmosphere before and after the Civil War. There is much evidence of how well the negroes liked it.[1]

[1] See for example Dett, p. 208, *Slave Songs*, p. 14, and Scarbrough, p. 13.

No. 293
NO MORE STORMY CLOUDS, OSH 278

Hexatonic, mode 4 A (I II — IV V VI 7)

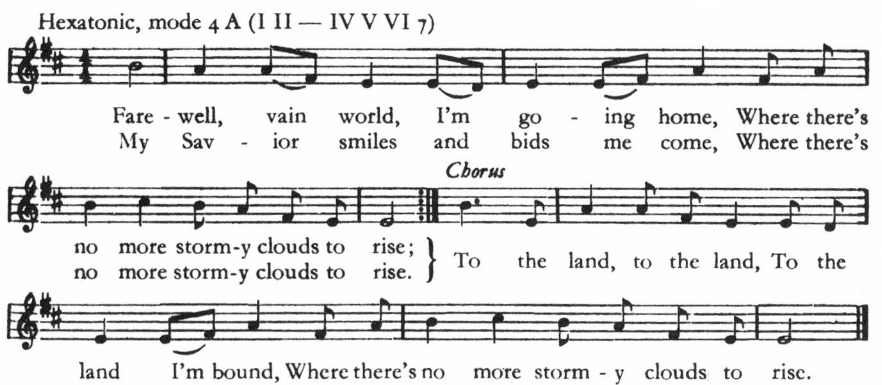
Fare - well, vain world, I'm go - ing home, Where there's
My Sav - ior smiles and bids me come, Where there's
Chorus
no more storm-y clouds to rise;
no more storm-y clouds to rise.
To the land, to the land, To the
land I'm bound, Where there's no more storm - y clouds to rise.

Further stanzas of the anonymous text are given under 'Golden Harp' in *Spiritual Folk-Songs*. For a list of some of the many refrains and choruses which have been sung with the basic verse-text, see *White Spirituals*.[1] H. S. Rees of Georgia recorded the song for the *Sacred Harp*. In the early editions of that song book the tune was treated mistakenly as aeolian. I inserted the raised sixths (*c*-sharps) following the way they were sung at the convention of the United Sacred Harp Singing Association, Atlanta, September, 1936. 'Green Bed' is a related tune.[2]

No. 294
PALMS OF VICTORY, SOC 53

Heptatonic aeolian, mode 2 (I II 3 IV V 6 7)

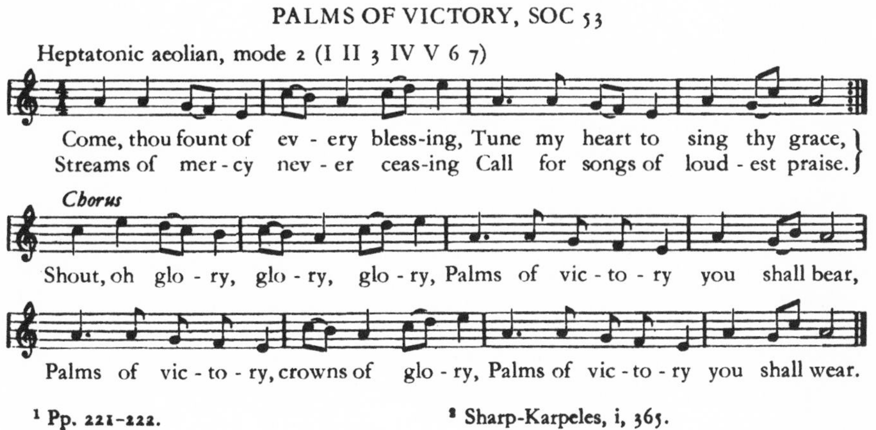
Come, thou fount of ev - ery bless-ing, Tune my heart to sing thy grace,
Streams of mer - cy nev - er ceas-ing Call for songs of loud - est praise.
Chorus
Shout, oh glo - ry, glo - ry, glo - ry, Palms of vic - to - ry you shall bear,
Palms of vic - to - ry, crowns of glo - ry, Palms of vic - to - ry you shall wear.

[1] Pp. 221-222.

[2] Sharp-Karpeles, i, 365.

Further stanzas of the verse text by Robert Robinson, 1735–1790, are given under 'Olney.' in this volume. The song is attributed in the *Social Harp* to Henry F. Chandler and dated 1854. The same chorus text is used in 'Deliverance Will Come' in this volume.

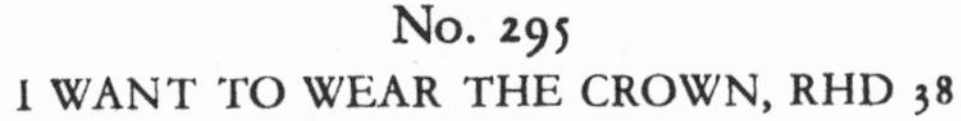

No. 295

I WANT TO WEAR THE CROWN, RHD 38

Hexatonic, mode 2 A minorized (I II 3 IV V — VII)

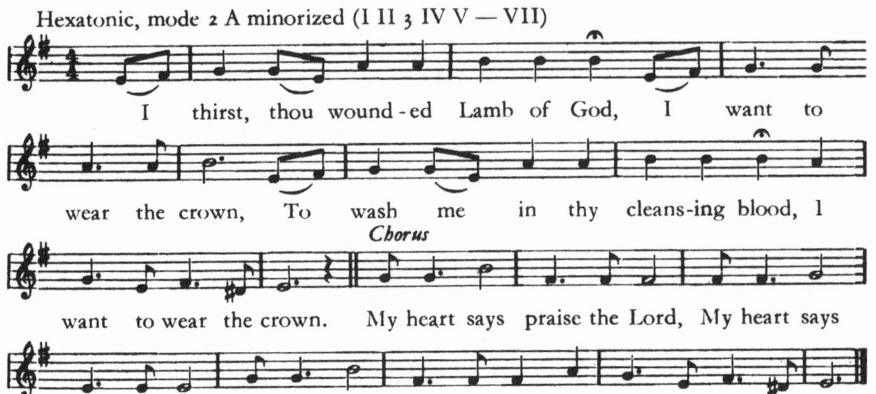
I thirst, thou wound-ed Lamb of God, I want to
wear the crown, To wash me in thy cleans-ing blood, I
Chorus
want to wear the crown. My heart says praise the Lord, My heart says
praise the Lord, My heart says praise the Lord, I want to wear the crown.

When gracious Lord, when shall it be,
I want to wear the crown;
That I shall find myself in thee,
I want to wear the crown.
Chorus

Thee, only thee, I fain would find, *etc.*
And cast the world and flesh behind, *etc.*

Thou, only thou, to me be given,
Of all thou hast in earth or heaven.

Take my poor heart and let it be
Forever closed to all but thee!

Seal then my breast and let me wear
That pledge of love forever there.

And blessèd Jesus when I die,
My soul thou wilt receive on high.

O let my spirit soar away,
To sing thy praise in endless day.

The three stanzas below then follow, in *Revival Hymns*, preceded by the editorial note: "The original of this hymn will be valued by many, if not all Christians."

When I was down in Egypt land,
I heard tell of the promised land.

My dungeon shook, my chains fell off,
Glory to God my soul did cry.

But little did I think he was so nigh,
He spoke and made me laugh and cry.

The Boston editor felt it necessary to explain some of these "original" expressions as merely figurative. Egypt land means, he asserted, "a state of [spiritual] darkness"; the promised land is "the inheritance of the saints in light"; the unsaved is in a "dungeon of unbelief and chained by sin". The convert may "laugh and cry for joy; everyone, however, must not expect to have just this exercise".

In Ingalls' *Christian Harmony* of 1805, p. 90, nearly forty years earlier than the above recording the last couplet reads

I little thought he'd been so nigh,
His speaking made me smile and cry.

The tune appears also in the *Millennial Harp*[1] but in a major key; the verse text being the same, but that of the chorus different. In the *Wesleyan Psalmodist* 'Shouting Victory' is a variant tune with a different text. Compare the above and its variants with the Welsh 'Farewell to Llangower' which also occurs in both major and minor aspects.[2]

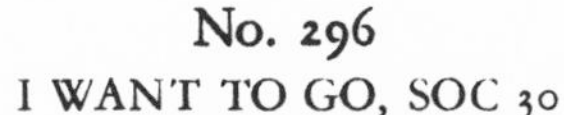

No. 296

I WANT TO GO, SOC 30

Heptatonic aeolian, mode 2 (I II 3 IV V 6 7)
When I can read my ti - tle clear to man-sions in the
skies——, I'll bid fare-well to ev - 'ry fear And wipe my weep-ing eyes.
Chorus
I want to go, I want to go, I want to go to glo - ry;
There's so man-y tri - als here be - low, They say there's none in glo - ry.

[1] Part i, 66.
[2] JWF, i, 43f.

18

Further stanzas of the text by Isaac Watts, 1674–1748, are given under 'New Indian Song' in *Spiritual Folk-Songs*. The song is claimed in the *Social Harp* by its compiler, John G. McCurry, and is dated 1851. The first phrase of the tune is found in 'The True Lover's Farewell'.[1]

No. 297

LOVING KINDNESS, OSH 275

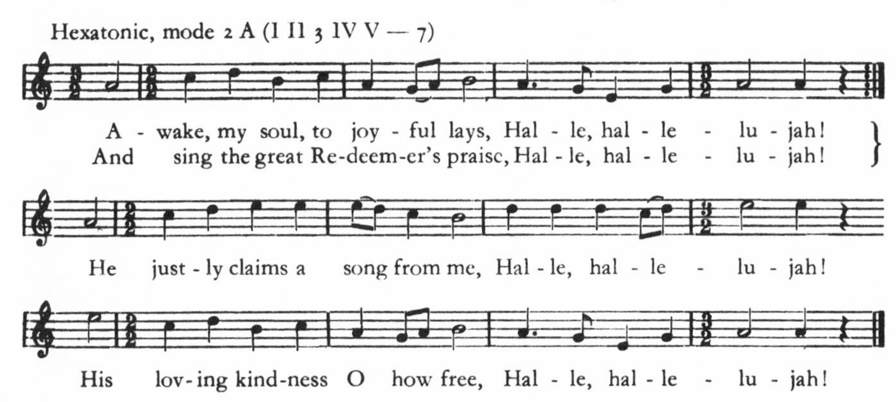
Hexatonic, mode 2 A (1 II 3 IV V — 7)
A - wake, my soul, to joy - ful lays, Hal - le, hal - le - lu - jah!
And sing the great Re-deem-er's praise, Hal - le, hal - le - lu - jah!
He just - ly claims a song from me, Hal - le, hal - le - lu - jah!
His lov-ing kind-ness O how free, Hal - le, hal - le - lu - jah!

He saw me ruined in the fall,
Yet loved me, notwithstanding all.
He saved me from my lost estate,
His loving kindness, O how great.

Though numerous hosts of mighty foes,
Though earth and hell my way oppose,
He safely leads my soul along,
His loving kindness, O how free. [strong?]

The above text, excluding the refrains, is by Samuel Medley, 1738–1799. The song in its above form was ascribed in the *Sacred Harp* to J. P. and S. R. Penick, country song leaders in Georgia before the Civil War. An old Irish song in Petrie[2] shows noteworthy similarities to this tune. Compare also 'I Want a Seat in Paradise' and its related tunes.[3]

[1] JFSS, ii, 55.
[2] No. 1164.
[3] *Spiritual Folk-Songs*, No. 240.

No. 298

IT WAS FOR YOU THAT JESUS DIED, REV 405

Hexatonic, mode 2 A (1 II 3 IV V — 7)

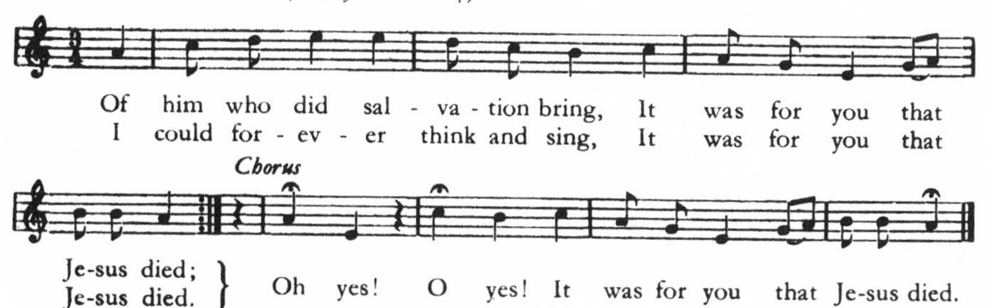
Of him who did sal - va - tion bring, It was for you that
I could for - ev - er think and sing, It was for you that
Chorus
Je-sus died;
Je-sus died.
Oh yes! O yes! It was for you that Je-sus died.

Arise, ye needy, he'll relieve,
Arise, ye guilty, he'll forgive.
Chorus

Ask but his grace and lo! 'tis giv'n,
Ask, and he turns your hell to heav'n.

Though sin and sorrow wound my soul,
Jesus, thy balm will make it whole.

To shame our sins he blush'd in blood,
He closed his eyes to show us God.

Let all the world fall down and know
That none but God such love can show.

'Tis thee I love, for thee alone
I shed my tears and make my moan.

Where'er I am, where'er I move,
I meet the object of my love.

Insatiate to this spring I fly,
I drink, and yet am ever dry.

Ah! who against thy charms is proof?
Ah! who that loves can love enough?

The editor of the *Revivalist* borrowed the song from *Devotional Melodies.* See McCutchan, No. 188, as to the remote source of the basic text which was first in Latin (ascribed to Bernard of Clairvaux) and translated into German by Anthony Wilhelm Boehm before being translated from German to English (1722) by John Christian Jacobi.

No. 299
LOVE THE LORD, OSH 375

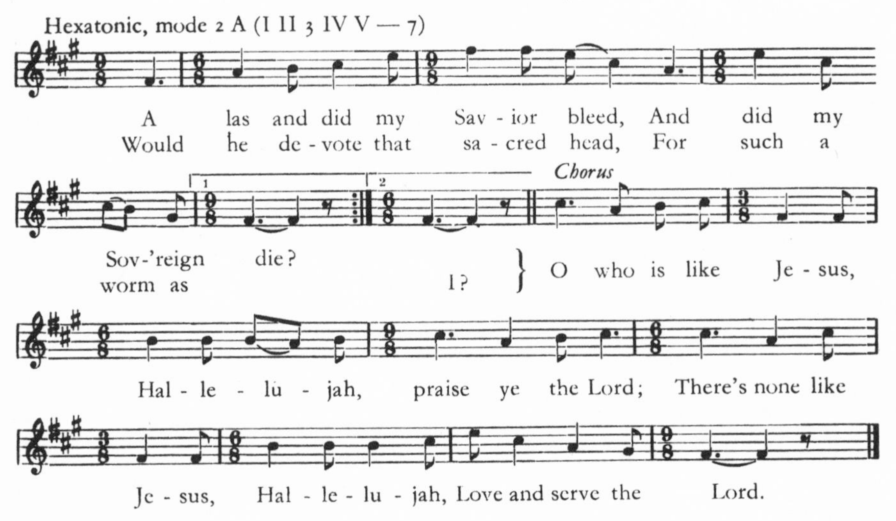
Hexatonic, mode 2 A (I II 3 IV V — 7)
A las and did my Sav - ior bleed, And did my
Would he de - vote that sa - cred head, For such a
Chorus
Sov-'reign die?
worm as I?
O who is like Je - sus,
Hal - le - lu - jah, praise ye the Lord; There's none like
Je - sus, Hal - le - lu - jah, Love and serve the Lord.

The verse text by Isaac Watts is associated with a tune ascribed to J. P. Rees. It appeared first in the 1859 edition of the *Sacred Harp*. The barring, involving measures of different length, is mine. The original notation had exactly the same note and rest values and had them in the same sequence, but the tune was cut up regularly into six-eight measures.

No. 300
ON MY JOURNEY HOME, OSH 498

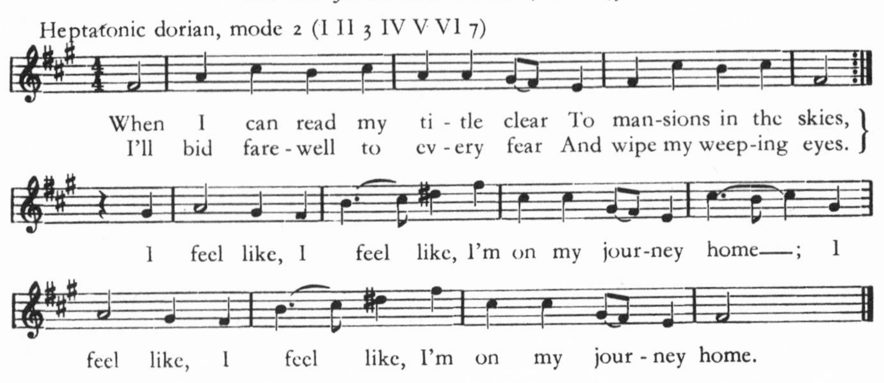
Heptatonic dorian, mode 2 (I II 3 IV V VI 7)
When I can read my ti - tle clear To man-sions in the skies,
I'll bid fare - well to ev - ery fear And wipe my weep-ing eyes.
I feel like, I feel like, I'm on my jour-ney home—; I
feel like, I feel like, I'm on my jour - ney home.

Further stanzas of the text by Isaac Watts, 1674–1748, are given in *Spiritual Folk-Songs* under 'New Indian Song'. The tune is ascribed in the *Sacred Harp* to Freeman Price. The *d*'s are natural in the *Sacred Harp*. I have sharped them as I heard them sung at the United Sacred Harp Singing Convention in Atlanta, Georgia, September 10, 1938. Since those singers are the carriers-on of the uninterrupted song tradition, etablished in Georgia long before B. F. White gleaned from it for his *Sacred Harp*, I assume that their singing is traditionally correct and that the notes are wrong.

Bibliography

Alderice, Catherine. Manuscript four-shape-note song book written in or near Emmittsburg Maryland, between 1800 and 1830.

Allen, William Francis; Ware, Charles Pickard; and Garrison, Lucy McKim. *Slave Songs of the United States.* C. 1868, reprinted New York, Peter Smith, 1929.

Baptist Harmony, The. Compiled by Staunton S. Burdett, Pleasant Hill, South Carolina, 1834.

Baptist Hymn and Tune Book, 1857.

Baring-Gould, S. *Songs of the West.* London, Methuen, 1890 to 1928.

Belden, H. M. Ballads and Songs Collected by the Missouri Folk-Lore Society. Columbia, University of Missouri, 1940.

Bennett, William W. *Memorials of Methodism in Virginia.* Richmond, 1871.

Benson, Louis F. *The English Hymn.* Philadelphia, Presbyterian Board of Publication, 1915.

Bible Songs. Compiled by M. B. DeWitt, Nashville, 1865.

Bolton, Dorothy G. and Burleigh, Harry T. *Old Songs Hymnal.* New York, Century Company, 1929.

Botkin, Benjamin Albert. *The American Play-Party Song.* Lincoln, Nebraska, 1937.

Broadwood, Lucy, and Fuller-Maitland, J. A. *English Country Songs.* London, Leadenhall Press, 1893.

Buchanan, Annabel Morris. *Folk Hymns of America.* New York, J. Fischer and Brother, 1928.

Chapple, Joe Mitchell. *Heart Songs Dear to the American People* etc. New York, Chapple Publishing Company, 1909.

Chase, George Wingate. *The Masonic Harp.* Boston, Ditson, 1858.

Chase, Richard. *Old Songs and Singing Games.* Chapel Hill, University of North Carolina Press, 1938.

Christian Harmony, The. Compiled by William Walker, Spartanburg, South Carolina, printed in Philadelphia, 1866.

Christian Harmony or Songsters Companion, The. Compiled by Jeremiah Ingalls, printed Exeter, New Hampshire, 1805.

Christian Lyre, The. Compiled by Joshua Leavitt, eleventh edition New York, 1833.

Christian Science Hymnal. Boston, 1932.

Christian Songster etc., *The.* Compiled by Joseph Bever, Dayton, Ohio, 1858.

Church Harmony (Supplement, *Kirchen-Harmonie).* Compiled by Henry Smith, Chambersburg, Pennsylvania, 1834.

Columbian Harmony, The. Compiled by William Moore, Wilson County, Tennessee, printed in Cincinnati, 1825.

Combs, Josiah H. *Folk-Songs du Midi des États-Unis.* Paris, 1925.

Davis, Arthur Kyle. *Traditional Ballads of Virginia.* Cambridge, Harvard University Press, 1929.

Dearmer, Percy. (See *Oxford Book of Carols).*

Delaware Harmony. Compiled by Azariah Fobes, Wilmington, Delaware, 1809.

Dett, R. Nathaniel. *Religious Folk-Songs of the Negro.* Hampton, Virginia, Hampton Institute Press, 1929.

Dolph, Edward Arthur. *Sound Off.* New York, Cosmopolitan Book Corp., 1929.

Elson, Louis C. *Shakespeare in Music.* Boston, 1900, seventh impression 1914.

English Musical Repository, The. Edinburgh, 1811.

Erk, Ludwig C., and Böhme, Franz M. *Deutscher Liederhort.* Three vols., Leipzig, edition 1925.

Federal Harmony, The. Compiled by Asahel Benham, New Haven, 1790.

Folk Hymns of America. (See Buchanan, Annabel Morris).

Gibbon, John Murray. *Melody and the Lyric.* New York, Dutton, 1930.
Gilchrist, Anne G. Articles in JFSS, expecially *The Folk Element in Early Revival Hymns and Tunes,* vol. viii, pp. 61—95.
Golden Harp, The. Compiled by George W. Henry, Auburn, New York, 1855.
Good Old Songs. Compiled by C. H. Cayce, Thornton, Ark., printed in Martin, Tennessee, 1913.
Greig, Gavin, and Keith, Alexander. *Last Leaves of Traditional Ballads and Ballad Airs.* Aberdeen, 1925.
Hymns. Compiled by Joseph Hart, fourth edition, London, 1765.
Hymns and Spiritual Songs, A Collection of, (for the use of Primitive Methodists, generally called Ranters). Pocklington, before 1820.
Hudson, Arthur Palmer. *Folksongs of Mississippi.* Chapel Hill, University of North Carolina Press, 1936.
— *Folk Tunes from Mississippi.* Edited by George Herzog and Herbert Halpert, published by National Service Bureau, Federal Theatre Project, WPA, New York, 1937.
Huber, Kurt, and Kiem-Pauli. *Alt-Bayerisches Liederbuch.* Mainz, Edition Schott, 1937.
Harp of Columbia, The. Compiled by W. H. and M. L. Swan, Knoxville, Tennessee, 1848.
Harp of Columbia, The New. Compiled by Marcus Lafayette Swan, 1867, an unnumbered edition printed in Nashville, Smith and Lamar, 1911.
Harp of the South, The. Compiled by Lowell Mason, publ. by Mason Brothers, New York, between 1855 and 1859.
Hesperian Harp, The. Compiled by William Hauser, Wadley, Georgia, printed Philadelphia, 1848.
Jackson, George Pullen. *Spiritual Folk-Songs of Early America.* New York, J. J. Augustin, 1937.
— *White Spirituals in the Southern Uplands.* Chapel Hill, University of North Carolina Press, 1933.
Journal of American Folk-Lore. New York, American Folk-Lore Society.
Journal of the (English) *Folk-Song Society.* London, 1899-1931. (New Series, see following title.)
Journal of the (English) *Folk Dance and Song Society.* London, 1932—.
Journal of the Irish Folk Song Society. Dublin, 1904—.
Journal of the Welsh Folk Song Society. Bangor, Wales, 1909—.
Knoxville Harmony, The. Compiled by John B. Jackson, Madisonville and Pumpkintown, Tennessee, 1838.
Lightwood, James Thomas. *Hymn-Tunes and their Story.* London, 1905.
— *Methodist Music of the Eighteenth Century.* London, Epworth Press, 1927.
Lute of Zion, The. Compiled by I. B. Woodbury, New York, 1853.
Lyric Gems of Scotland. London, Bayley and Ferguson, no date.
McCutchan, Robert Guy. *Our Hymnody.* New York, Cincinnati and Chicago, Methodist Book Concern, 1937.
McDowell, L. L. *Songs of the Old Camp Ground.* Ann Arbor, Michigan, Edwards Brothers, 1937.
Masonic Harp, The. (See Chase, George Wingate.)
"*Mercer's Cluster*". Popular title for *The Cluster of Divine Hymns and Social Poems.* Compiled by Jesse Mercer, Augusta, Georgia, *ca.* 1817.
Metcalf, Frank J. *American Writers and Compilers of Sacred Music.* New York, Abingdon Press, 1925.
— *Stories of Hymn Tunes.* New York, Abingdon Press, 1928.
Methodist Hymnal, The. Nashville, Publishing House of the M. E. Church South, 1935.
Methodist Hymns. New York, 1842.
Millennial Harp, The. Compiled by Joshua V. Himes, Boston, 1843.
Missouri Harmony, The. Compiled by Allen D. Carden, St. Louis, Missouri, printed in Cincinnati, 1820.
Modern Language Notes. Baltimore, Johns Hopkins University.

Musical Instructor, The. Compiled by Nathan Chapin and Joseph L. Dickerson, Philadelphia, 1808.
Musical Quarterly, The. New York, G. Schirmer.
Newell, William W. *Games and Songs of American Children.* New York, Harper and Brothers, 1911.
New Jersey Harmony, The. Compiled by John McCulloch, Philadelphia, 1787.
Ohio Harmonist, The. Compiled by Alexander Auld, 1850.
Olive Leaf, The. Compiled by William Hauser and Benjamin Turner, Wadley, Georgia, printed Philadelphia, 1878.
Original Sacred Harp, The. Edited by Joe S. James, Atlanta, Georgia, 1911.
Original Sacred Harp, The. Denson Revision, Haleyville, Alabama, 1936. (See also *Sacred Harp.)*
Our Familiar Songs and Those Who Made Them. Helen Kendrick Johnson. New York, Holt, 1889.
Oxford Book of Carols, The. Edited by Percy Dearmer, R. Vaughan Williams and Martin Shaw. London, Oxford University Press, third impression, 1931.
Petrie, George. *The Complete Collection of Ancient Irish Music.* Edited by Charles Villiers Stanford, London, Boosey and Company, 1903.
Primitive Baptist Hymn and Tune Book, The. Compiled by John R. Daily, printed in Madisonville, Kentucky, 1902.
Publications of the Texas Folk-Lore Society. Austin, Texas.
Repository of Sacred Music. Compiled by John Wyeth, fifth edition, Harrisburg, Pennsylvania, 1818.
Revival Hymns. Compiled by H. W. Day, Boston, 1842.
Revival Hymns and Plantation Melodies. Compiled by Marshall W. Taylor, Cincinnati, 1883.
Revivalist, The. Compiled by Joseph Hillman, Troy, New York, 1868; revised and enlarged edition, 1872.
Richardson, Ethel Park, and Spaeth, Sigmund. *American Mountain Songs.* New York, Greenburg, 1927.
Richard Weaver's Tune Book. London (?), 1861.
Sacred Harp, The. Compiled by B. F. White and E. J. King, Hamilton, Georgia, 1844, printed in Philadelphia, 1844. Especially consulted were the editions of 1859 and 1869. (See also *Original Sacred Harp.)*
Sacred Melodeon, The. Compiled by A. S. Hayden, Cincinnati, c. 1848.
Sacred Melody. John Wesley, London, second edition, 1765.
Sandburg, Carl. *The American Songbag.* New York, Harcourt, Brace and Company, 1927.
Scarbrough, Dorothy. *On the Trail of the Negro Folk-Songs.* Cambridge, Harvard University Press, 1925.
Scots Musical Museum. Compiled by James Johnson and Robert Burns, Edinburgh, 1787-1803.
Sears, Clara Endicott. *Days of Delusion.* Boston and New York, Houghton Mifflin Company, 1924.
Shaker Music. Albany, New York, 1875.
Sharp, Cecil J. *English Folk-Carols.* London, Novello, 1911.
— *One Hundred English Folksongs.* Boston, Ditson, 1916.
Sharp, Cecil J., and Karpeles, Maud. *English Folk-Songs from the Southern Appalachians.* Two volumes, London, Oxford University Press, 1932.
Shindler, Mary Stanley Bunce Dana. *The Southern Harp.* Boston, Parker and Ditson, 1841.
Shoemaker, Henry W. *Mountain Minstrelsy of Pennsylvania.* Third edition, Philadelphia, 1931.
Singer's Companion, The. New York, 1854.
Slave Songs. (See Allen, William Francis.)
Smith, Reed, and Rufty, Hilton. *American Anthology of Old-World Ballads.* New York, J. Fischer and Brother, 1937.
Social Harp, The. Compiled by John G. McCurry, Andersonville, Georgia, printed in Philadelphia, 1855.

Social Hymn and Tune Book, The. Philadelphia, 1865.
Songs of Grace. Compiled by E. S. Lorenz and I. Baltzell, Dayton, Ohio, United Brethren Publishing House, 1879.
Songs of Scotland. Compiled by Pittman, Brown, and Mackay, London, Boosey and Company.
Southern and Western Pocket Harmonist, The. Compiled by William Walker, Spartanburg, South Carolina, printed in Philadelphia, 1846.
Southern Folklore Quarterly, The. Gainesville, Florida, The University of Florida, 1937—.
Southern Harmony and Musical Companion, The. Compiled by William Walker, Spartanburg, South Carolina, printed in New Haven, Connecticut, 1835. Consulted also edition of 1854.
Spiritual Folk-Songs of Early America. (See Jackson, George Pullen.)
Sturgis, Edith B., and Hughes, Robert. *Songs from the Hills of Vermont.* New York, G. Schirmer, 1919.
Supplement to the Kentucky Harmony. Compiled by Ananias Davisson, Rockingham County, Virginia, 1820.
Taylor, Marshall W. (See *Revival Hymns and Plantation Melodies.)*
Tillett, Wilbur F., and Nutter, Charles S. *Hymns and Hymn Writers of the* (Methodist) *Church.* Nashville, Smith and Lamar, 1911.
Union Harmony, The. Compiled by William Caldwell, Maryville, Tennessee, 1837.
Union Harmony, The. Compiled by George Hendrickson, Mountain Valley, Virginia, 1848.
Union Harp and History of Songs, The. Compiled by Joe S. James, Douglasville, Georgia, 1909.
United States Harmony, The. Compiled by Allen D. Carden, Nashville, Tennessee, 1829.
Vannest, Charles Garrett. *Lincoln the Hoosier.* St. Louis, Chicago, Eden Publishing House, 1928.
Virginia Harmony, The. Compiled by James P. Carrell and David S. Clayton, Lebanon, Virginia, printed in Winchester, Virginia, 1831.
Virginia Sacred Musical Repository, The. Compiled by James M. Boyd, Winchester, Virginia, 1818.
Wesleyan Harp, The. Compiled by A. D. Merrill and W. C. Brown, Boston, 1834.
Western Harmony, The. Compiled by Allen D. Carden, Nashville, Tennessee, 1824.
White, Newman I. *American Negro Folk-Songs.* Cambridge, Harvard University Press, 1928.
White Spirituals in the Southern Uplands. (See Jackson, George Pullen.)
Wilkinson, Winston. *The University of Virginia* (manuscript) *Collection of Folk-Music.* Reposes in the library of the University of Virginia, Charlottesville, Virginia.
Wyman, Loraine, and Brockway, Howard. *Lonesome Tunes.* New York, Gray, 1916.
Zion Songster. Second edition, 1827.

List of Abbreviations of Titles

BB *Old Songs Hymnal* (Bolton and Burleigh)
BS *Bible Songs* (DeWitt)
CH *Church Harmony* (Smith)
CHH *Christian Harmony* (Walker)
CHI *Christian Harmony* (Ingalls)
CL *Christian Lyre* (Leavitt)
COH *Columbian Harmony* (Moore)
DH *Delaware Harmony* (Fobes)
FH *Federal Harmony* (Benham)
FHA *Folk Hymns of America* (Buchanan)
GH *Golden Harp* (Henry)
GOS *Good Old Songs* (Cayce)
HH *Hesperian Harp* (Hauser)
HOC *Harp of Columbia* (Swan)
HSM *Harp of the South* (Mason)
JAFL *Journal of American Folk-Lore*
JDSS *Journal of the* (English) *Folk Dance and Song Society*
JFSS *Journal of the* (English) *Folk Song Society*
JIFS *Journal of the Irish Folk Song Society*
JWF *Journal of the Welsh Folk Song Society*
KNH *Knoxville Harmony* (Jackson)
LZ *Lute of Zion* (Woodbury)
MH *Millennial Harp* (Himes)
MHL *Methodist Hymnal* (1935)
MOH *Missouri Harmony* (Carden)
MQ *Musical Quarterly*
OL *Olive Leaf* (Hauser and Turner)
OSH *Original Sacred Harp* (James)
PB *Primitive Baptist Hymn and Tune Book* (Daily)
REV *Revivalist* (Hillman)
RHD *Revival Hymns* (Day)
SAM *Sacred Melodeon* (Hayden)
SFQ *Southern Folklore Quarterly*
SH *Sacred Harp* (White and King)
SHD *Original Sacred Harp* (Denson Revision)
SKH *Supplement to the Kentucky Harmony* (Davisson)
SOC *Social Harp* (McCurry)
SOG *Songs of Grace* (Lorenz and Baltzell)
SOH *Southern Harmony* (Walker)
SWP *Southern and Western Pocket Harmonist* (Walker)
UH *Union Harmony* (Caldwell)
UHH *Union Harmony* (Hendrickson)
UHP *Union Harp* (James)
USH *United States Harmony* (Carden)
UVW *University of Virginia Collection of Folk-Music* (Wilkinson)
VH *Virginia Harmony* (Carrell)
VSM *Virginia Sacred Musical Repository* (Boyd)
WH *Western Harmony* (Carden)
WHM *Wesleyan Harp* (Merrill and Brown)

Index of Songs by Titles

Index of First Lines